"An explosive historical narrative. With Sedgwick's deft, clever writing, this true story of the dangerous and dramatic world of the Founders becomes as gripping as any novel."

—Matthew Pearl, *New York Times* bestselling author of *The Last Bookaneer*

"The famous duel has been recounted before, but never with such illuminating attention to the layers upon layers of ambition, vanity, talent, honor, and pigheadedness that marked the antagonists . . . a master storyteller."

—H. W. Brands, *New York Times* bestselling author of *The Man Who Saved the Union: Ulysses Grant in War and Peace*

The case of dueling pistols owned by Hamilton's good Federalist friend New York senator Rufus King. Similar to the Robert Wogdon flintlock pistols used in the fatal duel between Hamilton and Burr, these were made by H.W. Mortimer. They were never fired but demonstrate that such equipment was de rigueur for a gentleman of the political class and indicate the elaborate machinery involved in defending one's honor.

WAR OF TWO

ALEXANDER HAMILTON, AARON BURR,

and the DUEL THAT STUNNED THE NATION

JOHN SEDGWICK

NEW AMERICAN LIBRARY
New York

NEW AMERICAN LIBRARY
Published by Berkley
An imprint of Penguin Random House LLC
375 Hudson Street, New York, New York 10014

Photo credits: Page iv: Pair of Flintlock Dueling Pistols, c.1780–1800, H.W. Mortimer & Sons. ©
Collection of the New-York Historical Society, USA/Gift of Mr. and Mrs. Gherardi Davis and
Ellen King/Bridgeman Images. Page xxiv: A northwest prospect of Nassau Hall, with a front view
of the president's house, in New Jersey. Engraving by Henry Dawkins after William Tennent, 1764.
Rare Book Division, New York Public Library, Astor, Lenox and Tilden Foundations. Page 132: The
Inauguration of George Washington, American School (19th century). © Collection of the
New-York Historical Society, USA/Bridgeman Images. Page 246: View of New York from
Weehawken, New Jersey, After William Henry Bartlett, c. 1840. Granger, NYC. Page 344: Cipher
Letter from Aaron Burr to James Wilkinson, July 29, 1806. Courtesy, The Newberry Library,
Chicago. Call # Graff 503. Page 407: Alexander Hamilton Letter to Theodore Sedgwick, 10 July
1804. Page 1 and 2. Original manuscript from the Theodore Sedgwick Papers. Collection of the
Massachusetts Historical Society. Additional photo credits can be found on page 435–36.

The excerpt "Only we two are one" is a portion of a line from "Re-statement of Romance," a poem
by Wallace Stevens, from *Wallace Stevens Selected Poems*, edited by John N. Serio, Alfred A. Knopf,
a division of Random House, Inc., 2009; reprinted from *Ideas of Order* by Wallace Stevens,
copyright 1936 by Wallace Stevens, copyright © renewed 1964 by Holly Stevens.

ISBN 9781592409693

THE LIBRARY OF CONGRESS HAS CATALOGED THE HARDCOVER EDITION OF
THIS TITLE AS FOLLOWS:

Sedgwick, John.
War of two: Alexander Hamilton, Aaron Burr, and the duel that stunned
the nation/John Sedgwick.
p. cm.
Includes bibliographical references and index.
ISBN 9781592408528 (hardcover)
1. Burr-Hamilton Duel, Weehawken, N.J., 1804. 2. Hamilton, Alexander, 1757–1804. 3. Burr,
Aaron, 1756–1836. 4. United States—Politics and government—1801–1809. I. Title.
E302.6.H2S27 2015
973.4'60922—dc23
2015014275

Berkley hardcover edition / October 2016
New American Library trade paperback edition / October 2016

Printed in the United States of America
1   3   5   7   9   10   8   6   4   2

Cover photograph of Alexander Hamilton © DEA Picture Library/Getty Images.
Cover design by Stephen Brayda.
Interior text design by Tiffany Estreicher.

FOR RANA

Only we two are one

—Wallace Stevens

The powers of Hyde seemed to have grown with the sickliness of Jekyll. And certainly the hate that now divided them was equal on each side. With Jekyll, it was a thing of vital instinct. He had now seen the full deformity of that creature that shared with him some of the phenomena of consciousness, and was co-heir with him to death: and beyond these links of community, which in themselves made the most poignant part of his distress, he thought of Hyde, for all his energy of life, as of something not only hellish but inorganic.

—ROBERT LOUIS STEVENSON,
The Strange Case of Dr. Jekyll and Mr. Hyde

CONTENTS

PART TWO

The Battle Is Joined

PART THREE

To the Death

PART FOUR

AND THEN THERE WAS ONE

AUTHOR'S NOTE

ONE FALL AFTERNOON several years ago, I was in the reading room of the Massachusetts Historical Society, a splendid brick bastion in Boston's leafy Fenway neighborhood. I was prowling through the society's extensive collection of Sedgwick family papers for a book I was writing about my family's history when the head librarian, Peter Drummey, came up and tapped me on the shoulder and said he had something to show me.

"We've got this one on display up front," he whispered. "Come, you should see it." He led me through a series of rooms to an exhibition space showing the society's prized holdings in long glass cases. Peter stopped beside one of them and pointed toward a wrinkled letter, yellowed with age, its once-black ink long since faded to brown, that was propped up on glass. "There. Take a look."

I bent over the case. "New York, July 10, 1804," I read out.

My Dear Sir

I have received two letters from you since we last saw each other—that of the latest date being the 24 of May. I have had in hand for some time a long letter to you, explaining my view of the course and tendency of our Politics, and my intentions as to my own future conduct. But my plan embraced so large a range that owing to much avocation, some indifferent health, and a growing distaste for Politics, the letter is still

considerably short of being finished—I write this now to satisfy you,
that want of regard for you has not been the cause of my silence—

"Wait, this isn't—?" I asked.

Peter nodded. "Yes—Alexander Hamilton's last letter. Written the night before he was shot." By the sitting vice president Aaron Burr, he need hardly have added, in the famous duel at Weehawken, New Jersey, in 1804, an event that Henry Adams called the most dramatic moment in the politics of the early Republic.

"And look, it's to one of yours." He beamed. "His good friend and legislative ally Theodore Sedgwick." Of course—the name was scrawled hastily across the bottom.

I'd known about the letter, but I'd never seen it. Theodore was my great-great-great-grandfather. A career politician, he'd helped push Hamilton's economic agenda through the House when he was a representative from Massachusetts, and ultimately rose to become Speaker of the House for the fateful election of 1800 that wrested control away from his Federalist Party and turned it over to Thomas Jefferson and the Republican "Jacobins," as he thought of them, alluding to the bloodthirsty radicals of the French Revolution. Much to Hamilton's distress, Theodore had tried fruitlessly to steer the election to Burr, a friend from the Berkshires. Still, Theodore had been one of the only politicians who'd remained a trusted friend of both men, which was why Hamilton was writing him then.

We will return to the letter later, in its time. Taken out of context, it may seem tangential and, unusually for Hamilton, wildly overblown. It is likely to defy expectations as to why Hamilton crossed the Hudson at daybreak and faced his doom. In a few choice sentences, Hamilton offered a better explanation about his part in the duel, and a better prediction of what would come from it, than he did anywhere else. Theodore Sedgwick never responded, since by then there was no one to respond to.

When earlier members of the family encountered the letter, they could see its value to history, for several added urgent notations on the back before they passed the letter down to the next generation. All conveyed the same message: *This letter must be preserved.*

The Fatal Dinner

Searching for the true origins of the fatal hatred between Alexander Hamilton and Aaron Burr is like trying to trace the wind to its source. It is easier to detail how the gusts are knocking tree limbs about. There was never any question that Burr shot Hamilton in anger. As for why, everyone turned to a remarkable series of letters, eleven in all, that Hamilton and Burr, or their surrogates, volleyed back and forth in the run-up to the slaughter and that filled the newspapers afterward. The letters have much of the quality of legal arguments, as befits the work of the two most prominent lawyers in the city, as each tried to pin the blame on the other, and they make up a duel of their own, a war of words.

While each man clearly disdained the moral character of the other, the issue at hand was far more limited, and more precise, as it turned, remarkably, on a single word, spoken in haste at a dinner party in Albany that February, in the midst of an abominable winter that, from November to May, was the coldest and snowiest on record. Only the steep roofs of the city's Dutch houses were clear of the otherwise endless freezing white. The event was held at the State Street home of a powerful local judge named John Tayler, whose mouth seemed always down turned in displeasure. He ran nearly everything in town from the waterworks to the local New York State Bank, which he'd conveniently located directly across the street, and he was at work on plans for a new granite statehouse a few blocks away. The city had long been so Dutch that, it was said, even the dogs barked in

Dutch. The Reformed Protestant Dutch Church still commanded one end of State Street—but a sturdy new Episcopal church had risen at the other, reflecting the developing political tensions of the city.

Tayler had invited in a few gentleman friends who were staying in the city for an ample repast before a roaring fire. The men duly arrived by sleigh on the snow-packed street. Their cheeks must have been raw as they came stamping into the front hall, their top hats and capes dusted with white. Federalists all, they dressed in the Federalist fashion; for clothing, too, was divided by party. Unlike Republicans, these good Federalist men all wore traditional knee-high silk stockings and buckled shoes, eschewing the blowsy shirts and crude trousers affected by the Republicans. *Or worse.* Even on formal occasions, President Jefferson was known to lounge about the President's Mansion in a dressing gown and slippers.

The purpose tonight, however, was not mere conviviality. Since this was Albany in an election season, and one that featured the almost lubricious prospect of the disgraced vice president Aaron Burr's attempt to seize the governor's chair, the topic would be politics and, for a diversion, more politics. But for its designation as the state capital, after all, Albany would have remained what it once was: a nice piece of land along the Hudson, rich in strawberries. And these men possessed political opinions of value. Among them were the eminent James Kent, chief justice of the New York State Supreme Court, and the Dutch aristocrat Stephen Van Rensselaer, the eighth patroon, or lord of the manor, a onetime candidate for governor himself whose estate, Rensselaerswych, once encompassed all of Albany. But the prize guest of the evening was Alexander Hamilton.

In his younger days, Hamilton had cut a girlish figure, wasp-waisted, slim limbed, with none of the manly chest you'd associate with an orator who could dominate a hall for hours. He'd had a dancer's grace, too, pirouetting and gesturing as he kept up an endless stream of talk. (No one had ever talked as much as Hamilton—the world might have drowned in his words.) Now it was only the talk anyone remembered. At forty-nine, he'd aged noticeably, thickened up, slowed. Even his electric, violet-blue eyes had dimmed, like a fire that had burned down to embers. And his hair, once a lustrous strawberry blond—a token of his Scottish heritage, it was said—had gone pale and brittle, but Hamilton still wore it straight back, clasped in his trademark club behind.

America was still a thinly populated country of only a few million free whites, most of them clumped in a few cities from Georgia to the Massachusetts coast that was not yet called Maine. If the elite weren't related by blood or marriage, they'd served together in the war or gone to college together. So here, Hamilton knew Kent from his earliest days as a lawyer, and he knew Van Rensselaer because Van Rensselaer was married to Hamilton's wife's sister. But, of course, familiarity doesn't always guarantee warmth. Among intimates, a slight can cause a cooling, and then chill into an icy fury, and so the political world of the young America was driven by the dual polarities of Anton Mesmer, the German physician who believed that everyone and everything is held together by a magnetic force. Those who loved, loved like newlyweds. Those who hated, hated like demons. Thinking he was among men he loved and who loved him, Hamilton ventured an opinion of a man he didn't. When questioned about Burr's candidacy for governor of New York, Hamilton was dismissive, but, being Hamilton, he expressed himself with memorable acuity. He said that he found Burr to be "dangerous." He said other things too, but that was the only one that mattered.

Hamilton had said so many words, it was probably inevitable that he would say a wrong one. This was a wrong one, and no more words from him could make it right. For there was another man there that night, one whom Hamilton failed to take into account. It was Tayler's young son-in-law Dr. Charles D. Cooper, who was staying over. He was so taken by Hamilton's fevered denunciations of the vice president that he did something dangerous. He jotted down a summary for a political friend in Manhattan, and that man—unidentified—must have found the comments of larger interest, for he passed them along to the *Evening Post*'s editor, William Coleman, who was eager to run them, but with a disclaimer in case Burr take offense and make a challenge against him. The editor persuaded Hamilton's father-in-law, the former New York senator General Philip Schuyler, to add a line expressing doubt that Alexander Hamilton would say anything so harsh about Burr after he'd pledged neutrality in Burr's gubernatorial contest. That was a howler. Everyone knew that Hamilton had been anything but neutral in that election.

Up in Albany, Dr. Cooper read the Schuyler note in the *Post*, and he took offense at Schuyler's insinuation that he'd gotten the story wrong or possibly had made it up entirely. Furious, he wrote a stiff letter to the Federalist *Albany Register*, to reiterate that Hamilton absolutely had called Burr "dangerous," and that was not all. He added, tantalizingly, "I could detail for you a still more despicable opinion which Mr. Hamilton has expressed to Mr. Burr."

Still more despicable.

That did it.

As Burr told a friend later, with the lightly veiled anger that was the purest expression of his breeding: "[Hamilton] had a peculiar talent of saying things improper and offensive in such a manner as could not well be taken hold of." Dr. Cooper's letter in the *Register* didn't come to Burr's attention for a full two months, in the middle of June, by which time Hamilton had succeeded in snatching the governorship from him in humiliating fashion: Burr lost by the greatest margin of any gubernatorial candidate in the state. Burr was not inclined to be forgiving. He intended to extract from Hamilton the full meaning of Cooper's words, if he had to use pincers to do it.

On June 18, 1804, he dispatched a note to Hamilton at his law office in New York.

> Sir:— *I send for your perusal a letter signed Charles D. Cooper, which, though apparently published some time ago has but very recently come to my knowledge. Mr. Van Ness, who does me the favor to deliver this, will point out to you that clause of the letter to which I particularly request your attention.*
>
> *You must perceive, sir, the necessity of a prompt and unqualified acknowledgement or denial of the use of any expression which would warrant the assertions of Dr. Cooper.*
>
> > *I have the honor to be,*
> > *Your obedient servant,*
> > *Burr.*

With that, the game was on. Those eleven letters passed between them, but when the third, from Burr, declared that he had been dishonored, it became clear that the men would be headed across the Hudson to the dueling ground in Weehawken to resolve the matter at dawn with pistols.

→►◄←

BUT IT IS the rare lethal dispute that stems from a single word, or even several words. And, while "dangerous" was insulting, and "despicable" more so, the words merely evoked a string of calumnies that Hamilton had leveled against Burr at every presidential election up through the last one, the epic contest of 1800, when Jefferson and Burr tied in the Electoral College, throwing the matter to the House of Representatives. While Hamilton had always disdained Jefferson, he loathed Burr so utterly that he fought to counter every attempt by the Federalists to cut a deal with him that would award him the presidency, not Jefferson. It is a mark of Hamilton's aversion to Burr that he embraced the Antichrist instead.

> *As to Burr, there is nothing in his favour. His private character is not defended by his most partial friends. He is bankrupt beyond redemption, except by the plunder of his country. His public principles have no other spring or aim than his own aggrandizement.... If he can, he will certainly disturb our institutions to secure to himself permanent power and with it wealth. He is truly the Catiline of America.*

As every classicist knew, the dissolute Catiline was one of the greatest traitors of the classical age, leading troops against the Roman Republic in a monstrous conspiracy that was foiled by Cicero, the canny orator in whom Hamilton may have seen a little of himself.

But Hamilton's political antipathy dated back to the presidential contest of 1792, when Burr rather audaciously put himself forward as a vice presidential candidate for the nascent Republican Party against the Federalist incumbents, Washington and Adams. At that point, Burr had been elected New York assemblyman, then appointed attorney general by the governor, who later persuaded the Assembly to make him senator from New York just the year before his vice presidential bid. He was hardly a political threat to the Federalists, and certainly not in a campaign against Washington. Yet Hamilton savaged him:

> *I fear [Burr] is unprincipled both as a public and private man. . . . I take it he is for or against nothing but as it suits his interest or ambition. . . . I am mistaken if it be not his object to play the game of confusion and I feel it a religious duty to oppose his career.*

A *religious* duty, no less. Divinely inspired, and permanent. And this for a man who went on to garner just one electoral vote, from South Carolina.

While Hamilton did not hesitate to say such things, and more, against Burr, Burr never responded in kind, preferring to answer Hamilton's contempt with silence, which may have been all the more infuriating. Hamilton's vituperation was unanswerable in any case, as it stemmed from something far deeper than any transient political disagreement but may have been embedded in his psyche. But in seeing evil in Burr, he brought some out in himself. The duel did not derive from circumstances, but from the essence of who these men were and aspired to be.

Who you are can depend on where you are, just as what you seek can depend on where you've come from. The past is always pertinent. Hamilton came to America alone at sixteen, a penniless immigrant, from the West Indian island of Saint Croix, the only one of the original Founding Fathers not born on the continent; Burr was raised comfortably in New Jersey, the son of the second president of the college that became Princeton University, and the grandson of the greatest theologian of the age. "I have never known, in any country," John Adams once declared, "the prejudice of birth, parentage and descent more conspicuous than that in the instance of Colonel Burr." As for the illegitimate Hamilton, Adams derided him as "the bastard brat of a Scotch peddler."

The differences followed from there. Eager for acclaim, Hamilton was resplendent in dress and fair in coloring, with those violet eyes; reserved, Burr dressed most customarily in black, his eyes were black too, bottomless, and he wore his fine dark hair straight back, to reveal a luminous white forehead. In argument, Hamilton could take four hours to say what Burr could say in thirty minutes. Burr was the one with the common touch, whereas

Hamilton could sound superior. All the same, Burr was the furtive one, writing many of his letters in code and keeping no notes. Hamilton was a straight party man; Burr was impossible to categorize politically. Hamilton believed in an almost neoclassical sense of order, balance, and regularity; Burr was a dreamy and impetuous romantic. While both devoted themselves to the ladies, Hamilton strayed only once in his marriage, catastrophically. Burr remained faithful in his but was an epic lothario outside of it.

There were plenty of similarities, of course, but they may have only encouraged the antagonism. They had nearly identical builds, both short and slender—Hamilton about five-seven and Burr an inch less—and may both have felt they had something to prove. They were just a year apart in age, with Hamilton the elder, which may have encouraged a kind of sibling rivalry. Both were extraordinarily intelligent—quick, insightful, articulate, educated. But in the small public arena of a young country, their rare talents may have only pulled them into tighter conflict as they ascended into an ever narrower circle of influence. Personally magnetic and immensely capable, they were born leaders, a fact demonstrated both in war and in peace, but in politics they had sharply contrasting styles and skills, as Hamilton was brilliant at backroom politicking while Burr was the first political candidate to campaign openly for his office, rather than leave the electioneering to surrogates. Each envied, and feared, the abilities of the other.

Their rivalry became a study in contrasts by which each man came to define the other, and be defined by the other, as light defines shadow, or up defines down. Each was what the other was not, Hamilton the man who would never be Burr, Burr the man who would never be Hamilton. The differences, however, were oddly complementary, like the competing images of an optical illusion: Both couldn't be taken in simultaneously, but neither could be removed, either, without destroying the picture.

So, no, the duel did not start on the morning of July 11, 1804, with a stray word from Hamilton earlier that year. Conflicts do not begin at the end. It had begun like a cancer, imperceptibly, and only gradually turned lethal. A mild irritation had evolved into disdain, then into dislike, then into a hatred, and finally into a war that transcended all reason and eclipsed everything else. When the two men faced each other down at sunrise at Weehawken, each did it to save himself. If one was to live, the other had to die.

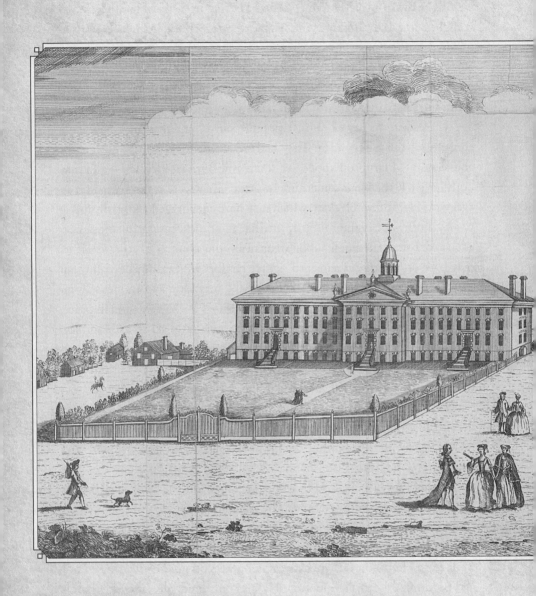

Nassau Hall, the College of New Jersey, later Princeton University, in 1764, five years before Burr was admitted at the age of thirteen. To the right stands the president's house, where Burr's father and grandfather died before Aaron Burr was two. When Hamilton realized he would be older than Burr had been when he'd graduated from the college, he attended King's College, later Columbia University, instead.

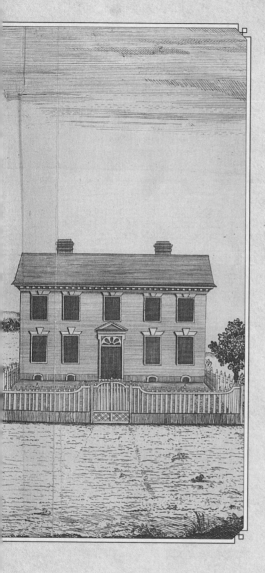

Part One

THE ROOTS OF THE HATRED

ONE

In the Hands of an Angry God

I N EARLY JUNE of 1752, a wizened figure, cloaked in black, made his slow way north from Newark, New Jersey, to Stockbridge, a farming village arrayed on either side of a broad, rutted street on the edge of civilization in the chilly Berkshires of western Massachusetts. It was a treacherous three-hundred-mile journey that could take a week—by sail up the Hudson to Albany, then east by wagon through pine forests that were said to be thick with Mohawks.

The traveler was the thirty-eight-year-old Reverend Aaron Burr Sr., president of the College of New Jersey, later Princeton University, which had been founded recently in Elizabethtown. A kindly character with a penetrating gaze, he was unusually forceful for someone so slight. He possessed a vast storehouse of classical knowledge, some humor, and, according to a contemporary, a "*lofty style*," the italics suggesting this was not entirely a compliment. He was coming to Stockbridge in search of a wife, and he had every reason to think he would find one.

Pastor of the First Church of Newark, the most prominent church in New Jersey, since he was twenty-two, he'd taken over the presidency of the college after the death of its founder, four years into the school's existence. He moved it from Elizabethtown to Newark, and, without compensation, taught eight students the Hebrew Bible, Greek and Latin, rhetoric, natural and moral philosophy, history, divinity, and politics. After boosting the enrollment to nearly fifty, he'd undertaken to move the college to the village of Princeton. He'd been raising the funds for a proper campus by running lotteries in local towns, soliciting potentates like New Jersey's royal governor, Jonathan Belcher, and importuning a variety of English aristocrats eager to educate the colonists.

He'd come to Stockbridge because he had set his eye on Esther Edwards, a cheerful, moon-faced beauty of twenty. He'd met her only once, six years before, when she was barely a teenager, but he'd never forgotten her spirited ways. To some at the college, the prospect of their esteemed president betrothed to a flirtatious twenty-year-old was unnerving, but Burr himself had no reservations. He'd allotted three days to the task of securing Esther's assent at the snug Edwards house on Main Street, and that is precisely how long it took. Esther was quite candid when she told a friend why she'd agreed: to gain "a bedfellow." Then she added with a silent cackle, "'Tis better to Marry than to—!" The nuptials were set for Newark a fortnight later.

The whole operation was conducted so briskly that Burr had plenty of time left over to devote to Esther's father, Rev. Jonathan Edwards. A Calvinist theologian of vast renown throughout the colonies, he was also a prominent member of the New England elite, the so-called River Gods who governed every aspect of life—political, judicial, military, and much more—in the wide plain of the Connecticut River valley that pushed up into western Massachusetts. Serene looking despite his wiry intensity, Edwards had a high forehead that conveyed an almost eerie intelligence, all-seeing eyes, and a slender mouth that rarely curved into a smile.

Back in 1734, Edwards had unleashed a bone-shaking religious fervor, known as a Great Awakening, that ripped like a wind out from his pulpit in Northampton, down through the valley's broad reach, as far east as New Haven, and southwest into New York and New Jersey. It had begun with an impassioned funeral sermon he had delivered at the service for a young man who had died in agony of pleurisy, every breath labored, as if his chest was being crushed by a force he couldn't see. To Edwards, that was God's punishment for his wasting his precious youth, as so many did, in a life of "levity and vain mirth," rather than in devotion to the Lord. Let his death be a lesson to young people everywhere, Edwards thundered. That made an impression, but when a young wife died shortly after, his sermon struck the parish like lightning. For this woman had devoted herself to God—and everyone noticed that she had died without a flicker of distress. Proof, Edwards said, "of God's saving mercy." With that, Edwards's evangelism swept up the young, who inspired their parents to rededicate themselves to the church. In short order, the ways of God became the only topic in Northampton. "Other discourse," Edwards noted approvingly, "would scarcely be tolerated in any company." As his message of God spread parish by parish, throughout the northern colonies, Edwards became something close to a divinity himself.

In 1736, when he was a recent Yale graduate, Aaron Burr Sr. had been inclined toward a scholar's life, but with the Great Awakening, "God saw fit to open my eyes" to religion. Or Rev. Edwards had. Burr might have been one of the wayward youths Edwards had fulminated against, a young man "polluted," as Burr himself put it, "by nature and practice." Newly penitent, Burr declared himself the recipient of "the Divine wrath I deserved." To restore himself, he accepted the call.

It was on a visit to the Reverend Edwards in Northampton that Burr had first met Esther. By the time Burr came courting his daughter, Edwards had fallen victim to some of the very passions he had unleashed. In 1750, the congregation had tired of his frightful severity and cast him out of the church he had once ruled. It was in exile that Edwards came to Stock-bridge, amid the wilderness of the chilly, low-slung Berkshires. Here he presided over the town's Congregational church and served as a missionary to the Stockbridge Indians who had settled there among a clutch of hut-wigwams to receive religious instruction and social guidance from the English in that "praying town." Rather than seek to stir another awakening, Edwards devoted himself to towering religious works like *The Freedom of the Will* and *The Nature of True Virtue*, which pushed theology deep into psychology and onto the verge of metaphysics.

Edwards's driving interest was in man's relationship with God, but he never entirely acknowledged that that was never mutual. While God could plumb the soul of the believer, the believer could never discern the mind of God. He must take God's love on faith, no matter how many cruelties he visited on the faithful. All human suffering was deserved, Edwards argued, punishment for sins that God alone could detect.

In his most memorable sermon, "Sinners in the Hands of an Angry God," Edwards depicts the errant soul as a helpless spider dangled by the Almighty over the fires of hell. Terrifying as the prospect of being cast forever into this burning pit might be, it is far worse, Edwards insists, to contemplate God's disgust at what makes that act so necessary.

> *The God that holds you over the pit of hell, much as one holds a spider,*
> *or some loathsome insect, over the fire, abhors you, and is dreadfully*
> *provoked; his wrath towards you burns like fire; he looks upon you as*
> *worthy of nothing else, but to be cast into the fire; he is of purer eyes*
> *than to bear to have you in his sight; you are ten thousand times so*
> *abominable in his eyes as the most hateful venomous serpent is in ours.*

The ferocious imagery of damnation aside, the sermon captures the terrors of daily life in Stockbridge, and throughout the colonies, where the Christian settlers were supposed to count themselves lucky whatever happened, even if they were scalped by marauding Indians, slaughtered by the militant French, or assaulted by one of the many contagions that swept through the colonies. To Edwards, it was meant to be reassuring that, despite such perils, God alone decides the settler's fate. To him, the true hazard is not sickness or war, but sin.

The clucking in the college over the difference in age between the Burrs did not quickly dissipate. While one student found Esther "amiable in her person, of great affability and agreeableness in conversation," that was a minority view, and local wags found much to dislike in a dainty young thing with her "Calimaco gown" and "Corded Dimity." Her husband had to warn her to "expect to hear, & Bare a great deal of ill nature."

Esther resolved to take all of it, and more, to be the wife of such a wonderful husband. As she wrote her bosom Boston friend Sally Prince: "Do you think I would exchange my good Mr. Burr for any person or thing on Erth! No sire! Nor for a Million Such worlds as this yt had no Mr. B——r in it." Whenever they were apart, she counted the minutes until his return. "O my dear it seems as if Mr. Burr had been gon a little Age! & it is yet but *one Fortnight*!" she wrote Prince when Burr had gone to visit Prince's father and her own. "I imagine now this Eve Mr. Burr is at your house, *Father* is there & some others, you all set in the Middleroom, *Father* has the talk, & Mr. Burr has the *laugh*, Mr. Prince get room to stick in a word once in a while." Life wasn't a complete delight for Esther in the president's tight, hip-roofed house under the buttonwood trees between his Presbyterian church and the town jail. As the wife of the president-cum-parson, Esther was obliged to bake "Mince-pyes & Cocoa-nut-Tarts" for thirty at a moment's notice. And there were existential worries. In the sweaty heat of summer on July 9, 1755, an entire English regiment headed by General Edward Braddock was annihilated when it staged an attack on the French stronghold of Fort Duquesne, outside Pittsburgh. If their British protectors could be destroyed there, they certainly could be slaughtered in Newark—and then what? "O the dreadful, awful news!" Esther fairly shrieked to Sally Prince. "General Braddock is killed and his army defeated. Oh my dear, what will, what must become of us!" She tried to think of it as God's justice. "O our sins, our sins—they are grown up to the very heavens, and call aloud for vengeance, the vengeance that the Lord has sent—'Tis just, 'tis right." But her heart wasn't in it.

Her husband took up her father's line as he bellowed from the Newark pulpit that the Duquesne massacre only portended worse calamities to come, all of them richly deserved. "Our men slaughtered! Our *wives* and *daughters* delivered to the lusts and fury of a lawless soldiery! Our helpless *babes* dashed against the stones!" It was too much for Esther. " 'Tis very probable that you and I may live to see persecution," she soberly told Sally Prince, "and may be called to give up everything for the cause of God and a good conscience—even to burn at the stake."

In 1754, Esther had given birth to her first child, Sarah, whom neither parent admired, Burr predicting she'd be a "numbhead," and Esther insisting, rather tepidly, she'd be "above middling on all accounts." In the snows of early February, two years later, the Reverend Burr was off attending to his pastoral duties—leaving Esther, almost nine months into her second pregnancy, feeling that the "Sun does not give as much light as it did when my best Self was at home." Heavy with child, she lumbered through the snowdrifts to a friend's that chilly Wednesday evening, February 5, to keep her spirits up. The next morning she was feeling "very poorly unable to write." That afternoon, her husband still away, she delivered Aaron Burr Jr.

Aaron proved a weakly baby, prone to flu and other illnesses. His health gradually improved, but Esther was not drawn to him. "A little dirty Noisy Boy," she called him, fairly hissing. "Very sly and mischievous." It was with some reluctance that she admitted he was more energetic than Sally, "and some say handsomer, but not so good tempered." He must have cried, fussed, refused to be calmed, for she concluded: "He requires a good governor to bring him to terms."

After Aaron turned one, Esther bundled him up for the long journey by sled to Stockbridge to show him to her parents. A frightening passage anyway, it was made all the worse by the terrible news from August 10 that the British Fort Oswego in upstate New York had fallen to the French and Indians. Worse still was the duplicity: As terms of the surrender, the French general Montcalm had assured the English soldiers that they would be unharmed once his troops entered the fort. The French observed the agreement, but once the soldiers were inside, the Indians sprang on the defenseless English, scalped dozens of them, butchered others, and made off with the rest.*

To Esther, it was all too awful. In her imagining, Indians were everywhere. The Mohawks were keen to take revenge on the turncoat Stockbridge Indians and their English keepers. Esther imagined she could see savages flitting in the shadows of the thick, leafy woods all around, their faces streaked with war paint, bows drawn to pierce her and her baby Aaron with arrows, or butcher them both with tomahawks, all amid fearful screams of battle, knives at the ready to scalp her and who knew what else.

At the family house on Main Street, the Reverend Edwards tried to reassure her that God never punished without good reason. If the English had suffered, it was because they deserved it. From the pulpit, he insisted to his anxious parishioners that it would be far worse to lose God than to lose their lives. Esther found that some comfort, but still, she decided to return home directly with young Aaron; it was too frightening to stay. Before she left, her father instructed her to remain close to God and all would be well.

---

* The cruel duplicity finds its way into James Fenimore Cooper's novel *The Last of the Mohicans.*

"What a mercy that I have such a Father!" she declared after she left. "What a guide!"

When she returned, the new college in Princeton was almost complete, a staggering accomplishment, a new Jerusalem. The main building, Nassau Hall, rose three stories and was 176 feet long and a third as wide. Esther was sure it was the biggest "on the continent." A handsome president's house stood beside. The students responded with such enthusiasm that it seemed the college was experiencing an "awakening" all of its own, Aaron Burr Sr. noted proudly. "Religious concern has been universal. Not one student excepted."

The next summer, 1757, Burr Sr. rode to Stockbridge to tell his father-in-law the thrilling news in person. By now, though, the town was virtually under siege. The French and Indian forces had taken the British fort at Lake George, less than a hundred miles away—close enough, Burr wrote Esther, that they could "hear the firing at the fort" in Stockbridge. Rev. Burr decided not to tarry, but hurried home again, arriving at their impressive new Princeton quarters as the leaves fell in October. He'd hardly gotten there before he had to set out again to Elizabethtown, ten miles distant, to see what he could do about exempting a student from military duty.

When he returned this time, he was crushed to discover that New Jersey's governor Belcher, loyal supporter of the college, had just died at seventy-five. "Such a loss," he lamented to Esther.* Already exhausted from his travels, he felt obliged to labor over the funeral sermon, but the strain brought on a burning fever that left him delirious. "The whole night after he was irrational," Esther reported. Weak, blurry, Burr was determined to deliver the oration in Newark all the same. When he came back, he was ghostly pale. Drenched with fever, wheezing, white, he collapsed into bed and never rose again. He died three weeks later. He was forty-two.

Esther was devastated. As awful as it was to lose her bedmate, she was

---

* Back in 1750, when Belcher had been stricken with "the Common paralytic disorder," or palsy, he had, at Burr's instigation, been given shock treatments inspired by Benjamin Franklin's electrical globe. His health, however, only worsened.

frightened she would not set a proper Christian example for her children, as her father had made clear was essential to warding off such calamities. "I am afraid I shall conduct myself so as to bring dishonor on my God, and the religion which I profess!" she wrote her mother. "No, rather let me die this moment than be left to bring dishonor on God's holy name." Pathetically, she begged her not to "forget their greatly-afflicted daughter (now a lonely widow), nor her fatherless children." She tried to see by her suffering that God was close by. And he sometimes truly seemed to be. After burying her husband, Esther told her mother, "God has seemed sensibly near"— and shown her the way to deliverance. "God has given me such a sense of the vanity of the world, and uncertainty of all sublunary enjoyments as I never had before," she announced. "The world vanishes out of my sight! Heavenly and eternal things appear much more real and important, than ever before."

In the midst of these trials, Aaron Jr. came down with a raging fever of his own that left him churning on the bed, his hair drenched with sweat. Esther took that as a sign of God's love too. He wished to claim her boy. It was all too beautiful, to be immersed in so much divine love. "I was enabled to resign the child," she wrote her father. "God showed me that the child was not my own, but his." Her husband dead, the boy's life ebbing—the very gloom was thrilling. "He enabled me to say, *Although thou slay me, yet will I trust in thee*." "One evening, in talking of the glorious state my dear departed must be in," she confided to her father, "my soul was carried out in such long desires after this glorious state, that I was forced to retire from the family to conceal my joy." It was beyond happiness. "When alone, I was so transported and my soul carried out in such eager desires after perfection, and the full enjoyment of God, and to serve him uninterruptedly, that I think my nature would not have borne much more." She ended: "I think I had a foretaste of Heaven."

It was the full flower of her father's preaching. Hell may be below, but God was above, and one need only reach for him. The Reverend Edwards himself came to Princeton to take over the presidency vacated by his son-in-law and to occupy the house in which he'd died. He had been in Princeton only a few months, when, to protect himself from an epidemic of smallpox that was sweeping through the colonies, he had himself inoculated by a Philadelphia physician, Dr. William Shippen, the founder of the medical college there, and a good friend of the family. Edwards had been a naturalist before he was a theologian, and he wished to demonstrate the value of medical science to the academic community. The inoculation was a fairly simply matter of slicing open a small wound, inserting a few pustules of the disease, and letting the body develop immunity as it healed. By a quirk, the technique had been brought from Africa by a "Negro-man" owned by the prominent Puritan minister Cotton Mather, and it may have taken on a tinge of divine providence. In this case, however, the inoculation did not confer immunity. It gave him the full-blown disease.

Smallpox is hideous and excruciating, as the pox bubble up, lifting off bloody sheets of crusty skin, torturing the sufferer in his bed, every movement a dagger slice of pain. Worse for Edwards, the pox encrusted the roof of his mouth and throat so thickly he couldn't speak above a whisper, and eating or drinking was impossible. But Edwards bore it all stoically, unmoving, his eyes on the ceiling, his afflictions a sign of God's tender, embracing love. He rasped to his daughter Lucy, who had rushed down from Stockbridge: "It seems to me to be the will of God that I must shortly leave you." He told her to thank their mother for producing "a most uncommon union" with him, and he directed his children, after his death, "to seek a Father, who will never fail you." The end came on March 22. Dr. Shippen attended him; he said he had never seen anyone go with such "continued, universal, calm, cheerful resignation."

Esther was inoculated successfully, but she soon came down with a fever that produced such hellish sweats and violent headaches that her mind floated free of reality altogether. Unmindful of her two children, she babbled incoherently for two weeks until she died, too, on April 7. She was twenty-seven. At the news, her friend Sally Prince fell into a pit of mourning for her beloved "Burrissa," who "held the empire of my breast." But she resolved to love the Lord all the more.

TWO

Contentment

I N 1745, ON the West Indian island of Saint Croix, three weeks' sail from New York, a cheerful, rather flirty sixteen-year-old redhead named Rachel Faucette lived with her mother, Mary, on a small plantation called the Grange. It was owned by Rachel's sister Ann and her prosperous husband, James Lytton. It was perhaps an hour's climb by horse up from the main port of Christiansted, with a fine view of the Caribbean and a steady breeze to counter the dusty island's baking heat. Mary had come there with Rachel to escape her husband, John Faucette. A French Huguenot, he'd come to the nearby island of Nevis to escape the brutal French persecution after the religiously tolerant Edict of Nantes had been summarily revoked at the end of the previous century. John Faucette had learned doctoring, enough to pass himself off as a healer, and probably as a veterinarian, too. The couple had seven children, but despite John's medical skills, five of them died from one or another of the many contagions—malaria, dysentery, yellow fever—that burned through the island. That was hard enough for both parents to bear, but when some land investments soured, dropping the family into poverty, John Faucette turned bitter, then outright cruel, and Mary decided to take Rachel and leave him. The abuse from him must have been extreme, for she obtained from the island's chancellor the right, rarely granted, to "live apart for the rest of their lives," and also won a writ of "supplicavit," enjoining her husband not to injure her physically or to "vex, sue, implead" her legally.

But the agreement also required Mary to renounce all rights to her aging husband's property after his death; her share would go to Rachel instead. While she did receive a scant annuity, it would be hardly enough to keep the two from starvation. A marriageable daughter was about the only asset Mary possessed.

A Dane lived on the next estate, lower down the hill. Thirty years old, Johann Michael Lavien was tall, pale, and handsomely dressed in laced vests and dress coats, and, while he was neither vigorous nor charming, he expressed a romantic interest in Rachel that was welcomed by her mother, Mary, if not by her. To Mary, Lavien seemed like the perfect man to restore her fortunes: a well-to-do planter who'd been highborn in Danish society and retained his standing in the Danish court. To Rachel, there was something drooling about Lavien that made her uneasy. As was said later, he seemed to have the "mouth of a shark."

Nonetheless, Rachel married Lavien at the Grange, with her sister and brother-in-law attending, and they settled next door on the broad estate he called Contentment. As soon as the couple was wed, the name proved bitterly ironic. For far from being highborn and prosperous, Lavien came to the marriage possessing little more than the fine clothes he'd worn to win Rachel, and his property was mortgaged to the hilt. Like so many other islanders, he'd come to Saint Croix to make a fortune in the sugar trade, only to lose whatever money he had. By marrying him, Rachel had taken a similar gamble, with a similar result.

No longer was he the genteel, courtly man he'd seemed to be while wooing. "A coarse man of repulsive personality," sniffed a Hamilton descendant. In the records at Saint Croix, he spelled his last name half a dozen ways—Lovien, Lawine, and so on—probably to disguise his origins as a Sephardic Jew, not that such a background would have been a liability on an island like Saint Croix with a significant Jewish population. Still, his reversal of fortune did for him what a similar turn had done for Rachel's father. It made him angry, and then mean, and then Lavien took it out on his wife. Rachel bore it for five miserable years, and then, in her desperation, left him, and even abandoned their son, Peter, not much more than a toddler. In his fury, Lavien brought the Danish court down on her, charging her not only with marital abandonment, but also with the worse crime of adultery, as he insisted that she had committed "errors" while they lived together, not just afterward. The fact that Rachel did not dispute the charge suggests it must have been true. That left the Danish authorities with no choice but to clap her in prison—a grim, dark, low-ceilinged hell in the Christiansted fort by the boisterous harbor. There, kept alive on cornmeal mush and an occasional scrap of cod, she sprawled on a dank stone floor, staring out a window slit through some sharply tipped iron bars at a slender patch of sky.

When she was released months later, she fled the island and made for nearby Saint Kitts to start afresh. Despite her tortured history, Rachel was still pert and enticing at twenty-one, and men noticed, one of them a Scotsman named James Hamilton, who, like Lavien, had come to the islands to make a fortune in the sugar trade and largely failed. Unlike Lavien, however, his lineage was genuine: the son of the fourteenth laird of the so-called Cambuskeith line of Hamiltons, who traced their lineage back to a twelfth-century castle ironically also called the Grange. James Hamilton was raised in Kerelaw Castle, an ivy-draped pile by the Firth of Clyde with a view of a rolling green landscape, where the Hamiltons owned half the arable land in the parish.

Since James was one of eleven children, including nine sons, and nowhere near the oldest, he had no chance of becoming the fifteenth laird, and he utterly lacked the qualities of industry and imagination to make up the deficit. "Bred to trade," his grandson John Church Hamilton admitted.* He was hired out by an older brother to work in an inkle factory producing linen tapes, but James didn't catch on, and, all his options exhausted, he went to sea.

Sugar was so profitable that competence was not essential to success, but it did help. James was undercapitalized and unlucky, but most of all he was inept. His brother John sent enough money to keep him from starving—but not enough to allow him to leave. The islands became his

---

* John Church Hamilton was Alexander Hamilton's fifth child and the one most devoted to his memory. William Henry Harrison's aide-de-camp in the War of 1812, he married the daughter of a wealthy New York merchant, freeing him to write a series of unreadable tomes about his father, and to place a bust of him in Central Park.

prison, just as they were for Rachel. Hamilton was working a menial job in the harbor at Saint Kitts when he met Rachel sometime in the early 1750s. Both were in social free fall—Rachel by her jail stay and Hamilton because of his financial failings. But Rachel had a flair, nicely symbolized by her flaming red hair, and obvious gumption to have risked everything to flee a husband she loathed. And James Hamilton's aristocratic pretensions might have given her soul a lift. Relationships outside of marriage weren't approved on Saint Croix, but they were common enough, and the two felt no obligation to withdraw from each other for lack of a marriage certificate. To start over, Rachel and Hamilton crossed to Nevis, the island from which her mother had fled, and where she'd inherited from her father, recently deceased, a small, two-story stone cottage by the sea in the port town of Charlestown. The thick limestone blocks of the house were a product of the slave economy. (With free slave power, heavy blocks were no more expensive than light ones, and held a tighter seal.) Cramped and ill lit, the house was not pleasant on the bottom floor, which they reserved for themselves, but this was the tropics, and, for all but sleeping and the most private acts, life was lived in the open air. And it was here, on January 11, 1755, that Rachel squatted over the earthen floor, a midwife hovering over her, straining to give birth to a son whose name would reflect James Hamilton's frustrations and his aspirations both. He would be Alexander Hamilton, named for James's father, the fourteenth laird, and heir to the Grange. Alexander was the couple's second son after James, who'd been named for *his* father and was two years older. Alexander would be the couple's last child.

→>-<←

ON A MAP, the island of Nevis was nearly a perfect oval, just seven miles across. Viewed from the sea, however, it seemed to go almost straight up, a steep, greened-over, jagged-topped volcano that rose more than three thousand feet to disappear into the swirling clouds. If Saint Croix and Saint Kitts and the other Leeward Islands were flat and peaceable, Nevis was bulked up, an angry god that cast a dark shadow across the sea.

In 1755, Nevis was home to about a thousand European settlers, most of them planters like Johann Lavien and James Hamilton who'd come to make or restore their fortunes. But they were vastly outnumbered by the ten thousand "nigro" slaves, a churning mass of African muscle imported by slave ships that unloaded their wares in the harbor not far from the Hamiltons' stone house, their cargo to be paraded into the town square, where they would be displayed in cages, often naked, for bulk purchase. The slaves worked the sugar fields that made Nevis some of the richest land in the world.

In 1755, Nevis and the five other sugar-producing Leewards exported goods of greater value than all thirteen American colonies combined, and when the English were trying to decide whether to give France all of Canada or the single sugar-producing island of Barbados, it was a very close decision. Once reserved for sweetening the tea and coffee of European nobles, sugar had become more pervasive, and the trade infinitely more lucrative, as the sweetener found its way into cakes, candy, jam, pastry, and innumerable other sweets for which the middle class had developed a craving. Just in England, the importation of sugar jumped from 10,000 tons a year in 1700 to 150,000 tons a century later. Sugar was white gold.

With sweetness the lure, Nevis became a global trading center, as if it weren't on the edge of the world, but at the very center of it. African monkeys and mahogany trees, Indian mangoes, Tahitian breadfruit, Spanish oranges—everything on the island seemed to come from somewhere else. Only the monstrous iguanas were native-born. They were five feet long, with green-and-gold scales that were metal hard; it could take three bullets at point-blank range to kill them. And, of course, the slaves came to enrich the planters, receiving nothing but misery in return. They worked under a broiling sun from dawn to dusk, felling the trees, clearing the fields, planting the sugarcane, then hacking off the cane from a plant that grew head high, and hauling it off to windmills that powered rollers to squeeze out the sweet juice—and sometimes caught a hand or an arm in the process. The juice was boiled down to precious granulated sugar, which was then exported by ship. Primitive and unabashed, many of the Africans worked naked, giving their masters all the more flesh to sting with their whips. One especially sadistic planter, Edward Huggins, established the island record for cruelty when he gave a male slave 365 lashes and brought his whip down on a female for 292 more. Brought into court for malicious conduct, Huggins was exonerated: His slaves were his property to do with as he liked. Worn-out by their misery, two of every five imported slaves died within five years of their arrival on the islands.

In the face of such horrors, the slaves were not placid, which is why half the cannons at that Christiansted fort where Rachel Faucette was imprisoned were trained inland. An Anglican minister named Robert Robertson in 1727 saw that whites and blacks were *both* enslaved, the blacks by their chains and the whites by their fear. The more fiercely the planters subjugated the slaves, the more determined the slaves were to seize their freedom, which brought on harsher measures still. Rev. Robertson noticed that as soon as the slaves stepped off the fetid slave ships that had brought them from Western Africa they sought to rebel—making them an early model of the revolution on the mainland to come. According to Robertson, they immediately schemed to "find ways of working off their Irons, and rise upon the Seamen, and snatching Billets of Wood, or whatever offers, knock them down, toss them over-board, turn their own weapons upon them, and mischieve them all they can; and these Insurrections are not sometimes to be quell'd without much Effusion of Blood, the Sailors being forced in their own Defence to fire upon and slaughter the slaves." In reprisal, the island laws were savage: If a slave raised a hand in resistance, that hand was chopped off. Any runaway who was caught would lose a foot. If he ran again, he'd lose the other. And any slave who attacked a white would be decapitated, but not before he'd been castrated, and ravaged by red-hot pokers.

Riding the volcano that was Nevis, everyone, black and white, faced the same tenuous existence of life amid the sea. Like most islands, Nevis was prone to fierce storms that seemed to whip up out of nowhere: Suddenly, the skies would darken, birds start shrieking, fish scatter to deeper water, and then the winds would come, ferocious ones that ripped through the island, turning life sideways, uprooting trees, smashing boats at harbor, and blowing down the houses in their path. Slaves working the fields knew to throw themselves to the ground and dig their hands into the earth to keep from being blown away.

And then there were the earthquakes. One started with a "strange, hollow noise," according to an eyewitness, and then the ground opened up

great chasms that could drop a man to the center of the earth, hissing gey-
sers shot boiling water twenty feet into the air, and a massive tidal wave
rose on the horizon, surged toward the shore, and crashed so hard up the
beach that its waters drove a third of a mile up the mountain, destroying
everything in their path. When the waters finally drained away, the capital
city of Jamestown was no more.

→>-<←

IT WAS AGAINST this background that Alexander Hamilton was raised—
a harsh world of angry weather, divided between those who whipped and
those who were whipped, with struggling, impoverished families like the
Hamiltons caught in between. The aristocratic Burr, even after that spate
of deaths, would have identified with the planters, in their fine houses well
up the mountainside, enjoying the sea breeze. Although Hamilton maintained the optimism of the talented, his life was hard, and it always would
be hard, a matter of constant, grinding toil, with little gladness in it. He
would forever live under the baking heat of the flatland, down with the
slaves.

A proud man whose eyes in portraits never engage with the viewer, but
look askance, trained on some distant object only he can see, Hamilton
seems always to be trying to set himself apart, and often, as in the celebrated John Trumbull portrait, to place himself above. From birth, he'd
strained to raise himself—to rise above his standing as a bastard. A harsh
word, "bastard," but one that he heard often from journalistic gadflies and
political enemies like John Adams, whose snub of him as "the bastard brat
of a Scotch peddler" quickly entered the annals of vituperation. Thinking
of his father's claims to the Grange, Hamilton once declared, "I have better
pretensions than most of those who in this Country plume themselves of
Ancestry," but then added a heartbreaking line, that his birth was "not free
from blemish." For, of course, his parents could not have been married at
the time of his birth; his mother had been unable to extract herself from
the odious Lavien. It would not be for another four years that Lavien
agreed to a divorce so he could marry again—to a local laundress, demon-
strating the depth to which he had sunk. Even then, Rachel was legally pro-
hibited from remarrying. So Alexander and James Hamilton were bastards,

and would remain bastards, and penniless ones at that. To the Danish court, they were termed "obscene." Or in Lavien's still more vicious term, they were "whore-children."

It was a stain that Hamilton could never wash off, as desperately as he tried, and so did his descendants as they laid on encomiums to Alexander's parents, as if adjectives could undo the ignominy. One hailed Rachel as a "woman of superior intellect [and] elevated sentiment," and another praised James Hamilton as a "dreamer," whose fancies at least had some elevation to them.

THREE

Platonic Love Is Arrant Nonsense

YOUNG AARON HAD recovered from his own fever by the time his mother died. Now orphans, he and his sister, Sally, two and five, were entrusted to the care of Dr. Shippen, the inoculant, who brought them to his home at the corner of Fourth and Locust Streets in Philadelphia, joining his own children there. Their grandmother Sarah Edwards was to collect them eventually, but, in mourning for her double loss, she was not able to come down from Stockbridge until six months later, in September of 1758. No sooner had she arrived than she contracted dysentery, a raging inflammation of the bowels that killed her.

It was a frightful string of calamities, and one made all the more troubling for its being visited on the family of the greatest theologian of the age. What sin was being punished? Did other believers have anything to fear? Or was suffering proof of election? Sally Prince spoke for many as she extolled Esther as "a mortified humble self-denied lively Christian." While she was unnerved at the idea that "God points his arrows at me," she decided she would "gladly . . . follow my dear beloved into the valley of DEATH." She set aside all doubts. "I want to lay low at the foot of God and resign to him."

It is impossible to know what the children thought. At nearly five, Sally would certainly have sensed the sweeping loss—not only of parents and grandparents, but also of her life in the grand president's house at Princeton and in the more humble Edwards quarters in Stockbridge. At two and a half, Aaron would have just started to emerge into consciousness and to store lasting memories. His first understanding of the world would have been of a dreadful vacancy. In his case, a double vacancy, as he was not only missing his parents, but missing the grandparents whose memories would have brought them back to life. It wasn't until long after, when Burr was in his sixties, that he found some letters of his mother's in her final derangement, when it appeared that Aaron's fever would take him from her, too. She made clear that she was content with that, for little Aaron did not belong to her at all, but to God, who was willing to "comfort" her by "enabling [her] to offer up the child by faith." By then, Burr had been exiled from the country and had nearly starved in Europe. So he knew suffering intimately, and he knew how hardship can be distorted into a perverse form of pleasure.

The children stayed on with Dr. Shippen for two years, until they moved in with their uncle Timothy Edwards. The oldest of Jonathan Edwards's three sons, he was, as a twenty-one-year-old bachelor, an unlikely choice. But now that his parents were dead, he'd already taken in several of his younger brothers and sisters. An aspiring merchant, he lived in Elizabethtown, New Jersey, on the shore of the Elizabeth River that opened onto Newark Bay. From there, a ferry made the twenty-seven-mile passage to New York City. Edwards soon took a wife, Rhoda Ogden, a respectable name in Elizabethtown, and they eventually added fifteen children of their own, making the house a small village of twenty-one children altogether.

Burr was not overly fond of his guardian, who must have been tremendously put-upon, and he played the rebel, as if the deaths cut any bonds to the strict Calvinism of his ancestry. At four, annoyed by something Timothy Edwards had said, he ran away and hid for "three or four days." At eight, irked by the "prim behavior and severe morality" of a female visitor, he climbed up into the boughs of a cherry tree and pelted her with cherries. At ten, he decided to bolt. He made it to the New York docks, where he prepared to go to sea as a cabin boy. When Edwards chased him down and spotted him on board one of the sailing ships, Aaron shinnied up the topgallant mast and refused to come down until, as he wrote later, "all the preliminaries of a treaty for peace were agreed on." Meaning that his irate guardian would not thrash him for his misbehavior.

Burr stayed put after that, spending much of his time on the Elizabeth River, close to home. There he'd swim, fish, or paddle about in his skiff with Matthias Ogden, an easygoing sandy-haired boy, technically his uncle as the brother of his aunt Rhoda, who would be a lifelong friend and the first of his political allies.

In the early years both Aaron and Sally were tutored by Tapping Reeve, a brilliant, wide-eyed scholar with womanly, shoulder-length hair who'd graduated from Princeton a few years before. In the one surviving portrait, he looks startled, but then, he was the kind of person whose eyes were more closely trained on his books than on life around him. A legacy from their father sent Sally to a girls' school in Boston, and Aaron to Elizabethtown Academy, a strict school of thirty boys where Aaron, small for his age, held his own with the other boys, being more argumentative. One of its founders was Reeve, who later pursued his interest in the Burrs by wooing Sally, an idea that Aaron found astonishing, since he always considered her a bore. Nonetheless, Reeve eventually married her and took her back with him to Litchfield, Connecticut, where he would establish himself as one of the great legal talents of the day, creating the nation's first law school.

At the ripe age of eleven, after two years of the academy, Aaron decided it was time to enter the college where his father and grandfather had been presidents. He appeared before the college's authorities to make his case. Burr never would be tall, but he must have seemed minuscule to those black-robed elders, especially with his elfin ears clapped on either side of an unimpressive little face with a narrow nose and dark eyes that were set so deep in bony sockets that they must have seemed like two tiny caves. The group took little more than one look at the lad and sent him home. To Burr, that was infuriating, and, to show them their error, he set himself to learn the entire first two years of the Princeton curriculum—Latin, the Hebrew Bible, and the Greek New Testament, as well as rhetoric, logic, mechanics, and on and on—in a single year, even though it would require an endless series of grueling eighteen-hour days, rising before daybreak and studying deep into the night by candlelight. With two years of the curriculum under his belt, he would enter as a junior, two years in. That would be his revenge, and that was the plan. But when he returned to Princeton in the fall of 1769 at thirteen to plead his case once more, the college had a new president, a rigorous Scot named John Witherspoon whose academic brilliance manifested itself in physical eccentricity—as he possessed a balding head that, to the younger students, looked like a top, narrow at the tip and fat in the middle. Unfortunately for Burr, Witherspoon brought new requirements for admission. Regardless of what Burr might have studied, as a candidate for the junior class he would have to pass a stringent set of exams of Witherspoon's own devising or go up against three classmates in an oral exam to determine if Burr was at their level. Burr chose the first, and he was granted admission—but only as a sophomore, not as a junior.

Burr was outraged, but he had little choice except to accept entrance as a sophomore, and to redouble the effort he'd put in at Elizabethtown. He would do the work of sophomore year, and of junior year, and of senior year, too. At that rate, he'd enter his senior year at fourteen, the youngest student ever to have that standing, and have all the work needed to graduate already done.

Still solidly Presbyterian from his father's time, Princeton, with its massive granite Nassau Hall, had a monastic, interior quality. There was a tavern in town, the Hudibras, that was located in a "commodious Inn," and a general store, but few other diversions. After the students were awoken by a servant's bang on the door at five thirty, the day began with a round of earnest prayers, and, from then on, prayers alternated with study and meals until the candles were snuffed out at nine. That is when, determined to make up that extra year, Burr bent over his books all the more—the Hebrew Bible, Tacitus, rudimentary mathematics, the pages a dull yellow in candlelight—until midnight or later. And if, in his exhaustion, his mind balked at the prospect of another page, he'd cut back on his meals to starve himself, in the belief that digestion was wearying him.

He did not complete the three years in one year as he'd hoped, but he did in two, passing the requirements for a Princeton degree at fifteen. He might have finished with Princeton then, but he remained. Rather than continue his studies, he chose to engage instead in what his close political ally and the editor of his posthumous memoir, Matthew L. Davis, primly termed "idleness, negligence and . . . dissipation." This at a time when the college was caught up in another of the religious convulsions called awakenings; Burr could not have been less interested. It was the first example of the erratic streak that became a Burr characteristic, as if his compass might point north one week and south the next. So it was here: Burr could not have worked harder to win the acclaim of the college, to say nothing of his late father and grandfather. Now he sought to antagonize all of them.

There was another activity in Davis's list of fripperies that may explain all the rest and would prove defining: "gallantry"—a courtly, and therefore deceptive, term for a casual involvement with the opposite sex. While Burr's friends made light of his numerous sexual conquests, they won the scorn of Davis, who could be quite prim on the subject.* Burr was an unabashed sexual enthusiast from puberty, and he enjoyed the close companionship of dozens if not hundreds of women, all of them willing if not enthusiastic. But to Davis he was a predator, whose victims were powerless to resist. "In his intercourse with females," Davis wrote, "[Burr] was an unprincipled flatterer, ever prepared to take advantage of their weakness, their credulity, or their confidence. She that confided in him was lost. No terms of condemnation would be too strong to apply to Colonel Burr." Why, Davis asked, did a man like Burr waste his time on such frivolities? "It is truly surprising how any individual could have become so eminent as a soldier, as a statesman, and as a professional man, who devoted so much time to the other sex as was devoted by Colonel Burr."

But Burr himself didn't regard these affairs as pointless at all. They were the point. "For more than half a century of his life they seemed to absorb his whole thoughts," Davis admitted. "His intrigues were without number. His conduct most licentious."

Intrigues. In retrospect, the word fits the shadowy Burr psyche. But sex is always a matter of discretion, a romp to be enjoyed behind closed doors, and sex outside of marriage especially so. It can't *not* be an intrigue. But if it is unmonitored, it is a matter for the couple alone to decide, an arrangement that puts the woman in a vulnerable position, as she can be far more compromised than the man. If it is hidden, it will also go unrecorded, which might have served Burr's interests.

---

* Davis compiled his memoirs shortly after Burr's death—and after Burr had been charged with both murder and treason, which may have colored Davis's judgment.

Was Burr dastardly—or loving? We'll never know. While the romances of most men of his station were primarily for their satisfaction, Burr thought of love more as a fair exchange, and a physical one at that. This may have been a rebellion against the astringent Calvinism of his father and grandfather, who, however joyfully lascivious they might have been in marriage, looked on sex outside of wedlock as an abomination. For all of his scattershot affairs, Burr wasn't just a deflowerer of women, someone who enjoyed the quest and lost interest when he had secured the prize—although plenty of women must have thought so. He genuinely loved women, and loved them so much that he wanted more of them. He delighted in idling with them, enjoying the free play of sex for hours. What would a man rather do than love? And, having loved, what man wouldn't want to remember? Burr not only dedicated himself to these romances, but kept records so he could savor them all again later, like a botanist thrilled with every detail of some rare woodland flower he'd spotted years ago and pressed into a book. His whole life, he carefully saved all his diary entries, his mementos, his love letters, his couplets, and stored them all in a kind of romantic treasure chest where he hoped they would be safe forever, his most prized possessions. Davis burned all of it, every scrap.

A few sexual details slipped into Davis's volume. The first of Burr's many romantic conquests most likely dates from this year of liberation, when he was fifteen, and it is included, presumably, because it fits Davis's thesis. As Davis tells the story, Burr seduced a young woman from Elizabethtown named Catherine Bullock and then cruelly abandoned her, leaving her to die, he says, of a "broken heart." Of course, heartbreak is not a medical diagnosis, and later research has suggested that the cause of death was tuberculosis. And, in any case, heartbreak is born of eagerness, not disgust. It's a fair guess that the relationship was brief and intense and ended by Burr, a statement that could apply to many of them. But that doesn't mean it was "licentious." Burr simply took his pleasure and then failed to give her enough in return.

His slight, chatty, Irish-born friend William Paterson, a Princeton graduate—and future Supreme Court justice—ten years older, wondered, like Davis, why Burr wasted so much time in Elizabethtown, when he could be improving himself at Princeton. Elizabethtown had always struck

Paterson as too tempting, with so many delightful young ladies about. "Perhaps," he told Burr, "the reason that I fear it, makes you like it. There is certainly something amorous in its air." It was a scent that Burr could detect in any breeze. Paterson admits that he wasn't immune, as he was himself just then hurrying to Philadelphia in pursuit of a certain "Miss ——," whom Burr knew, and perhaps knew *well*. "Platonic love," Paterson concluded, "is arrant nonsense."

Burr tried writing a few orations that year of idleness, and one of the more memorable touched on the subject of "the passions," which Burr considered the source of all action and feeling. "The passions give vivacity to all our operations," he declared, "and render the enjoyments of life pleasing and agreeable." He skipped over sexual passion, unsurprisingly, but may have alluded to it when he declared that no passions were inherently bad. Some were merely "unruly"—out of "balance"—and lacked "regulation." In short, they were missing that "governor" his mother identified. They characterized the "savage tribes," not "polished society." They weren't wrong, just out of place. He closed with a wish that no one fall victim to them. A wan wish, as it turned out, because he did.

Frisky and assertive, Burr became quite popular that last year. His fellow students called him "Little Burr," and they meant it affectionately. He formed many attachments with the other rising young men in American politics, such as James Madison, Henry Brockholst Livingston of the New York political family, and the spirited Henry Lee III, better known later as Light-Horse Harry. Burr joined the Cliosophic Society, founded by his friend Paterson, a literary group where students gathered with a few chosen professors under the eaves of Nassau Hall to discuss poetry and practice orations like "Passions."*

The Clio vied for intellectual supremacy with the American Whig Society, founded by Madison and the future poet Philip Freneau. Madison, always tin eared, derided the Clios as "screech owls, monkeys and

---

* Another one was about a duel involving a Colonel Gardiner who, when challenged, retorted: "I have courage to fight with feeble man, but I am afraid to sin against Almighty God." This would be Hamilton's attitude later.

baboons." One of the professors was Dr. Samuel Smith, a dry stick whom Burr could not abide. Burr was Clio president, up in the big chair, slouching onto one chair arm, since he was too small to reach both simultaneously, when Professor Smith arrived an hour late to a meeting. Burr insisted that the professor stand before him while Burr scolded him, saying that the students expected a "different example" from him. Later president of the college, Smith must have quivered with indignation. The dressing-down became college legend.

When the time finally came to graduate, Burr delivered a commencement address on the topic of "Building Castles in the Air." The text has been lost, but the thrust of it is evident—that a man needs to build a life on solid ground. This Burr did not do.

FOUR

The Prodictious Glare of Almost Perpetual Lightning

T HE YOUNG ALEXANDER grew into a slim, narrow-shouldered boy with tender skin unsuited to the tropics; reddish brown hair that surely came from Rachel; and darting blue-violet eyes. As an illegitimate, or "outside," child, Hamilton wasn't allowed to attend school with the other children on Nevis, but he may have been tutored by a "Jewess," one of the many who'd sought refuge on the islands for the same reason that Huguenots like Faucette did. Hamilton later claimed to have learned the Commandments in Hebrew. From Rachel, Hamilton came to appreciate the Anglican religion that drew her to church every Sunday, and he learned the French she'd learned from her father; he soon spoke it so fluently that he could later converse freely with the French diplomat Charles-Maurice de Talleyrand-Périgord, Napoléon's chief diplomatic aide. But the young Hamilton's mind sponged up everything—historical facts, English poetry, mathematical principles, medical diagnoses. His true schooling came from a set of thirty-four leather-bound books, whose titles have to be guessed based on what he knew: the plays of Shakespeare, Machiavelli's *The Prince*, Plutarch's *Lives*, the poems of Alexander Pope. All of them shaped his understanding of the world and informed his writing too, giving it the forceful, rather impatient style of an adult well before he was one.

Strained by poverty, his parents' relationship frayed over time from a constant bickering into open rages. Years later, Hamilton observed, "It's a dog's life when two dissonant tempers meet." His own marriage would be placid, despite the disruptions he caused. When Alexander turned ten, his father left to collect a debt for a Saint Kitts client, and he never returned. Rachel took the boys across the water to neighboring Saint Croix, vaguely in the shape of the dolphinfish that could be found in abundance off its shores. It was a selfish move on James Hamilton's part that brought his family nothing but woe. Still, ever after Hamilton was determined to be proud of his father. "You no doubt have understood that my father's affairs at a very early day went to wreck, so as to have rendered his situation during the greatest part of his life far from eligible," he later wrote a friend. "This state of things occasioned a separation between him and me, when I was very young." It just happened; no one's fault. But as the disappearance continued, the absence preyed on him. "What has become of our dear father?" he begged of his brother, James, more than a decade later, when his father had still not returned. He hated to think of him dying alone somewhere, untended, possibly starving. He'd send money—"to render the close of his life more happy than the progress of it"—if he only knew where.* His father had "too much pride and too large a portion of indolence," he finally acknowledged, but nevertheless he clung tight to the notion that his father was worthy. As he put it: "His character was otherwise beyond reproach."

In 1765, Rachel settled with her boys on the upper floor of a row house at 34 Company Street not far from the water in Christiansted, a sun-splashed town scented with salt air. She sold fish, flour, fruit, and other staples in a humble shop on the first floor. The store provided most of the family's income, and much of their meals, supplemented by any milk Rachel could squeeze from the goat penned in back. Rachel had inherited five slave women from her father, and she rented them out for the brutal work in the sugar fields. By now, those five had produced four children, which were hers, too. One was a boy named Ajax, who became

---

* By one account, he had ended up on the tiny Caribbean island of Bequia, not far from the South American coast, where he had somehow acquired twenty-five acres of land that proved useless, as sugarcane could not be grown. He likely died there of starvation.

Alexander's house slave, an uneasy relationship that spurred Hamilton's abolitionism later.

In search of cheaper rent, Rachel shifted the family about a number of times, until 1767, when they came back to live at 34 Company Street once more. There, Rachel came down with one of the tropical fevers that swept across the island, and it soon infected twelve-year-old Alexander, too. Somehow she scraped up money for a physician, but his treatment was as harrowing as the disease—bloodletting, emetics, purgatives—and possibly more destructive, as it left them both exhausted, bathed in sweat, and oozing blood and excrement. Alexander rallied, but his mother continued to writhe on the bed, the fever burning her inside and out. Finally, on the night of February 19, 1768, Rachel lay still.

Alexander rallied to attend his mother's funeral. The judge found public funds to outfit him and his brother with proper shoes and black veils, but that was all. As the mother of illegitimate children, Rachel was not eligible for the graveyard of the Anglican church she'd loyally attended. Instead, she was buried up the hill at the Grange, alone, under some mahogany trees. With his mother dead and father gone, Hamilton was no less an orphan than Burr. But he had no family members to rescue him. Instead, he had a family stigma to pull him further down.

When officers of the probate court swept into their rooms to inventory Rachel's estate, they made clear they were not securing it for her two penniless sons, Alexander and James, but for her legal heir, Peter Lavien, the son Rachel had borne her husband. In a final act of malice, Johann Lavien had seen to it that his son should get everything, even though, at the time of Rachel's death, Peter lived in some comfort in Beaufort, South Carolina, and had not laid eyes on his mother in eighteen years. So the last remnants of James and Alexander's mother disappeared—all except for those books, which Alexander's kind uncle James Lytton bought back for him; he kept them for the rest of his life.

Lytton's ne'er-do-well son, also named Peter, was appointed guardian for the two teenagers, and he proved a horror of his own. Recently widowed, he'd scandalized the island by taking a black mistress and having a mulatto child with her. When a series of businesses failed, landing him ever deeper in debt, he became so irregular in his habits that his brother had him declared insane. Not long after, he was found lying in a pool of blood in his bed, having either shot or stabbed himself to death. His will passed over the Hamilton boys too. John Lytton tried to do something for them, but he was struck down by a fever too, and died in his bed.

Hamilton avoided emotional details in his letters, and he recorded no reaction at the time, but many years later, in 1782, he wrote of his irritation that Peter Lavien had died in Beaufort without thinking of him in his will. "He dies rich, but has disposed of the bulk of his fortune to strangers," Hamilton complained. He was eager for *something* of his mother's legacy. "The amount is not very considerable, but, whatever it might be, I shall be glad to have it." Nothing was forthcoming.

Known in town to be studious and quick-witted, Hamilton caught on with the New York trading firm, Beekman and Cruger, that had supplied some of the goods in his mother's shop from its local office. Both partners were from established mercantile families in New York and would do much to widen Hamilton's view of the world. He caught another break when, improbably, a respectable King Street merchant named Thomas Stevens offered to take in both brothers, introducing them to a world of comfort they must have found unimaginable. Stevens had a bright, eager young son, Ned, who was two years older, but, with his flashing blue eyes and reddish hair, looked far more like Alexander than his own brother, James, did. Alexander never commented on the resemblance, but many others did. Thirty years later, Hamilton's friend Timothy Pickering could not believe the similarity between Hamilton and Ned Stevens, who later became a doctor in New York. "I thought they must be brothers," he wrote. When he passed that along to Stevens's brother-in-law, James Yard, Yard was unimpressed, as he'd heard that "a thousand times."

Although Hamilton died believing he was descended from Scottish lairds, he was likely the son of his new patron, Thomas Stevens of Saint Croix. Paternity would explain not only the uncanny likeness, but also the extraordinary gesture of extending guardianship to a non-relation. Properly, Alexander Hamilton was likely not Alexander Hamilton at all, but Alexander *Stevens*.

If Rachel had indeed been unfaithful, that would explain Lavien's outrage and his insistence she be thrown in prison—depriving her of the ability to marry again and thus making Hamilton legitimate. Still, Lavien hadn't been the one to damage Hamilton's reputation. Rachel had done that, and then bestowed on her son the name of the man she betrayed.

→>-<←

THE JOB THAT Beekman and Cruger had in mind would have crushed an experienced wholesaler, to say nothing of a twelve-year-old. The firm supplied the island with everything from timber and shingles to pork and black-eyed peas—hundreds of items altogether, virtually everything that islanders needed but could neither grow nor make on their own. And, as for the goods and produce the island could grow to excess, Beekman and Cruger would ship it out to dozens of ports around the world. All of this was overseen by Alexander Hamilton, starting at age twelve.

Shipping was a matter of records, orders, inventories, prices, and weights, and nothing crossed the seas, bound for Saint Croix, or from it, without the details passing through the Beekman and Cruger office at the corner of King and King's Cross Streets, just up from the harbor in Christiansted, not far from the fort where Hamilton's mother had been imprisoned. At first, Hamilton's work was supervised by the owners, but then David Beekman quit the business and Nicholas Cruger returned to New York, leaving Hamilton to run the office largely by himself. He didn't just keep track of the paperwork, but handled the negotiations, assigned the cargo, and examined the goods themselves, coming and going, to make sure they were up to standard. All weights and measures were carefully recorded and compared, the results noted and filed. Hamilton also had to determine the most expedient sea routes, sometimes over a thousand miles, and the right type of ship, keeping in mind the proclivities of the captain and crew, who ranged widely in talents and temperaments, none of which were very appealing, and had to work out the various payments in more than a dozen different currencies, from Dutch stivers to Spanish pieces of eight. All of the records had to be set down in faultless penmanship in the ledger book, backed by an occasional stinging letter to enforce the agreements. "Believe me, sir, I dun as hard as is proper," he assured Cruger, who oversaw his activities from New York.

It was at that desk that the young Alexander Hamilton left his "obscene" childhood behind. If this transition was born of necessity, it was also a product of his desire to make himself exemplary, with circumstances to match. If Burr assumed his mantle, Hamilton created his.

Not that it was easy overseeing blustery men many times his age, and many more his weight, while he teetered on the edge of nervous exhaustion from the weight of his cares. "I am so unwell," he confided to Cruger just a few weeks after starting in, "that it is with difficulty I make out to write these few lines." Nonetheless, he let Cruger know that he'd sold "30 bbls. flour more." He rode his captains hard, cautioning a Captain Newton, off in "Curracoa," to be "very choice" in the mules he selected, and to beware of the pirates along the "Guarda Costa" on his return. "Remember," he added. "You are to make three trips this Season & unless you are very diligent you will be too late—as our Crops will be early in." Before Newton could return, another ship appeared with seventy mules, but Hamilton assured Cruger by letter that the other mules would never sell, since the rival concern was demanding hard cash, and "Cash of all kinds [is] scarce here." Sure enough, the other mules didn't sell—but Newton's didn't either, since many of them had sickened en route.

It was a heady experience for a boy, but one he detested for his knee-scraping subservience to distant owners who'd left him with grueling, around-the-clock pressures and little hope that he would ever improve his situation. As he peered out from his King Street office at the human chattel being unloaded from Africa, he must have thought he had more in common with the burdened slaves than with their whip-wielding masters. Adding to Hamilton's frustrations, Thomas Stevens had sent his son Ned to New York to be educated at King's College while Hamilton labored on. "I contemn the groveling condition of a clerk," he wailed to Ned, "to which my fortune, etc. condemns me, and would willingly risk my life, though not my character to exalt my station" (that "though not my character" is pure Hamilton). He went on:

> *I'm confident, Ned, that my youth excludes me from any hopes of*
> *immediate preferment, nor do I desire it, but I mean to prepare the way*
> *for futurity. I'm no philosopher, you see, but I may be justly said to*
> *build castles in the air. My folly makes me ashamed and beg you'll*
> *conceal it, yet Neddy we have seen such schemes successful when the*
> *projector is constant. I shall conclude [by] saying I wish there was a war.*

The castles make for an interesting point of contrast. Hamilton admitted to building them when he wasn't, and Burr decried doing it when he was.

And, of course, there would be a war.

→>‹‹

FOR ALL OF Hamilton's complaints, he did have time for a little frivolity, and he spent it much the same way Burr did: pursuing women. If Burr recorded his activities in boastful letters, Hamilton resorted to rhymed couplets, and subtly suggestive ones at that.

> *So stroking puss's velvet paws*
> *How well the jade conceals her claws*
> *And purrs; but if at last*
> *You have to squeeze her somewhat hard,*
> *She spits—her back up—prenez garde;*
> *Good faith she has you fast.*

Not bad for sixteen, both for a style that anticipates Byron and for a knowing way with women's sexual ardor that suggests that, even then, he had enough experience to detail the intricacies of love. He was a quick study, after all.

His literary skills proved his salvation, and quite unexpectedly. The island was savaged by one of the ferocious, drenching hurricanes that periodically roared in from the sea. Most of the islanders scurried indoors to safety, but Hamilton ventured outside with a notebook and, bracing himself, scribbled some notes for a letter to the island's *Royal Danish American Gazette*. Hailing the storm as "the most dreadful hurricane that memory or records can trace," he went at it with a literary force that nearly matched its subject. "The roaring of the sea and wind—fiery meteors flying about in the air—the prodictious glare of almost perpetual lightning—the crash of the falling houses—and the ear-piercing shrieks of the distressed, were sufficient to strike astonishment into Angels." This wasn't just a storm; it was a message from the heavens: Humans were "vile worm[s]" that could use some humility.

A bravura performance, from one seemingly determined to deliver his own revenge on a world that had been so hard on him. In this scenario, Hamilton may have been a worm, only too aware of his pathetic limitations as a tiny clerk in a counting house, abused by fate. But, because of his knowledge, he was not a vile one—or a humble one, for that matter. He envied the hurricane's wrath, its ability to waste the vile worms he detested. That was the inner message in his letter, wound tightly inside the outer one.

On an island not known for its literature, the composition was bound to command some attention, but the very elements that made him feel so frustrated and ashamed—his youth, his clerkship—made it a sensation, and it quickly won the attention of a Falstaffian minister, Hugh Knox, who'd drunk away his youth in New York City and then fallen under the sway of Rev. Aaron Burr Sr., of all people. The elder Burr reformed him by offering personal instruction in the Presbyterian faith, and then handed him off to the synod, who dispatched him to a small circle of hell—the hollow caldera of the remote volcanic island of Saba in the Leeward Islands. Only a few miles from Saint Croix, it had infrequent contact with any of the other islands, making it only a little more hospitable than the moon. Knox did his penance there for seventeen years, attending to the spiritual needs of the few villagers. Finally released from this purgatory, he returned to Saint Croix in time to read Hamilton's gale-force prose and see a boy in desperate need of an education—at the Princeton of the now-deceased

Burr Sr., Knox imagined, since its new president, Witherspoon, had put out the word that the college was seeking worthy students from just such far-flung places as Saint Croix. Knox got up a fund from the West Indies governor Ernst Frederick Walterstorff and various Lytton relations, and it was done. Within a week, Hamilton was aboard a packet bound for America, never to return.*

---

* It's not clear what Hamilton took with him, but he likely took this: the story of an unusual duel. Although it had taken place three years before Hamilton was born, it was a legend on the island. It involved a peppery local lawyer named John Barbot and a brusque planter from Saint Kitts, Matthew Mills. Squabbling over a piece of land, Mills called Barbot "an impertinent puppy," a remark that brought the men to the dueling ground. There Barbot rushed his fire and shot Mills in the chest, killing him instantly. While duels were legal, it was not allowed to practice ahead of time or to shoot a man before he was ready. A jury found Barbot to have done both, and it sent him to the gallows. It was a rare duel, one that left both men dead.

FIVE

Refinement

W HILE BURR DAWDLED at Princeton, Hamilton sailed into New York Harbor in the fragrant city heat of early summer 1773. No place in the world was so frenzied, so bustling. From the fortified Battery by the Hudson along the East River, the shoreline piano-keyed with wharves—Albany Pier, Murray's Wharf, Beekman Slip, and a dozen more all the way around to the clattering shipyards well to the east—the sea air alive with squawking gulls, the rattle of cartwheels, the rude shouts of dockhands, the operatic cries of passengers searching for their ship, the yells of the newsboys, the patter of visitors in every conceivable language. It was a meeting of the Old World and the New, but it was a scene like no other along the coast, or in the world, for people came to New York to make an entrance into a new life in a city that called itself new, because it was new and always would be. Since 1760, the city population had swelled by almost a quarter to just under twenty-five thousand, beginning a stampede of immigrants that would soon push New York past Philadelphia as the most populous city in America.

It was made for Hamilton. The city would define him, and he would define it. Although he shifted his residence with the seat of government, from the moment he set foot on the dock, he never thought of anywhere else as home. Others might gape at the turbulence of such a rambunctious city; Hamilton was keen to throw himself into it and ride its waves. Even at sixteen, he was not one to be cowed. A handsome lad with those electric eyes and an erect bearing, he had grown used to staring down big-chested sea captains over shoddy merchandise and poor performance, and he was not likely to be put off by noisy New Yorkers. The proper John Adams of Massachusetts was appalled by New Yorkers and their unmannerly ways. "With all the opulence and splendor of this city, there is very little good breeding to be found," he sniffed. "We have been treated with an assiduous respect but I have not seen one real gentleman, one well-bred man, since I came to town. At their entertainments there is no conversation that is agreeable; there is no modesty, no attention to one another. They talk very loud, very fast and altogether. If they ask you a question, before you can utter three words of your answer they will break out upon you again and talk away." But that's Adams at his fussiest. Hamilton would talk away. He was home.

→>⋅<←

EVEN AS ITS population grew, New York had fewer people than Saint Croix, and only half the land. But most residents were crammed onto the southern tip of the island by the harbor, where oddly angled streets ran past shops stuffed with fine goods; coffeehouses loud with political talk; taverns full of noisy, cussing patrons; and churches of every denomination, their spires dominating the sky. But the pews were emptying, as the awakenings receded. In Manhattan, God was passing out of style.

Inflated by the sugar trade, Saint Croix's port did more business than New York's, but New York's economy, boosted by the first stirrings of industrialization, generated a much broader range of goods to send to the sugar islands, receiving their sugar, rum, and slaves in return. The activity created a rivalry with the mother country that was starting to grate on both sides—and would lead to a conflict that would define the age. To regain Britain's edge, King George had pushed through the Stamp Act of 1765, imposing stiff duties on English paper goods, and would soon squeeze the colonists further with the fabled Tea Act, which stoked outrage throughout the colonies, and no less in New York, which drew so much wealth from British trade.

For all of its new immigrants and rising patriotic sentiment, New York was still, at heart, an English city, and as Hamilton wandered about a fashionable neighborhood like the one along Queen Street, he might have imagined himself in London's Mayfair. Shops offered fine glassware, European furniture, leather-bound books, and other luxury goods of an energized economy. Wealthy merchant families like the Beekmans and Crugers built palatial homes. The ladies attired themselves in the latest London fashions—cloaks, hooped petticoats, and bonnets of India damask or Venetian poplin—while the men were decked out in "gallant" wigs, cravats, silk handkerchiefs, walking sticks, toothpick cases, and the occasional sword. The best families in Manhattan, exactly sixty-nine in total, owned elegant carriages, chaises, and phaetons, all of them relatively new presences to the city streets, to whisk their passengers to the Governor's Ball, the charmingly informal "turtle feasts," a card table for a private game of whist, some Haydn at the New York Harmonic Society, or the New Theater on Nassau Street to see *Richard III*, or, for a thrill, *The Intriguing Chambermaid*.

The growing economic disparity between rich and poor had given rise to a new word to clarify the social distinction: "refinement." Just the word was refined, as only the rich used it, and employed troops of professionals to create it. Elocutionists instructed their charges to lengthen their vowels with more breath and to eliminate crude expressions like "Split me, madam" from their conversation. To instill social grace, dancing masters were enlisted to give their clumsy, gawky students a smoothness of motion. Smoothness was key. In a herky-jerky world, the aristocrat needed to be smooth. Class was certainly not new to New York, but it was new on this scale, and it had never before been a choice. For Hamilton, the choice was easy.

Whatever else Hamilton brought with him to America, he possessed only one article of value—a list of Rev. Hugh Knox's connections among the Presbyterian elite. Given the city's social stratification, for a young man from the West Indies—a place so foreign that many people expected him to be a Negro—it would be impossible to get anywhere without such entrée, and he could never have created it on his own. Foremost among the Presbyterians was the Reverend John Rodgers, a pompous figure who carried a gold-headed cane as he completed his rounds making loving gestures to the poor. At that point, Hamilton was bent on attending Princeton as Knox had intended. When they met, Rodgers must have mentioned that his son had recently attended the college. In fact, he had roomed there with a young man with a notable pedigree. Aaron Burr Jr., son of the former president—perhaps Hamilton had heard of him? Rodgers might have added that Burr was a remarkable boy who'd entered Princeton at thirteen and finished his studies just two years later, which was nearly a record. That, in turn, might have provoked Rodgers to ask Hamilton how old he was. Either then, or shortly afterward, Hamilton subtracted two years from his age—a curious development for a boy who had previously felt too young. Now he was no longer a year older than this Burr, but a year younger.

It was Hamilton's first awareness of Burr, and it shaped him almost ineradicably, as Burr may have come to embody that elusive gentility Hamilton saw everywhere about him but could not think how to obtain. Rodgers must have advised Hamilton that, no matter how eager he was, he could not go directly to Princeton without formal schooling. This delay made the age adjustment all the more imperative. Hamilton agreed to attend Elizabethtown Academy, just as Burr had. Or, perhaps, because Burr had.

A mere coincidence at first, and the substance is a matter of some speculation, this virtual meeting of Burr and Hamilton through Rodgers. It might have been the work of that spider of Jonathan Edwards. But this spider is not at God's mercy; men are at the mercy of *it*. In the world of Burr and Hamilton, after all, God is not the prime mover, leaving the spider to cast its silky, invisible web as it will. And sometime in 1773 the first wisp wound about these two proud, unsuspecting young creatures, joining them, and then the spider began the slow work of binding them, loop by loop, ever tighter in an unnatural embrace.

SIX

In the Roseate Bowers of Cupid

H AVING LIVED IN Elizabethtown since he was four, Aaron Burr had long since ceased to notice it. To a boy from the tropics like Hamilton, though, the chill in the air that fall, the turning leaves, and the first skim of ice on the Elizabeth River, all of it would have been astonishing, to say nothing of the grand brick houses in the center of town, the proper estates farther out, apple and pear orchards that extended to the rolling hills, the geese tottering about with long sticks tied sideways to their necks to keep them from escaping through the fence, or the town's academy, a fine two-story building topped by a gleaming cupola, the first schoolhouse Hamilton ever entered.

Late that summer, Burr came home from Princeton, on one of his regular forays to visit one beauty or another, and he may have overlapped with Hamilton there when he was settling in. More likely, they didn't cross paths, reflecting the radically different stations they occupied in those days, with Burr a longtime resident at the center of this elegant town and Hamilton a visitor on the outskirts.

Through Knox, Hamilton had won an introduction to the cerebral William Livingston, tall and lean enough to be dubbed the "whipping post"—a troubling image, surely. He was a member of the powerful and moneyed Hudson River clan. Livingston would go on to become the first governor of the state of New Jersey, but he also wrote romantic poetry and was not averse to stoking a political controversy on occasion. Outraged that the Crown was bent on setting King's College above the harbor, interrupting some of the finest views in the city, he raged against the school as a "contracted receptacle of bigotry." When this had no effect, he created the New York Society Library as a counterweight to this royal imposition and made plans to sell his finely wrought town house in Manhattan and move to Elizabethtown, where he'd build a fifteen-room extravaganza for himself with the evocative name of Liberty Hall on a sumptuous 120-acre estate. Hamilton stayed with him in the city, and when the estate was complete that spring, Hamilton visited regularly, his first immersion in extravagance. It must have been alluring: the vast, rolling expanse, the Georgian architecture, the orchards, classical statuary, English gardens. There was almost too much to take in.

Fitting its name, Liberty Hall was a place of some abandon, and Hamilton watched another visitor, the smart young New Yorker John Jay—the future Federalist whose political life would be interwoven with his own—in open pursuit of Livingston's delightful young daughter Sarah, just sixteen, whom a cousin described as an "opening rose." The witty Gouverneur Morris, himself a ladies' man, watched the suitors moon about, "one bending forwards rolling up his eyes and sighing most piteously. Another at a distance sitting side long upon his chair with a melancholic and despondent phiz [sic]." Jay prevailed, marrying Sarah the following spring and snatching the political influence that was her patrimony.

Hamilton fell hard for Sarah's older sister, Catharine, known as Kitty, a spritely version of her more demure younger sister. Kitty was in her early twenties, making her several years older than Hamilton, but, ever since those Saint Croix poems, he'd never lacked confidence in romance either. He wanted Kitty to know that his mind brimmed with other things besides cleverness.

He slipped her a provocative note:

> *I challenge you to meet me in whatever path you dare. And, if you have no objection, for variety and amusement, we will even make excursions in the flowery walks and roseate bowers of Cupid. You know I am renowned for gallantry and shall always be able to entertain you with a choice collection of the prettiest things imaginable.*

It's quite pushy for a sixteen-year-old, let alone one who is pretending to be fourteen, and not just for its teasing sexuality. Somewhere between a tickle and a nudge, it shows off his powers of persuasion, as it appeals to Kitty's sense of adventure, literary imagination, femininity, sensuality, material desires, and hunger for sex. While most of Hamilton's writing seems *very* written, even from a young age, with balanced phrases and choice metaphors, this one has all the directness of actual speech, and you can hear him whisper this devilishly in her ear in the drawing room. And, as speech, it penetrated. Kitty did not ask him to stop. Most likely, Kitty Livingston was his first conquest in America. He'd entered her circle.

Another character who drifted through Liberty Hall was William Livingston's uproarious brother-in-law, William Alexander, who called himself Lord Stirling on the strength of a highly dubious Scottish earldom. Like all the Livingstons, Lord Stirling would reappear in the war, ultimately dying of diseases brought on by drink. He went William many times better with a thousand-acre estate in nearby Basking Ridge, complete with stables, gardens, and a deer park in the manner of an English country estate, where he bred horses and made wine, among other aristocratic pursuits.* But Hamilton's interest in anyone of rank was compounded by his fascination with Lord Stirling's daughter, also a Catharine, although she was dubbed "*Lady* Kitty," to distinguish her from her cousin. Just as Burr might have done, Hamilton dallied with both Kittys shamelessly.

And finally, in this teeming Elizabethtown milieu, Hamilton was drawn to another local power, Elias Boudinot, an innkeeper's son who, in his piety, created the American Bible Society and would rise to become the president of the Continental Congress after John Hancock. Boudinot also appreciated the finer things, arranging for readings of biographies and histories, while his wife, Annie, wrote verse that later won the compliments of George Washington. Hamilton was virtually adopted by the Boudinots, so much so that when the Boudinots' infant daughter, Anna Maria, was

---

* For all his rampant Anglophilia, Lord Stirling would soon serve loyally as a brigadier general for the revolutionary side, although not well if Aaron Burr—who surfaced in his military retinue—is to be believed. Burr claims Stirling was chiefly devoted to tippling, his tankard endlessly refilled by his obsequious aide-de-camp, James Monroe.

stricken with a fatal illness, Hamilton sat by her bedside until the end came, and, afterward, wrote an affecting elegy.

> For the sweet babe, my doting heart
> Did all a mother's fondness feel;
> Careful to act each tender part
> And guard from every threatening ill
>
> But what, alas, availed my care?
> The unrelenting hand of death,
> Regardless of a parent's pray'r
> Has stopped my lovely infant's breath.

It is striking that it is written from the mother's perspective. Possibly, he was thinking of his own mother, Rachel, who abandoned her young son, Peter, when she fled her brutal husband, and then removed herself from her two other sons when she died. It's a tale of loss from both sides, for he feels for the dying child too.

The emotional range of his writing—by turns empathic, aspirational, mimetic, hortatory, and seductive—is impressive for a teenager, and all the more so because the sensitive Hamilton is so rarely in evidence outside the page. Hamilton—or Ham, as he was then called—was primarily a man of action, driven to achieve; his strongest feelings stemmed from ambition, and indignation when his aspirations were not met. To judge by his letters, he did not usually bother with introspection. One imagines that if the later Hamilton were to stumble across this elegy, unaware of who had written it, he might have been puzzled that anyone would trouble himself to express such feelings.

Hamilton attended the academy for only six months before he decided he was ready for college. That was intended to mean Princeton. But Hamilton was now a boy in a hurry. Like Burr before him, Hamilton had an interview with President Witherspoon. By now Witherspoon had started to emerge as a fierce patriot, one who would later sign the Constitution and take pride in the fact that the Constitutional Convention held more graduates from Princeton than from any other college. At that point, however,

Hamilton wasn't a patriot and didn't think he'd ever become one. Having grown up on Nevis, he was an English subject, and that meant more to him than it did to his fellow colonists in America. He called himself an Anglican and had no objection to the aristocracy, in England or anywhere else. Coming from poverty, he sought to *join* the aristocracy, which is why he'd been so at ease at Liberty Hall. If a war of independence required hating England, Hamilton would never take up arms. No, he had, he said, "strong prejudices" in favor of the British point of view. So Hamilton told Witherspoon no, he wouldn't enter Princeton. Instead, he would follow Ned Stevens to King's College. Lord Stirling, the brother-in-law of William Livingston, may have helped his admission, since he was on the governing board (of the college Livingston detested, no less). It was the first decision that Hamilton made on his own, without any outside influence, and he acted not on exigency, but on desire. He wished to be a King's College man, with everything that that entailed—set in Manhattan, not New Jersey, of Anglican belief, aristocratic in outlook, and with fealty to the Crown. Of these, the most enduring attachment would be to Manhattan, the great, throbbing beast that would always inspire him. As the seat of commerce, it was the perfect training ground for a future secretary of the treasury, and it wouldn't hurt him to enter that endless gladiatorial contest that was life in the city—and take on all comers.

SEVEN

Six Slayloads of Bucks and Bells

AFTER GRADUATING FROM Princeton at sixteen, Burr was in no hurry to get on with his life. Instead, floated by that modest legacy from his father, he lolled about Nassau Hall for a full year more, idling over the classical texts, much to the distress of his guardian, Timothy Edwards, who didn't approve of too much leisure. When his books bored him, he drifted back to Elizabethtown to return to that summertime life with his strapping friend Matthias Ogden, the uncle he loved like a brother. In the warm weather, the two would laze in the Elizabeth River as they had done in his youth, swimming in its gentle currents or paddling about.

Or he'd chase women, of course. Elizabethtown seemed to have no shortage of flirtatious young ladies eager to dally with someone like Burr, who was now beginning to develop that air of dark mystery that countless women would find alluring. By now, Burr was free to take advantage of it, since his uncle Timothy had taken Aunt Rhoda and the remaining young children off to Stockbridge. She'd turned tubercular, and he was hoping the Berkshires' cool inland air might be better for her tender lungs. In Stockbridge, Edwards bought a dry goods store on Main Street across from the property of one of the last Stockbridge Indians, the others having been dispossessed of their lands by the English, who'd pledged to provide for them, and made a slow, sad migration west out of town. He later oversaw the sale of the Indian's house lot to a broad-chested lawyer and rising politician named Theodore Sedgwick, who built on it a fine Federal-style house, the largest in town, for a growing family that would eventually include seven children. The confidence of the house matched his own. It was in Stockbridge that Sedgwick would meet Aaron Burr, and, seeing a rising political star, befriend him.

This was the summer that Hamilton dallied with William Livingston at Liberty Hall. Burr surely knew Livingston, since he'd delivered the funeral oration for Burr's father. If Burr didn't come around to Liberty Hall, it was because Burr didn't need to cultivate someone like Livingston; he already had. He preferred to focus on bosom friends like Ogden—and, of course, on any ladies he might find.

Now, what to do with his life? Just to ask the question was a luxury, and Burr spent some time pondering. For him, the choices boiled down to three: the law, medicine, or the ministry. To Burr, none seemed attractive. Most of his Princeton classmates picked the ministry, as it was stable and prestigious, and his ancestry cried out for him to follow their example. His background gave off "an almost suffocating odor of sanctity," as one friend put it. Burr himself could scarcely have been less interested, but he had to acknowledge the expediency. So he found his way to Rev. Joseph Bellamy, a disciple of his grandfather's, no less, who ran a small divinity school out of his home in Bethlehem, Connecticut.

Immense and imposing, with a booming voice that seemed to ring down from heaven, Bellamy had a history of intimidating would-be ministers and sending them packing before the first day was out. Slight as he was, Burr was not frail, and he didn't back down. He learned his texts, firing back a smart answer to every one of the sly Socratic questions posed by the overbearing reverend, and soon bragged to Matt Ogden that he had Bellamy "completely under [his] thumb."

Typically for him, now that success was in hand, Burr started to feel bored by the whole religious enterprise and was eager for some fun. Idling at a local tavern one snowy winter afternoon, he noticed "six Slayloads of Bucks and Bells," a cheery group from nearby Woodbury who'd come by horse-drawn sleigh, furled in blankets, their faces bright with the wintry air. Burr gave them his full attention. "And," he rejoiced, "a happier Company I believe there never was; it really did me good to look at them. They were drinking Cherry-Rum . . . and I perceived both Males and Females had enough to keep them in Spirits—the Females especially looked too immensely good-natured to say NO to anything." Burr could always tell the noes from the yeses, or thought he could. "And I doubt not the Effects of this Frolic will be very visible a few months hence." Nine months, to be more exact.

That was January of 1774. A month later, Burr told his guardian he was tired of the ministry and he was going to try the law instead. He'd decided to learn it either from Timothy Edwards's brother Pierpont Edwards or Sally's husband, Tapping Reeve, Aaron's former tutor. Both were impressive lawyers, but Reeve more so, and he was now starting his law school, a one-room affair in Litchfield.* Edwards, growing frustrated with the whims of his ward, declared himself "indifferent" to Aaron's choice. So it was done: He'd study with Reeve.

Burr moved in with Reeve and his own sister, Sally, to their white, pillar-fronted house in Litchfield on a street lined with sycamores, and he became Reeve's very first law student, making use of his extensive law library and receiving his instruction. Burr proved to be an able student, but he did not devote himself exclusively to his studies. "I have now and then an affair of petty gallantry," he confided to Ogden, who would not have been surprised by the news.

One such affair was hardly petty. It took place in Fairfield, forty miles away, at the home of his cousin Thaddeus Burr. Ostensibly, Aaron rode over for a few familial visits, but the purpose was actually to woo the stylish socialite Dorothy "Dolly" Quincy, who was visiting there. This required some daring, for Miss Quincy was already spoken for—by John Hancock, no less, the rich and formidable Boston merchant who would soon serve as president of the Continental Congress. Not a man to trifle with, obviously. For Hancock, the attachment to Dolly was not casual. "Be fully convinc'd," Hancock declared to his intended, "that no Distance of Time or place can ever Erase the Impression made & the determination I have formed being

---

* Burr was not only the first graduate but also the most prominent one, although the list also includes Senator John C. Calhoun, the educator Horace Mann, and Supreme Court Justice Levi Woodbury.

forever yours." The stentorian tone suggests why Dolly wasn't so sure of that attachment, and Burr saw a chance to ruffle her skirts, steal a few kisses, and possibly more. Dolly was utterly infatuated. She complained that she scarcely had "a moment alone" with this "handsome young man" who kept riding over from Litchfield to see her. The affair had elements of Restoration comedy—the charming young rake seeking to cuckold a rich and stuffy elder—but it caused his cousin Thaddeus "the most bitter anguish," as he was terrified that Hancock might be furious to find out about the affair being carried out under Thaddeus's roof.

It came to nothing, as Burr soon shifted his attention to a wealthy "young Miss ——,"* provoking him to confer with Ogden about the wisdom of marrying for money. Matt conceded it was "alluring" but told him not to "let fortune buy you peace, or sell your happiness." So Burr turned his attention to yet *another* "Miss ——," this one a "fountain of melody" who had written a musical composition he told Ogden he was desperate to find. It was, Burr said, "the work of her own hands." The notion is suggestive, and it becomes all the more so for being written to Ogden in code, as if the real intimacy was not between Burr and the miss, but between him and Ogden.†

Burr was on to yet another new love just weeks later: "What would you

---

* To the frustration of posterity, many of the names have been redacted from the surviving letters in Matthew L. Davis's edition of Burr's *Memoirs*.

† It thus follows a habit that dates back to Burr's first secretive letters to his sister and would be the mode hereafter for Burr's sensitive correspondence. While it is true that letters were notoriously open to public perusal, it is unusual for someone so young to be so clandestine. Hamilton hardly ever wrote any personal letters in code, and Washington never. At this point, the cipher's schoolboy simplicity is rather charming, as the code was a simple "acrostic," as Burr terms it, by which every letter of the alphabet is translated to another one, following a key that both parties possess. As Burr's duplicities multiplied, and he had ever more secrets to keep from more people, he would strengthen the encryption significantly. William Paterson once teased Burr that his feminine "hand" was too "sleek & ladylike," and later made clear the implication as he referred to his own writing: "When the itch of scribbling seizes me, I hardly know when to stop. The fit, indeed, seldom comes upon me; but when it does, though I sit down with a design to be short, yet my letter insensibly slides into length, and swells perhaps into an enormous size. I know

say if I should tell you that —— had absolutely professed love for me," Burr asked his good friend. "Now I can see you with both hands up—eyes and mouth wide open. Trust me, I tell you the whole truth." By then, it's doubtful Ogden could be surprised by anything in this department. The better question is how Burr could be so successful with women and yet so indifferent to them. And why, knowing Burr's reputation, would any woman seek to add her name to his list? The identifier "——" seems apt, for all Burr's women in these accounts end up a blank. His only lasting relationship is with Ogden, with whom he seems to join arms as he declares, "The world is before us."

---

not how it happens, but on such occasions I have a knack of throwing myself out on paper that I cannot readily get the better of."

EIGHT

Holy Ground

I N THOSE DAYS, King's College, later Columbia University, consisted of a single, handsome three-story building that, much to William Livingston's distress, commanded a hill on the southern limits of the city, offering splendid views of the water. To its stolid president, Myles Cooper, the former chaplain of Queen's College, Oxford, the elevation was proof of its "commanding eminence," for you could see down to the harbor, across the Hudson River to the farmland of New Jersey, and out past Staten Island to the open sea. For all the expansiveness, the college was still in the grip of the city—and its many earthly temptations. Just outside the front gate past Saint Paul's Chapel stood the "Holy Ground" where hundreds of perfumed "ladies of pleasure" abounded for undergraduates who dared to vault a high wall to enjoy them. Hamilton was undoubtedly one; his sexual desires were fully the equal of Burr's. As John Adams hatefully rasped later, Hamilton possessed "a superabundance of secretions which he could not find whores enough to draw off."

The one three-story building contained the entire college: President Cooper's quarters, rooms for twenty-four students, a chapel, library, kitchen, dining hall, and classrooms. Student rooms were often shared, and Hamilton was thrown in with Robert Troup, a tubby orphan from Elizabethtown who would become a lifelong ally. A friend of Aaron Burr's too ("That great fat fellow," Burr called him), the amiable Troup was one of the few men besides the Berkshireman Theodore Sedgwick who would be able to stay close to both. In the tight quarters of King's, the two students shared the same bed, too. At first, Hamilton studied medicine, starting with Professor Clossey's lectures on anatomy—or "physic," as it was known—possibly at the recommendation of Hugh Knox, who had a fascination for such things. Never a doctor, of course, Hamilton did retain a deep understanding of the essential functions and structure of the body, one that may have provided a helpful model for the nation's economy, with its bloodlike money flows and skeletal financial institutions. But then he shifted to mathematics, whose Professor Harpur may have introduced him to the political philosophy of the formidable Scot David Hume, which proved critical to his understanding of government. Hamilton continued scratching out poems and attended the college's Anglican services. Troup used to see Hamilton drop down on his knees in the little chapel to pray aloud "both night and morning," leaving his friend "moved by the fervor and eloquence of his prayers." If Burr had the literary-minded Cliosophic Society, Hamilton had a weekly debating club he started with Troup and Ned Stevens, where Hamilton made his first forays into oratory. Troup said that Hamilton "made extraordinary displays of richness of genius and energy of mind."

Whenever the colonists' struggles with the Crown came up in conversation, Hamilton always took the British side. He "admired" the English constitution, said Troup, who considered his friend "originally a monarchist." Such attitudes would haunt him.

→> ◄ ←

BUT THAT WAS before the revolution broke into bloody conflict. In New York, the colonial Assembly had asserted much earlier in the century that the colonists' rights to their own property were not to be surrendered to any distant king. The question remained: Who owned America? Was it the king's to administer, and tax, as he pleased? Or was it the colonists' to manage on their own, without interference from the Crown? The issue split into a hundred pieces of contention, from the obligations to serve in the British army to the freedom to assemble to the place of the Anglican Church. And the slights had been building, first into indignation, then to open hostility, and finally to a fury that could never be contained.

The rage burst forth in December 1773, just as Hamilton started college. In Boston, New York's rival city well up the coast, a hardy band of rebels, many of them liquored up, and all clothed crudely as Mohawks with buckskins and face paint, rowed out into Boston Harbor in the dead of night to sneak aboard three British ships lying at anchor. There with tomahawks they burst open more than three hundred chests of tea and dumped the contents overboard, making a statement about taxes and tyranny that would reverberate throughout the colonies.

Troup contended that Hamilton, astounded that such a large furor could stem from such a small tax, rode to Boston to investigate the matter and came away impressed with the "superior force" of the "American claim." The sequence may be off, and the conversion oversimple, but there is no question that Hamilton started to reconsider his loyalist views. Exactly how thoroughly he converted, then or ever, is an issue that Hamilton would spend a lifetime addressing. The fact was, Boston was not New York. Boston was free to defy its imperial warlord, but New York was not so eager to abandon its English ties. After the Tea Party, Hamilton continued to attend a Tory college, observe Tory religious beliefs, admire Tory culture, and sympathize with Tory politics, much as before. But just the word was telling, for Tories were defined by what they weren't. They weren't the daring patriots devoted to the new cause of American independence, but loyalists to the old cause of the Crown, which, as the war approached, was proving to be an increasingly rare and risky devotion.

Furious at the Tea Party antics, the Crown imposed on the colonists a set of draconian regulations that became known as the Intolerable Acts. They shut down the Boston port, choking off all trade, until the colonists paid for the spilled tea; forbade public assemblies and jury trials; suspended other rights of a free people; and unleashed a regiment of stiff British troops under the bovine General Gage to patrol Boston's streets to enforce these new regulations.

If this was intended to contain the outbreak of liberty, it did the opposite, as Bostonians turned their calamity into a cause and sent out riders to enlist the support of other colonies through "committees of correspondence," which led to the convening of the First Continental Congress in a craft guild's brick Carpenters' Hall in Philadelphia in September.

The news of the British assault on Boston swept through Manhattan like an island hurricane, leaving the city "as full of uproar as if it was besieged by a foreign force." Hamilton had returned to his books, but he could not remain oblivious to the political winds whipping past the college. It seemed the city was engulfed in handbills and rallies and frenzied talk of rebellion.

At first, Hamilton was unsure where he stood. While New York's rebel leaders promoted a boycott of British goods in sympathy, the more moderate worried this would only bring the British down on New York too, and Hamilton was not yet ready to sever his Tory ties.

To promote the boycott, a band of militants called the Sons of Liberty called for a mass meeting on July 6, 1774, on the common by King's College. The war had come to Hamilton. It was time to pick a side.

Ahead of the meeting, Hamilton spent some time strolling under the shade trees by the college quietly talking to himself, trying to think the question through. Despite his Tory disposition, he could not help being affected by the emotional power of the patriot cause, with its quest for liberty. He had already dashed off an article or two for the Boston newspapers in favor of the Tea Party, trying out the stance. As he told Troup, "I [had been] prejudiced against the measure." But now was the time to commit, and as he went through the arguments under the trees, his mutterings were loud enough to draw attention to what passersby called "the young West Indian." He was rousing himself to speak.

The meeting had been called by a former merchant privateer named Alexander McDougall, now the streetwise founder of the Sons of Liberty. He had been imprisoned for assailing the New York Assembly as a gang of traitors to the patriot cause—and then proved so popular in jail he had to schedule appointments for his visitors. "I rejoice that I am the first sufferer for liberty since the commencement of our glorious struggles," he declared when he was freed. McDougall became the symbol of liberty, and his appearance that afternoon by the Liberty Pole at the Fields was electrifying. But that was just symbolism. As Hamilton listened to the speakers bellowing into the wind, he found the arguments against the British to be surprisingly feeble, and, unable to wait his turn, he started to speak up, unbidden, from the middle of the crowd, first timidly, unsure, and then loudly, firmly; and finally he could not stop, bringing forth a great tumbling river of argument that washed over the crowd. At nineteen, Hamilton was not the most prepossessing speaker, or the most fully voiced, but he was the most persuasive—forceful, compelling, assured—and somehow all the more so for being so boyishly slender and obviously young. When he finished, people in the crowd looked about, searching for someone who knew the lad, and finally the cry went up, "It's a collegian! A collegian!"

And a patriot. By backing the rebels on the Fields that hot July afternoon, and doing it so firmly, he set himself on a course for life. Indeed, McDougall and the others were so taken by their collegian, they didn't ask Hamilton just to join, but to join the leadership.

But he was still in college, so he aided the cause with arguments that he scribbled out in the third-floor room he continued to share with Troup, the heat rising with the warm weather. When an Anglican rector named Samuel Seabury, writing as "A Westchester Farmer," claimed that the patriots were starting a trade war with England, the pamphlet inspired such wide disgust that scraps of it were tarred and feathered and stuck to whipping posts. But Hamilton took him on in "A Full Vindication of the Measures of the Congress." The essay promised to leave the farmer's folly "exposed, his cavils confuted, his artifices detected, and his wit ridiculed," and it largely did. Hamilton slyly allowed that he was "neither merchant, nor farmer," never hinting he was actually just a callow student, and insisted he wrote only because "I wish well to my country." He defended the Tea Party, laid out the economic case for a break from England, and went on to observe that any war would not go well for the mother country, as foreign armies rarely win wars of attrition. And then he tossed in the sort of observation that revealed, once again, the fact that for someone so inexperienced, Hamilton could sound very sage. "In common life, to retract an error even in the beginning is no easy task," he observed. "Perseverance confirms us in it and rivets the difficulty."

In some desperation, Seabury did his best to rebut "A Full Vindication." Hamilton rebutted that with "The Farmer Refuted," this time, in his fresh confidence, deploying a sharp wit to go with his icy intelligence, and the farmer quit the field for good.

In Boston, the British resolved to crush the foment by the colonists, dispatching eight hundred redcoats to round up the revolutionary leaders Samuel Adams and John Hancock and then seize a cache of munitions in Concord and Lexington. When, along the way, the British troops encountered a clutch of armed farmers known as minutemen, they let loose a few blasts of grapeshot, and in moments, eight colonists lay dead. The war was on.

The stunning news raced down the coast. In New York, protesters swarmed the streets and, late one night, their outrage amplified by drink, surged toward King's College, by now a symbol of Tory contempt. There, with torches blazing and drums pounding, they surrounded the college's one building, bent on rousting President Cooper—his scholarly self-assurance having long since elided into rank arrogance—out of bed so they could tar and feather him. A sympathetic alumnus had raced ahead to warn Cooper to flee, and the man had awoken Hamilton and Troup too, since their room was close by. When Cooper froze in terror, Hamilton hurried down the stairs to hold off the insurgents. He arrived on the front steps just as the assailants were advancing on the school building, ready to seize their prize and hustle him away to be stripped and tarred. Despite Hamilton's growing reputation, the mob took him to be little more than a schoolboy. But when he started to reason with them, to point out that nothing would be accomplished by abusing Cooper, they quieted, and then Hamilton went on from there. Only a few words have survived, but they catch the burden of it, as Hamilton asserted that taking Cooper would only bring "disgrace and injure the glorious cause of liberty." As if to demonstrate just how out of touch Cooper was, he then poked his head out his third-story window and, not realizing that Hamilton was trying to save him, demanded that nobody listen to the boy because he was "crazy."

The mob never did get its hands on Cooper, who fled the college in his nightgown and finally found his way to a ship back to England, never to return. For all of Hamilton's decisiveness, the scene reveals his ambivalence too, as he defends a questionable Tory from a drunken mob of patriots. Which side was he on? The patriot side is the short answer. The longer one—his own. For every word, every gesture, says what his placement atop that stoop does: I am with you, but I am above you. And I say so not because of my birth, but because of my genius.

NINE

A Fever for War

WHILE HAMILTON SAW the war approaching from hundreds of miles away, Burr seemed largely unaware of the coming conflict until the winter of 1775, a few months before the Battles of Lexington and Concord, when he found out that a mob of several hundred people had torn down the house of a suspected loyalist in Great Barrington, just over the Massachusetts border from Litchfield. With axes and saws, the rioters had chopped the house down like a pine tree. The ringleaders were from Burr's Litchfield, and, after they returned to town, they'd been captured there by the sheriff, "*without resistance*," Burr marveled to his friend Matt Ogden, indicating they probably did not have his sympathy. But then the mob regathered and galloped into town on horseback bearing white clubs, the emblems of their cause, to free the leaders—only to discover they'd been locked in jail. With that, Burr broke off the story and turned whimsical, as if this event were of no consequence. "I shall leave here a blank, to give you (perhaps in heroics) a few sketches of my unexampled valour, should they proceed to hostilities; and, should they not, I can then tell you what I would have done."

It's a bit of a tease, this lurch into hypotheticals, leaving it to Ogden to fill in the facts. The truth is, like Hamilton, Burr was unsure where he stood regarding the monumental issue of his day. By 1774, the students of Princeton had burned in effigy the Massachusetts royal governor and formed their own militia, but Burr's elitism may have outdone his rebellious nature. When Hamilton faced a similar dilemma, his gut instincts kicked in with those speeches that marked him forever as a patriot leader, even though he'd shielded Myles Cooper from the intruders. When Burr heard the story of *his* endangered loyalist, he felt no need to intervene. It was just a story.

Then, in April, came Lexington and Concord, and this time Burr did not hesitate. Electrified by the news, Burr wrote Ogden to fly with him on horseback to Cambridge to join the war. When Ogden replied that he couldn't just yet, Burr waited while he read up on military history and tactics to prepare himself to be an officer in the conflict. Then, two months later, came word of the American triumph at Bunker Hill, and, terrified he might miss out on the war, he rushed to Elizabethtown and demanded that Ogden come with him at once, and the two galloped to Cambridge, where the Continental Army was massing on the common.

It was not an inspiring sight. Almost seventeen thousand strong, the troops were little more than a mass of farmers stretched out across a vast, mud-soaked township of sagging tents, dripping wash, foul latrines, and fleshy whores. As Burr moved among this ragtag assemblage, he could see that smallpox, dysentery, and countless other diseases had spread like slow wildfire through the ranks, leaving hundreds of the men lounging bare chested on sweat-soaked blankets. Harsh words born of pique or boredom led to fistfights that sometimes burst into small riots. Even the ones who weren't sick or hungry were unmanageable, all were ill equipped, and it defied the ability of the officers to bring order. "A scene of idleness, confusion, and dissipation," Matthew Davis called it.

George Washington had assumed command only a few days before Burr arrived. A tall, deep-voiced, oddly serene Virginian who'd distinguished himself as a soldier in the French and Indian War, he'd been a planter for the last decade or more and had never led any troops into battle. With scarcely any staff, he was overwhelmed by the task of organizing so many farmers into a fighting army.

Burr wandered the camp in a kind of daze, astounded at the squalor. When he approached Washington's senior staff, he repeatedly emphasized that he was a *gentleman* volunteer, a man of lineage, of education, and he produced letters to that effect from prominent citizens including Hamilton's mentor Elias Boudinot from Elizabethtown, now a member of the Congress. He identified Burr as "the only son of our old worthy Friend President Burr," not needing to explain what he was president of. He added grandly that young Burr was bent on "improving his youth to the advantage of the country."

It might not have been wise to emphasize what Burr sought to gain from his service. But even he could see there was no use for such a letter, and he made no effort to put it in Washington's hands. With that realization, something broke within him. Burr was ever a tower that was not always fully supported by its base, and at the thought that the war might not be the answer to his dreams, and that the grandeur that he imagined was his due might elude him, the whole thing came crashing down. Burr tumbled onto his cot, pulled his sheets about him, and lay there like a dying man.

Davis called it a "fever," and there were plenty of infections passing through the camp. And Burr had always been sickly, ever since he was very young, prone to periods of exhaustion after intervals of tremendous effort. But there had been no particular effort this time, only the shock of what he'd seen at the camp and his sudden hopelessness about his prospects. Like Hamilton, he could be oversensitive, taking to heart what others might shrug off. He brooded, letting dark thoughts congeal until they became a great weight within him. But it quite likely manifested itself for him as something physical that went beyond lethargy, a migraine, perhaps, that began with a pounding headache, like the thudding of an ax, timed to his heartbeat, then spread to a swelling of his eyeballs as if being pushed from within, wheezing nausea, a burning fever, a fatigue accompanied by a fretful tossing about. The military career that was supposed to crown him with glory was drowning him in muck.

He lay on his cot for some time—until one day he heard Ogden talking to some soldiers outside the tent about an "expedition" of some kind. Roused, Burr was curious to know more. He shouted for Ogden, who came in to explain that some troops were to embark on an expedition to take Quebec from the British. Almost impossibly audacious, it would mean pushing through hundreds of miles of the Maine wilderness to mount a surprise wintertime assault on a fortress atop a towering cliff that was thought to be impregnable. If this mission succeeded, it could lead to the liberation of British Canada. But anyone could see it was far more likely to fail, and fail miserably. That was Burr's kind of plan.

General Washington had already approved the mission, and an American contingent of several hundred men headed by Brigadier General Richard Montgomery was already headed up the Hudson to take Montreal. Montgomery was a large, affable Irishman, much appreciated by the troops for his easy authority, who'd been in the British army before coming over to the American side. The other contingent would be headed by Colonel Benedict Arnold. Slick and muscular, given to dares and stunts, Arnold projected an exciting sense of dash that had not been dimmed by the recent death of his darling young wife, and he was fresh from seizing Fort Ticonderoga from the British, the greatest victory of the young war. Now he was seeking men for the march on Quebec. Both contingents would ultimately defer to the Northern Department of General Philip Schuyler, the blustery aristocrat from Albany.

His blood up, Burr volunteered and then plucked some of the hardiest and most enterprising soldiers he could find from the sprawling mass of volunteers to form a "mess," or small company, to join him. Not to be left out, Ogden signed up, too, and gathered some men of his own, and both companies marched with the rest of Arnold's men forty miles north to the embarkation point at Newburyport. There, Burr assured his sister in Litchfield that he "was equal to the undertaking"—and happily noted that the villagers gave a special welcome to "gentleman volunteers" like himself. When she passed on word to their guardian, Edwards, about her brother's military plans, Edwards was staggered at his ward's folly and insisted he quit this nonsense at once. When that didn't work, Edwards had a number of Burr's friends plead with him to be sensible. "You will die," wrote one. "I know you will die in the undertaking; it is impossible for you to endure the fatigue." But this only urged Burr on. Danger was the whole point. Finally, in desperation, Edwards tried to bribe Burr, with gold, no less. Burr's answer: No.

Before their departure by sail, Burr joined some other officers for a service led by the Princeton clergyman Samuel Spring at the First Presbyterian Church, the only time Burr had ever been known to attend church since the death of his parents. Afterward, they all descended into the crypt, where lay George Whitefield, the flamboyant open-air preacher who had spread the fervor of Jonathan Edwards's Great Awakening of 1740. The men pried open the coffin lid to gaze upon the hallowed remains, touching them "with great solemnity." The body was little more than dust, but much of the clothing was still intact, and the officers cut it to pieces to carry with them as "a precious relic," blessed by the Almighty, to protect them. For Burr, it was an unlikely joining of his religious lineage and his own quest for valor, but one that reflects the solemnity with which he viewed this potentially fatal undertaking. When the group emerged, they were greeted by an adoring throng that lined the street to cheer the mission on.

As plotted out on the map of a keen-eyed British military engineer named John Montresor, who'd nearly starved to draw it one freezing winter, down to shoe leather for nutrition, the mission seemed preposterous. More than a thousand raw recruits would journey six hundred miles into the frigid wilderness. They'd sail by packet up the Atlantic Coast into the Maine interior, then board two hundred flat-bottomed, squared-off bateaux, each one more than twenty feet long, to push a hundred miles up against the current of the twisting ice-cold Kennebec. They'd then ride down the ominously named Dead River, along the way hauling the heavily laden boats up from the riverbanks, through the woods, and down into the water again to avoid dangerous rapids or thundering waterfalls, and make one last exhausting portage hacked out of the woods to Lake Mégantic and then to Chaudière Lake beyond. Finally, they would cross the wide Saint Lawrence to the meeting point of the two armies by the cliffs of Quebec. The place names indicated the vagueness—Great Carrying Place, Seven Mile Stream. Little of this route had ever been traveled by white men aside from Montresor, and almost none of it had been settled except by Indians. Everything depended on the accuracy of the map and Arnold's ability to follow it. He'd allowed provisions for twenty days to cover a 150-mile trek to Quebec City. If it took much longer, the men would likely die of starvation and exposure in the deepening winter.

From his days on the Elizabeth, Burr was comfortable on a river, but none of his fellow soldiers figured he was anyone to count on. So Burr outfitted himself in rugged clothing—heavy boots, woolen trousers, a double-breasted jacket, a short, fringed coat—and then added a foxtail hat, plumed with a jaunty black feather. All of it intended, he admitted, to "help my Deficiency in Point of Size." For arms, he carried a "Tomma-hawk" and a musket with a fixed bayonet. Ogden and his men joined Burr in one boat, along with Rev. Spring, among three or four others.*

A last-minute scramble delayed the departure until October 2, peril-ously close to the onset of winter. But Burr set off aboard the sloop *Sally*—"the very name I hope prosperous," he wrote his sister—and before the first day was out he'd made it up the Kennebec to Gardinerston for the shift to bateaux. Rowed by a pair of oarsmen, and a couple of others who worked poles to protect the boat from rocks, they weren't particularly maneuverable and proved too small for their men and the material they needed to carry, bringing the water up perilously close to the gunnels. Because of his experience, Burr took charge of one boat as captain.

At first, life on the river must have seemed luscious in the golden para-dise of a fall forest, but before long the river revealed what the maps didn't—that the water ran dangerously shallow in some places, was clogged with boulders and downed trees in others, and sometimes came up un-expectedly on ripping rapids, uncharted turns, or monstrous falls that swamped boats and required dozens of brutal portages deep into the tan-gled forests. Only gradually did Arnold realize that John Montresor's map was unreliable in more critical ways, having been deliberately distorted by the British military to deceive the Americans.

Worse still, the boats were leaking. Built in haste, they had been made of green pine, which shrank as it seasoned, opening up wide cracks in the floor that admitted ice water that rose up the men's shins, and then brought more water surging over the gunnels. "You would have taken the men for

---

* By one account, Burr was accompanied by a beautiful Abenaki princess named Jacatac-qua. Part Indian and part French, she was supposedly helpful to Burr because she knew the backcountry, and she was keen to provide the help because she was in love with him. Despite Burr's alarming reputation for gallantry, she joined him in his bateau, along with her hound. Sadly, this seems too good to be true, since she appears in none of the near-contemporary accounts, and, distrustful of Indians, Washington was opposed to using them on such an expedition.

amphibious animals," Arnold reported, "as they were a great part of the time under water." When the temperatures dipped below freezing as fall deepened, a Captain Thayer added that his clothes were "frozen a pane of glass thick." All the sloshing water made the boats nearly impossible to steer, and it ruined what was left of their provisions, primarily peas and salted beef. The men tried to scoop up fish and shoot game, and when their efforts failed, their hunger was so fierce they shot the dogs they'd brought and roasted them over a fire.

And then the rains came. Torrential, freezing rains that raised the river as much as eight feet, the water surging over the banks and tumbling madly over the boulders on the riverbed, halting the progress of Arnold's flotilla and leaving everyone soaked to the skin and white with cold. But as winter came on, the temperature continued only to drop, and the snow fell, turning the whole world white. Exhausted, frozen, starving, some men were reduced to drinking a sickening broth of boiled shoe leather; others tried a "water gruel" of melted candles. Still, up against the frigid waters of the fierce Kennebec they struggled, poling against the current only to find hundred-foot waterfalls sending up spray in their faces, or some riotous rapid shooting at them. Many of the men died of slow starvation, exposure, or illness, and many more vanished into the woods to save themselves. On it went, the snows getting heavier, the rations lighter, the progress slower.

It was Burr's first chance to demonstrate his hardiness, and "Little Burr," as he was still called, was used to going without food from his college days. Eager for a test, and for recognition, he welcomed the hazards, the fiercer the better, almost as if the outcome didn't matter, and he soon won the trust of men who'd seen an overeducated stripling with a boastful feather in his cap and misjudged him. At one point, once he'd finally reached the Dead River and was pulled along by the swift current, he didn't see the men on the banks signaling for him to stop—there was a waterfall ahead. He blithely kept on until it was too late, and over the falls he went in his bateau, tumbling straight down twenty feet into the foam below. One boatmate was killed on impact, everyone was battered, but Burr was not seriously harmed, and he slogged to shore and then kept on, without complaint. If anything, he seemed to welcome this ordeal of manhood and the chance to abandon his dignity, and so establish it.

Finally, on October 29, Arnold's team spotted the first houses along Chaudière Lake, meaning that Quebec was in reach. Of the original 1,100 men, only 650 had survived the passage. But by then, Montgomery had captured Montreal, and he was to be coming downriver with supplies and reinforcements. Arnold continued to the Saint Lawrence and soon saw the city rising on its promontory across the river.

The British had filled the river with their own patrol boats to intercept any force that tried to cross. Somehow, Arnold found enough canoes to ferry his men past the British patrols. But on the Quebec side, the British had gotten wind of Arnold's plans and brought in heavy reinforcements. Even with Montgomery's men, the American forces were outnumbered two to one; the defenders were fresh, experienced, and numerous, and they were seemingly ready for any attack. But the Americans had come too far to turn back. Arnold sent Matthias Ogden under a white flag of truce to climb up to the citadel and try to bluff the British commanders into surrendering to superior forces, but the British sent off a cannon blast before he could even enter the city's main gate.

The vainglorious Arnold still seethed from the indignity of being passed over for the head of the Northern Department, whereas Montgomery would never keep track of anything as absurd as rank. But both men had a reckless side, and they both eschewed caution. They decided their only choice was forward, into the teeth of the opposition, no matter what. They'd storm the citadel, hoping to overwhelm the defenses with a full-out assault. The men would have been excused if they'd had a bitter sense of foreboding. To rouse themselves, they pinned a piece of paper to their uniforms—LIBERTY OR DEATH.

High on a rocky promontory, the city's defenses made Quebec a virtually impregnable fortress, probably the most forbidding in all North America, and guarded by sixteen hundred men. Climbing up three hundred feet from the riverbed, the attacking forces might have some surprise on their side, and they planned to have more by waiting for heavy weather to conceal their movements. When the first snowstorm blew in on December 31, Montgomery and Arnold began their ascent from two sections of the river, but the storm proved blinding and brought sheets of ice that impeded the climb. Still, some of the men might have reached the top but for a few young Quebec defenders, about two-thirds of the way up. While others fled in panic at the sight of the hundreds of rebels swarming their position, one stayed long enough to set off a cannon, and on that one blast, the entire campaign turned. Quebec's defenders higher up scrambled to repel the assault, raining down grapeshot on the nearly defenseless men below.

Arnold himself was felled by a musket ball that cut through the back of his leg and left him unable to walk. He was carried to the army's hospital while men were slaughtered all around him in a fusillade of musket shot and cannonballs raining down from a height. Burr was right behind Montgomery, making for the gates. Montgomery turned and shouted reassurance. "We'll be in the fort in two minutes!" Then he raised his sword to signal his men to charge a log house he assumed was lightly defended. But the British inside let loose a burst of artillery and grapeshot that cut Montgomery to ribbons. He staggered backward and died where he fell, his sword arm still raised. Two aides fell too, but not Burr. Rather than retreat to safety, he hoisted the larger man's body onto one slim shoulder and struggled with it through the heavy snow toward the American lines, creating the first iconic moment of the young war. It was the chaplain, Spring, who first described the feat "amidst a shower of musquetry," and then another Princeton classmate, the poet Hugh Henry Brackenridge, took Burr's act to another, possibly more dubious plane in his poem "The Death of General Montgomery, in Storming the City of Quebec," which has Burr falling on the general's corpse and kissing his face before hoisting it onto his back.

The assault on Quebec was a tragic failure. Fifty died, thirty-four were wounded, and 372 were captured, including virtually everyone under Arnold's command, and this was after his deadly bushwhack up through Maine. But Montgomery's heroic death offered some redemption, as he pressed on into the teeth of the enemy. In dying, he became the first tragic hero of the revolution. Burr acquired noble stature too. As another Princeton graduate, William Bradford, a future state supreme court justice, told him, "Your praise is now in every man's mouth." The Connecticut reverend Joseph Bellamy's chatty son Jonathan wrote Burr of a dream he'd had in which Burr had become Montgomery, to "stand up, clasp your hand upon your sword, look so fiercely . . . it almost frightened me." But the whole vision filled Bellamy with "exquisite delight." Stockbridge's Theodore Sedgwick, who had new reason to befriend Burr, praised the "young, gay, enterprising martial genius." Just the idea of it marked the culmination of the fierce ordeal that had come before, where Burr had survived the rigors of the wilderness and passed that most fundamental test of manliness, endurance. While he'd used his family credentials for preferment, he'd earned this accomplishment entirely on his own—"dirty, ragged, moneyless and friendless," as he proudly said later. In the process, Burr attained the glory he'd sought. In the course of just a few wintry months, he'd emerged from dreamy adolescence to steely manhood and seized patriot consciousness as a man of honor.

TEN

Liberty or Death

W HEN HAMILTON HEARD the news from Lexington and Concord toward the end of April 1775, he rushed to enlist, joining a uniform company in Manhattan dubbed the Hearts of Oak and headed by a Captain Fleming, who immediately set to work turning the rough volunteers into polished soldiers. Hamilton memorized Fleming's instructions, and every morning, he pulled on a makeshift uniform of a short green coat and a cocked hat emblazoned with the same motto Burr bore on his chest, "Liberty or Death," and shouldered his musket to go practice in the Saint George's graveyard. There, among the mottled stones, he'd march about for an hour or more, halting here or there, as if he'd spotted the enemy, to ram some powder and shot down the musket barrel, take aim at an imagined redcoat, and pretend to fire. His friends soon marveled that he'd become "exceedingly expert."

Still a student, and always a student, Hamilton read everything on soldiering that he could find, just as Burr did. This was new terrain, and for their own sakes as much as for their country's, they would both have to master it. If Burr's reading smacked of the armchair general, Hamilton dug into technical details as if war were a piece of engineering. He thought ahead to the eventual peace, too, jotting down in his paybook, his son recalled, "tables of political arithmetic, considerations on commerce, the value of the relative productions which are its objects, the balance of trade, the progress of population, and the principles on which depend the value of a circulating medium."

But a revolution is a battle of ideas, and Hamilton began to put forth his in open letters, including an early one on the Quebec Act passed by Parliament the previous year. Burr may have raised a musket against it, but Hamilton lifted a pen. Hamilton saw the act, ostensibly a guarantee of full religious freedom for Catholic French-Canadians, as an affront to colonists everywhere in the New World, as they would now have to contend with creeping papacy, the expansion of byzantine French law, and an encroachment of the province of Quebec well south of the Great Lakes down the Ohio River. As such, it was yet another example, Hamilton argued, of the British ministry's "dark designs" to enlist the pope and his black-robed clerics in a "systematic project of absolute power" over all of Canada—and who knew where else from there. His letter went even beyond that dire specter, to demonstrate the necessity of disentangling church from state in the new America. Hamilton was only twenty, but he was already showing the vast and subtle reach of his mind—fiercely polemical, but exquisitely sensitive to the delicate interplay of religion, economics, culture, politics, and war.

In Manhattan, Hamilton was well positioned to feel the tensions between the colonies and the Crown, for, of all the thirteen colonies, New York was the one in the most tenuous balance between the revolutionaries and the loyalists. It seemed a puff of air would shift it from one side to the other. After the rousing fights in Lexington and Concord, the invigorated revolutionaries threw out the Tory-dominated Assembly and put in a patriotic Provincial Congress, which proudly sent its representatives to the Second Continental Congress gathering in secret in the grandly Georgian statehouse in Philadelphia, no spectators allowed.* Under the leadership of Boston's irascible John Adams, the Congress was frantically trying to put a proper Continental Army in the field. He'd nominated Washington, already a delegate to the Congress, to serve as commander in chief. Well positioned as the hero of the French and Indian War and a resident of mighty Virginia besides, he was clearly anticipating the appointment, as he

---

* Despite the tip toward rebellion, the New York delegation would not be empowered to vote for independence and abstained, leaving it the only colony not to sign the Declaration of Independence.

appeared in his military uniform, and he'd be chosen without significant opposition on June 15, 1775.

When New York's representatives returned to the city later that month, they proudly brought Washington with them. Hamilton was in the crowd lining Broad Street watching his new commander in chief pass by in a fine carriage drawn by a pair of shining white horses. Hamilton could see little beyond a massive Roman head pointed resolutely forward, never once acknowledging the crowd, and the bright purple sash that slanted across his blue uniform. Tall and stately, Washington always conveyed tremendous self-assurance, his posture rarely deviating from plumb vertical. It was as if, amid the battles and intrigue, he alone remained above the fray. "No Harum-scarum, ranting, swearing fellow," went one assessment, "but sober, steady, calm."

Beside him rode General Philip Schuyler, the commander of the Northern Forces under whom Burr would soon serve—via Montgomery and Arnold—in Quebec. Tremendously wealthy through a propitious marriage into a Dutch merchant family, he had created a vast estate, with a fine brick mansion in Albany. No one ever called Schuyler handsome. He was fleshy and thickset, with beady eyes under shaggy brows on either side of a prominent nose. But he was imposing, and wherever he went, he left his stamp. In two years, he would be Hamilton's father-in-law.

While this was a moment for some pomp, Washington did not tarry. After a brief appearance in the city, he pressed on to Cambridge hoping to rouse the sodden soldiers that would so distress Burr to capitalize on the tremendous victory at the Battle of Bunker Hill in nearby Charlestown, which had put a scare into the British.

Besides, New York was hardly a parade ground. Hamilton could see that it was a prime military target. Valuable in itself, this jewel of an island was also the gateway to the fertile Hudson River valley, land of the Dutch barons, and fervidly patriotic New England to the east. If Quebec secured the Saint Lawrence for the British, Manhattan guarded the Hudson for the Americans. But Manhattan would be almost impossible to defend, as the ferocious Royal Navy could bomb the island from almost any direction, while the Americans lacked a single serviceable ship to fend them off. Worse, Manhattan was not solidly patriotic, but riddled with Tories or

Tory sympathizers, all of them emboldened by a proclamation from their king that the colonists were in open rebellion. This made for spies everywhere. No plan for the city's defense would remain secret for long.

The schism also made for turmoil that put Hamilton back in the discomfort of divided loyalties. Just as he'd protected the granny Myles Cooper, he helped out a Tory printer named Rivington who'd printed too much loyalist opinion in his *New-York Gazetteer* for the liking of a gang of patriots, who burst in his door one night to ransack his house and destroy his print shop. They apparently didn't realize that Rivington printed patriot articles, too, including the work of Hamilton. Appalled by the "contempt and disregard of all authority," Hamilton complained bitterly about the ruffians to John Jay, whom Hamilton had known from his wooing days in Elizabethtown, despairing that such an attitude could lead to chaos. It would create a mob, in short. Slovenly, liquored up, ignorant—they were like a pack of wild dogs that would never obey. Hamilton found that terrifying; it was his worst fear of democracy.

If anyone had any doubts about British sea power, they got a better idea that August when the *Asia*, with sky-high masts and iron sides studded with sixty-four guns, breezed into New York Harbor. It was like watching a mountain sail by, but it did not draw a single shot in opposition. The *Asia* dropped anchor offshore, furled its sails, and remained there as if to fish, not more than a hundred feet from the Battery. From there, a single well-aimed blast from one of its cannons could have burned down the whole city, but the *Asia* held its fire. At that point, England needed to show restraint. If it rained down too much destruction on the city, it would rouse the patriots to a fury and lose the sympathy of the loyalists on whom it depended.

Although Hamilton was not yet a soldier, he already thought like one, and he realized that the seamen on the *Asia* might try to make off with the patriots' only cannons, by Fort George, down by the Battery. Late one night, he led some other students to the shore, where they all roped themselves to the heavy cannons and like oxen hauled them back up the hill to the common by the college. There, for safekeeping, they buried them under the Liberty Pole. They were still at it, hauling and burying, when dawn broke and the officers of the *Asia* could see what the students had done. In a fury, the ship let loose with its big guns on Hamilton and the others. The students scrambled to safety, but Hamilton realized that his jovial friend Hercules Mulligan had left Hamilton's musket down by the fort. Hamilton dashed through the firestorm to retrieve it, wrote Mulligan, "with as much unconcern as if the vessel had not been there." Hamilton returned unharmed to the college. In frustration, the *Asia*'s gunners dropped a few cannonballs on the Fraunces Tavern, opening a gaping hole in its roof. But the gesture was largely futile—no one was inside at that hour, and it served only to raise the ire of its many patrons.

The war for New York was on.

→‒◂

ALEXANDER MCDOUGALL, FORMERLY the leader of the Sons of Liberty, now a colonel in the hastily formed First New York Regiment, picked Hamilton to be captain of an artillery company. Hamilton had to round up his own men, and, together with the silly and ubiquitous Mulligan, he collected twenty-five in the first afternoon and soon had sixty-eight. Many of the men were immigrants who entered their names in his ledger only as wobbly *X*'s, but Hamilton accorded everyone the same pay and rations, regardless of background. Hamilton did, however, insist they all look sharp "to stimulate [their] vanity." As he explained: "Smart dress is essential [or a] soldier is exposed to ridicule and humiliation." He dug into his own education fund to outfit his soldiers in handsome sky-blue coats with shiny brass buttons and gleaming white shoulder belts. And, following Captain Fleming, he trained the men hard. This won Hamilton the admiration of General Nathanael Greene, who saw Hamilton working his men on the parade ground one afternoon. An iron forger who was himself self-taught in military ways, Greene was impressed by how much this young captain seemed to know about soldiering without ever having gone to war. He would remember that later.

An ingenious onetime bookseller, the gloriously fat Henry Knox had somehow managed to sled the army's massive guns all the way from Fort Ticonderoga to Boston, from where they blasted the hated British ships to break the siege of the city. The ships flew north to mass in Halifax, Nova

Scotia, and then stormed down the coast under the command of the rheumy-eyed Admiral Richard Howe, bound for New York, bearing much of the British army with them. As the ships approached, they seemed to darken the skies with their vast sails, and many of the city's patriots fled in a panic, leaving the city's Tories to exult in their newfound dominance.

To repel the invaders, Washington had relied on the intemperate General Charles Lee. A man of considerable military experience in England, he had developed a fevered eccentricity in America, engaging in a duel that cost him two fingers, traveling with a pack of barking hounds, and marrying an American Indian woman—and, for all this, winning himself the derisive epithet "Boiling Water." Lee had expected to be named commander in chief and was not pleased to come in second, which may have dampened his enthusiasm for the task of defending the city. He put his few guns on Governors Island out in the bay, in Red Hook along the Brooklyn shore, and along the New Jersey coast of the Hudson; and he sank some decommissioned ships at the mouth of the Hudson too. But it was a paltry effort. Lord Stirling, that inflated cousin of William Livingston, threw up heavy wooden barriers to close off the city's streets, and his men dug an earthworks that ran clear across the city from the Hudson to the East River to disrupt an invasion from the north. Hamilton's company set to work building a small protective fort atop Bayard's Hill, which once stood near present-day Canal and Mulberry Streets.

Despite such barriers, Washington didn't think his men could keep the British out of New York for long, not with their numbers and prowess. He was tempted to burn the city to the ground to keep the enemy from seizing anything of value. But he didn't want patriots to see Manhattan engulfed in flames. Instead, in April of 1776 he hurried back from Cambridge to personally oversee the city's protection, which did not endear him to General Lee. Washington set up headquarters in a fine mansion on Richmond Hill, a gentle rise not far from the Hudson.

→>-<←

AFTER THE DISASTROUS Quebec venture, Burr was obliged to linger on there by the Saint Lawrence the entire bone-chilling winter while Arnold waited for a chance to avenge his losses and take the fort, but that chance never came. Ogden meanwhile had received orders to return to New Jersey. When he received no letters from his friend, Burr became increasingly fretful. Rivalrous, Burr wanted Ogden to do well, but not too well, not while he was bivouacked in the snow for months. When he finally learned in May that Ogden had been promoted to lieutenant colonel, Burr's envy burned through as he lectured his friend on the hazards of success. "Promotion, the caresses of the great and the flatteries of the low are sometimes fatal to the noblest minds," he counseled. He assured Matt that *he* would never abandon him. "Rely on the sincerity you never found to fail," he declared.

As it happened, Ogden had not forgotten Burr. Rather, he'd done for Burr what Burr would likely never have done for him. He'd secured Burr a chance to experience one of those "caresses of the great"—by serving on the staff of General Washington. Washington responded to the good word from Ogden by issuing Burr an invitation to meet him at Richmond Hill in early June. Burr had been released to New York by the time that message arrived, and he arrived at Washington's headquarters with alacrity. The tall, taciturn commander looked over this intrepid young soldier and briskly appointed him a member of his staff—or "family," as he preferred to say, stressing the loyalty and intimacy of the arrangement.

Burr was gone ten days later, never to speak of the matter again. Nor did Washington. So it is unknown what transpired. Obviously, Burr rubbed Washington the wrong way. Burr's coppery self-assurance and innate hauteur may have irritated a commander in chief; his air of mystery may have incurred mistrust from a man who lived by candor; or his passion for romance may have struck Washington as unsoldierly. Or it might be that Burr simply did not find himself suited for a desk job and preferred to win glory in the field. In the face of any such profound difference, Washington was not inclined to make an accommodation for someone so untried, and Burr was never one to conform. Ever after, Washington dismissed Burr as an "intriguer" and never again welcomed him into his inner circle. Burr never returned to Richmond Hill during the war, but afterward, when he emerged as a prosperous lawyer in the city, he purchased Richmond Hill as his own estate.

ELEVEN

When in the Course of Human Events

T RUST WAS ESSENTIAL, for there were indeed intriguers everywhere. In June of 1776, the former royal governor and other loyalists in New York City had gotten to a member of Washington's personal guard, Sergeant Thomas Hickey, and persuaded him to use his proximity to murder Washington, whereupon other conspirators would descend with knives on his staff officers. The plot was exposed in time, and Hickey was taken to the gallows, defiant until nearly the end, when he burst into tears at the sight of the noose dangling before him. Hamilton had been sending dispatches back to readers on Saint Croix, and he delivered an excited account of the "barbarous and infernal plot" but ended on a more sober note: "It is hoped that the miscreants now in our possession will meet with a punishment adequate to their crimes."

There was an eerie stillness to New York through the month, as the few thousand patriots who dared remain waited for the British fleet to come. And then, on July 2, the British sailed into the harbor—an unimaginably vast armada of three hundred ships that clogged the sea with their massive, battle-ready hulls and filled the skies with their flapping sails, altogether a prodigious sight. Staring from rooftops, the motley Continental Army watched agog. "I thought all London was afloat," said one soldier. The ships anchored off New Jersey's Sandy Hook, tauntingly visible from the city, and then, to a lively tune that echoed contemptuously across the water, they disgorged an astounding thirty-two thousand redcoats, including more than eight thousand of the fearsome Hessian mercenaries, a vaster count than the population of New York even at its height, let alone then, when so many citizens had fled. Washington had put that beefy Bostonian Henry Knox in charge of the fortifications, and he'd shifted Hamilton's artillery company, now bolstered by thirty-two-pounders, to star-shaped Fort George down on the Battery. From there, Hamilton had a clear line of sight at this display of might across the water and wisely kept his guns silent.

Two days later, as if in response, came July Fourth, when America officially broke from England with a ringing declaration of war from Philadelphia called the Declaration of Independence. The announcement went unnoticed elsewhere that day since it took riders several days more to fan out through the colonies with the news. As it happened, Hamilton passed the Fourth hunting for a pocketbook he'd left somewhere around the fort. It was stuffed with nearly all the money he possessed, but he could be clumsy about such things. He ended up placing an advertisement for the missing item in one of the loyalist newspapers, the only ones still operating, which was likely greeted only with derision. The pocketbook never turned up.

Washington received a full copy of the Declaration several days later and ordered it to be read out to the regiments "with an audible voice." It was just words, not ships or guns or soldiers, words that may have seemed beside the point, like responding to a cannonball with a puff of feathers, but those words had power, and they did much to counter the daunting arrival of the British armada. "When in the course of human events . . ." The words were a lyric that created its own music. For all the swelling rhetoric, the most powerful line was probably the first one about the "thirteen united States of America." Not colonies of Britain, but states of America. The break was made. Never before in all of history had a colony turned against the mother country, let alone tried to establish itself as a democracy, a form of government that had not been tried since the Romans, *and* put forth high-flown principles about liberty and equality among all men, universal principles that had never before, anywhere in the world, been considered a basis of existence. Yet this document did all this in a manner that was both credible and inspiring. Hamilton heard Thomas Jefferson's words in his dress uniform with the rest of his artillery company on the New York Common, the confident, lyrical phrases spreading through the troops like a fresh breeze. Everyone listened in awed silence, stirred by the sudden contact with eternity, and then, electrified, many of the soldiers burst off the common to go rampaging through the streets, knocking down British pub signs, tipping the massive equestrian statue of George III—gilded, in Roman garb—off its pedestal, and hauling it away to melt down for bullets.

->-<-

WHEN HAMILTON RETURNED to his post at Fort George, he was alert for any sign that the British were preparing to bombard the city, and on July 12, the sign was unmistakable: a huge forty-four-gun warship, the *Phoenix*, and a smaller frigate, the *Rose*, raised their sails, detached themselves from the rest of the fleet, now anchored off Staten Island, and made for the Hudson, firing their big guns on the city as they went. Fort George took a heavy pounding, which Hamilton tried to return with his own much smaller cannon—until catastrophe struck. One of his cannons exploded, sending hunks of red-hot lead everywhere, killing six of his men and injuring maybe a dozen more. It appeared the gunners had gotten drunk to celebrate the Declaration and failed to swab the cannon shaft properly. Afraid he might be held responsible, Hamilton was furious. But already admired by his superiors, he faced no official reprimand.

With the British assault, Washington ordered the last New Yorkers, about five thousand in all, to leave the city, turning New York into a ghost town except for the soldiers girding to defend it. Anticipating an invasion of British troops but not knowing where, Washington spread his own meager forces out over Manhattan and across the East River to Brooklyn. Hamilton was with his artillery company posted at Brooklyn Heights, ready to move in any direction. But the British only pretended to be preparing an invasion on Manhattan. The crafty General Sir William Howe—brother to Admiral Howe, who directed the fleet—was in charge of the invading land forces, and he shifted his troops to the undefended Long Island coast, well to the east.

After the falling-out with Washington, Burr by this time had found a more congenial post, as aide-de-camp to General Israel Putnam, or "Ol'

Put," as Burr called him, the kind of nickname he would never have given Washington. Although Burr's was fundamentally a desk job, Putnam gave him freedom to take the field, and, sensing the British might land on Long Island, he'd gone prowling out there largely on his own. Convinced that was the invasion point, Burr raced back to Putnam, who rushed his troops there, but it was too late. The British were already pouring onto Long Island, overwhelming the sparse resistance, and then pushing inexorably toward Brooklyn, slaughtering any Americans they encountered along the way. Burr dropped back with Putnam's men to Brooklyn, too, and there Washington scrambled to shore up the city's emplacements along the East River, barring the way to the prize of Manhattan.

Hamilton and his artillery company were up in Brooklyn Heights when the British attacked the patriots arrayed haphazardly about Brooklyn, and he could do little to halt the redcoats' merciless advance. The invaders were bent on pushing all of Washington's army into the East River. By luck, the skies darkened late that afternoon, a drenching rain started to fall, and General Howe suspended his attack, figuring he would kill off the rest of Washington's army in the morning. But the night was moonless, the waters of the East River were enfolded in darkness, and the rain muffled the movements of Washington's men. Washington was able to evacuate what was left of them to Manhattan in dozens of commandeered skiffs, while the exhausted British soldiers slumbered not far away. Hamilton's men stood guard while Burr's company rowed across. His own squad was one of the last to be ferried across, but, when his men were safely across, Washington himself took the final boat.

Hamilton and Burr may have intersected hours later, after Burr learned that a brigade under Knox's command had been caught behind the British lines near Bayard's Hill Redoubt, a fort up from the Hudson on the far side of the island. It was still pouring rain, and well past midnight, making it all the more difficult to find his way about. But from his visits to a country home nearby, and his rambles through the woods, most likely with a young lady, Burr picked a trail to the redoubt where he could safely gather Knox's men. Hamilton and his men were in the vicinity, drowning in rain, and they may have needed Burr's help, too, although neither man mentions it. Hamilton may not have wanted to portray himself as the rescued and not the rescuer, and Burr's records are spotty in any case. If it did occur, it was the first actual contact between the two men, and the second looping of the spider's thread. Burr's commander, Brigadier General Gold Selleck Silliman, wished to keep his men at the fort, thinking escape was impossible, but Burr insisted he lead them away before the enemy converged on them. When Silliman refused, Burr charged off in a fury—only to double back to say that he'd received instructions from Washington for him to evacuate the position. That wasn't true, but Silliman thought it was, and he obediently followed Burr up to Washington's temporary headquarters in Harlem Heights. Hamilton found his way there, too, rain drenched and furious to have been separated from his horse, his baggage, and his company's cannons. It was his first meeting with Washington, and it would lead to a collaboration that would win a war and create a country. It was Burr's last. Having been banished from Washington's so-called family, he would never restore himself to the commander in chief's good graces. So when Hamilton and Burr met on the Heights, one was coming, the other going—establishing a pattern that would govern their interactions for the rest of their lives. Washington hovered over them both, not just inspiring Burr to purchase Richmond Hill but stirring Hamilton to build his dream house, the Grange, on the Heights.

From there, the men could see clear down to the city by the harbor, swarming now with fevered British troops and angry loyalists looting stores and burning buildings by the square block, sending up thick black plumes of smoke that rose to the low, gray clouds. King's College had been commandeered by the British army, and all the school's books torched, adding poignancy to the conflagration.

→>-<+-

WHATEVER HE'D MADE of Burr, Washington could not fail to be impressed by this precise young captain Hamilton. When Washington retreated from New York in October, he ran into the British at White Plains, and the redcoats ripped the Americans apart while a military band played. Only Hamilton's artillery company, up on a high ledge, performed brilliantly, as his men were able to pick off dozens of redcoats wading across the Harlem River.

Forced again to retreat, Washington at least tried to hold the Hudson by erecting defensive forts on either side of the mouth of the river and running a vast chain across the water. But on November 16, when Washington was at Fort Lee on the New Jersey side gazing across at Manhattan's Fort Washington, he watched through his spyglass in horror as the fort was stormed by a mass of British and Hessian soldiers, who butchered the Americans before his eyes. Fort Lee fell soon after. All the Hudson was Britain's.

Washington withdrew to New Jersey to save what was left of his army. He'd thought of taking on the British at New Brunswick by the Raritan River but decided to send his troops splashing across the river in full retreat, while Hamilton's company provided artillery cover. From there, Washington crossed the Delaware into Pennsylvania, playing possum, waiting to hit the British with surprise attacks on more favorable terms. For all Hamilton's bravado, he collapsed under the strain, just as Burr had, that December. Desperate for a victory to boost morale, Washington roused Hamilton from his sickbed, and, ignoring the bitter cold and deep snow, the two men joined Lord Stirling's company to pole a cargo boat back across the ice-cold Delaware and then haul two cannons eight miles through heavy snow to the British camp at Trenton. There, the day after Christmas, the Americans caught a Hessian detachment drowsing by campfires, tipsy from yuletide ale.

Hamilton's artillery company fired off a series of thundering cannon blasts that shattered the camp and sent the groggy soldiers stumbling out into the snow. Woozy and baffled, a thousand Hessians were captured, by far the greatest American victory in the war.

Flush with that conquest, Washington chased the British to their encampment in Princeton, where the troops were billeted in the vast Nassau Hall of Rev. Aaron Burr Sr. At least one American was able to idle at the sight. A senior officer recorded this image: "I noticed a youth, a mere stripling, with a cocked hat pulled down over his eyes, apparently lost in thought, with his hand resting on a cannon, and every now and then patting it, as if it were a favorite horse or pet plaything." Then the stripling let loose with ferocious cannon blasts that drove two hundred British soldiers out into the yard to surrender.

After the battle, much of Washington's army pushed on to winter quarters in Morristown, forty miles north of Princeton, but Hamilton's artillery company made camp in the snow on the Pennsylvania side of the Delaware River, in Bucks County, to protect the fledgling colonial government in Philadelphia from any attack by Howe's army. Still unwell, Hamilton himself retreated to the city, where he recuperated from an undescribed disease that Hugh Knox later called "a long and dangerous illness." He was still ailing when this item appeared in the *Pennsylvania Evening Post* of January 25, 1777: "Captain Alexander Hamilton of the New York Company of Artillery, by applying to the printer of this paper, may hear of something to his advantage." Hamilton didn't have the strength to find out what, but he soon received the explanation from Washington, who sent him a note inviting Hamilton to join his staff as an aide-de-camp with a promotion to lieutenant colonel.

Lying back on his cot, still weak, Hamilton wasn't entirely pleased. He'd always longed for the glory of a field command, the kind that Burr had possessed, not a desk job—"confined from morning to evening, hearing and answering . . . applications and letters."

But there was no saying no, and Hamilton soon was able to rouse himself to find Washington's Morristown headquarters in Jacob Arnold's tavern, a stout building with a wide front porch, a rabbit warren of tight rooms and smoky fireplaces. The bare wooden floors must have drummed with all the heavy boots and deep voices. Twenty aides bent to tasks during the day, a half dozen sleeping to a room at night. Washington chose his men well: his personal lawyer Robert Hanson Harrison, Tench Tilghman, Richard Kidder Meade—they were all quick men, shrewd soldiers, and smart horsemen besides. Impressive as the others were, it wasn't long before Hamilton, with his abundance of talents, emerged as Washington's "principal and most confidential aide," and the general's voice boomed regularly throughout the house with one command: "Call Colonel Hamilton!"

At night, Hamilton shared the officers' quarters with the commander. The two could hardly have looked more different. At six foot four, the heavyset, grim-faced Washington towered over the slender, youthful Hamilton, his ample hair that strawberry blond. Washington communicated best by *not* speaking—Adams said he had a "gift of silence." No one ever said that of Hamilton. "A bright gleam of sunshine," General Nathanael

Greene called him, although another said Hamilton's intensity drove others to "fear and hate him cordially." Energetic, cogent, knowledgeable, quick-witted, a brilliant writer, he was made for impossible tasks. He had ready access to a tone of absolute authority, whether he'd been steeped in a subject for half an hour or for a lifetime; his writing voice had dropped a register to capture the basso profundo of a taciturn Virginian twice his age. As Hamilton's mastery of military details expanded and solidified, Washington relied not just on his writing skills, but also on his judgment. The first dispatches revealed the range of the job: a bid to reduce the sentence of Lieutenant Colonel Archibald Campbell of the Seventy-First Regiment of the British army, who was being held prisoner in Concord, Massachusetts; a request to Major General Horatio Gates to inoculate two Virginia brigades; a letter to Benedict Arnold to discuss his plans to invade Rhode Island; a note to Brigadier General George Clinton that he should decide for himself where to place the cannons on the Hudson River; and so on. The dispatches were an education in the vast cosmology of war. Four days into it, in Washington's name, Hamilton settled on the essential principles of prisoner exchange with the British in a letter to be forwarded to General Howe, the British Parliament, and King George III. Having dispensed with the details, he rounded off the letter on an orotund note that was not exactly Washington's style but must have pleased him nonetheless, as Hamilton signed off by invoking "the principles of justice and humanity, and conformable to the most civilized customs and usages, for the greater ease, convenience, and security of all captives belonging to the armies under our respective command." And then, with a flourish, Hamilton signed his own name directly below, as if he were Washington's coequal:

By His Excellency's   *Given under my Hand and Seal*
command.   *at Head Quarters in Morris Town*
Alexander Hamilton   *this 4th. day of March 1777,*
Aid De Camp   *Go: Washington*

By March 10, he was confidently writing to his old associate General Alexander McDougall when Washington was ill not just over Washington's signature, but in his place. "Though he has grown considerably better than he was," Hamilton informed McDougall, "I find he is so much pestered with matters, which cannot be avoided, that I am obliged to refrain from troubling him on the occasion; especially as I conceive the only answer he would give, may be given by myself."

While this was a relationship of convenience, it had its psychological component. The orphaned son and the childless father of his country—it is hard to shake the notion that Hamilton had found a father, and a family, too. But to Hamilton, just to put it that way would have invoked a paternal encumbrance he did not welcome. The last surrogate father, Thomas Stevens, had not lingered in his affection after Hamilton left the island for New York. To Hamilton, a son was subservient, and to him subservience was never appealing.

With no children of his own, Washington did not have a father's knack anyway. Pressured by events, he showered on his staff the wrath he withheld from others—when he didn't withdraw into an icy silence. He preferred, as he once said, "to let my designs appear from my works than by my expressions." By "works," he meant "acts." If the two men were father and son, they were remote, wary ones, their many differences consigning them to opposite sides of a wall that neither acknowledged. Washington called his aide "Colonel Hamilton," who referred to him as "Your Excellency."

→>-<←

AND THEN, IN October 1777, the skies around Morristown lifted and brightened, for John Laurens arrived on the scene. A handsome, trim, spirited young man, he was about Hamilton's age, but nearly as highborn as Burr; his father, an aristocratic Charleston planter, would soon succeed Elias Boudinot as the president of the Continental Congress. Laurens had attended school in Geneva, where he'd learned to fence, draw, and dabble in philosophy; he was brilliant and cocky and fun and blazingly quick—with a remark, an idea, a gambit—which fit his sleek, wiry body and bright eyes. He'd prepared for the law but hated the idea of getting "my Bread by the Quarrels and Disputes of others." Like Hamilton, he had no shortage of "secretions," and he'd had a fling with the daughter of an English friend of his father, a girl named Martha Manning, and this led to "an important Change in my Circumstances." He seems to have had no feelings for Manning whatsoever, but Laurens felt obliged to marry her quickly, before her father required him to stay in England as a condition of marriage. Five months into the pregnancy, the two were duly wed, and shortly after daughter Fanny's birth, he was gone to fight for his country. He never saw his wife again, and never met his daughter.

Sailing from England, he arrived in Charleston in April 1777, after the victories at Trenton and Princeton, and that summer, with a note from his father, he applied for a position on Washington's staff and was appointed an aide-de-camp too. Seeing him, Hamilton must have thought he was seeing himself with an aristocrat's self-assurance. One portrait shows Laurens with one hand on his hip, the other on the hilt of a long, graceful sword. Laurens must have seen in Hamilton what comes of a man who can create himself. From the first, they were nearly inseparable, almost like lovers. The fraternal tightness recalls Hamilton's bond with Ned Stevens, and even evokes his relationship with Burr; that's the darkly obsessive version, but it operated at a similar depth of manly intimacy. Laurens, Stevens, and Burr were all of the same physical type—short, slender, alert, sensitive—and all of them, in their different ways, captivated him.

Shortly after he arrived, Laurens's wife, Martha, begged him to allow her to sail over with their daughter, but Laurens insisted such a sea voyage was too dangerous. He would remain with his other family, Washington's, with Hamilton. He was drawn to several other members of Washington's staff, especially Richard Meade, to whom he professed an "unbounded and inviolable attachment." It was a world of men, and Laurens delighted in it. He had an extraordinary devil-may-care approach to soldiering, as if he really did not care if he lived or died. In his first battle, at Chadd's Ford, intended to keep Howe out of Philadelphia, Laurens was hit by a musket ball that passed clean through the flesh of his shoulder and then took a whack from a spent ball on his side, which produced only swelling. Yet he still volunteered to dump lit straw against the front door of a large stone house to smoke out a hundred redcoats crammed inside. That gambit failed, but he lived to regale everyone with the recounting of it.

But it was Hamilton he loved. It wasn't long before Laurens was freely addressing him as "My Dear"—and his letters were answered, "I love you." For educated men like Hamilton and Laurens, male friendship had a classical overlay, by which manliness could include tenderness and sensitivity. It is highly unlikely that Laurens and Hamilton took their affection for each other into the physical realm of what was called "sodomy"—a hanging offense throughout the thirteen states and not likely to be treated any more leniently by Washington in wartime.

Letters require distance, and there is little record of their intimate life when Laurens and Hamilton were together. It wasn't until two years later, when Laurens left to recruit black soldiers in South Carolina for the war effort, that Hamilton wrote down what was in his heart, and his letter reveals a man who was quite undone. If Hamilton had striven to create himself as the decisive commander of his own heart, the letter shows that, when it came to love, he was as vulnerable and unsure as any conscript. He writes:

> *Cold in my professions, warm in my friendships, I wish, my Dear Laurens, it might be in my power, by action rather than words to convince you that I love you. I shall only tell you that 'til you bade us Adieu, I hardly knew the value you had taught my heart to set upon you. Indeed, my friend, it was not well done. You know the opinion I entertain of mankind, and how much it is my desire to preserve myself free from particular attachments, and to keep my happiness independent of the caprice of others. You should not have taken advantage of my sensibility to steal into my affections without my consent. But as you have done it, and as we are generally indulgent to those we love, I shall not scruple to pardon the fraud you have committed, on condition that for my sake, if not for your own, you will always continue to merit the partiality, which you have artfully instilled into me.*

It is a startling letter, so startling that it might read like a piece of romantic comedy at a gentlemen's club, with hairy-chested men throwing on ladies' dresses and speaking in falsetto. But this is Hamilton, and it seems he is finally uncorking years of longing, which take on a sexual cast but may be simply an eagerness for a spiritual union with someone worthy of it. The letter "approached the tenderness of female attachment," Hamilton's son acknowledged uneasily, but if so, it is only because we ascribe such yearning to the female side of our being. It is love, but it is more than that, as it draws on years of silent yearning for someone who can meet him where he is. Laurens, because he is Hamilton in another guise, is one of the few to qualify as an object of his desire.

Soon after Laurens's arrival, a third young officer, this one the ascendant young French nobleman the Marquis de Lafayette, galloped into their midst, drawn to the mystique of Washington, the cause of liberty, and a chance for *la gloire*. Offering contacts in the French court and bearing a letter of introduction from Benjamin Franklin, he wrung from Washington, increasingly inundated with French seeking to bolster their social credentials with military ones, an appointment as an honorary major general, a title that granted the bearer everything except troops and pay. A ravishing nineteen-year-old, with lightly arched eyebrows and a powdered wig that smelled of nobility, Lafayette could be flighty and whimsical, but he was fearless and would do anything for victory.

Hamilton, Laurens, Lafayette, all three of them young, brash, brilliant, and glamorously handsome, quickly formed a three-way attachment that was unusual by the standards of a ragtag army. It was advanced by Lafayette's native French, which both Americans spoke freely, creating for themselves a private line of communication, a kind of whisper no one else could hear. But there was a common panache, too, like that of Dumas's Three Musketeers, in the view of Hamilton's grandson, if a gruesome war of attrition had room for such plucky chivalry.

→⤙

THAT SUMMER OF 1777, encamped in the highlands above the Hudson River, Washington was mystified to discover from a variety of dispatches that the British troops had vanished. Apparently, sometime in July, Howe had boarded more than eighteen thousand men onto 267 ships in New York Harbor and sailed them out to sea past the horizon line. They could have been bound for almost anywhere on the American coast, if not for their home port in England, but another month revealed the answer: Chesapeake Bay, and from there most likely to seize the capital city of Philadelphia, rout the Continental Congress meeting there in the statehouse, and further demoralize the already frightened colonists and their bedraggled army.

Washington was determined to defy the British and make a stand at the quiet, meandering Brandywine Creek, just past the Schuylkill outside Philadelphia, where the British would need to pass if they were to attack the city. But first he had to unchain Hamilton from his desk at Morristown and dispatch him to destroy a flour mill in the vicinity before it resupplied the enemy with bread to feed its troops. Accompanied by the unforgettably named "Light-Horse Harry" Lee III, a brisk cavalry officer whom Burr had known at Princeton, and a few other cavalrymen, Hamilton located the mill on the river shore and quickly set it ablaze. But the fire drew the attention of several dozen helmeted British dragoons—mounted infantrymen—who approached at a gallop. Lee and some of the soldiers tried to draw them off by bolting across the fields, but the British let them go and doubled back to pursue the easier prey: Hamilton, who'd scrambled into a flat-bottomed boat berthed by the shore to make his crossing. A hail of grapeshot dropped his horse into the muck and ripped up the boat, an unwieldy vessel that was making slow headway across the water. One of Hamilton's men gave out a scream as he was shot dead; another was ripped open by grapeshot. Seeing some of the dragoons jump into another boat to chase them, Hamilton ordered his men to leap over the side and swim for it. Safe and dripping on the far shore, he dashed off a panicked note for a horseman to take to John Hancock, saying Congress ought to leave Philadelphia "immediately without fail." The British were descending on the city.

Then he gathered his men and rushed to rejoin the army, where Washington's family had given him up for dead and greeted him with tears. Before ordering Philadelphia's evacuation, Washington assigned Hamilton the rough duty of going from house to house requisitioning supplies—blankets, clothes, for the desperate soldiers—from the hard-pressed inhabitants, and doing it "with as much delicacy and discretion as the nature of the business demands." A sensitive task that Hamilton performed flawlessly, depriving the British of essential supplies and delivering them to the Americans, every item duly noted in his account book, a receipt delivered to its owner.

Meanwhile, Laurens was at Chadd's Ford on the Brandywine, where

Washington expected Howe to cross, as he'd given every indication of doing, and press on to Philadelphia, twenty-five miles to the northeast. But it was another of those feints that too often fooled the Americans, and Howe, in a heavy mist well before dawn, wheeled due north and rushed to outflank the Americans' right by crossing Jeffries' Ford well upstream. When Washington hurried to block them, Howe's Hessians went at Chadd's Ford after all, which Laurens had been left to hold under the command of General Nathanael Greene, and which he did valiantly amid all the terror that the Hessians could bring down upon him. Lafayette was there, too, and he was shot in the leg, but he was astonished that Laurens survived the carnage. "It was not his fault he was not killed or wounded," he marveled afterward. "He did everything that was necessary to procure one or t'other." As the Continental forces fell back, the British poured into Philadelphia in late September as the congressional delegates fled. Hurrying off by carriage, John Laurens's father, Henry, spotted the injured Lafayette and rushed him to surgeons in Bethlehem.

TWELVE

The Malcolms

WHILE HAMILTON HAD moved into the affections of Washington back at Harlem Heights, Burr had brooded over the fact that Washington did not offer more appreciation for his saving Silliman's brigades from being destroyed or captured, likely bound for hideous incarceration in the hellhole of a British prison ship. It was an "intentional slight," he groused. So it wasn't a good time for his old friend Ogden to tease him about his slow progress up the ranks, as Burr was merely a major, whereas Ogden was a lieutenant colonel, one step up, on his way to becoming a full colonel. Burr claimed to be "happy in the esteem of my good old general," Ol' Put. When the promotion finally did arrive, it made Burr only a lieutenant colonel, when Burr had been expecting far more. Burr had no compunctions about complaining about it directly to Washington, declaring himself "constrained," as he said, to "observe" that he would now have to suffer the indignity of reporting to officers "younger in the service and junior officers in the last campaign." Was he being punished for some "misconduct"? He didn't mention the specifics: his heroism at Quebec, his valor in the retreat from Manhattan, but asked only, and rather pathetically, hadn't his conduct been marked by "uniform diligence"? Surely this was an "accident," as "a decent regard to rank is both proper and necessary." If Burr saw this as a plea for justice, Washington considered it an affront from a subordinate who had an inflated view of himself.

Bad as it was to have received such a limited promotion, it was worse to have been moved from Ol' Put to the newly formed regiment created by a jumbo-size New York merchant named William Malcolm, who knew everything about commerce and nothing about war. Colonel Malcolm had bought a colonelcy by recruiting, outfitting, and equipping what amounted to a private regiment—dubbed the Malcolms, appropriately—out of his own pocket. Malcolm needed a tutor in war, and he wasn't entirely pleased to discover a slim, dark-eyed boy sliding down off his horse to shake his hand as his aide-de-camp. But Malcolm soon knew better. The boy knew how to fight. Malcolm left the training of his raw recruits to Burr while he retired with his family to his country home, twenty miles from the action. "You shall have the honor of disciplining and fighting the regiment," he told Burr, "while I will be its father." So Burr took it upon himself to create some soldiers, drilling them, bolstering them with small comforts he purchased himself, and whipping them as necessary.

When they were finally ready for combat, the Malcolms were given the task of guarding the "back door" to the forts along the Hudson through a fourteen-mile gap in the Ramapo Mountains. Burr was still training his Malcolms when, late in September, a band of marauding loyalists from New York swept through Bergen County, just south of his outpost, ripping up farms as they went, trampling crops, breaking fences, and scattering horses and cattle. Thinking the Malcolms too green, General Putnam had advised Burr to hide them in the mountains. But Burr would have none of that. Battle ready or not, he would take his men to the enemy, and that September, as the summer light was fading, he sent them on a forced march deep into the enemy territory of Bergen County. Leaving his men to rest along the Hackensack River, Burr pressed on alone later that night to reconnoiter. Stealing through the fields in the moonlight, he came across an enemy picket of thirty men, all asleep except for two lonely sentinels. He crept back to gather some soldiers and quietly led them back to the site. As they approached, one sentry called out for Burr and his men to halt and identify themselves. Burr raised his pistol and shot the man dead. Then he waved his men on, and in moments they took all the rest of the sleepy picket as their prisoners.

When the news broke about Burr's work, hundreds of farmers clamored to join his Malcolms, but there was no enemy for them to fight. The loyalists had slunk back to New York. Now Washington had new plans for Burr and his Malcolms—to join him for the winter in the frozen hell of Valley Forge.

→>-◄-

WHILE HAMILTON WAS with Washington in Monmouth, New Jersey, the Americans won the first great victory of the war. Unfortunately for Washington, he was not the general involved. Rather, it was the insufferable Horatio Gates who had beaten "Gentleman Johnny" Burgoyne, a craven toady who never gave his full attention to the battlefield if there was a voluptuous young lady or a chilled jeroboam somewhere in sight, as there usually was. The battle was in upstate New York, in Saratoga, and Gates had so thoroughly overwhelmed the redcoats that the patriots had taken prisoner nearly six thousand of them, making this the Americans' most explosive victory since Trenton, and infinitely larger. The French, ready to come in against their perennial enemy if they could be beaten, were now ready to take the American side, dramatically increasing the chances for victory.

Saratoga could not have come at a better time—or enhanced the reputation of a worse general. For all Washington's talk of "family," his generals were never part of it. A fractious lot, most of them were more interested in buffing their reputations than in advancing the cause, and Gates was probably the best example. After Saratoga, Gates was lionized as America's preeminent general, ignoring that Washington deserved that distinction. The matter came to a head when Washington needed more troops to carry the battle to the enemy in Pennsylvania, but Gates wanted to keep his troops in New York. Washington sent the only man he trusted for such a sensitive assignment.

Hamilton set off at a full gallop to Albany, covering sixty miles a day and stopping only to sleep or confer with generals in the field, including Burr's mentor General Israel Putnam. On November 5, with winter coming on, he finally hurried in to see Gates. For all of Gates's bulk, Hamilton saw a man without substance—vain, stuffy, feeble. English by birth, he was an illegitimate son of a duke's maid, which might have aroused Hamilton's sympathy but did not. Overstuffed, with spectacles that slid down his nose, Gates was called "Granny" Gates for a reason.

At first Hamilton tried to persuade Gates that Washington needed two of Gates's brigades while Gates did not. But Gates had no interest in giving in to an overweening schoolboy. Hamilton persisted: *Washington must have them*. Finally, Gates allowed he might be able to part with one of the three brigades in a General Patterson's regiment, but Hamilton knew he'd selected the worst of the three and demanded better. Finally, Gates relented and allowed him to take the better. But Hamilton was still not satisfied, and, with considerable exasperation, Gates gave him the full two he sought, one from Patterson, one from Putnam.

On his return, Hamilton discovered that Putnam had not delivered on his promise. "I am astonished," he began, plainly furious. "And alarmed beyond measure to find all his Excellency's views have been hitherto frustrated and that no single step of those I mentioned has been taken to afford him the aid he absolutely stands in need of and by delaying which the case of America is put to the utmost conceivable hazard." It was brilliant to make this Washington's request, not his, and make clear that Washington was asking not for himself, but for the good of the country.

Putnam saw no choice but to oblige him. It was another triumph over a powerful elder who might have obliterated him. Washington was overjoyed, but Hamilton was utterly drained by the negotiations, so spent he could scarcely stay on his horse and had to stop in Windsor, Connecticut, to rest. There, shivering from icy chills and a burning fever, he dropped into bed at the home of a friend named Dennis Kennedy. His condition was so extreme, it looked to Kennedy like Hamilton might not survive, but after several frightening days the fever finally broke, and he was able to continue on his way.

→>-<←

LEARNING OF BURR'S experience at using relatively untrained troops to defend natural passageways, Washington put him and his Malcolms in the Gulph, an opening cut by a slender stream through the low hills encircling the patriots' winter camp at Valley Forge. It was a freezing-cold, sodden, nasty place that made for a devil's Christmas all too reminiscent of the Quebec campaign, and it froze whatever soldiers it didn't kill. The idea was to keep the British from bursting through and hacking the patriots to bits with artillery and musket fire. But the spot was so raw and desolate, the previous occupants had taken to staging false alarms, just for some excitement. Burr would have to teach the men some discipline. In the dead of winter, the men were not overjoyed by the relentless drilling that Burr required, or by the fact that he had a way of sneaking up on them when they least expected it. Finally, some of the men decided they'd had enough and had the remedy: murder him. But Burr had spies among the mutineers, and he emptied all their cartridges. At parade the next day, when the leader leapt out of line with a shout, "Now is the time, boys," aimed his musket at Burr, and squeezed the trigger—it produced nothing more than an ominous click. Burr unsheathed his sword and brought it sharply down on the man's arm, nearly severing it. The surgeon detached it later, with nothing for the pain.

While Burr was off with his Malcolms at the Gulph, Hamilton was quartered with Washington and the other officers in the handsome stone house of Isaac Potts, while more than ten thousand men, many of them scarcely clothed, many more half dead from hunger or disease, did their best to shelter themselves from the brutal cold in makeshift cabins of branches and loose timber. The snow was streaked with blood from men going barefoot, their skin rubbed raw, and, as the famine worsened, the corpses mounted. Burdened by the strains of war in any case, Washington's spirits drooped at the suffering of his troops. His struggles were compounded by the threats of insurrection against him by the vainglorious General Gates. His cause was being pushed by a scheming brigadier general, Thomas Conway, an Irishman who'd trained with the French army, pushing the Gates cause to a broader conspiracy of the so-called Conway Cabal (with Burr a quiet sympathizer). When Washington got his eyes on Conway's sneering critique of him, meant only for Gates, he responded with uncharacteristic fury. At the height of his power, he could have pounded the two men into the ground, but now Washington had to watch while Congress appointed Gates president of its Board of War, making him Washington's supervisor. And it made Conway inspector general. It was as if their coup had succeeded.

At Valley Forge, as Hamilton gradually recovered his health after the trials of early December, he turned increasingly to those books he toted around with him, expanding his list of classics to include philosophers like

Bacon, Hobbes, and Montaigne even as he boned up on the essential principles of economics with a massive, two-volume *Universal Dictionary of Trade and Commerce*, divined political essentials from the Greeks and Romans, and amused himself with the tales of ambition in Plutarch. Even in the midst of an unbearable winter, with pain and starvation all about him, he spent every free minute poring over his books, questing for a bigger future for himself in this rich, new country he was then beginning to imagine.

→>-<←

THAT WAS NOT the end of the political machinations against Washington, for by that June, there was another general spoiling to take his place as commander in chief: Charles Lee, the one who had been passed over once before. Nearly two years back, he'd foolishly gotten himself captured by the British in a tavern and had only recently been released. But that didn't keep him from returning to his noisome ways as a self-appointed military genius. Despite his absurd mishap, he would not let go of the idea that he knew better than Washington how to fight a war, and he immediately took to overruling the battle plan for the critical fight with Howe's army at Monmouth Court House in Freehold, New Jersey. When Washington refused to oblige, Lee went ahead into battle—only to defy Washington's order to strike at the British rear guard, and retreat instead. Infuriated, Washington leveled Lee with a blast of profanity "till the leaves shook on the trees," as another general put it.

With that, Washington ordered Lee to remove himself from the fray, while he took over, riding one resplendent horse after another, as each one dropped in the hundred-degree heat. The only officer to come close to keeping up with him was Hamilton, who was as happy as a colt to be on the battlefield again, tearing this way and that, urging some troops on, instructing others to pull back, until finally his horse was shot out from under him, and he pitched forward to the ground, hurt badly enough that he couldn't continue.

→>-<←

LEADING ON HIS Malcolms, the dark-eyed Burr fought valiantly at Monmouth too. Serving under Lord Stirling, now a major general, Burr spotted a small company of redcoats trying to slip away from a bombardment, emerging from a copse at one end of a ravine below him. Burr signaled his men to give chase, when one of Washington's aides raced up with orders to stay where he was. That left all the Malcolms terribly exposed to cannon fire, annihilating Burr's second-in-command, knocking Burr's horse out from under him, and leaving all the men to roast in the heat. Delirious from heatstroke and stricken with violent headaches, Burr retired from the field of battle and never returned to it. He wrote Washington afterward asking to "retire from pay and duty" until he was well again, and Washington granted the request "until your health is so far reestablished as to enable you to do your duty"—a crisp message that may have been penned by Hamilton. Although the fight at Monmouth was in June, Burr wasn't ready to report for service again until the end of November, for he had something he deemed more important to attend to. When he was able, Washington asked him to perform some reconnaissance, gathering information about the British troop movements along the Hudson. In this, Washington knew his man. Burr did well in the shadows.

→>-<←

NEITHER SIDE EMERGED victorious at Monmouth, but Washington ended up routing his errant general Lee by slapping him with a court-martial for ignoring the orders of his commander. Hamilton was one of the witnesses against Lee, and his testimony in the trial, which ran twenty-six laborious sessions, revealed his temper. Lee himself performed the cross-examination, accusing Hamilton of saying one thing in the field and another in court. "I did not," Hamilton fired back. "I said something to you in the field expressive of an opinion that there appeared in you no want of that degree of self-possession, which proceeds from a want of personal intrepidity." Even in a fury, Hamilton was never shy about the most baroque expression. The court found Lee guilty of three counts and suspended him from command. But Lee would not let the matter drop and encouraged his minions to go after Washington and Hamilton, too. One of his supporters was Burr, who had reasons of his own to be irritated at Washington. His endorsement of Lee has been lost, but Lee's reply gives a pretty good idea of what was in it, as Lee says that in his retirement from the military, he would return to Virginia and grow tobacco—a dig at the commander in chief, who had once done that and aspired to again—"which I find is the best school to form a consummate *general*." After Lee repeated such vituperations in print, John Laurens decided that enough was enough and challenged him to a duel.

Duels were surprisingly common during a war that offered plenty of killing already. To a French observer it was a "rage" that had reached an "incredible and scandalous point." But they did at least offer a means of resolving disputes quickly, without a cumbersome court-martial. Theoretically, by the code of honor that governed duels, only the man who'd been directly accused—Washington, in this case—could make such a challenge, but when Laurens spoke for him, Lee accepted. Laurens picked Hamilton as his second.

The duel was fought on December 23, 1778, in a snowy wood outside Philadelphia. Every duel is fought by its own rules, and these were especially murderous, as the two duelists stood at the customary ten paces, pistols in hand, and then walked *toward* each other and commenced firing when they were just six paces apart. From there, it might seem impossible to miss, but nerves are a factor even for military men, and once the two men started to close on each other, only Laurens was able to hit the mark, bloodying Lee on his right side. After a hit, both sides have the option of demanding a second round; at first Lee did demand it, and Hamilton wanted to honor his request and finish off this usurper. But then Lee reconsidered and issued a statement saying that he "esteemed General Washington" and would never again speak ill of him. Laurens deemed this satisfactory, and he and Hamilton galloped away to share the glorious adventure with their third musketeer, Lafayette, at a nearby tavern.

THIRTEEN

A Lady with a Beautiful Waist

E VEN MORE THAN most wars, the Revolutionary War was horrendously destructive—to minds, bodies, property, and order—but it was creative, too, and Hamilton and Burr both saw their essential personalities forged and hardened by the conflict. Hamilton had wished for a war, and now it was doing everything he'd hoped, vaulting him to the military pinnacle as Washington's indispensable man, and it did only a little less for Burr, as it gave him the confidence to trust his instincts, no matter how unconventional. Both men were tested—Hamilton by the strain of running a war and Burr by the fearful dangers of fighting one. The war fostered Hamilton's sense of order; it brought out Burr's quiet savagery.

And then it delivered them something else.

→>·<←

IN DECEMBER OF 1779, General Washington shifted his encampment from Princeton to the farming village of Morristown. Protected by a low ring of mountains, it was just twenty-five miles west of New York City and allowed Washington to monitor the massive British army and quickly contest any move General Gage might make on Philadelphia. But it was hardly a pleasant refuge. Fierce as the preceding winter in Valley Forge had been, this one immediately threatened to be far worse, as the temperatures started plunging in late fall, and blizzards would eventually heap up as much as six feet of snow in twenty-eight snowfalls, leaving his men—about eighty-five hundred altogether—shivering in frigid huts they'd hewed out of the woods and gnawing on sticks or sucking a tea of boiled boot leather for sustenance. Any soldiers who schemed to save themselves at the expense of the regiment were whipped nearly to death if their plans were uncovered.

Already depressed not to have been offered a field command by Washington, and saddled with the endless letters and ledger accounts of his administrative duties, Hamilton had not been cheered by the change of scene, although his lot as an officer was infinitely better than that of the enlisted men. With Washington and the rest of his senior staff, Hamilton was billeted in Judge Jacob Ford's mansion, a stately white house with green trim that commanded the village. He slept upstairs in a room with two others and worked out of the wooden hut adjoining. In a letter to Laurens he declared himself "disgusted with everything in this world but yourself and very few more honest fellows." The next line revealed the profound depths of his distress: "I have no other wish than as soon as possible to make a brilliant exit. 'Tis a weakness, but I feel I am not fit for this terrestrial country."

Sensitive to the plunging morale of all the officers, the ever-kindly Martha Washington had the idea of inviting some fashionable young women from town for a series of dinner dances and other social amusements. The Continental Army had often been trailed by "camp ladies," and the normally good-natured frontiersman John Marshall, the future Supreme Court judge, decried the "lewdness" he'd sometimes witnessed. But these pretty, well-coiffed visitors, in their fine European fashions, were a cut above, as Hamilton—never oblivious to the ladies—immediately noticed. Their cheeks reddened by a few miles' sleigh ride, their hearts beating with excitement, they could not fail to gain a soldier's attention.

For these cheerful soirees, Hamilton—apple-cheeked, and resplendent in his brown uniform with yuletide-red vest—often manned the punch bowl and provided the toasts, the better to survey the crowd, and then helped lead the "dancing assemblies" at a nearby storehouse. Washington always claimed that he would never "give in to such amusements," as an example to the men, but he often attended all the same, cutting a fine figure in a black velvet suit.

If Hamilton was crisply decisive about practical matters, in love he could be flighty, drawn to this one, then that. At first he was taken by a slender beauty named Cornelia Lott, much to the amusement of his fellow officers, one of whom composed a teasing ditty: "Now Hamilton feels the inexorable dart / And yields Cornelia all his heart." Cornelia soon gave way to a young lovely remembered only as Polly. Then a series of . . . others, as a military friend arranged for Hamilton to visit a nearby boardinghouse where he might find welcome from "a lady with a beautiful waist." With them all, Hamilton would woo them in person but follow up by letter, his hand racing excitedly across the page.

Such puppyish eagerness was charming, especially from Washington's cultivated and fine-featured top aide. With those keen eyes of his, no one doted like Hamilton. But his gaze rarely rested on anyone for very long. "In youth and maturity Hamilton loved the ladies, and they him," one early biographer concluded. "There was scarcely a one he could not charm, and none who could not deceive him. They were susceptible to him because of his attentiveness and flirtatious pleasantries, his polished manners, his gracefulness as a dancer, his wit and his good looks."

He was no cad, but women too often misunderstood the exact nature of his ardor. The most intimate details of these encounters have been lost, but in the depths of winter, with little privacy, official discouragement of frolicking, and scant access to the French "cundums," as they were often spelled—the word rarely being printed—it isn't likely that Hamilton was able to consummate many of these attachments. Hamilton was a man on the prowl and had been ever since he was a randy teenager on Saint Croix. No wonder Martha Washington named her frisky tomcat Hamilton. Out of jealousy, his male friends called him "Little Hammy" and dismissed his magnetism as a kind of parlor trick. Still, there was never any shortage of women to oblige him.

For Hamilton, however, romance was not a frivolous matter, and his more serious affairs had a military quality, as if the flirtation was a way to test a woman's defenses and determine the value of her assets. For Hamilton, without family or property, the right wife was key to his aspirations. While he had not yet seen her, he knew what she looked like, and, more important, he knew her qualities. And in knowing those things without knowing *her*, Hamilton revealed much.

In April of 1779, he'd laid it all out to John Laurens not long after that astonishing proclamation he wrote that amounted to a love letter to *him*. No sooner had he plighted his troth to Laurens than he drastically changed tone and direction and asked him for a favor: to find him a wife. Laurens could do that, Hamilton implied, since he was already down in South Carolina picking black soldiers for the army. The whole matter is all topsy-turvy, as it is introduced with a bit of jejune humor regarding the length of his nose, but revealing all the same.

For the matter of matrimony was indeed on his mind, so much so that the joke soon wore thin for him, leaving him in the awkward position of asking a man he loved to find him a woman he might love more. But that didn't keep him from laying out exacting specifications for the perfect wife.

> She must be young, handsome (I lay most stress upon a good shape), sensible (a little learning will do), well bred (but she must have an aversion for the word ton), chaste and tender (I am an enthusiast in my notions of fidelity and fondness), of some good nature, a great deal of generosity (she must neither love money nor scolding, for I dislike equally a termagant and an economist). In politics, I am indifferent what sides she may be of; I think I have arguments that will easily convert her to mine. As to religion, a moderate streak will satisfy me. She must believe in god and hate a saint.

Delivered presto like this, this jumble of requirements may sound comic, but the pushy monosyllable *must*, much repeated, is the giveaway, since it is the most characteristic expression in the Hamilton lexicon. Such demands, after all, are characteristic of a man accustomed to dashing off a hundred sets of instructions a day.

Without sisters, with a mother who died young, with a history of all-male environments culminating in the military, Hamilton had little intimate knowledge of the female of the species, and the idea that women were to be appraised from the outside in was standard for proper young gentlemen. Lord Chesterfield, the English self-styled philosophe whose famous letters to his illegitimate son were the last word on the subject of proper behavior, declared that women were more "binding" than "book," and men the reverse.

Still, for all his flirtatiousness, Hamilton's fundamental interest was financial security. At bottom, a woman's worth was her worth to him, and the tone of the letter turns serious when he discusses her material qualifications. Any wife of his had to be seriously rich. "As to fortune, the larger stock of that the better," he wrote Laurens, all humor draining away. "You know my temper and circumstances and will therefore pay special attention to this article in the treaty. Though I run the risk of going to purgatory for avarice, yet as money is an essential ingredient to happiness in this world—as I have not much of my own and as I am very little calculated to get more either by my address or industry—it must needs be that my wife, if I get one, bring in at least a sufficiency to administer her own extravagances."

It was a rare confessional: A love that floated free of the material world didn't appeal to him largely because he couldn't afford it. That realization must have clouded over him, because he quickly tries to make a joke of it. If Laurens doesn't find him such a belle, his bosom friend should advertise for one in the "public papers." There, to improve his chances, Laurens should be sure to include Hamilton's own "qualifications"—"his *size*, make, quality of mind and *body*, achievements, expectations, fortune, &c." The winking italics are all Hamilton's. "In drawing my picture, you will no doubt be civil to your friend; mind you do justice to the length of my nose and don't forget, that I—" Here the paper breaks off again.

In closing, he throws the whole business up into the air as a *"Jeu de folie."* As he says: "Do I want a wife? No—I have plagues enough without desiring to add to the number that *greatest of all*." He assures Laurens he went into the silliness about wives only to extend the letter to *him*— "lengthening out the only kind of intercourse now in my power with my friend." The sexual implications of that sentence were surely not lost on either of them.

Speaking of matrimony, Hamilton concluded by saying he included a couple of letters from Laurens's wife, Martha, whom he'd abandoned after she'd given birth in England. "I anticipate by sympathy the pleasure you must feel from the sweet converse of your dearer self in the enclosed letters," Hamilton added, in a line that requires an ironic reading. He was doing to Laurens what Laurens was doing to *him*, namely, undercutting any interest in matrimony by invoking the thrill of their own "dearer selves." Then, as if it might be news, "She speaks of a daughter of yours." The rest is illegible, as the page has been torn, possibly by the recipient.

The letter raised so many questions about Hamilton's fundamental desires that it left his descendants in a quandary about how to handle it. Alexander's son John, the family keeper of his memory, was so distressed by the mercantile calculations in his choice of spouse—John's mother, after all—he wrote himself a note, "I must not publish the whole of this," and left the financial portion out of his account. Hamilton's grandson, the New York City alienist Allan McLane Hamilton, omitted the letter altogether.

FOURTEEN

Beauty Is Woman's Sceptre

W HEN IT CAME to love, Aaron Burr would never have been as calculating as Hamilton, even if he was feeling a little pinched. From his
days on the prowl in Elizabethtown through his dangerous dalliance with
Dolly Quincy, now Mrs. John Hancock, and into unknown philandering
in the war, Burr had a deep well of romantic experience to draw on. Even if
his aristocratic background had faded into the past, he still was confident
that any woman would be thrilled to have him, and he had only to take his
pick. His desires were never theoretical but made up a permanent state of
hunger.

Unlike Hamilton, he was not so utilitarian, or so crass, as to write out
his particular qualifications for the ideal wife. Nonetheless, he had plenty
of ideas about womanhood, most of them anticipating Mary Wollstonecraft, the mother of Mary Shelley, who wrote the first and most persuasive
feminist tract, *A Vindication of the Rights of Woman*. "Women are every
where in [a] deplorable state," she would write; "for, in order to preserve
their innocence, as ignorance is courteously termed, truth is hidden from
them, and they are made to assume an artificial character before their fac-
ulties have acquired any strength. Taught from their infancy that beauty is
woman's sceptre, the mind shapes itself to the body, and, roaming round its
gilt cage, only seeks to adorn its prison."

Burr never thought of women as mere beauties in service to men's
desires, even as he played with them. Instead, Burr held to the heretical

belief, shared only by John Adams in the circle of Founding Fathers, that women were fully the equals of men, just as capable in intellect, just as sensible, and just as deep in feeling. While they may have been intended for male pleasure, they were not just pretty baubles, but fully realized individuals. Not bindings, they were books.

While the editor of Burr's posthumous memoirs, Matthew Davis, is committed to the idea that Burr is a cad, one of the few romances he describes from the war years gives another impression. Burr was a lieutenant colonel on General Putnam's staff when he met a charming young English girl, Margaret Moncrieffe, who was the daughter of a British brigade major posted on Staten Island. As a foreign national, Margaret was being detained in Burr's hometown of Elizabethtown near Putnam's headquarters.

Davis doesn't specify what happened between Burr and Moncrieffe, but he presents this story as an example of Burr at his worst. And the encounter has the earmarks of the outrageous: Moncrieffe was fourteen. But Moncrieffe did not consider herself victimized, either then or years later when she recalled the incident for her memoirs. When Burr appears in her pages, it is as if the sun bursts through the clouds. Every word makes clear that she loved him then and loves him still. "May these pages one day meet the eye of him who subdued my virgin heart. . . . To him I plighted my virgin vow. . . . With this conqueror of my soul, how happy should I now have been!" It's unclear if a fourteen-year-old was simply consumed with fantasies for a handsome American officer, or whether something actually happened between them, but Burr's own account suggested the former. "Eccentric and volatile," he called her, but also "endowed with talents, natural as well as acquired." Initially charmed by her, he wrote over the signature of General Putnam an invitation for her to stay in his field headquarters. But then he had second thoughts. He found Moncrieffe to be unusually sophisticated and not a little sneaky. Once she was at military headquarters, Burr realized that she would be privy to military secrets. She could overhear conversations, pocket correspondence, study battle plans. At fourteen, she would be a very effective spy. Who would ever suspect? Perhaps it took someone inclined toward intrigues like Burr. He had her detained and then removed by barge to her father at British headquarters, presumably on Staten Island. "Bidding an eternal farewell to my dear American friends," she writes, "[I] *turned my back on liberty*." But Burr doubted that. While a seducer is interested in only one thing, Burr was able to focus on another.

→>-<←

IN THE FALL of 1778, Burr was detached from the Malcolms and received a brutal assignment to manage largely on his own. He was to preside over the Neutral Ground, a no-man's-land that was not controlled by either side, north of New York City near present-day Westchester County, whose residents were getting it from both sides—raids by heartless British "cowboys" and by brutal "skinners," or American brigands. The villages were being plundered of everything of value—food, livestock, household goods— driving the villagers to penury and starvation.

Washington assigned Burr to put a stop to it, eliminating the brigands and returning any stolen property to its rightful owners. Why Burr? Washington knew perfectly well that Burr had sided with Charles Lee and the Conway Cabal against him, and he may have seen this thankless assignment as fit punishment for Burr's disloyalty, but it might also be that Washington was giving him a lesson in sorting friend from foe. For the war was not entirely military; it was also political, stemming from a profound hatred between loyalists and patriots, a murky scrum that would continue long after the war was over. But unlike the military war, the political one had no clear battle lines, as each side had enemies in its midst. In Westchester County, it would be up to Burr to rout them out.

Arriving in a howling snowstorm, he immediately issued orders that every stolen article was to be returned to its owner, whether patriot or Tory, and the thieves chased down. Determined to bring order to the Neutral Ground, Burr threw himself into the dismal work, scarcely eating, not sleeping more than an hour at a time, through the night making the rounds of his commanders, a circuit of about twenty miles, never failing even in the worst winter weather, and it thoroughly exhausted him. As with the Malcolms, Burr was able to rouse a listless, inept crew of soldiers into a fairly solid fighting force. But it wasn't just the physical effort; it was also the emotional stress of bringing home to the thieves on both sides the blunt fact that their criminality would not be tolerated—and he conveyed this in the most persuasive way he could, through a savage ministry of unbearable pain: fifty lashes on their bare backs. Burr himself bore witness as the whip plucked out hunks of skin, spattering blood everywhere, while the half-naked thief hauled on his restraints and screamed with pain. In one case, Burr commanded that the plunderers—a pair of soldiers in the local militia—be whipped at the house they'd plundered and be imprisoned there "till they make satisfaction." Always, Burr was there when the suffering was dispensed.

Burr had never been a man of solid constitution. He would push himself until he'd used up all his reserves and then fall into torpor. Even short of a complete collapse, it seemed there was always a wasting of some kind waiting for him, whether it be the flu, the fevers known as agues, distempers, migraines, "eye trouble," or some mysterious ache or other. And those were just the physical ones; he was also prone to violent mood swings that sent him skyward with enthusiasm over some daring adventure and then plunged him into long fits of gloom. All of it, together, made close friends like Robert Troup worry that this time he was ready to take his "final farewell of this wrangling world." For he succumbed to a cluster of nervous complaints that left him scarcely able to rise from bed for well over a month. He tendered his final resignation from the army to Washington in April of 1779, and this time it was accepted, probably without regret. Hamilton may have handled that correspondence too.

With Burr, however, retirement was not quite so simple. With his Westchester County assignment, he was to keep to his miserable post every day, and, according to his order book, he did—every day except for two nights toward the end of his tour, when he stole away on a horse he named Ol' Put to gallop to the Hudson. Because of its strategic value, the British patrolled the river closely. Nonetheless, Burr took a boat across to New Jersey, where he rode on to Paramus, a journey of more than thirty miles. To see a woman, of course.

FIFTEEN

The Schuylers

WHILE HAMILTON WAITED for the perfect woman, he enjoyed his waltzes with the nameless ones. And then, in early February 1780, a woman appeared before him who so closely matched his dream lover that he would be forgiven to think of her first as an apparition. It was Elizabeth Schuyler, one of *the* Schuylers, and no one ever had to say more than that. She was the daughter of General Philip Schuyler, the former commander of the Northern Forces who'd overseen Aaron Burr's ill-fated Quebec campaign. Hamilton had first laid eyes on him when he paraded into New York with Washington, a paunchy figure with an endless nose. Hamilton had never been impressed with Schuyler's skills as a military man; neither had Washington. But Schuyler was rich. He was a descendant of one of the four immensely wealthy Dutch families that had settled in New York well over a century before and ruled upstate New York in Hamilton's time. The Schuylers lived outside Albany in a fine brick mansion they called the Pastures. And, through Schuyler's wife, the former Catherine Van Rensselaer, of that *other* great Dutch family, which possessed nearly a million acres of upstate New York, Schuyler had acquired a 120,000-acre estate in Claverack, up the Hudson, in Columbia County. He created a primitive industrial village on the edge of the Saratoga wilderness that would come to be called Schuylerville. All of this made Philip Schuyler one of the richest men in the colonies.

When Elizabeth made her entrance at Washington's headquarters, she was accompanied by a uniformed military escort and she bore letters of introduction from her father to Washington and to General Friedrich Wilhelm von Steuben, the colorful Prussian field officer who was imposing military discipline on the ill-trained soldiers.

Hamilton had to be wondering if this timid little beauty had somehow been conjured from his letter to Laurens. With her hair done up in what she later joked was her "Marie Antoinette coiffure," with jeweled earrings, Betsey must have dazzled in the candlelight: slight and trim, scarcely more than five feet, with dark flashing eyes that "threw a beam of good temper and benevolence over her whole countenance," a friend of Hamilton's wrote. "She is most unmercifully handsome," Hamilton wrote Betsey's sister Angelica that February, and then praised her "good nature, affability and vivacity. In short she is so strange a creature that she possesses all the beauties, virtues and graces of her sex without any . . . amiable defects." Not the way Betsey would have had him put it, but in keeping with the image that he created for himself as a connoisseur of fine wives. And Hamilton? "He exhibited a natural, yet unassuming superiority," wrote Betsey's younger sister Catherine. She recalled his "high, expansive forehead, a note of the Grecian mold, a dark bright eye, and the line of a mouth expressing decision and courage." It was, she concluded, "a face never to be forgotten." Betsey was staying with her aunt Gertrude, wife of Dr. John Cochran, an innovative physician who was attempting to develop a more reliable system of inoculations against the smallpox that was slaughtering American soldiers at an appalling rate.

Afterward, Hamilton could scarcely get her out of his mind, and the romantic intrigue undid him so much that he uncharacteristically forgot the pass code for reentry into the fortifications. He threw himself into courtship, at one point penning a sonnet entitled "Answer to the Inquiry Why I Sighed" that included the bloodless couplet "Before no mortal ever knew / A love like mine so tender, true." If the sentiment seems somewhat forced, it may be because the feeling was, at least at first. As his attachment deepened, he had a dream of finding her in Albany asleep on the grass—with another suitor stroking her hand. Somewhat archly, Hamilton "reproached him for his presumption and asserted my claim." Thereupon in the dream, Betsey awoke with a start, threw herself in Hamilton's arms, and covered his face with kisses, although he does not move to kiss her back. To Laurens, he called Betsey "a good-hearted girl" who is "not a genius," merely "agreeable." And concluded: "Though not a beauty, she has fine black eyes, is rather handsome, and has every other requisite of the exterior to make a lover happy."

Betsey was far more charitable in appraising him, and more insightful, too. While Hamilton's poetry did not move her, the attempt did. Years later, when she cataloged the qualities of Hamilton that won her heart, she mentioned ones that Hamilton himself would probably not recognize or appreciate. "Elasticity of his mind. Variety of his knowledge. Playfulness of his wit. Excellence of his heart. His immense forebearance [and] virtues." These were indeed his virtues, but they were not the ones he would have mentioned. Such insights are a mark of her love for a man who would repeatedly challenge it.

Rather than woo her, Hamilton set about to improve her. "I entreat you, my charmer, not to neglect the charges I gave you, particularly that of taking care of yourself and that of employing all your leisure in reading," he counseled. "Nature has been very kind to you. Do not neglect to cultivate her gifts and to enable yourself to make the distinguished figure in all respect to which you are entitled to aspire."

It was one thing to win Betsey and another to win her father. General Schuyler styled himself a democrat, but every utterance suggested otherwise. He once advised his son John, "Be indulgent, my child, to your inferiors." Schuyler was quite aware that Hamilton was not one of his kind. For a man of Schuyler's standing, it was a serious risk to let his daughter marry outside the clan. But the fact was, it had happened before, repeatedly. Three of Betsey's sisters had eloped, one slithering out her bedroom window to flee to Massachusetts with her lover, and all entered marriages without their father's consent. Betsey's beguiling older sister, Angelica, had fallen for an Englishman, born John Barker Carter, later John Barker Church, a short man with plum-like lips who'd been swanning about London as a man of means. From this side of the Atlantic, it was difficult to size him up, but General Schuyler had heard some alarming stories, like the one about Church's having fled to America because he'd killed someone in a duel. Everyone said it was much more likely that Church had fled bankruptcy, but he had a handsome pair of dueling pistols to show for it, ones that were made by the London firm of Wogdon and put to tragic use later.

That courtship had culminated in a mad dash to Angelica's grandparents, the Van Rensselaers, for immediate nuptials. "The *ceremony*," the society portraitist John Trumbull reported breathlessly, "passed at the Manor without the knowledge of the *Parents*." When they learned of the developments, the parents were beside themselves. General Schuyler "scarcely spoke a dozen words," it was reported, and Mrs. Schuyler was "in a most violent Passion and said all that Rage & Resentment could inspire." The marriage survived, but the Schuylers' fondness for Church took some time to kindle.

Schuyler was no fool, and he could see that whatever Hamilton lacked in breeding, he more than made up for in capability, and Betsey could do far worse. More to the point, *Schuyler* could do far worse. It would not hurt him to have an in with Washington or to latch onto a brilliant young man of such energy. Partly to oversee the courtship, the Schuylers moved down to Morristown themselves, and Hamilton paid them a call most every evening, often conversing in French to the burly but surprisingly cultivated general by the fire deep into the night. When Hamilton wrote to ask General Schuyler for his daughter's hand in marriage in February, he did not have to wait long for a reply. Agreed. Hamilton did not get too swept up in the good news, however. He didn't tell Laurens about his engagement for three months.

If there was any doubt that his marriage to Betsey might have been wanting in love, his obvious fondness for her sister Angelica did nothing to dispel it, for Hamilton fell for her hard. It showed what was in Hamilton's heart when it wasn't clotted with material calculations, and all the enthusiasm he'd first expended on Kitty Livingston, that great tumble of playfulness and mad passion, was now directed at an utterly unavailable woman who was not just married, but on course to be his sister-in-law. For all his calculating nature, Hamilton could be impetuous, and he had a powerful fondness for the self-destructive act. He couldn't help it; it was as if some hot lava just bubbled up inside him. The Schuyler sisters were born under different stars: while the firstborn, Angelica, took over the ethereal realms, Elizabeth laid claim to the social proprieties. If Elizabeth was about order,

Angelica was about fun. To Hamilton, Angelica was sunshine itself. The relationship revealed a gushing enthusiasm for a woman that ran the gamut from playfulness to desire and back again. From the first, he was so taken by Angelica, and so bad at concealing it, that many people assumed that they were the lovers. A friend congratulated him on his conquest. "No one has seen [Angelica] who has not been pleased with her and she pleased everyone."

In a portrait from these years, Trumbull captured much of what was so intoxicating about Angelica, with her bouffant hair, refined nose, and sophisticated air, all suffused with a shimmer of mischief. It was not just Hamilton who fell. She bewitched Thomas Jefferson and the lordly Robert Livingston, too. But, of course, she was married to another, that wildly wealthy John Barker Church, and so Hamilton must marry another, too. As the years proceeded, Hamilton tried to view the sisters as two halves of a whole, as he called them "my beautiful brunettes," but Angelica would continue to tantalize him as the woman he should never have.

But it was Betsey he did have, and the wedding service was held at noon on December 14, 1780, in the southeast parlor of the Pastures, the formal interior alive with brilliant light reflecting off the snow outside. With Hamilton's friends, including Laurens and Lafayette, all taken up by the war, it was only the Schuylers and their many relations who attended. But for James McHenry, a friend from Washington's staff, the groom was there alone, representing all that remained of his family.

SIXTEEN

But a Single Word, *Burr*

THE LADY WAS married, as it happened. Mrs. Theodosia Prevost. She lived in Paramus, New Jersey, well inland from the Hudson in a fine house called the Hermitage on an estate of nearly a hundred acres. Burr had probably known her since 1777, when he would have been one of a bevy of officers and gentlemen gathering for a taste of her elegant society, which offered a cultural oasis from the war, a place of music and fine talk. The relationship tightened in August 1778, when Washington picked Burr to escort Theodosia and three loyalist prisoners of war from New Jersey to New York, where he was to deliver the prisoners under a white flag to a British fort. It was a journey of five days in close quarters. And then he came for more.

It's unknown now what Prevost looked like. Betsey Schuyler was many times painted, but Theodosia Prevost's image is recorded only once, in blurry miniature, no more than a half inch high, beside the time on Burr's pocket watch. The explanation is made clear with the first detailed description of her appearance in the first Burr biography, published by James Parton in 1877. He does not equivocate. "The lady was *not* beautiful," he writes. He gives no details except this: "She was slightly disfigured by a scar on her forehead," although it likely came after the couple met. Nothing more about her appears in any of the contemporary accounts either, including Burr's own. Not her height, the color of her eyes or hair, her shape, delicacy, any of the usual feminine details. Still, she didn't lack for admirers, including future president the oafish James Monroe, who sent her a flirtatious note when she fell for Burr, calling her "the most unreasonable creature in existence" for being so obviously in love with Burr instead of himself.

Theodosia was an unlikely object for Burr's ardor in other respects as well. Raised in New Jersey in the wealthy Tory family of lawyer Theodosius Bartow, who died before she was born, Theodosia was married to a British officer, Lieutenant Colonel James Mark Prevost, and—shades of Margaret Moncrieffe—there were questions about her loyalty to the patriot cause. Her two sisters had married British soldiers, her brother had been imprisoned as a Tory sympathizer, Paramus was said to be a virtual province of the Crown, and there were plenty of cruel suggestions among begrudging patriots in town that she herself should be deported and her property seized. Prevost was ten years older than Burr, thirty-four to his twenty-four, and the mother of five children—significant impediments for a man seeking to have a family of his own. And she was of even more frail health than he. It seemed she suffered from an "incurable disorder of the uterus," a cancer that would kill her, but the symptoms sometimes left her crippled with pain in her abdomen, laudanum—a tincture of opium taken for pain—her only comfort.

Burr paid no heed to any of these drawbacks. For her medical complaints, Burr had, Theodosia marveled, only "friendly sympathy," never frustration, at least at first. That may have been one of the bonds between them. Of course, this may have been because he had plenty of ailments of his own. After a day of debilitating headache, he wrote her, "If you could sit by me, and stroke my head with your little hand, it would be well."

→>-<←

BY 1780, HE'D settled himself in Albany, studying with Titus Homer, a delegate to the Continental Congress, in preparation for the legal career he'd set aside for the war. The normal course of study took three years. He bargained with the legal authorities to make it one and a half, but even that meant excruciating sixteen-hour days—reminiscent of his brutal schooling—much of it peering at handwritten notes and blurry texts in the flickering candlelight. Because of the distance, his relationship with Theodosia was largely epistolary; anything more would have been adulterous in any case. Sorely pressed, he could promise to devote a quarter of an hour out of his day to write Theodosia. In return, he begged for half an hour of hers but allowed her to split it with the five children, who each should contribute a sheet, even, he wrote, if they set down "but a single word, *Burr*," to remember him by. And, when his day was finally done, he begged that she would "visit me in my slumbers."

Theodosia had something that Burr prized above everything else: a "cultivated mind." A clear thinker, well-read, and astute in the ways of the world, Theodosia offered Burr the brilliant and fully equal companion— the ideal woman described by Wollstonecraft—he'd lacked since college and probably even there. The lovers joined over books, a notion that would have left the Hamiltons mystified, and one that Burr himself would have found inconceivable before Theodosia appeared. In late 1781, Burr encouraged Theodosia to install a Franklin stove in a quiet back room, where she could have "a place sacred to love, reflection and books." Under her influence, the three had become nearly indistinguishable to him. Many of the letters that survive are devoted to discussing the merits of various philosophers, but the epistolary back-and-forth had an unmistakable sexuality, as Burr wrote sending her an "impulse of feeling" that expressed his "whole soul." Those were the letters Theodosia loved; she was bored by fine writing. "Candour" was what she craved, and the trust that it implied. "You have a heart that feels: a heart susceptible to tender friendship," she swooned. But she liked his intelligence, too, and, like a professor, graded it. "Your opinion of Voltaire pleases me," she announced, "as it proves your judgment above being biased by the prejudices of others. The English"—*her* English—"from national jealousy and enmity to the French, detract him."

"Burr was a lover of books, a lover of pictures, a lover of everything that distinguishes man from Puritan," Matthew Davis marveled of his friend, not that he was fully of that persuasion himself. "And it was rare, indeed, in those days, to find a lady in America who had the kind of culture which sympathizes with such tastes." The interests of most fine ladies, like Betsey, ran to quilting and knitting. And none of them were, says Davis, "familiar with the most recent expressions of European intellect, who could talk intelligently with him about Voltaire, Rousseau and Chesterfield." Davis sums Theodosia up with a tribute: "[Burr] used to say, in after years, that in style and manners [Theodosia] was without a peer among all the women he had known, and that if his own manners were in any respect superior than other men's it was due to her."

Still, Theodosia was certainly an unexpected choice by Burr; none of her predecessors were remotely like her. Perhaps because it was conducted by letter over a great distance, the courtship is nearly impossible to visualize. There is nothing to see: no walks in the woods, no outings to the theater, no snuggling in bed. There is instead a vacancy filled only by words, and it made a blank that their enemies moved to fill with their own dark speculations. The mystery of it evokes again the shadows that enclose Burr. The fact that no one knew for sure which side Mrs. Prevost, there in shady Paramus, was on makes one wonder how, or if, *he* knew—and whether that ambiguity was part of the appeal for a man who thrived on mystery.

This was not an academic matter. Just two summers before, in 1779, a Major John André of the British army was arrested as an accessory to the treasonous schemes of the almost insufferably ambitious Benedict Arnold, the onetime hero who had led Burr in the siege of Montreal. He was now revealed to be a vile traitor for divulging secrets about the American defenses at West Point, endangering countless American lives, if not the cause of independence. Alexander Hamilton was there when Arnold's plot was exposed. A man of darkness himself, Arnold slipped away to England, but André was tracked and captured and detained in an upstate tavern that served as a temporary jail. Curious to meet a man who seemed daring to one side and despicable to the other, Hamilton went to see him, and he came away impressed with this British major, so cool in the face of a terrible turn of fate.

The punishment for spying was death, but where Burr had insisted on setting out harsh penalties on his reprobates and watching them meted out, Hamilton now begged Washington instead to place André in a stockade for the rest of the war. Washington would not relent: Major André was to be hung. And Hamilton was there to watch his new friend be taken by cart to the makeshift gallows, where he was obliged to stand in the coffin that was soon to hold him forever. Hamilton's view of the scene was gauzy, but he detected a "smile of complacency" from André that "expressed the serene fortitude of his mind." André drew the noose tight around his own neck and bound his own eyes with a white handkerchief. Then, at a signal, the cart lurched forward, leaving André hanging from the rope, his legs kicking briefly in the air.

Although her husband fled to England, the histrionic Mrs. Arnold, to avoid suspicion, contrived fits of hysteria over her husband's duplicity, making it seem as though she didn't have the first idea about his treasonous activities. When attention finally shifted away from her, she paid a visit to her good friend Mrs. Prevost at the Hermitage. There, confident she was speaking to a British loyalist, she told her everything. She'd been in on her husband's plot from the beginning. She had herself passed on the critical documents, wrapped in precious millinery, to Major André. Theodosia told Burr, who told no one.

During this period, the two often communicated in a cipher of Burr's devising, one he would use regularly later on, when he had even more to conceal. It is hard to imagine that Theodosia, or any of his later correspondents, would think of such a stratagem, a painstaking matter for creator and translator alike, on their own, or make time for it. It is unclear whether this was intended to conceal the truth about Theodosia's loyalty or just to maintain the privacy of a relationship that had become a matter of increasing gossip. Either way, there was something about Burr—a heightened sense of exclusivity, or self-importance, perhaps—that sought out secrets, and kept them.

As the affair went on, there was much to bear for both of them, not the least of it the fact that people were starting to wonder about the fundamental propriety of an American soldier so plainly dallying with a married Englishwoman. Theodosia professed not to be troubled. "Our being the subject of much inquiry, conjecture, and calumny, is no more than we ought to expect," she told Burr. "My attention to you was ever pointed enough to attract the observation of those who visited the house. Your esteem more than compensated for the worst they could say. When I am sensible I can make you and myself happy, will readily join you to suppress their malice. But, till I am confident of this, I cannot think of our union. Till then I shall take shelter under the roof of my dear mother, where by joining stock, we shall have sufficient to stem the torrent of adversity."

But the fact remained that Mrs. Prevost was still married to Lieutenant

Colonel Prevost. He was never mentioned in her letters, and it's plain why. He'd disappeared from her thoughts practically the moment Burr appeared. Herself part of a military family, Theodosia had married Prevost, of Swiss descent, at seventeen, when he was a captain. Originally stationed in New Jersey, he was promoted in 1779 to become lieutenant governor of occupied Georgia, and before the year was out he was shifted from there to the West Indies (although not to Nevis or Saint Croix, the islands Hamilton had come from). Now a lieutenant colonel, lonely in the broiling, godforsaken islands where Hamilton was born, Prevost begged Theodosia to come down to him with their children. Theodosia's sister assured him she would, but Theodosia wouldn't think of it. Her life was in New Jersey, not the tropics; and, of course, there was Burr to think of. Instead, she sent her husband a lock of her hair, although it is doubtful he considered himself well compensated.

By then, the two lovers couldn't keep themselves from each other whenever they were together. Burr once wrote to his sister that Theodosia was curled up with him as he wrote, "And is this moment pinching my ear, because I will not say anything about her to you."

Theodosia was unwilling to go but unsure she could stay. Hence the lock of hair, the most tenuous declaration of affection. The whole situation was unbearable, made all the worse by the fact that this was a state and time that scorned divorce. If by a miracle she managed a legal separation, she would emerge from the marriage penniless, owning not even her clothes. It couldn't have helped the shaky health of either that neither could see a decent future for themselves.

SEVENTEEN

A Little Sorceress

AGAINST ALL EXPECTATIONS, Hamilton found a home with the Schuy-lers. To hear his father-in-law tell it, he'd become a virtual Schuyler himself. "You can not my Dear Sir be more happy at the Connection you have made with my family than I am," Schuyler exclaimed, with an epis-tolary clap on the back. "Until a child has made a judicious choice the heart of a parent is continually in anxiety but this anxiety vanished in the moment that I discovered w[h]ere you and she had placed your affec-tions.

"I am pleased with every Instance of delicacy in those that are so dear to me, and I think I read your soul," Schuyler went on, gently absolving Hamilton of his illegitimacy. "I shall therefore only intreat you to consider me as one who wishes in every way to promote your happiness and that I shall never give or loan but with a view to *Such* Great Ends."

A tenderness enters his letters to Betsey, too, a wistful longing that was new. With Washington in Dobbs Ferry, New York, Hamilton had been carousing with his fellow officers, when, he writes her, "I stole from a croud of company to a solitary walk to be at leisure to think of you, and I have just returned to tell you by an express this moment going off that I have been doing so." A love for Betsey had stolen over him.

You are certainly a little sorceress and have bewitched me, for you have made me disrelish every thing that used to please me, and have

*rendered me as restless and unsatisfied with all about me, as if I was
the inhabitant of another world, and had nothing in common with
this. I must in spite of myself become an inconstant to detach myself
from you, for as it now stands I love you more than I ought—more
than is consistent with my peace. A new mistress is supposed to be the
best cure for an excessive attachment to an old—if I was convinced of
the success of the scheme, I would be tempted to try it—for though it is
the pride of my heart to love you it is the torment of it to love you so
much, separated as we now are. But I am afraid, I should only go in
quest of disquiet, that would make me return to you with redoubled
tenderness. You gain by every comparison I make and the more I
contrast you with others the more amiable you appear.*

The more deeply Hamilton entered into his new family, the more he
chafed at his old one with Washington. He had resented the strictures of
his position for much of the war—confined to headquarters when other
officers, like Burr, could make a name for themselves in battle—and Washington had steadfastly refused to set him free. It was maddening: In October of 1780, Lafayette had wanted Hamilton to take charge of a company
to drive the British from Staten Island, but Washington refused, even after
Hamilton enlisted a pair of generals to plead his case. In some ways, Hamilton had become a victim of his own success. He'd become the indispensable man. But that didn't make the situation any easier to bear. If anything,
the unfairness of it all made it infuriating.

By January, Washington had established his winter headquarters in a
tight little farmhouse in New Windsor, New York, just off the Hudson,
where icy winds swept across to rattle the farmhouse walls and send snow
arcing up under the windows. For Hamilton, newly married, eager for his
wife's company, it was a place of utter misery. "I hate congress—I hate the
army—I hate the world—I hate myself," Hamilton moaned. "The whole is
a mass of fools and knaves." For Washington, it had been a miserable year.
The army had blundered into loss after loss, renewing calls for his removal.
In late spring, Hamilton had been distressed to discover that Laurens had
been captured by the British in a siege of Charleston, not far from the

grand house where he'd grown up. Laurens had begged Washington for reinforcements, but he had none to send, and it had fallen to Hamilton to give him the bad news. He began the letter "Adieu my Dear," and closed it with a plea for him to be careful "for the sake of Yr. affectionate A. Hamilton." Laurens was so outraged that Hamilton had to beg him to "play the philosopher" and not turn to "the dagger, nor the poisoned bowl, nor to the rope."*

Now, with another harsh winter upon them, mutinies had erupted among the ranks as soldiers refused to go any longer without shoes or proper clothing. With Hamilton's concurrence this time, Washington responded savagely, ordering the "most incendiary" leaders hanged. As ever, Martha Washington tried to boost everyone's spirits, and Betsey had come down from Albany to tend to Hamilton's, but it was no use.

One night after Betsey had returned home, Hamilton and Washington stayed up late preparing dispatches for some French officers, until they finally dragged themselves to bed, exhausted. Early the next morning, the offices once again humming with activity, Hamilton was descending the narrow stairs when Washington was coming up in search of him. Hamilton merely nodded to the general, said he'd be with him in a moment, and continued downstairs to speak to Lafayette. He returned to find Washington standing at the top of the stairs, glaring down at him. As Hamilton wrote his father-in-law, the exchange went:

---

* Hamilton was joking, but there was something extreme in Laurens's recklessness, as if he was seeking something in death he could not find in life. He'd seen two siblings die, a third had perished in his care, and his mother had died when he was still young. Then, in September 1780, Laurens's father, Henry, the former president of the Continental Congress, had been captured by the British at sea and removed to the Tower of London. But his obvious and impossible love for Hamilton may have encouraged this abandon, as he sought, in effect, to throw himself onto the pyre of his devotion. Even Hamilton's son John, usually obtuse where his father's emotions were concerned, observed that Laurens's quest for "higher excellence" was appropriate "in the warm conceptions of a mind deeply tinged with romance." And, in revealing his engagement to Laurens, Hamilton assured him that, while in marriage, he "had a part for the public, and another for you." Betsey was one thing, in other words, Laurens another.

*"Col Hamilton (said he), you have kept me waiting at the head of the
stairs these ten minutes. I must tell you Sir you treat me with
disrespect." I replied without petulancy, but with decision "I am not
conscious of it Sir, but since you have thought it necessary to tell me so
we part" "Very well Sir (said he) if it be your choice" or something to
this effect and we separated.* *

And that was it for the greatest collaboration of the war. Hamilton
stayed on for a month more, until Washington could find a suitable replace-
ment, but the two never again spoke of the impasse. Washington was mortified by the break, Hamilton somewhat relieved. "For three years past, I
have felt no friendship for him and have professed none," he bluntly
declared, because their "dispositions are the opposites of each other." Hamilton felt no inclination to "court" him. But he did feel guilty all the same.
To Schuyler, Hamilton did everything but tally the seconds to show that
Washington had been in the wrong, and he invoked Lafayette—who surely
did not want to get in the middle of this—as his star witness in the case.
"He can testify how impatient I was to get back, and that I left him in a
manner which but for our intimacy would have been more than abrupt. I
sincerely believe my absence which gave so much umbrage did not last two
minutes."

But then he returned to the core issue. "You are too good a judge of
human nature," he told his father-in-law, flattering him in his eagerness to
keep him on his side, "not to be sensible how this conduct in me must have
operated on a man to whom all the world is offering incense. With this key
you will easily unlock the present mystery." It is typical of all family quarrels for one member to assail another for his own traits, so it was probably
wise that Hamilton struck a reference to Washington's "self-love" from the
draft, and he might have dropped the incense, too. Hamilton could be
quite the preening rooster, and this was a reckless display of vanity.

---

* Unlike most surviving letters of Hamilton's, this one is a draft, and its tatter of cross
outs and reworkings reveals what is normally concealed, namely, the fidgety, unsure
Hamilton.

Still determined to win military honor, Hamilton continued to pester Washington for a field command, and after several months of entreaties, Washington finally set aside his pique and dispatched him to New York City.

But by the end of the month, his ambition had gotten the better of him again when Washington finally awarded him four light infantry companies. He was desperate to obtain glory in the field and wrote Betsey that he simply must go. So much for the seductive whispers; now it was time for a lecture. "I am obliged to sacrifice my inclination to my public character. Even though my presence should not be essential here, yet my love I could not with decency or honor leave the army during the campaign. . . . I must not now evince to the army, that the moment my circumstances have changed, my maxims have changed also. This would be an inconsistency, and my Betsey would not have me guilty of an inconsistency. Besides this my Betsey, The General is peculiarly averse to the practice in question." Any love for her is soft and temporary; his need for success is hard and fixed. For Betsey, it was one thing to be wooed, and another to be won.

He left the Schuylers in Albany, and shortly before Betsey's worst fears were realized: A terrifying mob of Tories and Indians swarmed the Pastures and then burst inside, seemingly bent on slaughtering everyone, including Betsey, now several months pregnant with the Hamiltons' first child. "Where is your master?" one of the men demanded of Betsey's sister Peggy, menacing her with his musket. Schuyler was hiding upstairs, but Peggy told the men he'd galloped into town to fetch troops. The credulous marauders fled at the prospect, leaving all the Schuylers unharmed.

By then, Hamilton was preparing to join Washington in his effort to retake Manhattan and avenge the rout that started the war, when word came in from Lafayette—who'd been shadowing the British forces as the rambunctious young commander of seven thousand French—that General Charles Cornwallis had gathered the bulk of the British army, about seven thousand men, in the port city of Yorktown, Virginia, along the York River. There they were protected from any naval assault by a wall of British ships.

Washington saw his chance: If the ships could somehow be driven off, Cornwallis's strength would be turned to his weakness, as he and his great mass of men would be pressed up against the sea, facing annihilation from both sides. Washington immediately got word to the mammoth French fleet commanded by Admiral François Joseph Paul de Grasse and harbored down in the Antilles to fly north to scare off the flotilla of British ships. Meanwhile, Washington snuck two thousand of his own men plus five thousand French out of Manhattan, past innumerable spies who never understood what they saw, and rushed them to Virginia.

Hamilton, now, like Burr, a lieutenant colonel, had been assigned a light infantry company, and he trudged down the coast with them to join the fray. Keyed up as he was to be part of the war, his eagerness sat uneasily with his desire to be with his pregnant wife. "I must go without seeing you," he told Betsey a few days before he left Manhattan. "I must go without embracing you. Alas I must go." An unusual gloom stole over him as he marched, and his apprehension grew. "Every day confirms me in the intention of renouncing public life and devoting myself wholly to you," he declared. "Let others waste their time and their tranquility in a vain pursuit of power and glory. Be it my object to be happy in a quiet retreat with my better angel."

In Williamsburg, the staging area for the Yorktown fight, Washington joined with Lafayette to assemble a vast American force, the largest agglomeration of the war, of more than fifteen thousand men, enough for a small city, for the last great push to rid America of redcoats. Laurens was there too. Freed in exchange for a British officer of equivalent rank, he'd been serving in Paris in an ambassadorial post to secure some crucial arms for the American side. He'd been sprung from the negotiations in time to take part in this last great showdown of the war. Hamilton was thrilled to be reunited at last with his exuberant friend.

From Williamsburg, Hamilton's brigade led the fifteen-mile march to Yorktown, up on a bluff overlooking a narrowing in the York River. The river opened into the Chesapeake Bay, which reached up through Maryland. By then, the great twenty-nine-ship fleet of the French under de Grasse had dispersed the British fleet that had defended Cornwallis's position. As soon as they were gone, Washington directed his men to enclose Cornwallis in semicircles of soldiers and trenches. They were digging his grave. Without his ships, Cornwallis knew the peril, and he desperately put his men to protecting his position with stout fortifications that rose so high they hid everything but the very tops of a few church steeples. He'd hoped these defensive walls would hold off the Americans until his navy could return to rescue him, but they created his own prison instead.

It was a classic siege, an ever-tightening knot, designed to cut the British off from supply lines, all the while pummeling them with cannon and artillery fire to press their faces to the ground in submission. But to get the guns in range for maximum effect, the Americans had to gradually tighten the range of the trenches. Washington had Cornwallis in his grip, but he still had to squeeze. At first, the men set up camp safely out of reach of the British guns, so Hamilton and his men could sleep out under the stars, if fitfully.

Then Hamilton's men helped dig a closer trench to the south. By custom, when a trench was complete, one of the officers in the company of trench diggers would lead a small celebration, waving a flag or offering a spirited tune, to show the company's mettle. Hamilton led this one, and he ordered all his men out of the trench to perform some brisk parade drills on level ground, in full view of the enemy. It was supposed to be a taunt, but it had a death wish in it, and his men were not pleased to be part of such a nervy display. Later, Hamilton told his men that if the British charged at them, to fire only once at a soldier as he tried to storm the trench, and then run him through with a bayonet, which would require veins full of ice water. Sure enough, when he sent out pickets for some predawn reconnaissance, they came tumbling into the trench, terrified to have spotted some British soldiers. Furious, Hamilton ordered them back out of the trench, and to return to their task.

In yet another blunder, Cornwallis had placed two sections of his fortifications well in front of the rest, leaving them dangerously exposed to attack. To take advantage, Washington planned to take a page from General Howe's book at Chadd's Ford, feint north, to distract Cornwallis, and then charge hard at the two redoubts from the south.

But who would have the chance for glory? Determined to be the man, Hamilton pestered Washington about it, relentlessly cajoling, demanding, until the general had little choice but to award the plum to his renegade former aide. Ecstatic at the news, Hamilton burst into his tent. "We have it!" he exclaimed. "We have it!"

Past midnight on October 14, the American artillery units let loose with a thunder of cannon fire well to the north, to make the British think the attack was coming from there. Meanwhile, Hamilton readied his men to the south. Since silence was essential to the surprise, Hamilton had ordered all guns unloaded and bayonets affixed. Then he gathered his men five deep in the long trench and waited for the signal—a burst of five French shells high into the night sky. When it came, Hamilton leapt out of the trench to lead his men forward, dashing two hundred yards across the rough field to the distant redoubts, which loomed up larger with every pounding step. Hamilton was the first to reach the far walls, and, scrambling up the back of one of his soldiers, he was the first to vault over the top and into the parapet inside. Behind him, his men snapped off the tips of the wooden pikes intended to impale invaders and used them as steps to climb over the top. At Hamilton's direction, the men raised bloodcurdling screams, making one terrified Hessian soldier inside think he was being overrun by a "whole wild hunt." Inside the fortifications, bayonets dripped red in the night light as the men did their bloody work, Hamilton's no less than the rest, and a few plaintive gunshots rang out from the British side. Then Hamilton's men overwhelmed the enemy with their sheer numbers, and the British and Hessians were soon begging to surrender to save themselves. Hot with battle, many of the Americans wanted to press the attack, but Hamilton insisted they avoid such "barbarity." Hamilton instead accepted the proffered sword of his British counterpart, Major Campbell, and Hamilton's last battle was over.

Once the Americans seized the fortifications, their guns could strike anywhere in Yorktown. Frantic, Cornwallis dispatched some men under Lieutenant Colonel Robert Abercrombie to break the center of the American line, but they were easily repulsed. Hunkered down, Cornwallis even tried to infect some black slaves with smallpox and send them out to wander among the American troops, to no effect. The patriots continued to pound Yorktown. Two more days passed, in which the British supplies ran down and diseases spread, and finally on October 17, a single red-coated drummer boy appeared on the parapet, followed by an officer waving a white handkerchief.

"Tomorrow Cornwallis and his army are ours," Hamilton crowed to

Betsey. And it was so. Cornwallis had tried to hold out for better terms, but it was hopeless: In the end he had to surrender his entire army of nearly ten thousand men to the Americans. Hamilton was there to watch the spectacle of the British withdrawal from Yorktown. Once proud, strutting, invincible, the redcoats were now beaten men for whom Hamilton had no pity. "I observed every sign of mortification with pleasure," he said. Officially the war would drag on until 1783, as the remnants of the British army retreated to New York City, which had always been their stronghold, and as Benjamin Franklin, in Paris, negotiated the peace that would mark the departure of the British from American shores.

Hamilton watched the surrender on horseback, and when the ceremony was complete, he galloped off to see Betsey in Albany, wearing out two horses in his eagerness. When he arrived at the grand Schuyler mansion, he dropped into bed and scarcely rose from it for two months. The Pastures was a vast house, broad enough for seven windows across and, within, a sixty-foot hall that set off a sitting room, drawing room, nursery, and vast dining room, with a grand, curving staircase leading up to the ballroom above, and it was beginning to feel like his home. A friend extolled the house in Byronic verse as a lover's bower:

> *All these attendants Ham are thine,*
> *Be't yours to treat them as divine.*

By January of 1782, Hamilton had roused himself enough for Betsey to present him with a son, Philip, named for her father, not his, but giving Alexander Hamilton a true family at last.

EIGHTEEN

In Ill Humour with Every Thing but Thee

A SMALL CITY OF sober Dutch homes, Albany was the first place where Burr had to confront the fact that his income was no match for his expenses. He'd come to secure for himself a moneymaking profession, expecting he might soon have a family to support. While Burr had taken his time to settle on his career, Hamilton knew immediately that his was to be the law. It suited every talent of his, from his mastery of detail to his brilliance at argument. Like Burr, he'd learn it in the state capital, since Manhattan was still under British control. For both men, the law was attractive for its income. Both of them were reckless with money in all ways—spending it freely on luxuries and overly generous to friends in need.

Although Hamilton was supposed to be the poor one, it was Burr who was in the financial bind, and not for the last time. While he didn't dwell on his finances, they defined him, if only by their precariousness, and when they appear in his journal it's clear they made him miserable, as they explained why he was in this remote city, so far from Theodosia, doing work he plainly detested, in merely "tolerable" quarters. One entry doubles as a letter to Theodosia. "A day completely lost," he grumped of a futile search for rooms, "and I, of course, in ill humour with every thing but thee." The next morning, he was down with a migraine that he attributed to a "hearty supper of Dutch sausages." He took "the true Indian cure," sweating out the malignancy in front of the fire and living on hot tea. But he admitted the best cure would be Theodosia herself. He finally found rooms, but they were too dreary for studying.

"Were my life at stake, [the law] could not command my attention." And then deliverance: A Schuyler relative, Philip Van Rensselaer, came to call, sniffed about Burr's digs, and pronounced them inadequate for a man of his qualities; he soon found Burr far better lodging with a pair of his wealthy spinster aunts. Delighted with the new place, Burr professed to find the aunts "obliging and (incredible!!) good-natured," each of them "the paragon of neatness. Not an article of furniture, even to a teakettle, that would soil a muslin handkerchief."

It was likely that General Alexander McDougall—the rebel patriot from Hamilton's college days whom Burr had served under in Westchester County—had put the Schuylers up to enlisting Van Rensselaer, since McDougall was close to General Philip Schuyler. That had prompted Burr to pay a call on the Schuylers while Hamilton was at Yorktown and Betsey was still flush with her pregnancy. Shaking his hand in greeting, and then gazing into the moonglow of Aaron Burr's face, Betsey could not possibly have imagined she was staring at the man who would be her husband's killer. Nonetheless, she must have dispatched her uncle Philip to look after Burr—something she could obviously not, as a lady, do herself.

Starting in on the law ahead of Hamilton, Burr did a favor for his future rival by persuading the five-man New York State Supreme Court to exempt returning soldiers from the requirement of three full years of legal study before applying to the bar, and permitting them to complete only six months instead. "Surely," he declared, "no rule should be intended to . . . injure one *whose only misfortune is having sacrificed his time, his constitution and his fortune to his country*." The truth was, any length of study was too long. He told Theodosia he much preferred to dive into "Rousseau's 4th volume," with its interesting ideas about jealousy. Theodosia believed it a natural human emotion, but Rousseau declared it fit only for "brutes and sensualists," and Burr let her know rather sharply (he could be stinging in his chastisements) he heartily agreed.

By then, he'd received a far greater, almost wondrous deliverance. In December of 1781, a friend directed Theodosia to a small item in *The York Gazette*: Lieutenant Colonel James Mark Prevost had died of yellow fever in Jamaica. When Burr learned the news he was still in Albany, frantically training for the law. He started keeping a journal of his love for Theodosia as a means of closing the gap of separation between them. The following spring, Burr finally won his license as an attorney and set up an office in

Albany, and, the last impediment cleared away, the two were set to be married in Albany, not far from Hamilton's wedding place at the Pastures.

Given the relative extravagance, one would be forgiven for thinking that Hamilton was the aristocrat and Burr the immigrant. To save money, Burr and Theodosia wedded in a joint ceremony with Theodosia's half sister Catherine de Visme, who was marrying a British physician who'd joined the American cause. Burr wore an "old coat," and Theodosia's gown "of suitable gauze; ribbons, gloves, etc.," as she put it, was borrowed from her sister. It cost them "nothing," Theodosia was delighted to report. "The attention of my Burr," as she always called him, "is not to be equaled," and "the air of Albany is healthy, beer in perfection." This was a marriage that was plainly not about money.

William Livingston, Hamilton's host at Liberty Hall, and an admirer of Theodosia's, sent word that he hoped the marriage would silence "the tongue of malice" that had been so noisy against the couple. They could only hope.

-+>-<+-

WHEN HE ARRIVED in Albany, Hamilton relied on the Burr exemption, and he was confident that six months of legal study would be more than ample. He decided not to follow the custom of seeking instruction from a practicing lawyer. He'd teach *himself* the law, relying only on occasional pointers from his old friend Robert Troup, whom he lived with in the Schuyler mansion, and he busied himself preparing a manual to teach others the essential points of the profession. *Practical Proceedings in the Supreme Court of the State of New York*, he titled it. He also penned some essays about how to reorganize the national economy, a subject he'd been pondering while the army was plagued by the funding efforts of the Continental Congress.

Neither man mentioned meeting the other in Albany. But Albany society was so tight, their interests so similar, their friends so overlapping, and their ages and marital circumstances so nearly identical, it is inconceivable that the two should have missed each other. If they had met, it would have been a remarkable moment, like the moment when twins meet in Shakespeare, only these twins were fraternal, not identical, with intriguing differences to complement their obvious similarities. Both men were still short enough that they'd never been able to shake the sobriquet "little" that had attached to both their names, and each was deceptively slight. Hamilton's chest was so slender it needed a medal to enhance it. Burr, always dreamier, counted less on his body to convey his character, and more on his dark, deep-set eyes.

→‑<‑

THEIR TIME TOGETHER in Albany was brief, barely a year, and punctuated on Hamilton's part by duties that arose from those essays deploring the confederate system of governance. He was asked to serve on the Confederation Congress, intended to reconsider the thorny matter of the dysfunctional Articles of Confederation, and in November of 1782, he trotted on horseback from Albany clear to Philadelphia, now much restored after its months of British subjugation. It was now a pleasing little London that combined sea-scented wharves with parasol-twirling ladies on tree-shaded streets. The work of creating a new nation held Hamilton's attention for only two months before he was begging Betsey, "Come my charmer and relieve me. Bring my darling boy to my bosom."

The meetings meandered interminably, and it got worse with the signing of a provisional peace treaty with Great Britain at the end of November 1782, further undercutting any need for national unity. The whole thing might have been a total loss for Hamilton but for his discovery of a wizened, monkish figure whose brilliance possibly surpassed Hamilton's own. It was James Madison, a thirty-one-year-old who might have been twice that. Fresh from a virtuosic display at the Virginia House of Delegates, he'd been the youngest delegate in Congress when he arrived two years before, an honor that now passed to Hamilton at twenty-eight. Unlike most of their confederates, Madison shared Hamilton's conviction that the government needed to be reorganized along federal lines with a powerful central government in place of the current squabbling duchies. The national government needed its own source of revenue if it was to maintain an army, and the states would wither if they didn't create a national market. The frustrations came to a head that June when the entire four-hundred-man officer corps of the Continental Army threatened to resign if its demands weren't met. Hamilton appealed to Washington to intervene, and when Congress still did not act, the officers poured into Philadelphia to seize military arsenals and then stormed into the statehouse to take some congressmen hostage, including a seething Hamilton. When he was finally released, he wrote an angry broadside asserting that the government had been "grossly insulted." He demanded the state militia offer protection from these belligerent army officers, but when that was not forthcoming, the Congress decamped to cramped and inelegant quarters in Princeton.

Hamilton was so disgusted with the state of Congress that it compelled him to think anew about a more powerful national legislature. The outgoing governor of Virginia, the tall, airy, bandy-legged Thomas Jefferson, thought that Congress should remain weak and simply meet less. Hamilton would certainly not let Jefferson have the last word on that.

→>-<←

HAMILTON PASSED HIS exams and was set to embark on a legal career in Albany until politics again intervened. His thoughts on taxation led to his being appointed as the receiver of continental taxes for New York, a post that placed him at the center of the debate about the future of the government and won him membership on a five-man committee in Philadelphia to reexamine the Articles of Confederation.

By then, Hamilton had long since put the war behind him. But John Laurens had not, still committed to the idea of raising a black army against the British. "Quit your sword my friend, put on the toga, come to Congress," Hamilton begged him. "We have fought side by side to make America free. Let us hand in hand struggle to make her happy."

Laurens never received this message. Trying to brush back the British from South Carolina that August, Laurens flouted orders to be cautious—not for the first time—and tried to ambush a small expeditionary force he'd spotted near the Combahee River. But the enemy was waiting for him in the tall grass, muskets at the ready. As soon as Laurens and his men drew near, the British sprang on them, firing. Laurens was cut down instantly.

When he heard the news in Albany, Hamilton was crushed to have lost a friend in a "trifling skirmish," as he told Lafayette. "You know how much I love him and will judge how much I regret him." That was an ending for Hamilton, not just for his friendship with Laurens, but also for that flow of deep and honest emotion that Laurens always seemed to inspire in him. When Laurens died, it was as if the true Hamilton died too.

In his suit of American broadcloth, President George Washington delivered his first inaugural address on the balcony of Federal Hall. He was said to be so nervous that he thrust his free hand into his pocket to conceal the trembling. Not yet in the government as treasury secretary, Hamilton watched from an upstairs window of his house down the street.

Part Two

THE
BATTLE
IS
JOINED

NINETEEN

Commentaries on the Laws of England

Although Cornwallis's British troops had marched smartly out of Yorktown to fife and drum, the last soldiers occupying New York City under General Guy Carleton drained away like the tide.* A jeering crowd turned out to watch the detested redcoats get ferried out to transport ships in the harbor for the long, desultory passage home. Before the last of them was gone, the rotund General Henry Knox led thousands of tattered soldiers into the liberated city. "*Our* troops," recalled one witness. "My heart and eyes were full, and I admired and gloried in them the more because they were weather-beaten and forlorn." Many of the onlookers sported "union cockades" of black and white ribbons as they roamed the streets ripping down tavern signs that expressed loyalty to the Crown. Royal street names fell too: Crown Street became Liberty, King became Pine. When the last of the British were gone from the city's shores, to a roar from the crowd, Knox raised the American flag to flap in the chilly air over a free Manhattan.

General Washington had ridden down from Tarrytown for the occasion, and General McDougall and other former Sons of Liberty escorted him past a jam of ecstatic New Yorkers to the Bowery to see the British

---

* It was Carleton who directed the defense of Quebec to begin Burr's war; he now ended Hamilton's.

ships finally raise anchor and leave the harbor. Then he toured the *new* New York to a raucous welcome, receiving thirteen toasts at the fabled Fraunces Tavern alone. At New York governor George Clinton's dinner for the French ambassador at Cape's Tavern, 120 guests downed 135 bottles of fine Madeira and 50 bottles of beer—and then, joy-struck, tossed sixty wineglasses and eight decanters into the fire in an alcohol delirium. The night was capped with a burst of fireworks: A "Balloon of Serpents and a Yew Tree of brilliant fire" shot up into the heavens, followed by an "Illuminated Pyramid, with Archemedian Screws, a Globe and vertical sun," and then, the grand, thundering finale: "Fame, descending," accompanied by a hundred blazing rockets. The celebrations turned solemn a week later when Washington paid a return visit to Fraunces Tavern to deliver a farewell to his officers. No orator, he said little, but silently embraced each man in turn.

→>‒<‒

HAMILTON WAS NOT among them. Just a few days before, he'd come down the Hudson by sloop from Albany with Betsey and baby Philip to Manhattan, to establish a legal practice there now that all the Tory lawyers had been officially turned out. They'd found rooms at 57 Wall Street, not far from the Fraunces Tavern on Pearl, so inconvenience was no excuse. Nor was Hamilton likely to have gone uninvited, as Washington never held grudges where his family was concerned. More likely, Hamilton was still smarting from the incident on the staircase. His pride was sizable, but it was also tender, and Washington had wounded it.

Another young lawyer, a newly confident Aaron Burr, moved down from Albany virtually the same day, and he'd settled with Theodosia and three of her children, with Theodosia, *fille*, to come the next year, into a house on Wall Street, a short walk from the Hamiltons, not that Burr was likely to pass that way. He referred to it as "next door but one to City Hall." The rent was to start the day the troops left the city. He and Hamilton were certainly not the only ambitious young lawyers bursting into Manhattan. Hamilton's roommate Robert Troup came, as did Morgan Lewis, another rising political star; James Kent, who would become one of Hamilton's friends; and Henry Brockholst Livingston of that overspreading political family. Perhaps fifty altogether, making up a blindingly talented cadre of New York lawyers who proceeded to define the city's law, and its politics too.

-><-

WHEN NEW YORK emerged from the war, it was still only inhabited for about a mile up from the Battery on the island's southern tip. Beyond that it was a scramble of wooded hills, opening into an occasional lonely farm. Many of the trees fringing inhabited Manhattan had been hacked away for firewood, leaving just skeletons behind. Farther north, the landscape was teeming with wolves and black bears, and every imaginable species of bird flew overhead—enough wildlife to make New York's forest one of the most abundant in America. And the island was bounded on either side by the pristine waters of the Hudson and East Rivers, which were a paradise of oysters and lobster.

Hamilton and Burr both lived near the ruins of the once-spectacular Trinity Church, now a ghost of itself, a grim reminder of the city's devastation. All the finer buildings that were still intact, churches mostly, had been put to crude military use by the British as prisons and storage dumps, and they'd turned much of the rest of the city into an armed camp, digging up the streets for trenches and erecting forts on nearly every rise, in preparation for an American assault that never came. The Great Fire of 1776, which the British had let rage, had claimed seventeen hundred buildings, many of them those grand mansions around the former Queen Street that had given the city whatever gentility it might have possessed. They lay now hollowed out, the walls crumbled, the beams blackened embers, the furniture ashes. "The Burnt District," the papers called it. In the hollows where proper buildings once stood, desperate New Yorkers had thrown up a village of shanties and rude huts that was called "Canvas Town." Rude as they were, many of them had been stripped bare like the trees: scavengers peeled off every stick they could reach to feed the fires against the icy winter.

At first, the peace only made things worse, for the city largely depended on the wealth and talents of the Tories, who had now evacuated en masse, either by decree or in fear of what the victors might do to them. Ten thousand altogether, many of them fled to Nova Scotia, where fugitive slaves went to tend them. Hamilton was one of the few citizens who saw the exodus as the city's loss, as he knew the Tories would be essential to the rebuilding effort, not to mention the restoration of the prewar refinement that had made New York society so appealing. Lamenting the mindless hostility of the patriot mobs, he wrote one of the highborn Livingstons: "Our state will feel for twenty years at least the effect of the popular frenzy."

New York craved renewal. The exuberant fashions, the shameless celebration of wealth, the jaunty, cosmopolitan worldview—all the distinctive New Yorkness that had started to emerge before the war, as the city became a thriving commercial hub, abuzz with immigrants, had been pounded by cannon fire, torched, and ground to dust by heavy-booted soldiers. But it had not been extinguished. That essential vitality had merely gone underground, like tree squirrels in a forest fire.

The city's inherent electricity first returned in the boisterous coffee shops that sprouted by the dozens around the city—Tontine's, most famously, which would soon evolve into the city's first stock exchange—as well as the hundreds of loud taverns that were sprinkled about, one to every city block, and often, it seemed, on every side of every city block. All of these were places for garrulous New Yorkers to jaw over politics, gossip, news, and business, creating the outlines of the new city.

Besides its energetic immigrants, taste for the new, and commercial impulse, New York still possessed a unique asset—a confluence of the Hudson River and the Atlantic Ocean that made it the center of the New World, and the cocky attitude that came with it. Hamilton was one of the first to see that, free of Britain, New York could remake itself as an international city, if it could replace the English system of government with a sound American one. Not yet truly a nation, America was a confederacy of jostling sovereignties, each one a jumble of statutes that had no force past its borders. Still, for a young lawyer, these were attractive circumstances: a wide-open job market with the established Tory lawyers all banished; an endless supply of cases in the postwar chaos; and plenty of work in interpreting the new laws coming out of Albany.

In the scramble, two men quickly emerged as the two finest lawyers in the city—Hamilton and Burr—and each was so impressive no one knew which to rate first. General Erastus Root, a fellow New York lawyer who often saw them in action, went so far as to call them "the two greatest men in the state, perhaps the nation." But, as in so many other aspects of their lives, their appeal was a matter of taste. The styles of the two men could scarcely have been more different. Hamilton, Root declared, was "flowing and rapturous," and Burr "terse and convincing." To be sure, Hamilton might have been *over*flowing in Root's opinion, as it might take him four hours to say what took Burr thirty minutes. In a legal battle, though, each man could land a memorable blow. Hamilton's good friend Troup was on the opposite side of one case and fretted to a friend: "I shall deem myself fortunate [if] we all get out of this cause [without] fighting. With my moderation of temper I hope to escape [Hamilton's] pistols as well as his sword." Burr's wrath came out more subtly, as his early biographer Parton noted a "vein of quiet sarcasm in some of his speeches," although, he hastened to add, Burr otherwise exhibited nothing but "courtliness" and "perfect breeding."

Hamilton cut the more airy figure, pirouetting about the courtroom with that dancer's body, beautifully clothed, gesturing gracefully, ever eloquent, and seemingly inexhaustible. His rhetorical elevation wasn't just to convey superiority (although it did have that effect) but to take the long view. To Hamilton, a case was about the principle of the case.

To Burr, a case was about the case. In the courtroom, he rarely moved, scarcely gestured. His silky hair up in a shell comb, his head lightly powdered, his face was a mask, free of smiles, frowns, grimaces, or any other threepenny theatricality. Let Hamilton deliver his arias of impassioned argument. Burr kept his voice a level monotone, and he let those deep, penetrating eyes of his convey any emotion the jury might seek. "Perfectly round, not large, deep hazel in color, [each] had had an expression which no one who saw it could ever forget," intoned a correspondent for the New York *Leader*. "No man could stand in the presence of Col. Burr with his eyes fixed on him and not feel that they pierced his innermost thoughts." To Burr, the law was whatever he could claim it was—"Whatever is boldly asserted and plausibly maintained." Instead of eloquence, Burr went for a conversational style, but always, wrote Parton, "the conversation of a well-bred, thoroughly-informed man of the world."

Because of their celebrity, Hamilton and Burr took part in virtually all of the major cases of the day, usually in opposition, but sometimes in collaboration. While Burr ceded to his rival the "palm of eloquence," Hamilton called Burr "a man of honor, influence and ability," which reveals his reservations. Burr's bluntness could be more effective. When Hamilton created one of his glorious cathedrals of argument, Burr delighted in kicking out the one essential support to bring the whole thing crashing down. Even when the two men worked together, there was not total unity, understandably enough. For one client they shared, Hamilton insisted on speaking last. Burr acquiesced, but then in his own summary covered all the points Hamilton was likely to make too, leaving his colleague almost nothing to say.

Hungry for money, Burr became a legal machine that took in the facts of the case on one side and spat out winning arguments on the other. He took everything that came: the client who sued a loyalist for a thousand pounds for enslaving him for five months; the one who sued the thief who stole his female slave for sex; the man who sued to recover a stolen horse; the politician determined to avoid the requirement to swear to uphold the new Constitution. Hating the work, Burr never spoke to Theodosia about his cases with pride, only with impatience. A "laborious piece of business," he called one, typically. It encouraged a dark, moody, embittered quality in Burr that made him, as he once told his daughter, a "grave, silent, strange sort of animal," adding, in a mystified third person, "We know not what to make of him."

Hamilton rarely paid attention to his fees, viewing his work as above mercenary interests. When a New York merchant sent him advance payment for five years of his services, Hamilton sent it back, with the note, "returned, as being too much." Burr always charged more than Hamilton, and got it, and kept it. When they both worked the complicated matter of *Le Guen v. Gouverneur and Kemble*, Burr took twenty-nine hundred dollars, and Hamilton fifteen hundred dollars for comparable effort. Charging the highest legal fees in the city, and handling the more cases, Burr commanded the highest legal income in the city, more than ten thousand dollars a year, significantly more than Hamilton, but he was usually in debt all the same, and that debt would eventually prove ruinous.

→>-<-

EVEN THOUGH COLONIAL law had derived from the British law that had been developed over centuries, it was retained after the revolution banished the British themselves. Sir William Blackstone's *Commentaries on the Laws of England* were as relevant after the peace as they had been before (when, in an oddity, they served as the key to the cipher Benedict Arnold used to communicate with the doomed John André of the British army). British law simply became the law, and all thirteen states carried on with it, just as before. Murder was still murder. But the country's new statutes that were being enacted by its various legislatures were another matter, and Hamilton had grown increasingly uneasy to see how they had been subverted by patriots bent on revenge against any remaining loyalists. Already distressed to see so many Tories flee the city, taking much of the wealth and talent of the city with them, Hamilton hated to see those who dared to remain be assaulted on street corners, or tarred and feathered, and then further brutalized by new laws condoning the confiscation of their property or canceling their citizenship. To Hamilton, this would not help America's standing in the world or build a lasting peace.

As a solitary lawyer and occasional essayist, Hamilton used the only tools he had to rectify matters. He seized on a small, obscure property case, *Rutgers v. Waddington*, that, to everyone but Hamilton, seemed hopelessly one-sided in favor of Rutgers. That was Elizabeth Rutgers, a well-connected, staunchly patriotic widow who'd fled New York ahead of the British invasion in 1776, abandoning a profitable brewery and alehouse she owned on Maiden Lane (not far, as it happened, from Burr's house). It stood unused for two years, when a couple of British merchants took over the property at the urging of the British occupational forces, and the merchants appointed Joshua Waddington to restore it as a pub for British troops. By then, thieves had made off with the boilers and much of the piping. But Waddington got the place going again, and, as agreed, paid rent to the British army. When the British evacuated the city with the peace in 1783, some hooligans burned the establishment down to the ground. Insisting she had been the owner the whole time, Elizabeth Rutgers demanded back rent for her property, and the Trespass Act, recently passed by the New York State Assembly, seemed designed to provide it. The law was extremely popular in the city—except to Tories, of course.

To see it otherwise was to refight the war from the other side, for it meant taking on patriotic opinion, state law, and commercial interests in the name of Tories who were still regarded as enemies of the state. To all of that, Hamilton was indifferent. Instinctively, he didn't think new laws should apply to past actions. He was convinced that Joshua Waddington was obeying the existing law when he paid rent to the British military during the war, and he shouldn't be forced to pay more rent just because the Assembly said so.

Hamilton had one advantage. The case was to be decided not before a jury, but by a Mayor's Court that consisted of five aldermen and New York's bustling new mayor, James Duane, who was part of the vast network of Livingstons—including Hamilton's early patron, William Livingston—that overspread the city. John Adams thought the mayor had a "sly, surveying eye, a little squint eyed," but Hamilton saw him more charitably. Orphaned early, Duane had been the ward of Robert Livingston, the future chancellor, raised in Livingston Manor in the Catskills, and then had married Livingston's daughter, whose fortune had funded his political career and afforded him a fine law library, which Hamilton had already made good use of. Hamilton played on the connection by enlisting two more Livingstons to his legal team—Brockholst Livingston and the genial Morgan Lewis, who'd married a Livingston.

For her part, Mrs. Rutgers enlisted her well-connected nephew Egbert Benson, the state attorney general, and Hamilton's friend Troup. Because of the quality of the legal talent, it is a surprise that Burr was not involved, but he didn't do political cases, and, despite the stakes, typically for him, voiced no opinion on the matter.

On further reflection, Hamilton decided the Trespass Act was fundamentally flawed. The Assembly had acted as if its laws were supreme, but Hamilton believed there were higher considerations here, like the laws of nations, the laws of war, and, in this instance, the terms of the Treaty of Paris signed by the Continental Congress, the highest representative body of the United States. All of these laws explicitly permitted the appropriation of property in wartime, and Hamilton argued that no state legislature could contravene such laws on its own, or the nation would disintegrate into vast warring fiefdoms, with no common governance. How could a state simply ignore a treaty signed by the Continental Congress? Hamilton asked. If it did, "then the Confederation is a shadow of a shade!" It was a case made for what Hamilton's friend James Kent called his "impassioned eloquence," which, once the trial was on, "soared far above all competition."

It was a powerful argument, powerfully presented, and the Mayor's Court sided with Hamilton. Waddington needed to pay back rent to Rutgers only for the period before he started to pay rent to the army. National and international laws did indeed need to take precedence over state ones.* The implication was unavoidable: A strong central government was needed to rein in the renegade states.

While the case brought Hamilton a major victory, it also delivered political consequences that were not so welcome, as it tagged Hamilton with an identification with royalists that, for a man born offshore, with no natural loyalty to the new nation, and aristocratic tastes besides, was already in play. Unsurprisingly, the case brought Hamilton any number of Tory clients on lucrative property cases, too. Burr, by contrast, took the patriot ones. The cases tipped Hamilton toward the interests of the upper classes, surrendering the workingmen to Burr. It was the beginning of the political divide between them. At first a personal campaign by Hamilton, the case became a cleaving point for the emerging politics of the city and had effects beyond the island, as well. It was, in short, typical Hamilton.

Although the war was supposed to drive out all things English, plenty remained, creating a constant grinding irritation between patriots and loyalists. Chancellor Robert Livingston wrote to John Jay in Paris, laying out the political landscape in early 1784 and pitting the two sides at two extremes: the Tories with their "avowed attachment to England"; the "violent whigs" bent on banishing them and seizing their property; and a few

---

* And this ultimately became a bedrock principle of the US Constitution, as its Supremacy Clause declares that national laws are paramount.

moderate Whigs in the middle who tried to preach tolerance to both sides. Although his enemies would label him a Tory, Hamilton would have placed himself with the moderate Whigs, along with his father-in-law, Philip Schuyler. His violent Whig opponents were known as "Clintonians" and fronted by the wily New York governor, General George Clinton, whom Hamilton was beginning to abhor. Heavy and slow moving but indestructible, he was the turtle of generals and would be the turtle of politicians too. Notwithstanding his providential marriage into the wealthy Tappan family of upstate Ulster County, Clinton styled himself as the yeoman friend to farmers and the implacable enemy of those land-rich lords of the Hudson to the north, the Livingstons, Rensselaers, and, of course, Schuylers. He'd been the one to push through the Trespass Act, which underlay the Rutgers case, as well as a bill depriving Tories of their right to vote and a chance to hold elective office, and, by one account, he personally ordered Tories "tarred and feathered, carted, whipped, fined, banished, and in short, every kind of cruelty, death not excepted."

When Clinton lost the Rutgers case, he demanded redress in the courts and at the ballot box, as he urged voters to back only those candidates who would keep the state free from "judicial tyranny" like that of Mayor Duane, or the legislature would be "nothing but a name." In October, the Assembly declared Mayor Duane's ruling in Rutgers "subversive of all law and good order," and it called on New Yorkers to replace Duane with a mayor who would "govern . . . by the known laws of the land." Duane was no Tory sympathizer; he'd been evicted from his home by the British in the war. Voters returned him to office, and that was largely the end of Tory hating by default. Two years later, the Assembly reversed its ban on Tory lawyers and its restrictions on Tory citizenship. A year after that, it revoked the Trespass Act altogether.

The passions that had been aroused by Rutgers were not so easily extinguished, however. They would find their way into the Constitutional Convention and emerge from it too.

TWENTY

Children of a Larger Growth

I F HAMILTON WAS a party man who moonlighted as a lawyer, Burr was a lawyer. If Hamilton's legal work derived from his ideology, Burr's ideology derived from his legal work, although the pattern was harder to discern. While Burr took plenty of patriot cases from the Trespass Act, he found numerous clients among the New York elite, especially in lucrative land cases, as the speculation boom was on. He represented the de Peyster family, which owned the largest tract of land on Manhattan; William Malcolm, the wealthy merchant who had acquired Burr to drill his Malcolms; some English clients who had contested property in Maine; the Livingstons; Elias Boudinot, whom Hamilton had known as a teenager in Elizabethtown; and even, later, Thomas Jefferson, for a case involving the speculator Robert Morris.

The common denominator was money. Burr took clients who could pay, and he preferred the clients who could pay more. Let Hamilton take cases that would remake the world. He would take the ones that would remake *his* world, making it a little nicer.

While Burr dismissed wealth as a "paltry object," he airily acknowledged to his wife, Theodosia, that it was "a means of gratifying those I love." He sought instead to be rich in the things money could buy. Refined, extravagant things: statuary, artwork, furniture, books. And conveyances especially, those fleet emblems of a man on the go. Like the New York elite before the war, Burr prided himself in flying about the city in "a nice, new, beautiful little chariot, very light, of an entirely new construction."

And he was very particular about where he lived. His first address at 3 Wall Street was one of the prizes of the city, considerably more splendid than Hamilton's house down the street, and set off a competition between them, first latent, then manifest, as to who could live better. For the location and charm, Burr's house was probably the most luxurious property in what had emerged as the city's finest neighborhood. *"Ver Plank's house"* he always emphasized, referring to the Dutch real estate baron who'd built it—and whom he would soon claim as a client. At 115 feet, it had the largest frontage on that section of Wall Street. As Burr's finances improved, he moved the family into a "more spacious" place on Little Queen Street and then to 4 Broadway before he finally found his dream house, Richmond Hill, at the end of the decade.

In those rocky postwar years, many of the country's first citizens, from Washington and Jefferson on down, were seriously overextended; Hamilton, of course, was no exception, even as he rose to take charge of the nation's finances as treasury secretary. But Burr seems to have gone into debt the most steeply, in 1785, shortly after he came to the city, when he started negotiating his first loans from family and friends to stay afloat. For the rest of his life, despite the assertions familiar to every chronic debtor that *this* was the year he would not just balance accounts but grow positively rich, Burr sank ever deeper into the mire of insolvency, moving on to more loans at higher amounts from an ever greater and ever wider variety of people—friends, relations, clients—that turned New York into a hell of lenders seeking to dig a hand into his billfold pocket.

He complained to a political friend, New York congressman Peter Van Gaasbeck, in the 1790s that he was "in the hands of usurers." But then, Gaasbeck was too, and hoped that Burr might free *him*. But Burr replied that he was in a worse way than Gaasbeck could imagine: "I have been ten days endeavoring to raise the pitiful sum of 500 dolrs without success and have now a note laying over in the Bank at NY for Want of it," he complained. "I should not trouble you with these details but that it must appear very singular to you that a man of my large possessions and reputed Wealth should not have a few thousand dollars to spare for a friend." It was a truth that people had trouble grasping. General John Lamb, a Son of Liberty, had met the young Aaron Burr on the Plains of Abraham, where the American troops of Generals Montgomery and Arnold were massed ahead of the ill-fated Battle of Quebec, and was impressed by "the fire of his eye, and his perfect coolness." When Lamb emerged as a man of means in the 1780s, Burr saw a soft touch; in two years, he'd lightened the general of forty thousand dollars before Lamb said his first timid word about repayment. Realizing a grand gesture was needed, Burr assured the general he'd provide the money forthwith by selling the only valuable asset he could—all his furnishings at Richmond Hill, a desperate measure surely, as it would leave his palace an empty box of blank walls and bare floors. Burr did indeed sell every stick of furniture in the house. But that netted scarcely four thousand dollars, and Burr retained the proceeds for other expenses, never passing a nickel to his creditor. A swarm of creditors descended on Lamb, bent on sending him to the hell of debtors' prison for their satisfaction. To his credit, Burr performed some legal maneuvers to save Lamb from such cruelty, but he never did repay him.

In his desperation, Burr did what most of the New York elite did when they came up short. He engaged in land speculation himself, most of it in western New York. He bought with borrowed money, requiring payments he couldn't make until the land was sold, often at a loss.* By the end of the century, when he was on the verge of the vice presidency, his only possession of any value was Richmond Hill, but that was fully mortgaged and devoid of furnishings. A year or two later, Alexander Hamilton wrote a friend that Burr owed "about 80,000 Dollars," or about eight years' legal salary. Hamilton was always aware of such things.

→>-<←

BUT BURR DID have a larger ambition, one that went beyond conspicuous consumption. If Hamilton busied himself in these years creating the

---

* He also served as lawyer for his former guardian, Timothy Edwards, regarding some land purchases from the Stockbridge Indians—once the flock of his father—where they had been driven off to in the "Ten Townships" grant of New York's Broome and Tioga Counties. Edwards's and his brother Jonathan's portion had been disputed by their partners, and the whole matter thrown to the New York legislature.

American nation, Burr was establishing his own little country of seven, a monarchy with Burr himself as the all-powerful king; his brilliant but ailing wife, Theodosia, as his queen; and his sparkling daughter, born in 1784 and the other jewel of his existence, also named Theodosia, as the crown princess. The five stepchildren whom Burr had inherited from Theodosia's marriage to the late Lieutenant Colonel Prevost were young courtiers. He put the boys, Frederick and Bartow, to work in his law office and often brought one of them on his travels as a kind of roving amanuensis. Burr had hoped for a larger family still, but Theodosia delivered two stillborns and a daughter, Sally, who died in infancy. Burr was traveling at the time of the tiny girl's death and suspected she'd died only because his wife, not wanting to distress him, had stopped mentioning her in her letters.

The love of Burr and his wife, Theodosia, burns through their letters. Alive, impassioned, sensual, their marriage must be the most total union of all the political matches of the day, easily eclipsing the forced and stylized raptures of Hamilton for his prim Betsey, although she doted ardently back. Rather, in its swoop and abandon, it evokes the Romantics of later years, the two Shelleys or Byron and Caroline Lamb. Burr's writing might have, as he said, a "natural bluntness," and neither he nor Theodosia shrank from reality, but rather both spoke their minds clearly and forcefully, with a keenness for each other on every page, even in the irritable passages. These were not infrequent, as Burr was off chasing money he loathed, leaving Theodosia home to manage a household that overwhelmed her. Nonetheless, after Theodosia mentioned the exquisite pleasure of the gentle caress of pooled water on her hands, Burr could scarcely contain himself. "It kept me awake a whole night, and led to a train of thoughts and sensations which cannot be described." Theodosia compared her sexual sensations to those of an opium eater. "Love in all its delirium hovers about me," she gushed. "Like opium, it lulls me to soft repose!"

The letters reveal the range of their book-fed minds, for which ideas shot off like fireworks, snapping and sizzling as they lit up the sky. Both of them were ardent feminists, inconceivable as that concept might have been in a time when women were scarcely above slaves in legal standing. Theodosia worshipped Russia's dynamic empress, Catherine the Great, who'd come to power after having her inept husband, Peter III, arrested. "The ladies should deify her, and consecrate a temple to her praise," she wrote Burr. "It is a diverting thought, that the mighty Emperor of the Turks should be subdued by a woman," she added, referring to the two Russo-Turkish wars that led to Russia's seizing Turkish territory on the Black Sea. "How enviable that she alone should be the avenger of her sex's wrongs for so many ages past. She seems to have awakened Justice, who appears to be a sleepy dame in the cause of injured innocence." Burr was entranced by Mary Wollstonecraft, the fountainhead of feminism, whose admiration for the French Revolution had led her to champion female equality. A fiercely controversial work, her *Vindication*, when published in 1792, expressed something essential but forbidden in the Burr psyche, namely, that women had all the depth and majesty of men—and it was a scandal that they should be so desecrated by society: "It would be an endless task," she wrote, "to trace the variety of meannesses, cares, and sorrows, into which women are plunged by the prevailing opinion, that they were created rather to feel than reason, and that all the power they obtain, must be obtained by their charms and weakness."

Burr would have agreed wholeheartedly, but Hamilton would have sided with her antagonist, Lord Chesterfield, who brazenly put forth the contrary view in one of his famous letters to his son, which Hamilton, and many of his circle, considered required reading for a gentleman: "Women . . . are only children of a larger growth; they have an entertaining tattle, and sometimes wit; but for solid reasoning, good sense, I never knew in my life one that had it . . . A man of sense only trifles with them, plays with them, humours and flatters them, as he does with a sprightly, forward child; but he neither consults them about, nor trusts them with, serious matters; though he often makes them believe that he does both."

Wollstonecraft fired back.

My own sex, I hope, will excuse me, if I treat them like rational creatures, instead of flattering their fascinating graces, and viewing them as if they were in a state of perpetual childhood, unable to stand alone. I earnestly wish to point out in what true dignity and human happiness consists—I wish to persuade women to endeavour to acquire strength, both of mind and body, and to convince them that the soft phrases, susceptibility of heart, delicacy of sentiment, and refinement of taste, are almost synonymous with epithets of weakness, and that those beings who are only the objects of pity and that kind of love, which has been termed its sister, will soon become objects of contempt.

This sentiment, radical as it was, came to be so deeply associated with Burr—acting upon it both as a husband to one Theodosia and as a father to the other—he must have believed it already, lacking only the terms to express it. Still, he found the ideas electrifying, and they became a core principle in a life that otherwise was short of them. He wrote his wife:

I had heard [Vindication] spoken of with a coldness little calculated to excite attention; but as I read with avidity and prepossession every thing written by a lady, I made haste to procure it, and spent the last night, almost the whole of it, in reading it. Be assured that your sex has in her an able advocate. It is, in my opinion, a work of genius. She has successfully adopted the style of Rousseau's Emilius; and her comment on that work, especially what relates to female education, contains more good sense than all the other criticisms upon him which I have seen put together. I promise myself much pleasure in reading it to you. Is it owing to ignorance or prejudice that I have not yet met a single person who had discovered or would allow the merit of this work.

It was this principle of female equality, that "women have souls," as he put it, that he applied assiduously to the upbringing of his young daughter, Theodosia, which may have been the greatest accomplishment of his life, as she ultimately ascended to a height of learning and sophistication and poise that was unmatched by nearly all women and most men. He bought a portrait of Wollstonecraft and kept it until shortly before he died, when he sold it to clear some last debts.

For all their range and intensity, the letters inevitably provide a skewed view of the marriage, as each spouse is viewing the other from afar, with a mixture of longing and vexation. If Burr had been able to control his spending, he might not have been away so much. But there was not enough work in New York City, and he soon had to rove about an expanding orbit from New York City that culminated in months-long sessions in Congress in Philadelphia. Hamilton followed a similar route, but tellingly he usually traveled the legal circuit in a kind of caravan with other lawyers including Kent and John Jay, who became lifelong friends. Burr always worked alone and traveled by himself. And his could be arduous journeys. He describes one hellish trip up the Hudson to Albany, made all the worse by one of the migraines that had plagued him since the war. "The headache with which I left New York grew so extreme, that, finding it impossible to proceed in the stage, the view of a vessel off Tarrytown, under full sail before the wind, tempted me to go on board," he wrote his wife in October 1788. "We reached West Point that night, and lay there at anchor near three days. After a variety of changes from sloop to wagon, from wagon to canoe, and from canoe to sloop again, I reached this place last evening." Once there, he was obliged to remain until the case was complete, and inevitably it dragged on longer than he could bear, "wearied out with the most tedious cause I was ever engaged in." From afar he could only fret about his wife's health, which was always a worry. He insisted that she walk twice around the garden before breakfast, and ride in the afternoon. "I shall be seriously angry if you do not," he assailed her. He is hardly reassured to learn that measles has broken out in the city. "You must assure me that I shall find you in good health and spirits."

Burr's own health was hardly secure. His letters are studded with references to the aches and troubles that had been routinely afflicting him after the war, and he rarely slept well. "I lay awake till after three o'clock this morning; then got up and took a large dose of medicine. It was composed of laudanum, nitre, and other savoury drugs, which procured me sleep till now: have no headache; must eat breakfast, and away to court as fast as possible."

But the real disease may have been Burr's relentless quest for more, particularly as manifested in his lust for land. At one point, he had his eye on a lovely estate outside Albany. Although called Fort Johnson, it was a private piece of property, and Burr was desperate to get his hands on it. Knowing his proclivities, Theodosia forbade him even to see it, but Burr couldn't help going. He wrote like a man possessed, revealing an attraction to this "amiable bower," as he called the property, that was nearly sexual, as it offered a luscious beauty for him alone to penetrate. "Oh Theo!" he exclaims; "there is the most delightful grove—so darkened with *weeping willows* that at noonday a susceptible fancy like yours would mistake it for a bewitching moonlight evening. These sympathizing willows, too, exclude even the prying eye of curiosity. Here no rude noise interrupts the softest whisper. Here no harsher sound is heard than the wild cooings of the gentled dove, the gay thresher's animated warbles and the soft murmurs of the passing brook. Really, Theo., it is *charming.*"

He continued in this vein for several more paragraphs, extolling the "cluster of lofty oaks," the "gentle brook." He reminded Theodosia of how much she'd admired the "lofty Apalachians" and added, "Here the mind assumes a nobler tone, and is occupied by sublime objects. What *there* was tenderness, *here* swells with rapture. It is truly charming."

He went on to fantasize about what they would do with such a property, planting "jessamines" and woodbine. He longed to possess the property, even though he couldn't think of any particular use for it, and Theo would be furious. That made him ponder why he could think *this*, and his beloved wife think *that*. What was it about his "singularity of taste" that ran so counter to hers? Philosophizing done, he bade her to summon her "fortitude" for what he was about to write, and apologized for it in advance. Surely, she was bracing herself for yet another heedless extravagance. But then, with one last evocation of the many stimulations of this forbidden land, Burr sharply returned to his senses, right there on the page. He wrote:

> In short, then, my dear Theo., the beauty of this same Fort Johnson, the fertility of the soil, the commodiousness and elegance of the building, the great value of the mills, and the very inconsiderable price which was asked for the whole, have not *induced me to purchase it, and probably never will: in the confidence, however, of meeting your forgiveness.*

Not? Not induced him to purchase? Burr was like an alcoholic who teasingly brought a brimming glass of whiskey to his lips while his wife watched aghast—and then pitched it into the fire, laughing at her fears. Herewith the Burr essentials—insatiable desires, exquisitely evoked and brilliantly defended, and then surrendered to the one thing larger—his wife's maternal hold over him.

Whatever message they might bear, the letters were a precious lifeline between them, and both of them clung to the missives, reading and rereading and then rereading again, as if the letter itself—each one a soft, fleshy sheet folded in on itself to be its own envelope—were by some transmogrification a representation of the sender, to be scrutinized and held like his or her face or hands. Their pens are both such tender, delicate instruments, their letters inscribe *them*. "'Tis impossible for me to disguise a single feeling or thought when I am writing or conversing with the friend of my heart," Theodosia confides. For too long, letters were all the Burrs had of each other. The thrill of fresh tales from the far side was electric. Once, receiving a fresh batch of Burr's letters for herself and the children, Theodosia propped them up on the mantelpiece and then invited the children to come down for dinner, and waited. It was Bartow, the oldest, who noticed the letters first. He gave out a yelp and lunged for his letter, and the rest of the children quickly followed suit, and finally Theodosia herself reached for hers. "The surprise, the joy, the exclamations exceed description," she wrote her husband.

> *The greatest stoic would have forgot himself. A silent tear betrayed me no philosopher. A most joyous repast succeeded. We talked of our happiness, of our first of blessings, our best of papas. I enjoyed, my Aaron, the only happiness that could accrue from your absence. It was a momentary compensation; the only one I ever experienced. Your letters always afford me a singular satisfaction;—a sensation entirely my own; this was peculiarly so. It wrought strangely on my mind and spirits. My Aaron, it was replete with tenderness! With the most lively affection. I read and re-read, till afraid I should get it by rote, and mingle it with common ideas; profane the sacred pledge. No, it shall not be.*

Burr felt no less, but it left him to a wretched sense of deprivation when fresh letters were not forthcoming, tipping his mood from exultation to pique. "With what pleasure have I feasted for three days past upon the

letters I was to receive this weekend," Burr wrote from Albany, where he
was on business, in 1789. "I was engaged in court when the stage passed.
Upon the sound of it I left court and ran to the post office; judge of my
mortification to find not a line from your hand. Sure, in the course of three
days, you might have found half an hour to have devoted to me. You well
knew how much I relied on it; you know the pleasure it would have given
me, and the disappointment and chagrin I should feel from the neglect. I
cannot, will not believe that these considerations have no weight with you."

Of course, without information Burr can't think why she hasn't written, and he filled in his ignorance with whatever distressed him most—
that, despite all her testaments of love, his wife didn't care about him. In
this case, however, she'd been unable to write because she had scalded herself on the side of her face, leaving a nasty burn that would disfigure her for
the rest of her life—and that might be the one Burr's biographer James Parton was thinking of when he appraised her. Either way, it might account
for the fact that Burr never had her portrait painted, although he had several portraits done of their daughter. Still, Burr's deprivation was such that
he was convinced that she had done this purposefully to hurt *him*. "I cannot help feeling a resentment which must not be in this way expressed. I am
sure your sufferings might have been prevented. I had promised myself that
they were at an end many days ago."

Beastly and petulant as he could be, Theodosia never held his irritation
against him, but always took it as a sign of his own suffering or ignored it
altogether. Whenever he was away, she wanted nothing except his return.
And when he did not materialize as she had hoped, she suffered unduly: "I
have counted the hours till evening; since that, the minutes, and am still on
the watch; the stage has not arrived; it is a cruel delay. Your health, your
tender frame, how are they supported! Anxiety obliterates every other idea;
every noise stops my pen; my heart flutters with hope and fear; the pavement
from this to the Cape's [the stage house] is kept warm by the family; every
eye and ear engrossed by expectation; my mind is in too much trepidation
to write. I resume my pen after another message, in vain."

TWENTY-ONE

Come My Charmer and Relieve Me

AT 57 WALL Street, the Hamiltons lived somewhat more modestly than the Burrs. While undeniably impressive, their three-story brick house wasn't all that eye-catching on a block of many such homes. And unlike Burr's Theodosia, Betsey was not the center of Hamilton's world. He was primarily a public man, keen on statecraft, while Betsey busied herself with the domestic arts, and fairly humble ones, making pot holders and sewing undergarments for the children. Betsey made sure that the larder was well stocked with fresh produce from Albany, courtesy of her parents, and laid in mutton and wine to entertain Hamilton's legion of friends and colleagues, most of them drawn from the legal and political ranks, who might drop in at any moment. Not for nothing was his first purchase after leaving the army a dozen wineglasses.

While Burr had just the one child, Hamilton would have eight, starting with the much-loved Philip, born when Hamilton was at Yorktown, and the rest coming along almost biannually after that, creating a solid sense of family, with himself the proud patriarch, that dispelled the last vestiges of his shiftless Caribbean childhood. After their third child, Alexander, was born, they adopted a cheerful little two-year-old named Fanny, the daughter of a Revolutionary War veteran and King's College graduate who had suffered a breakdown after the death of his wife. Of the two men, Burr was the sterner father, viewing childhood as preparation for adulthood, rather than, for Hamilton, the last stretch of freedom before the hard work begins. Both men were supremely erudite, but Burr concentrated on philosophical tracts, while Hamilton's reading was more playful, taking in Henry Fielding's novels and Jonathan Swift's satires along with the obligatory Chesterfield and Hume. He was a doting father, but he left it to Betsey to do the child raising. In a rare vignette, James Hamilton recalls her "seated, as was her wont, at the head of the table with a napkin in her lap, cutting slices of bread and serving them with butter for the younger boys, who, standing at her side, read in turn a chapter in the Bible or a portion of Goldsmith's *Rome*. When the lessons were finished, the father and the elder children were called for breakfast, after which the boys were packed off to school." By the time Hamilton took it upon himself to enlist the nation's first president, Betsey had delivered four of their eight children, most recently James. His brood brought out the giddy side in Hamilton, which had been invisible during the war. Now that his first-born, Philip, had developed into a ruddy-haired toddler, his father could scarcely contain his excitement. "You cannot imagine how entirely domestic I am growing," he told the revolutionary general Richard Meade. "I lose all taste for the pursuits of ambition. I sigh for nothing but the Company of my wife and my baby. The ties of duty alone, or imagined duty, keep me from renouncing public life altogether. It is, however, probable I may not any longer be engaged in it."

A decade later, his children would still receive the bulk of his devotion, but far less of his time. Unlike Burr, Hamilton took little interest in their intellectual development, concerned far more with their grades than with their learning. He laid out his expectations to Alexander Jr. after he sailed across the Hudson for boarding school in Trenton at nine: "I expect every letter from [your teacher] will give me a fresh proof of your progress, for I know you can do a great deal if you please," Hamilton intoned. "And I am sure you have too much spirit not to exert yourself that you may make us every day more and more proud of you."

Manners were another matter. When his daughter Angelica turned nine, she went upriver to live with her grandparents, the Schuylers, at the Pastures, their formidable home in Albany. "We hope you will in every respect behave in such a manner as will secure to you the goodwill and regard of all those with whom you are," Hamilton instructed the little girl. "If you happen to displease any of them, be always ready to make a frank apology. But the best way is to act with so much politeness, good manners, and circumspection as never to have an occasion to make any apology." Those words would prove ironic.

While the Burrs' letters plumbed their souls, the Hamiltons' barely skimmed the surface, limited by differences in style and orientation. While Hamilton was deeply analytical in his thinking, inclined more toward treatises than revelations, he was also the more passionate of the two, while Betsey was the more religious. For the bulk of their married life, she was the one in regular attendance at the family pew, number 92, in Trinity Church, just up the street from their Wall Street house, not he.

That discrepancy was mirrored by another. Betsey had a sisterly devotion to the flashy Angelica, the wife of that plump and dubious Englishman John Barker Church. Hamilton had been infatuated with her from the first. How far the relationship went is anyone's guess, but it went far enough to reveal that streak of abandon in Hamilton that threatened to undo all his efforts to establish himself, pushing him to the edge of annihilation, and ultimately over it. In his disorientation, he was left writing Betsey letters that were probably intended to be ringing assertions of his love for her but come across as something else. When he was still a newlywed in 1782, he assured Betsey "there never was a husband who could vie with yours in fidelity and affection," as if that needed to be stated. Even the love notes conveyed his eagerness for company, not necessarily for her. "Come my charmer and relieve me. Bring my darling boy to my bosom." To Angelica, his words were far more heartfelt. In 1785, when she left with her husband for London, possibly permanently, Hamilton struggled to keep his feelings in check. "I saw you depart from Philadelphia with peculiar uneasiness, as if foreboding you were not to return. My apprehensions are confirmed and, unless I see you in Europe, I expect not to see you again. This is the impression we all have. Judge the bitterness it gives to those who love you with the *love of nature* and to me who feel an attachment for you not less lively." Eventually, that distance left him less constrained, as he teased her: "I seldom write to a lady without fancying the relation of lover and mistress."

→> <←

NOT UXORIOUS LIKE Burr, Hamilton felt an affection for Betsey that had a tenderness that was almost maternal. In his memoir Hamilton's lifelong friend James Kent recalled a moment from their legal rounds when he was judge and Hamilton a lawyer. As they roamed about the state in pursuit of legal business, he and Hamilton often bunked in together at some meager inn or other, to economize, and, as friends, they might share a bed.

One freezing winter night, after a long day of hard travel, Hamilton stayed up late before the fire with some of the other lawyers traveling with them, doubtless expounding at length on his theories of government. Feeling ill, Kent retired early. Worried about him, Hamilton soon left the fire to find an extra blanket for the judge and take it back to their chambers. Finding Kent huddled on the bed, shivering, Hamilton tucked the warm blanket around him as he might a child and whispered to his sleeping friend, "Sleep warm, little Judge, and get well. What should we do if anything should happen to you?"*

---

* Having made a lover of Laurens, Hamilton seems here to be making a child of Kent. However puzzling this might seem to later generations, it seems not to have been puzzling at the time, as neither Laurens nor Kent took exception to Hamilton's overtures, taking them for gestures of loving concern only, and none of his political adversaries, so eager to pounce on any perversion, found them noteworthy either. Even so, such tenderness was unusual; it is hard to imagine Washington writing such things. It may be that the emotions of Hamilton's that were so unbounded in other arenas were no less unbounded in this: He was a man of grand passions who simply couldn't easily be confined to the tidy psycho-erotic categories of today.

TWENTY-TWO

You Will Become All That I Wish

WITH TWO GENERATIONS of college presidents behind him, Burr had been determined to continue the family's aristocracy of knowledge, if not of wealth, into a fourth generation, and turn a "little girl rosy-cheeked and plump as a partridge," as her mother called Theodosia at eight, into a crisply educated, highly disciplined paragon of femininity—a female Aaron Burr, one might even say—by her teens. "Go on, my dear girl, and you will become all that I wish," Burr wrote her that year, in words simultaneously loving and diabolical. In this ambition, Burr had been encouraged by the free-spirited French philosopher Jean-Jacques Rousseau, who'd declared in *Émile*: "All that we lack at birth and all that we need when grown is given by education." But Burr also revered Lord Chesterfield, whose instructional, if somewhat overbearing, letters to his son offered a model for his own epistles to Theodosia, and he would have said exactly the same, except for this: Education should be confined to males alone, as it would be wasted on "children of a larger growth," as Chesterfield termed females. To Chesterfield, women were literally skin-deep. They have, he writes, "but one object, which is their beauty; upon which, scarce any flattery is too gross for them to swallow." The man's role, according to Chesterfield, is to provide that flattery, which is easy enough. "Nature has hardly formed a woman ugly enough to be insensible to flattery upon her person; if her face is so shocking, that she must, in some degree, be conscious of it, her figure and her air, she trusts, make ample amends for it." There is more, but that was plenty for Burr's wife, Theodosia. "The indulgence you applaud in Chesterfield is the only part of his writings I think reprehensible. . . . If Rousseau's ghost can reach this quarter of the globe, he will certainly haunt you for this scheme." While his wife was alive, he heartily concurred about her views of women, especially where their daughter was concerned. Afterward, he reverted to the Chesterfieldian view, as the grown women of his many romances were rarely more than baubles to distract him from serious business.

If there had been any doubt, Burr was now convinced he was absolutely right to educate Theodosia just like a man. "If I could foresee that Theo. would become a mere fashionable woman, with all the attendant frivolity and vacuity of mind, adorned with whatever grace and allurement, I would earnestly pray God to take her forthwith hence," he wrote his wife. "But I yet hope, by her, to convince the world what neither sex appear to believe—that women have souls!" And he threw himself into the task as if he were sculpting the perfect woman in modeling clay. He made sure Theodosia could read and write by age three, then enlisted a cadre of tutors to teach her mathematics, geography, Latin, Greek, and French by eight. It was a punishing routine for the little girl—starting at five A.M., she worked on her writing for three hours and then pushed through the day's curriculum from there—but there is no indication she resented it. Rather, the more overweening her father, the more she loved him. "From her earliest years, she began to manifest a singular, almost morbid fondness for her father, who, on his part, was resolved that she should be peerless among the ladies of her time," wrote Parton, the adoring early biographer. Concerned with her physique no less than her mind, he set his "Miss Prissy" to galloping on horseback about the grounds with her favored half brother Frederick, now in his late teens; vigorous dancing from a French instructor; and skating on the pond. When she complained to her father that she kept falling, he just laughed. "Even if you should fall twenty times," he teased, "that teaches you the advantage of a hard head."

Inevitably, it fell to wife Theodosia to organize a phalanx of instructors for her daughter, all of them posing problems of their own, either in timing or in their own messy lives. None of it was easy when she was already running a vast home with four other children, copious grounds, and a dozen servants and workmen who seemed to consume more of her energy than they saved. Not to mention her own uncertain health. And so she complains to her husband:

Theo. never can or will make the progress we would wish her while she has so many avocations. I kept her home a week in hopes Shepherd would consent to attend her at home, but he absolutely declined it, as his partners thought it derogatory to their dignity. I was therefore obliged to submit, and permit her to go as usual. She begins to cipher. Mr. Chevalier attends regularly, and I take care she never omits learning her French lesson. I believe she makes most progress in this. Mr. St. Aivre never comes; he can get no fiddler, and I am told his furniture &c. have been seized by the sheriff. I don't think the dancing lessons do much good while the weather is warm; they fatigue too soon. . . . As to the music, upon the footing it now is she can never make progress, though she sacrifices two thirds of her time to do it. 'Tis a serious check to her other acquirements. She must either have a forte-piano at home, or renounce learning it. For these reasons I am impatient to go in the country. Her education is not on an advantageous footing at present. . . . The moment we are alone she tries to amuse me with her improvement, which the little jade knows will always command my attention; but these moments are short and seldom. I have so many trifling interruptions, that my head feels as if I had been a twelvemonth at sea. I scarcely know what I speak, and much less what I write. What a provoking thing that I, who never go out, who never dress beyond a decent style at home, should not have a leisure moment to read a newspaper. It is a recreation I have not had since you left home, nor could I get an opportunity by water to send them to you. Albany will be a more favourable situation for every conveyance. But I don't understand why your lordship can't pay your obeisance at home in this four week vacation. I think I am entitled to a reason.

In his reply, Burr provided no reason for his absence, but testily demanded the cause of her obvious ill health. "You seem fatigued and worried, your head wild and scarcely able, but do not name the cause." Whatever the cause, his educational program certainly didn't help, as he must have known. She should take the air more, he tells Theodosia. Try "gentle exercise" but avoid "extreme heat." Ride early in the morning, but walk later "on account of the dew." Anything. "The freshness of the air, and the sprightliness of all animated nature, are circumstances of no trifling consequence."

Theodosia came around, as she always did. "O! my love, how earnestly I pray that our children may never be driven from your paternal direction," she exclaimed. "Had you been at home today, you would have felt as fervent in this prayer as your Theo. . . . I really believe, my dear, few parents can boast of children whose minds are so prone to virtue. I see the reward of our assiduity with inexpressible delight, with a gratitude few experience. My Aaron, they have grateful hearts."

Burr pressed his advantage. There was no aspect of his daughter that he did not shape and reshape to his liking, and he could be merciless in his demands. He was doing it for her, but *to* her, too. Burr's earliest surviving letter to Theodosia, just eight, established a tone, as he snapped at her. "Why do you neither acknowledge nor answer my last letter?" he demanded. "That is not kind—it is scarcely civil." He did not ease off over time. At eleven, when Theodosia wrote a pathetic letter about her mother's desire for laudanum to ease her pain—writing, "It was what she had long wished for, and was at a loss to procure it"—Burr pounced on her phrasing. She should have struck that second *it*, Burr declared. Then the sentence would have been "perfect, and much more elegant." It must have seemed to Theodosia that she could do nothing right. Rather than say something of hers was marvelous, excellent, fantastic, he'd say only that it was better than her previous efforts, diminishing her achievement even as he extolled it. And then he was likely to sprinkle in a few criticisms, like her dropping an occasional word, to render "some clauses . . . absolutely unintelligible." And then came Nathalie, further complicating the picture. In the early 1790s, an eleven-year-old Parisian, Nathalie de Lage de Volude, her governess, Madame de Senat, and the madame's daughter came to stay with the Burrs at their Manhattan address, ostensibly for the young Theodosia's improvement. They arrived as destitute French refugees from the slaughter of the French Revolution. Nathalie had grown up in Versailles, the goddaughter of Louis XVI and Marie Antoinette. Such good fortune, of course, became a serious hazard during the Reign of Terror, when the king and queen were beheaded, along with more than fifty thousand of their royalist sympathizers. Nathalie's family scattered, her father to a royalist encampment and her mother to a ship bound for America, only to be swamped in a storm, barely making it back to Spain. Nathalie's two sisters remained in hiding on the continent. Nathalie came alone with her governess, who established a French academy for the New York elite, including the Hamilton children, before Burr swept them up. Then, taken by the beauty of French culture, eager to advance Theodosia's French, and entranced by the slender, brown-eyed Nathalie, he offered to relocate the school to his town house. Nathalie quickly became Theodosia's best friend—and main rival for her father's attention. After he chastised Theodosia for her posture and complained about her indifference to her lessons, he noted that Nathalie would *never* behave that way. "Observe how Natalie replies to the smallest civilities which is offered to her."

Burr observed her, no question. Late one night in November 1795, his mind no doubt loosened by Madeira, he wrote of Nathalie to his close friend Dr. William Eustis, saying that, as he wrote, he was staying up with her in the library during a storm. She sat beside him, reading "but more than half the time laughing & talking," he reported. "The loveliest creature that I know of her age."

Theodosia was only a year younger.

Late in 1794, Burr commissioned Gilbert Stuart to paint a life-size portrait of his daughter, shortly before his wife died. Stuart had done Burr himself a few years before, evoking the dreamy and poetic side, rather than the serious-minded lawyer and politician, and Burr was delighted. Completed in January, the portrait shows a charming, wide-eyed girl, dressed in silk, her hair coiffed, but it reveals little of the sophistication that Burr had labored to instill. The girl was plain. Burr was dismissive. "Your picture is really quite like you, still it does not quite please me. It has a pensive air; that of a love-sick maid." Afterward, he complained about *her*, deciding she was unladylike. "Your habit of stooping and bringing your shoulders forward on to your breast not only disfigures you, but is alarming on account of the injury to your health," he complained. "The continuance in this vile habit will certainly produce a consumption: then farewell papa; farewell pleasure; farewell life!" Coming a year after her mother's death, his words must have stung. But then, this may have been the way Burr grieved—assaulting the living with his anger at the dead.

As harsh as Burr may have been, his efforts did pay off spectacularly as, by the time she was ten, even before Nathalie arrived, Theodosia spoke decent French, could translate forty lines of Virgil a day, was proficient in "cipher," or mathematics, read widely in English, and whatever her father might say, wrote well for her age, in a nearly calligraphic hand. At fifteen, she captivated a visiting Englishman named John Davis, who'd been introduced by her father, for being "elegant without ostentation, and learned without pedantry," and other praise that is normally reserved for adults, to say nothing of her graceful dancing, her fluency in French and Italian, and her knowledge of Homer. Davis added, perhaps jealously, that a French poet named Martel had dedicated a volume of his poems to her. "Like her father, her person was small, while to its enchanting symmetry and expression of countenance illuminated by vast reading and general knowledge, her imposing mien and flashing wit made her the ruling spirit to every circle." She would be the new Theodosia, and just in time.

TWENTY-THREE

Two Men of Politics

BURR NEVER PLANNED to enter politics. But in April of 1784, Alexander McDougall, the fiery Son of Liberty who'd befriended Hamilton and later was Burr's commander during that Westchester ordeal, named him to his slate of representatives from New York City. It was a testament to his high standing as a lawyer and to his elite background. Under the state constitution of 1777, only free, adult men of significant property could vote, restricting the electorate to one man out of ten and excluding women and slaves entirely. Such restrictions allowed powerful political alliances to hold sway, making a seat more a matter of appointment than of election. Burr thought the title of assemblyman would add to his luster as a lawyer with only a little inconvenience, since the Assembly met in the Exchange building right by his law office. Even so, Burr didn't actually show up at the Assembly for nearly a month after his election, and sporadically after that. That entire first term, he offered no legislation, served on no committees, and scarcely bothered even to vote. Reelected for the term that began in January of 1785, he made an audacious, but hopeless, move to end slavery in the state. It went nowhere, and Burr continued to hold slaves himself.

Burr's turn in the legislative spotlight came when a group of New York "mechanics"—the common term for workingmen—sought articles of incorporation, giving them legal recognition as an entity. Burr was the only one of the city's nine assemblymen to be opposed. He might have feared incorporation would invite political manipulation or raise labor costs in the city, two objections he had raised in the past. Whatever the motivation, the move shifted him publicly to the other side of the class divide, as the mechanics attacked him for preying on "the weak, the poor, the helpless," and threatened to assault him and stone his house. When Burr's friends offered to stand by his house to protect it from harm, Burr insisted there was no need. "Gentlemen," he grandly replied, "I will live no longer than I can protect myself."

In April of 1787, when Burr's second term ran out, the Assembly adjourned sine die—or indefinitely. Like the rest of the political structure, it had to wait for the results of the deliberations in Philadelphia to know if it was to remain in existence.

→>-<←

IN APRIL TWO years before, Hamilton was reading the political news in *The New-York Packet* when something caught his eye. His name. It had been included on the list of candidates for the New York Assembly. It was a discovery similar to Burr's of the previous year, but Hamilton had no intention of seeking such an office, and he insisted his name be withdrawn. A year later, he reconsidered. Dispirited by the country's fading prospects under the anemic Articles of Confederation, he offered himself as a candidate for assemblyman from New York City. Riding on his military record and his reputation as a lawyer, he was elected along with Burr, who was then seeking a second term.

Hamilton was not particularly interested in the affairs of the city, however. He endorsed the mechanics bill without thinking. Even as an assemblyman, he was attuned to the larger national issues embedded in local conflicts. He took an interest in an otherwise obscure quarrel between Maryland and Virginia over rights to commercial passage down the Potomac. To Hamilton, this was the country's core liability: The states were not unified as a single, powerful nation, but splintered into thirteen rivalrous sovereignties. Just as Maryland squabbled with Virginia, New York was bickering with New Jersey and Connecticut, imposing duties and tariffs on goods passing through New York Harbor on their way to those neighboring states. While states were extorting revenue from one another, the national government was going bankrupt.

The Potomac issue was eventually resolved, but Virginia's governor, Edmund Randolph, saw the larger problem and invited representatives from the states to discuss the matter in Annapolis. Hamilton made sure he was one, but the moment he arrived, he felt unusual regret to be parted from Betsey, who had just given birth to their third child, Alexander: "Happy, however, I cannot be, absent from you and my darling little ones. I feel that nothing can ever compensate for the enjoyment I leave at home or can ever put my heart at tolerable ease.... Think of me with as much tenderness as I do of you and we cannot fail to be always happy."

Only twelve delegates from five states actually appeared. Of them, the dominant figure was not Hamilton, but the scholarly, beetle-browed James Madison, whom he'd met in the Confederation Congress. Madison believed in granting a central government the power of "coercion" over the states to bring order to what he termed "the present anarchy of our commerce." The argument became so rancorous that, when Hamilton showed his final summary to Randolph, the governor thought he'd better tone it down "or all Virginia will be against you." Hamilton's own governor, George Clinton, would be even less obliging. He didn't want New York (and Clinton himself) to defer to a higher power. By 1786, he'd already been elected three times to the governorship and hoped to be reelected many times more. Clinton had already earned the loathing of Hamilton for his Trespass Act, and the Clintonians started referring to Hamilton as "Tom S**t" and a "mustee"—the child of a white and a quadroon, the first of many smears on Hamilton's ancestry.

The Annapolis gathering led to the Constitutional Convention in Philadelphia in the broiling summer of 1787, with representatives from all the states. Leery of federalism, Clinton appointed two Clintonians to New York's three-man delegation to ensure that Hamilton would be outvoted. The fifty-five delegates spent their days on the second floor of the statehouse, the blinds drawn through the long hot summer to close out the sun and to preserve the secrecy of the proceedings. They passed their nights in cramped quarters at the Indian Queen Tavern on Fourth Street. The convention was, said the eighty-one-year-old Benjamin Franklin, piebald, pained by kidney stones, "the most august and respectable assembly" he'd ever taken part in.

Happy on his farm above the Potomac, Washington had not planned to attend the gathering but was lured out of retirement by the shock of Shays' Rebellion, that uprising of Massachusetts's hill-town farmers outraged by the heavy taxes imposed to pay the state's war debt. Their widespread marauding revealed the feeble powers of the new confederacy to control its citizens, to say nothing of repelling any foreign invasion. Determined to create a durable nation after the agonizing war, Washington presided silently over the gathering from a tall chair, the delegates fanned out before him, his visage alone lending gravity to proceedings that were otherwise both timeless and tedious. Uncharacteristically, Hamilton said little, but he commanded attention all the same. "His manners are tinctured with stiffness and sometimes with a degree of vanity that is highly disagreeable," a delegate from Georgia noted. "When he comes forward, he comes charged with interesting matter. There is no skimming over the surface of a subject with him." He was struck by the wide range of Hamilton's expression, too, at points as "didactic" as the ponderous British statesman Lord Bolingbroke, at others positively "tripping" like the comic novelist Laurence Sterne.

As the animating intellect, Madison took the minutes, often improving the remarks through his recording of them. Before the convention, he had listed the "vices" in the old Articles, chiefly that they failed to create a nation. This convention was to find the remedies. It soon became clear they were not to be produced by any revision of the Articles. They needed to be replaced by a new document that would create a new government as yet beyond imagining.

Throughout, Hamilton was uncharacteristically silent in deference to his elders, interrupting only to deliver a six-hour oration in an effort to find a middle course for the deliberations. While he lacked the resonance of a born orator, he was poised, quick on his feet, full of facts—and, to the regret of his audience that day, indefatigable. It was a bravura performance, but a disastrous one, as the speech would be reduced to a single idea that would haunt him forever. He declared the British government the finest in the world and recommended that the American president be an "elective monarch" who served for life subject to "good behavior." In his own notes, he went further, saying the position should be hereditary and "have so much power that it will not be in his interest to acquire more." In that setting, it was a blunder of the first order.

The political world was soon ringing with the news that Alexander Hamilton wanted an elected king. It wasn't implausible. An obvious elitist, he had an affinity for aristocracy. He'd taken the Tory side in that Rutgers case and in countless more property cases afterward; he'd spoken up for Tories, declaring that the city's prosperity depended on them. His cultivated manners needed only a few puffs of perfume to win him a warm welcome from any royal court. The issue, as so often for Hamilton, wasn't that he thought this way—many in the hall did—but that he felt obligated to tell the world at every turn. Unlike Burr, Hamilton could not bear to keep secrets.

In the end, Hamilton's royalist attitudes did not affect the deliberations. His speech, said one Connecticut delegate, "has been praised by everybody [but] . . . supported by none." The convention ground on through three more months, hung up primarily on the thorny matter of how to apportion power among a few large states, such as Virginia, and many small ones, such as Delaware. The solution was reached on July 16 with the so-called Connecticut Compromise, which came up with the distinction between a Senate where each state was equally represented and a House that reflected each state's size. With that breakthrough, the debate reached the end Madison sought—a new Constitution creating Madison's "coercive" federal powers over the states that would make that nation, bolstered by a strong chief executive, a bicameral legislature, and a Supreme Court to uphold the Constitution—altogether a beautiful system of checks and balances that seemed almost Newtonian in its ability to bring clarity and order to the distribution of power.

When the Constitution was being finalized in July, it should have been obvious that Hamilton was not a monarchist at heart, no matter what he might say. For no one worked harder to promote the ratification of a system of government where the people ruled. He immediately took on Governor Clinton, who'd made clear his opposition to the Constitution, assailing him in an anonymous article: "Such conduct in a man high in office argues greater attachment to his *own power* than to the *public good*." Clinton's henchmen divined the source and hit back, taunting Hamilton as a "superficial, self-interested coxcomb" who'd be nowhere without Washington. That struck a nerve, and Hamilton rushed to Washington for reassurances. "This," he told the general, "I confess, hurts my feelings, and if it obtains credit will require a contradiction." Caught between Clinton and Hamilton, Washington could only reassure his former aide by saying such charges were "entirely unfounded."

In September, Hamilton was chosen for the Style and Arrangement Committee with his friend Gouverneur Morris to render the Constitution in tight, orderly prose. A friend from his King's College days, Morris possessed, in equal parts, gallantry, levity, brilliance, and recklessness. He'd twice crashed his phaeton on a city street from driving too fast and once lost a leg in a carriage accident, replacing it with a distinctive, clonking wooden one that proved no significant impediment to his many amorous pursuits. In a lighter moment at Constitution Hall, Hamilton entered into a schoolboy wager with Morris to see if his friend dared actually to touch Washington, who had a notorious aversion to such intimacy. Morris gladly took him on. He approached Washington, bowed, declared he had never seen the general look so well, and then—as everyone watched, aghast—laid his hand convivially on Washington's shoulder. At that, the sun set. Washington "fixed his eye on Morris for several minutes with an angry frown." Morris quietly retreated. "I have won the bet," Morris told Hamilton grimly, "but paid dearly for it."

The Style Committee's job was to edit the final draft of the Constitution, clarifying, sharpening, and condensing. It reduced the number of articles from twenty-three to seven, and Morris, ever the stylist, added such touches as the soaring opening phrase, "We the People of the United States." And then thirty-nine of the original fifty-five delegates signed it and repaired to the City Tavern. The country had been made new.

Whatever his ambivalence about democracy, Hamilton did more than anyone in New York—and most of the country—to advance the cause, as he undertook to write, under the name Publius (for Public Man), more than sixty of the essays in the Federalist Papers designed to promote the new Constitution to a skeptical public. He first conceived of the idea on board a schooner bound to New York from Albany and set the first one down while still on the water. It begins with a clarion call, "To the People of the State of New York": "After an unequivocal experience of the inefficacy of the subsisting Federal Government, you are called upon to deliberate on a new Constitution of the United States of America. The subject speaks its own importance; comprehending in its consequences, nothing less than the existence of the UNION, the safety and welfare of the parts of which it is composed, the fate of an empire, in many respects the most interesting in the world."

It was the full Hamilton, as he markets his opinion as undeniable truth regarding the "fate of an empire." Produced at breathtaking speed, the writing was like breathing, inhaling information, expelling enlightenment. And so each sentence pushed back the darkness.

Just as the true Burr can be found in those fresh and quirky letters to his wife, the true Hamilton can be found here in his Federalist essays, all of them, one after another, pushing the cause of ratification the way Sisyphus pushed his rock, over and over and over, long past the time when anyone else would have given up. Hamilton's very indefatigability was the trait his opponents hated most, even as it inspired his supporters. He could summon more arguments faster than his opponents could possibly counter, and they ultimately wilted under the hail of his blows. In his telling, federalism would improve commerce, boost government revenues, raise a navy, create efficiencies, undo the anarchy, embarrassment, and impotence of national and state governments under the Articles, and do it lawfully and benignly, reflecting the will of the people. He continued on in this vein until his Federalist No. 85, which concluded: "A Nation without a national government is, in my view, an awful spectacle. The establishment of a constitution in [a] time of profound peace by the voluntary consent of a whole people is a prodigy, to the completion of which I look forward with trembling anxiety"—meaning eagerness.

The Federalist Papers ran in dozens of New York newspapers, pushing for the upcoming New York convention to ratify the Constitution and gain another of the nine states needed for adoption. Despite the firepower of Hamilton's Federalist essays, an early poll of the delegates showed that the proponents, or Federalists, trailed the Anti-Federalists forty-six to nineteen. Worse, the convention would be presided over by the bovine Governor Clinton, a man Hamilton called "inflexibly obstinate."

The convention was to be held in a Poughkeepsie courthouse. Before it started, Hamilton unleashed another barrage of essays, and New York's merchants—keen on the commercial possibilities of a federated nation—gave Hamilton a glorious sendoff from the city, culminating in a thirteen-cannon salute. As soon as he arrived, Hamilton attacked Clinton for running "a despicable and dangerous system of personal influence." Clinton replied this was state influence, not his own, and assembled a flock of subordinates to plead the case, but Hamilton outtalked them all. After the Clintonians lambasted the Federalist Chancellor Livingston for exaggerating the damage of the Articles, Hamilton teased them for treating Livingston as if he'd "wandered in the flowery fields of fancy." Their fears had overwhelmed their reason. "Events, merely possible have been magnified by distempered imagination into inevitable realities," he declared. "And the most distant . . . conjectures have been formed into . . . infallible prediction."

"A political porcupine," one observer called Hamilton, "armed at all points and brandishes a shaft to every opponent." The dispute became so heated that at one point an Anti-Federalist, Colonel Oswald, challenged Hamilton to a duel. Fortunately, cooler heads prevailed. Before New York could reach a vote, Virginia and New Hampshire both ratified, pushing the pro-Constitution tally past the nine states needed out of the thirteen for passage. Incredibly, the new Constitution was in. In Poughkeepsie, the news caused an earsplitting explosion of fifes and drums all around the hall. When the convention voted, even New York went along. Hamilton had done the impossible. He had turned a landslide defeat into a secure victory, as New York, despite all of Clinton's power, voted yes by three votes. Even if it didn't usher in the Constitution, the vote was key: As the country's most dynamic state, with the fastest-growing population and economy, it helped establish the legitimacy of the new government.

Hamilton's accomplishment was not lost on the city, whose commerce stood to gain much from a federal system of government that would encourage the free flow of its products. In the general excitement, New York put forth a "Grand Federal Procession," featuring five thousand exuberant workers, from bakers hoisting a ten-foot "federal loaf" to "Black Smiths" hammering iron anchors as they passed. All of them hungry for the prosperity the Constitution would bring, they marched in triumph down Broadway toward Great Dock Street and then took a wide turn about the southern tip of the city. The most stupefying sight was the federal ship *Hamilton*, a thirty-two-gun frigate, twenty-seven feet long, its towering masts bearing full, billowing sails. Seemingly pushed by the wind, the tall ship actually rode on heavy wheels (concealed behind blue drapes meant to suggest the sea) and was hauled by a team of ten horses. In the wild enthusiasm for Hamilton's accomplishment, there was loud talk of renaming New York City "Hamiltonia." At the climax of the celebration, the *Hamilton* paused by a lowly Spanish packet and fired off a booming salute to its namesake from all thirty-two of its cannons.

→>-<←

AND BURR'S POSITION on the Constitution? At a time when the political world was split like an apple between the Constitution-endorsing Federalists and their fervid opponents, the Anti-Federalists, Burr seems to have been that rare man in public life who did not take sides. As someone who enjoyed secrecy, he probably preferred to keep his options open—and not make enemies by taking a stand. But others detected the odor of opportunism.

While the votes he cast in the Assembly gave little indication of his political principles, probably the clearest revelation of his orientation came soon after, when, for a third term, he was invited to run with a slate of staunch Anti-Federalists headed by Melancton Smith, Hamilton's primary antagonist at the Poughkeepsie convention. Burr agreed, revealing himself only by the company he kept.

TWENTY-FOUR

A Dreaded Dilemma

AFTER THE CONSTITUTION was ratified, it was clear to everyone that only General Washington could serve as the nation's first president—and only Alexander Hamilton could persuade him of that fact. Always one to demur, claiming no interest in glory or preferment, Washington had ample reason to say no, as he was, at fifty-four, after eight years of war, settling at last into a comfortable semiretirement at his idyll on the Potomac. The life of a Virginia planter wasn't without its frustrations, what with its strained economics and morally problematic slaves, and the fact that a stream of visitors had turned him into a hotelkeeper. But he was spending it at last with Martha, a woman of simple pleasures and boundless good cheer. And there was something about the glorious expanse of Mount Vernon, with its endless views and bright possibilities, that soothed and inspired him after all the tumult of war. His property covered thirty thousand acres, or nearly fifty square miles, of rolling farmland, much of it extending upland from his own little settlement by the river. It could have been mistaken for a charming English village, with two dozen neat outbuildings clustered around a stately manor house that stood off a circular drive about a bowling green. Complete with a deer park, formal gardens, fruit trees, and a splendid vista of the wide river, it was a country estate that would not have looked out of place in Derbyshire. If it lacked Monticello's charm, Mount Vernon had majesty. It was all the empire Washington wanted.

As a confirmed New Yorker, Hamilton regarded such pastoral splendor as so much vacancy and must have felt mystified that the general would be drawn to it. Hamilton himself needed the jostle of society to feel alive and considered the countryside useless except as a field of battle. His Wall Street house was in a prime location, and thanks to his flourishing legal career he'd been able to furnish it rather grandly. He'd bought splendid Louis XVI chairs to go with a Federal-style mahogany sofa, a piano secured for him by his sister-in-law in London, a Dürer etching, some evocative Hudson River scenes by the British painter William Winstanley, and a pair of exquisite French flowerpots that Angelica had brought back from Paris. It may not have been the extravagant French-style salon of the Burrs, which he visited at one soiree or another, doubtless appraising the quality of the furnishings, but it was definitely impressive in its way.

When Hamilton settled down to his parlor writing desk to begin the business of cajoling a reluctant Washington into doing his duty, he was canny enough not to make a straight-out plea, which might have been rejected. Knowing his man, he began by merely touching on this immense topic at the bottom of a letter offering his general a two-volume set of his Federalist Papers. But he may have taken a peremptory tone that betrayed too much of Hamilton's impatience with a leader who, while illustrious, was never known for his dispatch. "I take it for granted, Sir, you have concluded to comply with what will no doubt be the general call of your country in relation to the new government," he declared, charging headlong into the breach. Then he recovered himself. "You will permit me to say that it is indispensable you should lend yourself to its first operations." But then he ended on a note of pique. "It is to little purpose to have *introduced* a system, if the weightiest influence is not given to its firm *establishment*, in the outset." When he responded two weeks later, Washington clung to the determination only to "live and die, in peace and retirement, on my own farm." But his objections seemed wistful, not definitive. Or so Hamilton preferred to think. And the same went for Washington's grumblings about his "increasing infirmities of nature." Hamilton knew that, having received huzzahs from one end of the country to the other for his military service, Washington would miss them when they receded. In some frustration, Hamilton declared that it would be "inglorious" if Washington did not answer the call of his country. Finally, Washington admitted to Hamilton that he faced a "dreaded dilemma." Having made such a beautiful gesture of surrendering power, how could he reach for it now?

That was easy, Hamilton knew: by not seeming to. Washington would not seek the presidency, but let it seek him. Hamilton would attend to all the unseemly details of electioneering, raising a national clamor for his service, leaving Washington only to bask in the adoration. In a last effort to escape the burden of office, Washington expressed the wan hope that he could limit his service to two years, then turn the country over to a younger and more vigorous man. The Constitution made no provision for early retirement, as Hamilton well knew, but he kept his silence, and the deal was struck.

If Washington *did* want to be the indispensable man in the new nation, Hamilton wanted to be only a little less than that, and he knew that Washington would be his ticket to power. Washington might be king, but Hamilton would be the kingmaker. For someone so preternaturally self-assured, Hamilton retained an eager boyishness that could be charming to those not put off by his political views, and ever since the war, he had always been indulged by this childless older man who would soon be called the father of his country. Washington was not unaware of Hamilton's edginess, but he forgave such faults in his prodigal son.

And so it began: From that moment forward, as in the army, Washington would depend on Hamilton as he depended on no other. He would never make a significant decision without Hamilton's advice, often doled out in ten-thousand-word installments, his quill flying, and he would never question that advice, no matter how it turned out. Washington had plenty of wise men in his circle—Thomas Jefferson, John Adams, Edmund Randolph, James Madison, all but the last of them in his cabinet, and all of them older, some substantially so—but it was Hamilton he turned to, over and over. He emerged as Washington's alter ego, the first among equals.

→>-<←

THAT FIRST PRESIDENTIAL election proved ungainly, largely because the Constitution's framers, frightened of divisive factionalism, had failed to see that the common patriotism of the president and vice president might *not* be enough to unite them to a common purpose, and they made no provision for letting a president and his preferred vice president run as a team. Instead, the top offices were assigned by a kind of popularity contest, with the presidency awarded to the highest vote getter, and the vice presidency to the next, regardless of the electors' intentions as to who should fill which office.

In the first election, it went without saying that Washington was to be president. But vice president? For that role, the tart-tongued John Adams was widely put forward by Washington's supporters, although exactly who first proposed him is open to question. It was clear enough why. As a New Englander he would balance the Virginian. Also, as a prominent Boston lawyer, he had been a staunch backer of the Declaration, and he'd lately been serving the Continental Congress as a member of the peace commission that brilliantly negotiated an end to the war with the Treaty of Paris. And if a winning personality was required, precious few in that contentious age would be eligible for service.

Hamilton was alert to character flaws that others would dismiss, and he'd had misgivings about Adams ever since Adams had sided with Horatio Gates in that attempted coup against Washington by the Conway Cabal. That was understandable, since loyalty to Washington was now essential. Hamilton was also suspicious of Adams's service in a country, France, that Hamilton considered politically degenerate. But, for now, he largely put those reservations aside. "Mr. A, to a sound understanding, has always appeared to me to add an ardent love for the public good," Hamilton told a friend tepidly.

Now, how to keep Adams from somehow lucking into the presidency? In a near panic, Hamilton asked a half dozen of Washington's electors to hold back their votes from him, but then he was afraid that might tip the vice presidency, or even the presidency, to the Constitution-hating "Pharaoh," George Clinton of New York. So Hamilton frantically wrote to supporters around the country to back Adams for vice president after all.

In the end, all went as Hamilton intended: Washington was elected president, and Adams vice president. But the peevish Adams did not fail to notice that, while Washington had been elected unanimously with sixty-nine votes, he had himself received just thirty-four. This shortfall left him "incensed" later when he discovered Hamilton's "dark and dirty intrigue" that had left a "stain" upon his character.

→>-<←

As HAMILTON'S STANDING increased, so did his ferocity. Having deprived Clinton of a chance at higher office, he set about to turn his portly antagonist out of his present one. Having been New York's governor since 1777, Clinton had a formidable hold on the state. But the groundswell of enthusiasm for the new Constitution he'd bitterly opposed gave Hamilton an opening, one that he planned to exploit at the next election, in the spring of 1789, when he and his father-in-law planned to "kill the governor politically," as the Massachusetts Federalist Samuel Otis put it. If it was an assassination, it would stem from a broader war among the political classes that fought to rule the state. There were three in all, and the early Burr biographer, Parton, identified them: the Clintons, at first George but then his nephew DeWitt; then the numerous and wealthy Livingstons, who overspread much of the state; and finally the Schuylers, that tight cluster of interlocking Albany-based families of which Philip Schuyler, the general turned senator, was the titular head. "The Clintons had *power*," went Parton's adage, "the Livingstons had *numbers*, and the Schuylers had *Hamilton*." Of these assets, Hamilton imagined himself the most valuable after almost single-handedly pushing through the Constitution. While the Livingstons held back this time around, the other two elements were very much in play. Hamilton's father-in-law, Philip Schuyler, might have been tempted to mount a challenge, but having fallen short in 1784, he was loath to try again. So Hamilton sought out another candidate and came up with the supreme court justice Robert Yates.

A hard, skeptical man, Yates was not an obvious choice. As a New York delegate, with Hamilton, to the Constitutional Convention, Yates had fired off fierce Anti-Federalist tracts under the nom de guerre Brutus, and then left early, disgusted by the whole idea of a Constitution that gathered so much power in the hands of a centralized government. He made straight for Clinton's office in Albany and poured out to him all the confidential deliberations, so Clinton might put a stop to them.

After the Constitution was ratified into law, however, Yates became a believer. The spectacle of a state supreme court justice who'd seen the light—and could draw support from both sides of the constitutional divide—had attractive symbolism for Hamilton. After he persuaded Yates to run, Hamilton himself took over the thirteen-man committee of correspondence to win statewide support and gathered everyone at Bardin's Tavern, one of the city's plusher drinking establishments, on Broad Street in Manhattan.

Hamilton's King's College friend the ubiquitous Robert Troup was there. So was William Duer, the crafty financier who would soon prove a vexation to Hamilton.

And so was the mysterious Aaron Burr. He always said he'd come to pay Yates back for supporting the measure that opened the New York bar to him (and Hamilton) after the revolution. But, with Burr, there was always more to it, and it was a better guess that the real beneficiary was Burr. He never liked to limit himself just to one side of a political issue. While Hamilton threw himself into the effort, writing to all the county committees in the state to warn them of Clinton's near treasonable stance regarding the Constitution, Burr left no record of what he did, or said, if in fact he did or said anything at all. Hamilton worked himself into a froth extolling Yates as a "man of moderation, sincerely disposed to heal, not to widen those divisions, to promote conciliation, not dissension, to allay, not excite the fermentation of party-spirit," and so forth. In a sharply divided state, Hamilton's plea for moderation was not always warmly received. In Ward's Bridge, where voters from Orange and Ulster Counties were assembled, freemen ordered Hamilton's letters "thrown under the table" in disgust, and Yates's nominating papers to be burned on "an elevated pole."

Hardly deterred, Hamilton hit the newspapers with anonymous attacks on Clinton under the byline "H.G." Fifteen in all, the diatribes savaged Clinton's military career as "cunning," with some cowardice thrown in, his governorship a warning that "the transition from demagogues to despots, is neither difficult nor uncommon" and his politics merely "a system of STATE POWER unconnected with, and in subversion of the union." The missives were electrifying, if only because they crossed the line that separated a legitimate political attack from a nasty personal smear. Federalists exulted that nothing had ever been read "with more avidity and with greater success," but the Anti-Federalists protested that "the torrent of scurrility . . . argues a want of every manly generous principle." In the end, Clinton survived, but narrowly, winning the election by just 429 votes. The close result left him in a quandary about how to reclaim the Federalists that now made up half the electorate. In the end, he turned for help to a compromise figure, a straddler, who had positioned himself for just that eventuality—Aaron Burr. Clinton selected him as his attorney general, an obscure but influential position that, ironically, involved squaring New York's state laws with the requirements of the new Constitution.

But it also involved something else. As attorney general, Burr served, ex officio, as a commissioner of the land office, which was overseeing the sale of the vast tracts of "unappropriated"—meaning unsold—land upstate. This was a major source of state revenue now that the federal government had taken over the collection of duties in the Port of New York. Typically, the land sold for nineteen cents an acre, but one massive exception was a parcel the size of Connecticut that was purchased by a speculator named Alexander Macomb. It went for just eight cents an acre. Speculation was rife that Governor Clinton had delivered such a sweet deal, but Burr's land office investigation proved helpfully inconclusive. Burr later acquired two hundred thousand acres from Macomb. The price is unrecorded, but any would have been prohibitive, as Burr was, as usual, virtually penniless at the time. Burr's political fortunes rose from there, with George Clinton's assistance. Macomb's did not, and when the Panic of 1792 deflated the market for land, he fell three hundred thousand dollars in debt and was sent to debtors' prison.

TWENTY-FIVE

To a Mind Like His Nothing Comes Amiss

WASHINGTON WAS INAUGURATED at the freshly designed Federal Hall in New York City at the stroke of noon on April 30, 1789. A broad, handsome, perfectly symmetrical building, Federal Hall was a prime example of the confident new Federal style—a variant of the Georgian style in London—just sweeping into fashion. It was designed by the French architect and civil engineer Major Pierre Charles L'Enfant, who was soon to create much of Washington City. It was a dazzling, inspiring design—the front portico emblazoned with an immense and triumphant eagle; Roman laurel leaves adorned the interior. Both were intended to wrap the new Republic in the symbolism of the classical Roman one. Along with grand meeting halls for the House on the ground floor and the Senate above, it provided an extensive library and a "machinery room" to display models of the new inventions the nation was sure to generate.

Washington crossed the Hudson in a velvet-lined barge and then rode to the hall in a canary yellow carriage that brought cries of delight from onlookers. When he emerged, his tall, stately figure was topped by an unsmiling visage under a powdered wig and adorned with a ceremonial sword dangling beside his suit of patriotic American broadcloth. He climbed to Federal Hall's second-story balcony to take the oath of office from the first chancellor of New York, Robert R. Livingston, before a vast crowd extending in every direction, their enthusiastic shouts like cannon blasts. Vice President John Adams stood beside the president, a roundness for his verticality, but dressed identically except for different buttons.

Washington shifted indoors to deliver his inaugural address. Now, under the weight of history, his fabled nerves betrayed him. His left hand thrust awkwardly into his pocket, his quivering right holding his text, he was so tight he could scarcely make himself heard.

Hamilton was not there to see any of it. Elected to no public office, he was obliged to watch from his balcony more than a block away down Wall Street.

→>⤙

HAMILTON AND BETSEY did attend the inauguration ball, held at a dance hall on Broadway, a lively affair with most of Congress and a range of foreign ministers in attendance, and an occasion to show off the new exuberance that had returned to the city after the hard years of war and occupation. A social observer named Brissot de Warville detected some creeping Englishness in the style and fashion of the ladies in particular, a trend Hamilton would have welcomed. "If there is a town on the American Continent where the English luxury displays its follies, it is New York," de Warville declared. "You will find there the English fashions. In the dress of the women you will see the most brilliant silks, gauzes, hats, and borrowed hair." To be sure, he spotted few "equipages"—especially elegant carriages—and the men dressed more simply, disdaining "gewgaws," but they loved the "luxury of the table."

Since Martha was still at Mount Vernon, delaying her entrance into public life, Washington paired off with Betsey for the dancing. The general did not dance, exactly, but walked through the steps, with a certain "gravity," she wrote, that may have befit his notion of a president.

But then, it was anyone's guess as to how an American president should comport himself. Was he an elected monarch, as Hamilton might imagine, maintaining a certain superiority? Or was he a powerful commoner, exhibiting more of a democratic touch? A Senate committee was convened to decide how Washington was to be regarded. Here John Adams, fresh from France, revealed his taste for titled nobility, and, after considerable deliberation, offered that Washington should be referred to as "His Highness, the President of the United States and Protector of their Liberties." Poor Adams never lived that down. One wag responded by offering the tubby vice president a title of his own: "His Rotundity," a barb that stuck. Eventually, Congress decided that the president of the United States should be addressed as "the President of the United States."

Now, how should Washington mingle with his fellow Americans? For this the new president turned to Hamilton, who revealed his own disposition by recommending a British "levee," or formal reception, for a brief, ceremonial appearance on Tuesday afternoons. Washington accepted the recommendation gratefully, and he soon appeared at the levees in a black velvet coat and satin breeches, drifting slowly about, bowing but never touching, and certainly never shaking hands, before he drifted away from the gathering after half an hour. The whole business was insufferable, but it preserved the illusion that the president was approachable and that the people's will was to be taken into account.

Hamilton also recommended occasional dinners of eight at which Washington should not stay the entire meal; and larger state affairs for members of Congress, his cabinet, and "distinguished strangers." The gatherings maintained Washington's social distance, a preference Hamilton may have remembered from their soldiering days. "Be easy and condescending in your deportment to your officers," Washington once told a young commander, "but not too familiar, lest you subject yourself to a want of respect."

→-←

THE CONSTITUTION MADE no provision for a cabinet, leaving all power concentrated in the president's office, and it took some time to piece out the proper channels for presidential authority. Pondering the matter in the fine city house on Cherry Street by the East River that had been commandeered from Samuel Osgood for the President's Mansion, Washington had Jefferson in mind for secretary of state, handling international relations, and General Henry Knox for War. His first choice for the powerful post of secretary of the treasury was Robert Morris, the ingenious, if overfed, speculator, born in Liverpool, who'd provided crucial financial aid to Washington's war effort and served as finance minister under the confederacy. He was now a senator from Pennsylvania, but his financial luck had started to turn against him, and he told Washington he needed to give his full attention to business. He recommended "a far cleverer fellow" for the post—a man Washington knew well. At that point, shortly before the inauguration, Washington had not considered Hamilton for the position, and not from any lingering ill will after the staircase contretemps. Washington simply imagined Hamilton too young for such an important post. As Washington told Morris with some exasperation, Hamilton had "no knowledge of finance." Morris disagreed: "He knows everything," he said. "To a mind like his nothing comes amiss." When Morris told Hamilton he was under consideration for the position at the political epicenter of the new nation, Hamilton expressed a calm satisfaction: "It is the situation in which I can do the most good." The salary of thirty-five hundred dollars would make things tight for a growing family, but Hamilton deemed it worth the sacrifice to set the country on a solid financial footing. But there was a third candidate, Robert R. Livingston, who had just sworn Washington in for his inauguration. Hamilton had already antagonized him by pushing Rufus King, the eloquent, Harvard-trained lawyer from Massachusetts, for one of New York's two Senate seats, and his father-in-law, Schuyler, for the other. Livingston believed one of the two spots had been due to him. In selecting King, Hamilton bypassed New York's mayor, James Duane, the judge in the Rutgers case, who was a Livingston by marriage. (Hamilton feared any successor to Duane might prove "injurious to the city," meaning to his political interests in the city.) The Livingstons resented an upstart handpicking New York's senators anyway, and they'd be all the more bothered if a Livingston wasn't selected as one of them. And now Hamilton himself was going to make off with the best appointive prize of all as treasury secretary? The Livingstons still represented the third great political faction in New York—and, like all politicians, they had good memories for slights. The Livingstons might have fussed over their political standing in New York, but Washington had larger concerns, and he passed over Robert Livingston for treasury and then rejected him for chief justice, too.

So it was Hamilton who emerged as secretary of the treasury on September 11, 1789, and he wheeled into action, selecting five assistant secretaries to serve him. The most notable was the skillful but dubious William Duer, who'd served on the previous Board of the Treasury under the Articles. Hamilton's staff would soon swell to thirty-nine, more than War and State combined. (At War, Henry Knox had just two.) When the government moved to Philadelphia the next year, the Treasury would cover an entire city block. Even as a military man, Washington could see that America would never be established by military power, but, as Hamilton would have it, by flourishing ports, fluid interstate commerce, ever-expanding markets, reliable currency, manageable debt, good credit, and the stout faith all of this would convey on both sides of its borders. At thirty-three, Hamilton made his youth an advantage, as he wasn't confined by tradition or pretense, was indefatigable, refused to stand on ceremony, and was as keen on the details of proper accounting as on the broadest principles of economic theory.

The first order of business was revenue, needed to stave off looming bankruptcy. That meant building a proper customs service at all American ports to collect the duties due the government. Remembering the deceptions of sea captains in Saint Croix harbor, Hamilton made sure his customs officers compared the ship's manifests to the actual cargo and reported any discrepancies to the local district attorney. To limit smuggling, he had cutters built to patrol the coast for illegal cargo drops.* He had his men census all of America's lighthouses, beacons, and buoys and record their state of repair. And he tallied the full value of all of the nation's exports.

Such a clear-minded approach could push away the inherent gloom of economics in the minds of most congressmen. As Massachusetts congressman Fisher Ames told his colleagues, the subject "presents to the imagination a deep, dark, and dreary chaos; impossible to be reduced to order without the mind of the architect is clear and capacious, and his power commensurate to the occasion; he must not be the flitting creature of the day." Hamilton would certainly not be that. When a newspaperman spotted Hamilton on a New York street one evening, he was struck by how

---

* That service evolved into the US Coast Guard.

much the secretary's normally brisk pace was slowed, his head tipped down; he was obviously deep in thought.

His step was heavier when Betsey and the children were away in Albany, as they often were in those first fall months, and it was heavier still when the delightful Angelica left that October. A decade into knowing her, his ardor burned as fiercely as ever, and his letters to her conveyed his desire with stunning openness that Angelica never quite matched. Declaring that her husband's "head was full of politics," having just been elected a member of the British Parliament, Angelica flirtatiously told Hamilton she wished her husband "possessed your eloquence."

Angelica returned alone to New York just before Washington's inauguration, and Hamilton could scarcely contain his excitement. At a ball, a garter of hers slid down from her thigh and onto the floor as she was dancing, and Hamilton gallantly swept it up in his fingers and then held it out before her. Angelica teased him that he must be a "Knight of the Garter," to which Angelica's sister Peggy wickedly added, "He would be a Knight of the *Bedchamber* if he could."

Hamilton was crushed that fall when one of Angelica's children fell sick back in London, and she felt obliged to immediately book passage home. He was at the wharf to see her off. "We gazed, we sighed, we *wept*," he wrote her afterward. "Amiable Angelica, How much you are formed to endear yourself to every good heart," he continued wistfully. "How deeply you have rooted yourself in the affections of your friends on this side of the Atlantic! *Some* of us are and must continue inconsolable for your absence."

Betsey loyally seconded her husband's sentiments in her own letter. "I have seated myself to write to you," she began, "but my heart is so saddened by your absence that it can scarcely dictate, my eyes so filled with tears that I shall not be able to write you much." She, too, longed for her sister's return, but she wanted her to broaden her attention. "Tell Mr. Church for me," Betsey wrote her sister, "of the happiness he will give me in bringing you to me, not to me alone, but to fond parents, sisters, friends, and to my Hamilton, who has for you all the affection of a fond own brother."

Next, Hamilton turned to the country's prodigious debt. It had already led to that frightening citizens' revolt, Shays' Rebellion, in the hill country of Massachusetts. That one had finally been crushed by the state militia, and the leaders sentenced to be hanged, only to be pardoned by John Hancock, now the Massachusetts governor. (One conspirator was forced to stand at the gallows with a noose tight about his neck, awaiting a drop that never came.) But it wasn't just Massachusetts that was buried in debt. Ever exacting, Hamilton calculated the existing national debt (foreign and domestic) to the penny—54,124,464.56 dollars, with an annual interest of 2,239,163.09 dollars. The map of insolvency across the states was a patchwork, but it lay mostly to the north, with the two largest states, New York and Pennsylvania, on the verge of bankruptcy. Southern states had a much lighter load, as they saw less of the war, and many had paid off their debt completely. The divisions threatened to tear the country apart, as it pitted large states against small ones, North against South, the investment class against the working class, city against countryside, and shrewd bond buyers against gullible soldiers who'd unwisely sold their war bonds.

Hamilton had been contemplating this issue since the war, when he was appalled that it was so underfunded by the government waging it. He'd read that, a century before, England had nationalized its debt through the Bank of England and then used the credit to create the imperial navy that built a vast empire. Might not the United States use credit to do the same? Not to build warships, but to construct canals, ports, roads, all the elements needed for America's commercial development. To show this debt would not be held in perpetuity, he would add "sin taxes" on stimulants like Madeira wine (thirty cents a gallon) and distilled spirits (twenty).

Just three months into his tenure Hamilton wrote his epochal *Report on the Public Credit*—forty thousand words long, dense with statistics, and overflowing with argument—and did it, as usual, by himself in his tidy longhand. Knowing the report was likely to be momentous, speculators had besieged him for advance word of his plans, and friends waylaid him for inside information, but he said not a word. Still, bond values soared by fifty percent in a matter of weeks on a prairie fire of rumors. Following protocol, the lengthy report was finally read out by a clerk to the congressmen jammed into the lower chamber of Federal Hall, the gallery stuffed with rapt spectators. In the report, the author—Hamilton—referred to himself as "he," or "the Secretary of the Treasury," creating a royal penumbra that he may not have minded. As ever, he relied heavily on the rhetoric of certainty. "States," he intoned, "like individuals, who observe their engagements are respected and trusted, while the reverse is the fate of those who pursue opposite conduct." Or, "In proportion as the mind is disposed to contemplate, in the order of Providence, an intimated connection between public virtue and public happiness, will be its repugnancy to a coalition of those principles." Burr's public speaking was always conversational—personal and colloquial. Hamilton's was oratorical—universal and timeless, if occasionally rather dense. It was a style he'd first tapped into publicly at nineteen for "A Full Vindication of the Measures of the Congress"—when he took on a loyalist's economic arguments against the war—and had been growing into ever since, but at points it still seemed one size too large.

The dead certainty in such complex matters was as reassuring to his friends as it must have been exasperating to his enemies, but impossible to dismiss either way. Throughout the reading, the congressmen remained silent, scarcely stirring, as they strained to make sense of all the abstruse economics that, for all of Hamilton's efforts at clarity, still seemed slightly out of reach. When the clerk was finished, there was a long, meditative pause before anyone spoke, but then the hall broke into a buzz that didn't stop for months. Several members of Congress emerged from the hall stupefied, incredulous at what seemed to them to be black magic.

They weren't completely wrong. For Hamilton was proposing a kind of alchemy that would transform a debt that had been a cause of shame and anxiety in the states into a public resource that could instill pride and confidence in the nation. The nation would assume the debt left over from the revolution, add its own international debt, and create a new fiscal entity, the public credit, that would issue bonds that could be bought and sold like stock—or pigs, or whiskey, or lumber, or anything else. Debit became credit; something owed became something owned. Nothing became something. It was head spinning. And most dramatically of all, that nothing would become the foundation of the new nation, the rock on which its future would be built.

It was almost too much. Benjamin Rush, the physician who had a second life in politics, reported himself "sicken[ed] at such vile notions." Debt was a pox on the nation, as it "begets debt, extravagance, vice and bankruptcy." Whatever the doubts of congressmen, speculators believed, and they quickly bid up the price of the bonds that made up this financial bedrock. One congressman claimed that three boatloads of speculators had immediately sailed south to scoop up the paper of the unsuspecting. It was Daniel Webster who came closest to grasping the truth of the matter, as he observed much later: "The fabled birth of Minerva from the brain of Jove was hardly more sudden or more perfect than the financial system of the United States as it burst forth from the conception of Alexander Hamilton." If the Declaration created the spirit of America, and the Constitution its laws, Hamilton's report created its system of finance. Further, if power is the ability to create and destroy wealth, his report made Hamilton the most powerful man in America. It unleashed a speculative frenzy, a bloodlust of greed that pushed America into the future and, arguably, has never stopped.

But of course it was one thing to bring forth a department report, and another to convert it into a law that would clear both houses of Congress. The political obstacles were nearly overwhelming. The bill of assumption, as it was called, was to turn the *Report on the Public Credit* into policy. In doing so, it ran into some heavy politics, as it inevitably favored northern states over southern ones, since the southern states had largely paid off their debts. And it favored the reviled speculators who'd bought the notes from the patriotic soldiers who had originally received them for their service to their country—or so went the rhetoric. While the bill was meant to unify the country by making the debt that went to creating the nation a national obligation, it was divisive in most other ways, underscoring the growing tensions between Federalists and Anti-Federalists by exposing what lay underneath: a yawning divide between the classes. For the first time, the nation had to see that every economic development made winners and losers. Assumption would heap joy on those who'd bought bonds and drop ashes on those who'd sold them.

By creating the economic basis for a strong central government, Hamilton's report made real the federalism evoked by the Constitution. And it created a party that believed in it—and made Hamilton that party's leader. Washington might be the apolitical king, but Hamilton was the highly political prime minister, and he would wield the greater power both to design policy and to execute it. Typically, Washington voiced no opinion on assumption, preferring to let his surrogates in the cabinet hash it out. He'd already suffered from a "malignant carbuncle" that had to be gouged out. The surgeon's knife plunged deep below the skin as Washington sat utterly immobile—a procedure so agonizing that Mayor Duane had hay strewn on the sidewalk to muffle any irritating clatter of passersby. Now, at this critical juncture, Washington fell gravely ill with pneumonia, drawing all the deeper into the silence that nearly always engulfed him. He was a majestic figure, but a remote one.

That left Hamilton to lobby frantically for the measure largely alone, buttonholing one congressman after another. "Mr. Hamilton is very uneasy," the gossipy Pennsylvania congressman William Maclay reported in his diary, "about his funding system. He was here early to wait on the Speaker and I believe spent most of his time running from place to place among the members." Hamilton knew the stakes. On the other side was Madison, his onetime confidant who was now, to Hamilton, a shocking apostate who would sacrifice the national prosperity for crass political advantage. Hamilton complained that Madison had become "personally unfriendly" to him and had conveyed "unfavourable impressions" to others. Then he added: "The opinion I once entertained of the candour and simplicity and fairness of Mr. Madison's character has, I acknowledge, given way to a decided opinion that it is one of a peculiarly artificial and complicated kind." Translation: Our friendship is dead.

Madison had his reasons. He argued that the original bondholders shouldn't be deprived of the profits after unscrupulous speculators outwitted them. "There must be something wrong, radically and morally and politically wrong," he declared, "in a system which transfers the reward from those who paid the most valuable of all considerations, to those who scarcely paid any consideration at all." But Hamilton argued it wasn't up to the government to save those luckless original bondholders from their misfortune, or to compensate them afterward, if indeed those owners could ever be found. If investors weren't allowed to keep their winnings, who would ever invest? When Madison forced a vote on that portion of the issue, he lost thirty-six to thirteen. He had not distinguished himself. "A creature of French puffs," Adams called him. But Hamilton didn't have the votes either. It made for an anxious time.

TWENTY-SIX

Another Long Nose

I N THESE YEARS of power, Hamilton had a protean ability not just to make enemies, but to create them out of that swirl of contradictory emotions that defines most politicians. As the New York attorney general, Burr was still outside Hamilton's ken. To Burr, the fight for assumption might as well have been occurring in China. For now, it was Madison who embodied all evil in Hamilton's mind. Soon it would be Jefferson, the secretary of state. Jefferson was maddeningly difficult to define when he joined the government in 1790. Washington was fairly desperate to have him, but Jefferson was standoffish and, when he finally agreed, took months actually to show up in New York, a year into the presidency, arriving at his abode on Maiden Lane with eighty-six crates jam-packed with French furniture and other pieces of European high culture. Jefferson never did fully declare himself on the subject of the Constitution, saying vaguely that he approved of some parts but not others, and, although the topic of the assumption raged across the country, he didn't offer an opinion on it, either.

Writer, architect, aesthete, scholar, Francophile, faux commoner, slaver, spendthrift, sensualist, he was so multifaceted as to disappear into a dazzling blur, like a French chandelier. He was a sharp writer, but one who was as good at expressing what he did not believe as what he did. Thus he could pen a sublime tribute to liberty and equality in the Declaration and be an unrepentant slaveholder who allowed an eleven-year-old black child to be whipped for failing to give good service in his Monticello nailery. He could be even more enigmatic in person. He rarely spoke "three sentences together," as John Adams complained about him in Philadelphia in 1776, or ever looked anyone in the eye. Rather than shake hands in the new custom, he bowed, avoiding physical contact, like Washington. And there was something disdainful about the way he lounged on a sofa, his long torso contorted, his gangly legs askew, as if he wasn't inclined to give others room, or care what they thought. He sucked out the secrets of the voluble, like Hamilton, to deploy later to their disadvantage. Like Burr, he craved being in the know. "We must fall on some scheme of communicating our thoughts to each other, which shall be totally unintelligible to everyone but to ourselves," he once wrote his friend John Page. He hoarded gossip but was so fanatical about preserving his privacy that his relationship with his slave Sally Hemings remained unconfirmed for two centuries. And there was this: Hamilton sang only for others; Jefferson sang for himself, lightly, even when he was reading.

It was Hamilton who gave him shape. He became politically what Burr became personally—Hamilton's diametric opposite, a left hand for his right, an "anti" for every "pro." With Burr, the antipathy may have been fed by their similarities. With Jefferson, it was their differences that did it. Just as Hamilton's slender frame made Jefferson seem long limbed and Hamilton's frantic scherzo pointed up Jefferson's stately largo, Hamilton's political faith—in a powerful central government, in commerce, in the elite, and in the virtues of England—came to be opposed by Jefferson in every particular, and with it, over time, a whole political philosophy was born: Jeffersonianism. On England, Jefferson could be especially scathing, as he lambasted the British as "rich, proud, hectoring, swearing, squabbling, carnivorous animals." Then again, as an indebted Virginia planter, he was in hock to London creditors, which would not have been endearing. But Jeffersonianism might better have been called anti-Hamiltonianism since it was the opposite of everything Hamilton endorsed. Eventually it flew under the banner of Republicanism and became a political party. Advanced in the House by Madison, much to Hamilton's irritation, it drew from the agrarian South, always suspicious of the financial North, gaining a political base that—amplified by the ugly clause in the Constitution giving slave owners a three-fifths share of a white vote for each slave they possessed—

they would retain for decades. So it was that Hamilton defined both sides of that politically contentious age, the side that was with him, and the side that was against.

In opposing Jefferson, as he came to do, Hamilton of course personalized the quarrel so that he didn't distinguish between his hatred for Jeffersonianism and his loathing for Jefferson. Jefferson had no great love for Hamilton either, but he had the self-control to conceal his feelings. "Each of us perhaps thought well of the other man," Jefferson said later, "but as politicians it was impossible for two men to be of more opposite principles." Since the two were the most powerful men in Washington's cabinet, this growing antagonism became a point of increasing tension for Washington when they met at his lavish house on Cherry Street. The talkative Hamilton would go on for nearly an hour, and Jefferson, often tongue-tied, would offer a flustered rejoinder that Hamilton would effortlessly bat down, leaving Jefferson to sulk moodily and Hamilton to carry on with his crowing. Hamilton couldn't quite see it, being inattentive to the moods of others, but Jefferson was smoldering.

All the while, there was a curious subterranean connection between the two men, although it is doubtful that either spoke of it to the other. In Paris, Jefferson fell in love with the graceful, whispery twenty-six-year-old Maria Cosway, her hair a tumble of yellow curls, her sinuous body designed to encourage advances. She was the wife of the prominent miniaturist painter Richard Cosway. Speaking no French, Jefferson joined the Cosways in the expatriate world, where he became transfixed by the decadent Parisian demimonde the Cosways spun about them. They threw outrageous parties for people like the transvestite diplomat and—it was said—spy, Mademoiselle la Chevalière d'Éon, whose superior fencing skills the Cosways wished to put on display. If the mademoiselle had demonstrated her art in the nude the effect could not have been more dazzling, but it was his hostess, Maria Cosway, who held Jefferson's attention. Jefferson had enlisted Hemings, a long-haired, light-skinned slave of fourteen who was known at Monticello as "Dancing Sally," to accompany his eight-year-old daughter, Mary, on her voyage across the Atlantic to Paris via London. While Jefferson's sexual relationship with Hemings seems to have begun in those years, Jefferson toured much of Paris with Cosway. Nothing escaped their gaze—gardens, ruins, architecture. To Jefferson, the world must have all seemed like an extension of Cosway, until the fantasy ended when he snapped his wrist while trying to vault over a fountain. Surgery followed, and then a painful convalescence, and Cosway left for London without seeing him again. When Jefferson left Paris for a jaunt across Europe, he couldn't stop thinking about the beautiful mystery woman, and the moment he returned home, he snatched up her letter before any of the others in the pile waiting for him. Right away he wrote her back, telling her that in Heidelberg he'd dreamed that he'd led her by the hand through a vast garden. He said no more but requested a similar confession back—one "teeming with affection," he wrote, "such as I feel for you." And then he closed with a suggestive joke with her about his long nose—the same one Hamilton had made years before. She didn't oblige him.

Needing secrecy for his amorous campaign, Jefferson enlisted Hamilton's sister-in-law Angelica Church, who was part of Jefferson's circle while she was in Paris, to be his courier, since Jefferson knew she was a close friend of Cosway's. If bringing her into the intrigue was a subtle overture to the fetching Mrs. Church, too, it worked. By playfully passing love letters back and forth between the two, she showed she didn't mind such dalliances.

As a lover of secrets, Jefferson had an uncommon desire for married women, enjoying the world of whispers as much as Burr. For him, always quietly lordly, it may have represented a double conquest—winning the wife and besting the husband. In his twenties, he'd fallen hard for the pretty young wife of his best friend from childhood, John Walker, later senator from Virginia. Jefferson had been John Walker's groomsman at his wedding and his executor afterward. Walker thought him a "friend of my heart." After Walker left his wife, Betsy, with Jefferson when he had to travel on some military business, Jefferson made some unmistakable advances and didn't back off after she made clear they weren't welcome. When Betsy discovered that Jefferson had slipped a love note into the cuff of her sleeve, she ripped it to pieces in disgust. Still, Jefferson did not relent. He often spent evenings at the Walkers', chatting with John and his friends but eyeing her. Once, after Betsy had headed to bed, Jefferson slipped away to sneak inside the Walkers' bedchamber, where she was undressing. Betsy screamed and shoved him away. "He was repulsed with indignation and menaces of alarm and ran off," a shocked John Walker reported later.

That ended that, but now it was more of the same. To Jefferson's frustration, Maria Cosway had turned chilly. She clearly had no intention of leaving her marriage for him, or of entertaining him on any other basis. So he pivoted and let Angelica know that he might be interested in her. To this a relieved Cosway gave her blessing. At Christmastime 1787, Cosway teased the American minister: "Have you yet seen the lovely Mrs. Church? If I did not love her so much, I should fear her rivalship, but, no, I give you free permission to love her with all your heart." With that, Cosway receded, although she did not completely disappear, and for some time, the two flirtatious young women hovered in Jefferson's imagination like twin angels. Reflecting an undivided passion for each of them, Jefferson had the artist John Trumbull, a friend of the Churches', do two miniatures of him—one to send to Cosway and the other to Angelica. The two women seemed to delight in the hold they had over this powerful man, but neither one seems to have gratified him. Once it was absolutely clear that Cosway wasn't interested in a romance, Jefferson lit his candle for Angelica and invited her to visit him in Monticello, or join him on an expedition to Niagara Falls, or ... anything. She knew better than to accept.

Meanwhile, of course, Hamilton had his own fascination for his sister-in-law, and that unspoken rivalry may have added a little fire to the political one. At one drawing room or another, doors closed, the gabby Angelica had likely given Hamilton an earful about the Cosway intrigue and may have added some tidbits about Sally Hemings, too. Despite appearances, Jefferson was not entirely ascetic, just as Hamilton would prove not to be just the devoted family man. Jefferson, however, proved to be far better at hiding this truth than Hamilton, and his elusiveness stoked Hamilton's fury all the more.

→><←

AS THE ASSUMPTION bill moved toward a final vote, it seemed that Jefferson was the only man in America coolly indifferent to the outcome. He called himself "a stranger to the whole subject," but that served him at a time when his loyalty to the administration was starting to run counter to

his personal philosophy, and he started taking offense at the peppery treasury secretary with a million ideas about how to create America. Jefferson
was more directly concerned with the final location of the nation's capital,
which he wished to shift farther south, bringing the center of power with
it. There was a proposal to move the capital to some land by the Potomac,
to a portion of Jefferson's Virginia. To Hamilton, the assumption bill was
the essential one. Without it, there might not be a capital.

As it was, each bill seemed so different—like an arrow and a glass of
water—that each was a distraction from the other, and neither seemed
headed for passage. With tremendous anguish, Hamilton saw the chances
for his bill slipping away—until one fine evening in that spring of 1790.

As Jefferson later told the story, he noticed someone skulking by the
front door to Washington's grand residence on Cherry Street, seemingly
unable to decide whether to knock or not. Looking closer, Jefferson saw it
was Hamilton of all people, and, for Hamilton, he was extremely bedraggled. His dress was "uncouth and neglected," Jefferson recalled. This is hard
to picture, but to Jefferson the appearance may have been only metaphorical. It wasn't really his dress but the man himself who was in tatters that
night. "Somber, haggard, dejected," he wrote of Hamilton, pounding home
the adjectives. Jefferson may have felt some sympathy for his fellow secretary, struggling to move his mountain of finance. But the lines also suggest
some pity, some condescension, which would have been far less welcome.
Jefferson asked what was the matter, and Hamilton raged at the insufferable pettiness of legislators who would prefer to see the whole country
crumble to dust rather than pass the bill that would secure its greatness
forever. And then Hamilton caught himself. Perhaps Jefferson could help
find a way out of this impasse? Was that possible? After all, Jefferson had
many more friends on his side of the political divide than Hamilton did,
starting with Madison. Could he bring some reason to this?

In due time, Jefferson invited Hamilton and Madison to his lodgings
on Maiden Lane to break bread. It may have been the wine, or the cheering
dinner, or the fact that Jefferson was spreading his wings over his two
guests, but Hamilton managed, uncharacteristically, to set aside his frustrations with his former friend, and Madison did the same. And they reasoned together to reach the obvious. Hamilton wanted the assumption bill

and Madison wanted the Potomac site. Clearly, there was room for a trade—and there was. The three men forged the deal that created the all-powerful central government that Jefferson later professed to decry, and placed the capital of it in his native Virginia. Hamilton agreed to back the capital move, and Madison would put his weight behind the assumption bill. Each would produce the requisite votes for the other. Done. It was Hamilton's last piece of cooperation with Jefferson or with Madison.

In his later years, Jefferson always regretted his part in the scheme, claiming he'd been "duped" by the secretary of the treasury into passing a bill that led to the ruination of the country by financial interests, and his irritation may have caused him to play Hamilton as pitiable, as if there were no other reason he'd get involved in something so heinous. If it did happen this way, it was ironic that a display of weakness should bring Hamilton the greatest victory of his political life.

But, of course, the deal made Jefferson, too. A powerful central government, built on debt, crawling with speculators—this gave Jefferson a monolith to inveigh against.

TWENTY-SEVEN

And We Had a Bank

A FTER HIS SUCCESS with assumption, Hamilton followed up with a system of collecting taxes, an expanded customs service, and, most audaciously, a national bank. At that point, there were only a few banks in the country, one of them the Bank of New York, which Hamilton had himself helped start several years before. The bank bill sailed through, thirty-nine votes to twenty, but it instilled a foreboding among its opponents—Madison and Jefferson foremost among them. To them, a national bank served the powerful northern commercial interests that the Republicans dismissed as vile speculators. Indeed, the prospect sent Jefferson into a frenzy, and he shot a fireball to the governor of Virginia, Henry Lee. After dismissing the US Congress as a "foreign legislature," the secretary of state raged that if anyone in a Virginia bank cooperated with Hamilton's new national bank, even as a cashier, that person "shall be adjudged guilty of high treason and suffer death." Jefferson garnered some support from his fellow Virginian Attorney General Edmund Randolph and then rode to Washington's mansion to insist he veto it as a violation of the Constitution. Although he had never endorsed the Constitution, he was, when it was convenient, a strict enforcer of its positions and believed that anything not explicitly recognized by it was forbidden. As the Constitution made no provision for a national bank, it was to Jefferson unlawful—as simple as that.

But Hamilton saw it differently, and he elaborated a novel legal theory to back him. Specifically, he discerned a "principle of intent" by which certain powers were "implied" if they were needed to enact ones that were "expressed." Thus, if the Constitution expected the government to collect taxes, borrow money, regulate trade, and raise an army, as it did, it had to be free to create a national bank to facilitate all that. "Every power vested in a government is in its nature sovereign," Hamilton declared, "and includes by force of the term a right to employ all the means requisite and fairly applicable to the attainment of the ends of such power." When Washington passed Jefferson's objections on to Hamilton, he gave his treasury secretary a week to refute them, and exactly seven days later, with Betsey his scrivener, Hamilton delivered to Washington a fifteen-thousand-word essay that answered all of Jefferson's objections in a manner that proved to be both ingenious and irrefutable[*] and left Jefferson and his allies fuming to have been outmaneuvered yet again. As Betsey Hamilton recalled for a visitor years later, "He made your government," referring to her husband. "He made your bank. I sat up all night with him to help him do it. Jefferson thought we ought not to have a bank, and President Washington thought so. My husband said, 'We must have a bank.' I stay[ed] up all night, copied out his writing, and the next morning he carried it to President Washington and we had a bank."

If Washington decided otherwise, Hamilton said he'd face "the singular spectacle of a political society without sovereignty or of a people governed without government." If Washington had been one to smile, he'd have smiled at that. He never showed Hamilton's rebuttal to Jefferson. Instead, he signed the banking bill into law.

→>-<←

WHEN THE NEW Bank of the United States issued its first stock in Philadelphia on July 4, 1791, it set off a near riot of eager purchasers. The city was in a pandemonium for paper profits. "Scriptomania" it was called, referring to the wild passion for the bank stock purchased as script. Hamilton had

---

[*] And enduring, as the principle of "implied powers" is a foundation of constitutional authority today.

expected the offering to sell out in a week. It went in an hour. Offered for twenty-five, the shares shot to twice that before the day was out and skied to nearly three hundred a month later. Public bonds, those investments in the national debt, also rallied. The clamor was decried by Jefferson, who saw more proof of Hamilton's northern favoritism and of his own conviction that the South was better off without such flashy forms of commerce. Hamilton saw it as another example of the economic Niagara that was there to power American business into the future. Still, he feared this was a bubble that would soon burst. Fortunately, he had devised that a "sinking fund," intended to pay off the national debt, double as an emergency fund to calm the markets in a panic. Sure enough, the bank securities and debt bonds both crashed resoundingly, sending alarms in every direction. Speculators were derided as "Hamilton's Rangers" and "Paper Hunters." In local newssheets, giddy "scriptomania" had given way to galloping "scriptophobia." James Jackson, a Jeffersonian from Georgia, denounced the speculators as "rapacious wolves seeking whom they may devour" and accused them of draining "the gallant veteran" of the "pittance which a grateful country had afforded him in reward for his bravery and toils." Hamilton summoned the other directors of the sinking fund and organized massive purchases of US debt through the Bank of New York, where he had personal relationships, having founded it himself. He asked the bank's cashier, William Seton, to buy up several hundred thousand dollars' worth of bonds and stocks. In a matter of days both markets had stabilized. But not everyone was made whole. When events settled, it became clear that this bubble was no accident, but the work of Hamilton's former number two at Treasury, the avaricious New Yorker William Duer. He had gathered the paltry savings of "shopkeepers, widows, orphans, Butchers, Carmen, Gardners," according to an associate, to try to corner the bond market. His mania fed a general exuberance for bonds, and when the price tumbled, he was not the only one to fall, although his fall was by far the most dramatic. According to the *Gazette of the United States,* Duer's debts reached a spectacular 1,583,000 dollars, of which he may have owed as much as 1 million to Burr's old client, the land speculator Macomb, now languishing in debtors' prison in Philadelphia, dubbed "the hotel with grated doors." But Duer's creditors were so numerous and so infuriated, it was partly for his own safety that he was removed from his house on Broadway to the New Gaol. Its upper two floors were given over to a debtors' prison that was almost tolerable once angry mobs quit pelting the place with stones.* There were many Duers in the vigorous young Republic, and their story makes for useful commentary about the exact nature of the élan vital that powered the Hamilton economy. Its zest could easily overwhelm its restraints. Burr was not the only one who required a governor.

→›‹←

ROUNDING OUT HAMILTON'S efforts to remake the national economy, he turned to the annoyance of all the different currencies coursing through. Washington himself computed his daily expenses in British pounds, and a panoply of foreign coins filled everyone's pockets. Just a week after the banking bill, Hamilton delivered a *Report on the Establishment of a Mint* to set the dollar as the standard unit of American currency. It was to be either a gold or silver coin, with smaller coins subdividing it into halves, quarters, tenths, and hundredths in a decimal system. He specified what the coins should look like—smaller but fatter than the foreign pieces, and adorned with the heads of presidents, done in fine workmanship. Each was a piece of the new country that every citizen could hold in his hand.

---

* Its denizens made up a little society that published its own newspaper and established its own court, of which Duer served as a judge. Duer had two rooms, one of them given over to two clerks who attended to his various petitions. He remained there for five years, released only briefly in 1797 to avoid the yellow fever epidemic. Returned, he pleaded with Hamilton for intercession, and Hamilton may have persuaded his friend Troup to sign a forty-five-thousand-dollar bond, springing Duer to live in the city. By then, Duer was painfully sick; it was a special torture to urinate. He died that May of 1799 of "putrid Fever," according to a relative.

TWENTY-EIGHT

Botanizing

Late in the spring of that dramatic year of 1791, Jefferson and Madison took a trip up the Hudson, sailing from New York City clear up to Lake Champlain, and then returning down the western edge of New England. "Botanizing," they claimed. The two great political leaders claimed they'd come to fish for trout and to shoot squirrels. Jefferson said he had a particular interest in examining the Hessian fly—a crop pest named for the Hessian troops that brought it in their bedding during the war—at the behest of the American Philosophical Society, of which he was a vice president, although he may have been teasing. Their itinerary, slicing through the northern Federalist stronghold, suggested that they were in search of a particular class of mammals, receptive to the new Jeffersonian persuasion, just beginning to be called Republicans. In Manhattan, Hamilton's good friend Troup saw "every evidence of a passionate courtship" of converts and warned Hamilton: "*Delenda est Carthago* I suppose is the Maxim adopted with respect to you." Hamilton was enough of a classicist to know the meaning: *Carthage must be annihilated.* And Hamilton with it. The trip would map the field of battle and recruit generals for the fight. The first was Philip Freneau, a Princeton schoolmate of Madison's, who'd unsuccessfully wooed Freneau's sister, Mary. Moody and romantic, the author of darkly sentimental verse that anticipated Poe, he'd served as a seaman in the Revolutionary War, only to be captured by the British and locked in the hellhole of a prison ship for six weeks. He emerged a savage anti-British propagandist, flaying George III as "the Caligula of Great Britain." In him, Jefferson saw the perfect man to counter the Hamilton-worshipping *Gazette of the United States*, which was edited by a former Boston schoolteacher named John Fenno, handpicked by Hamilton to advance the Federalist line. To Jefferson, Hamilton's *Gazette* dispensed nothing but the "doctrines of monarchy." With his *National Gazette*, he'd extol the Republican virtues of farming and France. Now, over breakfast in New York, invigorated by his immersion in the wilderness, Jefferson offered Freneau a State Department post as a translator, an obvious sinecure since Freneau barely even knew French. He'd also be paid to print government notices that Jefferson would send his way. The real job was to lionize Jefferson and slice Hamilton to ribbons.

Four columned, with a cheerfully flamboyant logo, the *National Gazette* flourished by playing up every imaginable claim against Hamilton, and many unimaginable ones, like the assertion that at a dinner of the Saint Andrew's Society on November 21, 1792, Hamilton rose to offer a toast to George III, declaring, "there was no stability, no security in any kind of government but a monarchy." The specificity of the date and place conveyed accuracy, but it fit too well Jefferson's caricature of Hamilton as a man "bewitched and perverted by the British example." Unlike Jefferson, Hamilton nearly gave his life to defeat the British, after all.

→> <←

AND THE OTHER man in New York that Jefferson and Madison entertained over breakfast? Aaron Burr. At first glance, he was an unlikely choice for such an honor. Just three years before, he had been a lowly attorney general, having been plucked out of even deeper obscurity by Governor Clinton for that post, and he might have remained there if, earlier in 1791, the New York Federalists, meaning Hamilton, hadn't run into some bad luck. By draw, the Senate seat that Hamilton had delivered to Philip Schuyler ran only two years; Rufus King received the seat that ran six. Now Hamilton's machinations to throw over the Livingston relation, Mayor Duane, for King came back to haunt him. Such were the byzantine politics of New York State that Clinton had quietly pushed King too, knowing that the clannish Livingstons would turn on Hamilton when their kinsman

Robert R. Livingston lost. Hamilton first learned of their fury when he was seeking Federalist support for his assumption bill, and even though the Livingstons stood to profit handsomely from it, they assailed it as an invitation to "stock-jobbing"—an insidious form of speculation. Afterward, the Schuyler-Livingston alliance against Clinton became a Livingston-Clinton alliance against Schuyler, or more precisely, against Hamilton. So—who would the Clinton-Livingston faction put forward against Schuyler in 1791?

Burr was the perfect man for Clinton for the same reason that Yates had been perfect for Hamilton in the governor's race. It was the quality that had come to identify Burr above all others. The quality of no quality. No political quality, that is. Having played both political sides—working for Yates in '89, serving Clinton since—Burr was no lightning rod, but a broad, flat meadow that didn't offer so much as a single tree to strike, while Schuyler was a high fortress of haughty superiority.

The election was decided in the Assembly where Burr had served. When a motion was put forth to offer Philip Schuyler to the federal Senate, it was defeated thirty-two to twenty-seven. When the name of Aaron Burr was offered, it passed by the same margin.

In Philadelphia, Hamilton was crushed by the news. He'd failed his father-in-law and his party—and, in his mind, he had only one person to blame. Burr. Now US Senator Burr. Any cordial relations with Burr evaporated, replaced by the most savage contempt. Not even Jefferson aroused him to such a height of indignation. Every reference to Burr in his letters is black with scorn. He never acknowledged his own part in the catastrophe by blithely alienating the Livingstons so fiercely that he kicked away his majority in New York and would never recover it.

Burr knew that his election would be "displeasing" to the Hamilton forces, but he never imagined the secretary would hold a grudge. "Burr is as far from a fool as I ever saw," his later associate Andrew Jackson once said, "and yet he is as easily fooled as any man I ever knew." It wasn't that Burr opposed Hamilton on principle; it was that he didn't. He rarely took a position on matters like the assumption bill, which Hamilton considered essential.

All this explained why Jefferson and Madison were so eager to meet with the junior senator from New York. They imagined Burr would do in the political world what Freneau did in newspapers: drive Hamilton to a frenzy of irritation, causing him to bring about his own ruin with no further help from them.

→⤚⤙←

WHEN BURR ARRIVED in Philadelphia in October 1791, he took a seat in the Senate chambers upstairs in the high-spired Independence Hall, ready, as his wife put it, to "commence politics." The irascible John Adams presided from a stiff chair beside a silk-skirted table, the thirty senators arrayed before him. In his thirties, Burr was not exactly handsome, but he was striking, and one imagines the other senators took a good look at this new man with deep-set eyes behind a sturdy brow, the thinning hair pulled back to expose the brilliance of his face, the proud, upright head above a swirling white cravat. Since minutes were not kept, and the public barred, it can't be known what Burr said, but it appears he took little part in the discussions. He could be quite brilliant at summarizing the arguments of others—or so said New York's other senator, Rufus King—but Burr rarely added any opinions of his own. Typically, when he broached the seminal topic of Hamilton's proposed national bank, he hedged. Writing Theodore Sedgwick, the now-haughty congressman from Massachusetts, he acknowledged the idea of a US Bank was "interesting," but the "promised advantages" were "problematic." Then he conceded he knew little about it, as he had not "read with proper attention" Hamilton's arguments, and would defer to Sedgwick's opinion, whatever it might be, since it was likely born of "deeper study."

Burr did diligent service on a variety of committees, the bulk of them concerned with the affairs of Indians on the western border. He was much more keen to write a definitive history of the War of Independence—*his* definitive history. To the purpose, he spent several hours every morning copying out lengthy extracts from the war archives in the Department of State—until Washington got wind of the project and, loath to let someone so impudent determine his place in history, had him barred from the archives.

TWENTY-NINE

Embryo-Caesar

A T THIRTY-SIX, HAMILTON was a young man on the verge of becoming an old one. For all his intellect, he had relied on his protean energy to attain his position and to hold it against all comers. As his hour lengthened, he was commanding attention less through his acts than through his stature. An anonymous dinner guest remembered an evening with Hamilton during this period. Ever the dramatist, Hamilton was the last to come to the table, but the group quieted when he appeared, and all eyes turned to him to extend their "respectful attention." He was dressed with a nearly royal flamboyance, with bright buttons, "the skirts of his coat . . . unusually long," "a white waistcoat, black silk small-clothes, white silk stockings." As Hamilton went around the table, the host introduced him to the few people he didn't know. "To each he made a formal bow, bending very low, the ceremony of shaking hands not being observed." In the politics of the era, hand shaking was considered a vulgar Republican custom. From Washington on down, Federalists did not touch. "His appearance and deportment accorded with the dignified distinction to which he had attained in public opinion. At dinner, whenever he engaged in the conversation, every one listened attentively. His mode of speaking was deliberate and serious; and his voice engagingly pleasant. In the evening of the same day he was in a mixed assembly of both sexes; and the tranquil reserve noticed at the dinner table, had given place to a social and playful manner, as though in this he was alone ambitious to excel."

Despite his prodigious power as secretary of the treasury, as chief adviser to Washington on every aspect of his administration, and as de facto head of the Federalist Party, Hamilton did not act the part of the confident potentate. To the contrary, the higher he rose, the more precarious his position seemed—at least to judge by his fury in defending it from men he perceived to be his enemies, who were growing numerous. That energy that had once been put to such constructive uses now turned inward, feeding the most destructive passions. Hence his fury at Madison for his apostasy and his outrage at Jefferson for his "dangerous" opinions. It was as if there were demons on every side.

And then there was Burr. With Burr the antagonism went beyond policy, for the threat was more than just political. To Hamilton, Burr must have been a ghoul, haunting him first at Elizabethtown, then at Princeton, in the war, in New York courtrooms, and now in government, and the conflict between them may have become existential—not that Burr would ever think this way. It is not so hard to imagine that Burr went so deep he threatened Hamilton's reasons for being, making him not just purposeless but vulnerable, and raising the specter that must have always been there, on some level, of a forced return to a beggar's life on Nevis. Hamilton would never forget how Burr had undone his father-in-law, snatching his prized Senate seat from him and ending his political career. That revealed a Burr that only Hamilton could see—the smug aristocrat unbound by the conventions of civilized behavior. And Burr's shameless disregard of proper political conduct was exasperating, as Hamilton saw him as a man devoid of political beliefs. But far from being punished for such errant ways, he was being rewarded for them, whereas Hamilton, the virtuous immigrant, was being treated like a nonentity.

Hamilton acted like a man filled with foreboding. His own greatness was starting to recede behind him; he had to have sensed that. Burr's lay ahead. Only a year into a highly ineffectual Senate term, he was already being touted in some corners as a vice presidential candidate in the coming election, and could the presidency itself be far behind? Burr made Hamilton feel like yesterday's man. As the Senate contest showed, he was too polarizing, too annoying, to win elective office. Jefferson had left State, Knox was about to leave War, and his own tenure at Treasury would not last much longer. He would soon return to a quiet private life as a New York lawyer, his only power his influence over the Federalist Party, and that was sure to wane if the party did, as it surely would if Adams—a man he viewed (in one of his typically unrestrained opinions) as a dyspeptic windbag—was elected to lead it.

While it was plain that Washington could hold the presidency for as long as he wanted, Adams's position as vice president was not so secure. And in the summer before the December election of 1792, the unstoppable George Clinton was urged to take Adams on. When the Old Incumbent—as he was called even at fifty-three—temporized, he left Burr an opening. He dispatched Melancton Smith—the Burrite whom Burr touted as "the man of the first Influence" in New York State—to make a foray into the South to test the political waters for Burr. But the national Republican caucus in Philadelphia got word and insisted that Burr stop. Adams scoffed at the gathering as expressing "the pure Spirit of Clintonian Cabal [and] of Virginia Artifices." But it was the first national political convention, and it forced Burr out in favor of Clinton. It was significant that the convention was largely inspired by opposition to Burr, not support for him. Burr dutifully dropped out of the race and pledged to "lend every aid in his power to C[linton]'s election." He sent Smith out to campaign throughout New England for Clinton, to no discernible effect, as Clinton would garner no electoral votes there.

Grateful for Burr's support, nonetheless, Clinton tried to repay him with an appointment to the Supreme Judicial Court of New York State. A shrewd move, as, in a stroke, it extended a bouquet to a rival and generously offered to ease Burr's financial burdens—and potentially retire a tenacious rival from politics forever. Burr declined. Money was an attraction, no question, but not enough of one. "There was not that instinctive shrinking from debt," wrote a somewhat mystified Parton, "that caution . . . which indicates the entirely honest man."

Increasingly preoccupied with Burr, Hamilton dispatched Rufus King to do some reconnaissance on his rival's popularity outside of New York. When King's report came back to reveal that Burr was indeed seen as a potential vice president both in the Federalist heartland of Connecticut and in the swing state of Pennsylvania, Hamilton was furious and dashed off a screed to an unnamed political correspondent. While he affected a nose-in-the-air detachment, the vitriol had force. Burr was so offensive, he made Hamilton long for Clinton, the lumpen Constitution hater Hamilton had spent more than a decade trying to unseat.

"Mr. C—— is a man of property, and, in private life, as far as I know of probity," Hamilton began airily. "I fear the other Gentleman [Burr] is unprincipled both as a public and private man. When the constitution was in deliberation, his conduct was equivocal; but its enemies, who I believe best understood him considered him as with them. In fact, I take it, he is for or against nothing, but as it suits his interest or ambition. He is determined, as I conceive, to make his way to be the head of the popular party and to climb per *fas et nefas* to the highest honors of the state; and as much higher as circumstances may permit."

Then he turned pitying, which is crueler. "Embarrassed, as I understand, in his circumstances, with an extravagant family—bold enterprising and intriguing, I am mistaken, if it be not his object to play the game of confusion, and I feel it a religious duty to oppose his career." A religious duty—from a man who was not then religious in any other way.

He concluded: "I have hitherto scrupulously refrained from interference in elections." That was hilarious, as he did little else now. "But the occasion is in my opinion of sufficient importance to warrant in this instance a departure from that rule." He was duty-bound. "I therefore commit my opinion to you without scruple; but in perfect confidence I pledge my character for discernment that it is incumbent upon every good man to resist the present design."

Like a man obsessed, Hamilton returned to the theme of Burr's perfidy as he anatomized his rival to another anonymous correspondent just a few days later.

> *As a public man, he is one of the worst sort—a friend to nothing but as*
> *it suits his interest and ambition. Determined to climb to the highest*
> *honours of the State, and as much higher as circumstances may*
> *permit—he cares nothing about the means of effecting his purpose. 'Tis*
> *evident that he aims at putting himself at the head of what he calls the*
> *"popular party" as affording the best tools for an ambitious man to*

*work with. Secretly turning Liberty into ridicule, he knows as well as
most men how to make use of the name. In a word, if we have an
embryo-Caesar in the United States 'tis Burr.*

As it happened, Hamilton had had no reason to fear. Having withdrawn from the race, Burr was not selected as a vice presidential candidate at the Republican caucus, needless to say. He did not receive even a single vote. The honor went instead to New York's perennial governor George Clinton. Hamilton ran the risk of building Burr up by tearing him down. As it was, Hamilton made a far greater impression on the delegates than Burr. "There is no inferior degree of sagacity in the combinations of this extraordinary man," one member declared. "With a comprehensive eye, a subtle and contriving mind, and soul devoted to his object, all his measure are promptly and aptly designed, and, like the links of a chain, depend on each other [and] acquire additional strength by their union." Hamilton was the man on the high throne, and the Republicans were already contriving a means to haul him down.

In the election, Washington was reelected unanimously with 133 votes as expected, but Adams came in second once again, this time with 77, to win another term of "the most insignificant office that ever the invention of man contrived," as he put it. Hampered by his late entry into the race, and by the Burr diversion, Clinton came in third with just 50 votes. Burr secured a single vote, from an elector in South Carolina.

THIRTY

Other Than Pecuniary Consolation

T HAT YEAR, HAMILTON was a balloonist at his height, admired by all who squinted up at him, commanding long views to distant horizons, imperious in his ether, but a man who would have to return to earth eventually. Descend Hamilton did, abruptly. The man who could do no wrong now could do no right.

When Hamilton moved with the capital to Philadelphia, he settled his family into a fine town house on elegant South Street. Still larger than New York, Philadelphia was in some ways faster, too. The puritanical New Englander Abigail Adams had been shocked to see all the women's flesh on display at dinner parties. "The arm naked almost to the shoulder," she complained to her husband. With his growing celebrity, Hamilton now seemed to expect the ladies' attention, whereas he had simply hoped for it before. The Bostonian Harrison Gray Otis noted Hamilton's "liquorish flirtation" with women at dinner parties, John Adams brayed at his "indelicate pleasures," and the Capitol architect Benjamin Latrobe went so far as to lambaste him as "an insatiable libertine."

In came the saturnine Mrs. Maria Reynolds. Hamilton met her early in the summer of 1791, when she was a fluttering beauty of twenty-three. Since fifteen, she had been married to a dubious character named James Reynolds, and they'd had a daughter, now eleven. During the war Reynolds had been a riverboat captain and an agent in the Commissary Department; with the peace, he'd taken a turn as a speculator, which had gone badly. For money, Reynolds had pushed Maria into prostitution, conducted in their marital bed, her gentlemen clients tacking their requests to the wall at the top of the stairs. It was for a more regular source of funds that James Reynolds thought of Hamilton. He was, by widening reputation, libidinous.

No physical description of Maria exists aside from Hamilton's once terming her "a Beauty in distress." If not fully beautiful, she was at least alluring, and it's a fair guess that Maria Reynolds did not look much like the prim, matronly Betsey Hamilton. She had some social connections: She was related to the New York Livingstons, ironically enough, through her sister's husband. The tortured grammar and hilarious spelling of her letters make it clear she was a long way from gentry. Rather, Maria was like a lot of women in a time of upheaval—poor, ill educated, unemployable, trapped in a bad marriage, and eager to improve her luck. But she had a slyness to her, one that was obscured by a jumpy manner that sometimes lurched into screaming hysteria. (Curiously, Hamilton had similar qualities, although his hysteria was manifest as furious indignation.) But Maria Reynolds's quicksilver moods, shifting from light-fingered seduction to pounding rage, may have been part of the enchantment for Hamilton, even as they were part of the hazard, too. They allowed him to soothe her.

The long, tortured melodrama began one evening that summer of 1791 with a knock on the door of the Hamiltons' fashionable brick house, not far from the cooling breezes of the Delaware River. Hamilton opened the door and discovered a young woman who, obviously in some distress, asked to speak to him, alone. Since his wife and children were home, Hamilton quietly ushered Reynolds into a side parlor off the entrance hall, and he closed the door. A telling gesture, that secrecy. He knew to keep this visitor from his wife. Once the two were secluded, Maria Reynolds introduced herself and then blurted out the story her husband had crafted for her—that James Reynolds had treated her "very cruelly," presumably with his fists, then abandoned her, for another woman no less, and left her "destitute." Was it raining that night—or does it only seem as though it was, since damp clothes, chilled skin, and dripping hair would do much to convey the sensual appeal of this beleaguered young woman. Hamilton immediately saw a woman in need; it didn't occur to him until shortly afterward that she could be taken advantage of. Perhaps Hamilton saw his mother, another fallen woman who'd been treated harshly by fate. Hamilton's grandson, the alienist Allan McLane Hamilton, sees his ancestor's own sexual fall as a mark of distinction. Only men of the "highest order of intelligence [would] impulsively plunge into the underworld in obedience to some strange prompting of their lower nature." More likely, Hamilton's prompting was quite familiar.

Hamilton said only that her situation was "very interesting" and offered to bring "a small supply of money" with him to her home a few blocks away, on South Fourth Street. They did not discuss what the money would purchase.

Then: "In the evening, I put a bank bill in my pocket and went to the house. I inquired for Mrs. Reynolds and was shown upstairs, at the head of which she met me and conducted me into a bedroom. I took the bill out of my pocket and gave it to her. Some conversation ensued from which it was quickly apparent that other than pecuniary consolation would be acceptable."

"Other than pecuniary consolation"—surely one of the more artful terms for adulterous sex, and comical for a treasury secretary. This passage appears in the Reynolds Pamphlet, Hamilton's oddly unabashed account of the affair that he wrote years later when he needed to clear his name. For Mrs. Reynolds, of course, pecuniary consolation would be of primary interest. While she might profess otherwise, she did not live to be ravished by the treasury secretary. It was he who hoped there was more to it.

Hamilton provided the nonpecuniary sort of consolation over and over, first in her bedroom, separate from her vanished husband's, and then, once Betsey took the children to her father's in Albany in mid-July, in the Hamiltons' bedroom upstairs at home. As the summer went along, Hamilton sent his wife a loving letter begging her to stay in the country for her health, or the children's, all the while exclaiming how much he missed her. "I am so anxious for a perfect restoration of your health that I am willing to make a great sacrifice for it," he told her.

If Hamilton had allowed himself to think that Maria was indeed all his, and that her husband had indeed fled the scene, he soon received a rude awakening when Maria gaily told him that she and her husband had affected a "reconciliation" and they would live together as man and wife once more. This could not have been good news, but Hamilton professed to be pleased.

His mood must have darkened when Maria told him that her husband traded on private information from sources in the Treasury Department. Things only got worse when James Reynolds showed up at Hamilton's door. He is nowhere described, but the evidence suggests a blunt, rough-hewn sort of man who was not Hamilton's type. Reynolds expressed no outrage at Hamilton's relationship with his wife and made no immediate effort to exploit the connection but mentioned he had the name of the Treasury Department official who had fed him tips. Perhaps Hamilton would like to know who it was? Hamilton must have nodded, for Reynolds told him: the notorious speculator William Duer.

As it happened, Duer had left his office in disgrace almost two years before en route to far greater shames to come, making Reynolds's information very much old news. Reynolds made a request anyway—for a job at Treasury. Not inclined to oblige him, Hamilton regretted to say that nothing was available. Reynolds left irritated.

Reynolds acted as if his wife and Hamilton were just good friends, but Hamilton couldn't believe anyone could be so stupid. But then, he was foolish enough to believe Mrs. Reynolds was in love with him. If she was extracting money from him, he preferred to think it was only because she was being forced to by her husband. She herself had a different stratagem: She played up the desperation of her circumstances, knowing that Hamilton would respond to a woman in need. "I need not acquaint that I had Ben Sick all moast Ever sence I saw yo as I am sure you already no it Nor would I solicit a favor wich is so hard to obtain were It not for the Last time," Maria Reynolds began one wheedling letter. The lure is clear, and rather sophisticated. She isn't going to ask for money; she is going to make Hamilton want to offer it. "Yes Sir Rest assured I will never ask you to Call on me again I have kept my Bed those tow dayes and now rise from My polliow which your Neglect has filled with the sharpest thorns." Her pain will be Hamilton's. "I can neither Eat or sleep I have Been on the point of doing the moast horrid acts at I shudder to think where I might been what will Become of me." Hamilton is *killing* her. "Let me Ingreat you If you

wont Come to send me a Line oh my head I can rige no more do something
to Ease My heart or Els I no not what I shall do for I cannot live."

Altogether, it is quite a plea—and it plays on all of Hamilton's sensitivities. However ferocious he may have been in political circles, he was kitten-
ish in domestic ones, especially where women and children were concerned.
But now any kindness to Mrs. Reynolds, of course, was an unkindness to
Mrs. Hamilton. He vowed to forswear the pleasures of the lady, but whenever he tried to disentangle himself, she voiced such noisy, tearstained hysteria that Hamilton had to hurry to her, if only to keep her quiet. "All the
appearances of violent attachment, and of agonizing distress at the idea of a
relinquishment, were played with a most imposing art," Hamilton complained later, too late. At the time, Hamilton couldn't believe a woman
would be so calculating. But he couldn't stay away. "My sensibility, perhaps
my vanity, admitted of real fondness," he admitted. He was determined to
withdraw, but cautiously.

THIRTY-ONE

Sober Among the Drunks

T HEODOSIA'S WORSENING ILLNESS deterred her from leaving New York to join her husband in Philadelphia that December of 1791, when Hamilton's tawdry affair had been going on for six months, so Burr lodged alone with an elderly mother and her daughter, both widows, who must have made poor company. The mother was so utterly stone-deaf, Burr wrote Theodosia, that the woman had asked him *not* to bellow to make himself heard—"for fear of injuring [his] lungs." He found greater sociability in a circle of illustrious wives who were aglow over the dashing new senator's clever insights and sly humor, and he quickly became so popular with the ladies that Theodosia grew alarmed when she got wind of it. He tried to reassure her that the "reports of my life style are... much too absurd to gain belief." But the truth was, as he admitted, that he had received "many invitations to dine &tc." For a man so skilled at deception, whom he was hiding, and what, she could not have guessed. For during this period he was using his reputation as a gallant as cover for far more shadowy activities than romantic ones. For he sent, via a certain "Mrs. Gilbert," a number of light, teasing letters to his friend Peter Van Gaasbeck detailing a variety of frolics with different women in town. Anyone who intercepted such a letter would simply assume that, since this was Burr, it was about some harmless romantic misadventures. But a closer look would reveal that Burr's tone, ordinarily mellifluous, turns oddly stiff in places, and no "Mrs. Gilbert" was known to exist in his orbit. More likely, these letters hid behind Burr's caddish reputation to convey coded messages directing Van Gaasbeck to engage in financial speculations of the sort that Burr was increasingly keen on as his finances grew ever more desperate. And if these meant investing in the Hamiltonian banks that his Jeffersonian colleagues decried—who would ever know?

When Theodosia finally did visit early the following year of 1792, she brought a "companion," Mrs. Mary Allen, known to all the Burrs as "Mama," who likely doubled as a nurse for the increasingly frail Mrs. Burr, and the two were installed with her husband at the widows'. Whether it was the rigors of her illness, the agonies of a long, jolting trip, her prejudice against the dour Quakers, or her growing resentment of the gay social life her husband enjoyed without her, Theodosia responded to Philadelphia with a loathing unusual for her, calling it "the most inhospitable region that ever was inhabited." She complained bitterly about everything from the tedious streets to the dull parties that might glory in displaying a "footman with a silver breadbasket." Anticipating this reaction, Burr had offered to have her stay at his cousin's house ten miles out of town, but Theodosia wouldn't hear of being closeted away in the woods. Still, the whole prospect of her visit, combined with the "absurd and irrational way of life," had shaken her husband's own delicate health and left him "sitting with my feet in warm water, my head wrapped in vinegar and drinking chamomile tea." When Theodosia departed with her "Mama," she never returned. The next time she saw her husband, months later, it was in Trenton, New Jersey.

→>·<←

AFTER HIS WIFE'S departure, Burr moved to a boardinghouse run by Mrs. Mary Coles Payne, whose toothsome daughter Dolley lived nearby with her husband, the lawyer John Todd, and their two small boys. Bright and curvaceous, she was the sort of woman who would command any man's attention, and she took a firm hold of Burr's. When the vicious yellow fever epidemic burned through Philadelphia in 1793, Todd and one of the boys both died of it. A murderous disease of black vomit and jaundiced skin, it killed twenty Philadelphians a day, leaving corpses in the street, and, after the statehouse doorman was found dead one morning, scattering the members of the state legislature who'd assembled to reassure the citizenry that all was well. Hamilton came down with the fever, and he immediately retreated with Betsey and the children to a summer residence on a hill outside of the city. There, in a startling twist of fate, he was attended by Ned Stevens, Hamilton's doppelgänger from Saint Croix, now a distinguished Philadelphia physician. Like the newspapers, dress, and so much else, the treatment of the disease took a political cast. Hamilton had little faith in the esteemed Republican doctor Benjamin Rush, who dashed about the city, treating the afflicted with what Hamilton considered the feudal techniques of bleeding and purging, which offered few cures. Stevens addressed Hamilton's case more benignly, letting the body heal itself, as he prescribed only gentle sedatives and an antiemetic of chamomile flowers. It worked. While Hamilton convalesced, Washington sent a note of paternal concern, plus six bottles of "vintage wine." Jefferson snickered to Madison about how the "timid" Hamilton surely suffered only from "autumnal fever." The Federalists received a lift when, after Hamilton recovered in just five days, he publicized Stevens's methods—an implicit rebuke to Rush, who fired back that Hamilton's "remedies" were no more popular in Philadelphia than his "funding system" was in Virginia. He likewise refused to believe Hamilton had ever had yellow fever at all. From Hamilton's perspective, the yellow fever had one unquestionably good result: It so disrupted the city's economy that it wrecked the finances of the *National Gazette* and put its sharp-quilled editor, Philip Freneau, out of work as a political saboteur.

Burr took his own advantage of the scourge. He provided legal services, gratis, to the distraught widow, Mrs. Todd, and became her "trusted friend and advisor," as he put it, and possibly more, as well. The intimacy was such that she named Burr the sole guardian of her surviving son in the event of her death. Burr introduced her to his party leader, James Madison, whom Hamilton by now could not abide. But Burr could see the service could be helpful. Madison was known to be in the market for a wife, but he was still embittered by the humiliating rebuff of Kitty Floyd, the sixteen-year-old daughter of a New York congressman, after they'd become engaged a decade before. Thomas Jefferson had pushed Floyd on his acolyte as possessing "every sentiment in your favor which you could wish." For all his intellect, Madison was rather stony—a "gloomy, stiff creature," one political wife termed him, "the most unsociable creature in existence." Floyd's rejection had cut Madison so deep, he expunged every reference to the courtship from his correspondence. But Burr had reason to think he was ready to attempt matrimony once more, this time with the greater confidence of a statesman. Not only did Burr press Madison's case, but so did Martha Washington, and the young widow could not help but be dazzled by all the attention. As she scribbled excitedly to her friend Eliza Collins, "Aaron Burr says that the great little Madison has asked to be brought to me this evening." They met by candlelight, and they were both enthralled, although he perhaps a little more. He was forty-three, she twenty-six. They were married in September. Since Jefferson was widowed, Dolley Madison served as hostess for a range of presidential events during his administration. And when her husband was elected president, Dolley played the role for real, setting the elegant standard for first ladies that would survive for generations.

→>-<←

WHILE BURR DIDN'T bother much with governance, he was fascinated by politics, and brilliant at it, divining where the real power lay and then grabbing some of it for himself. He could tell who was on the rise and who was set to fall and could sense the seismic shifts in the electorate before they were evident to anyone else. And, with his gift for common speech and his unforgettable black eyes, he knew how to attract attention from powerful men who thought they could advance their cause by advancing his. Burr knew it wouldn't hurt his prospects to furnish Madison—second to Jefferson as the most powerful man in the emerging Republican Party—with a curvaceous young bride and was brazen in doing so. And there was something about the way Burr conducted himself—so poised, and yet so self-contained—that had the look of a comer.

Just a year into Burr's Senate career, the patriot-physician Benjamin Rush enlisted Mr. John James Beckley—the multitentacled Republican functionary and close confidant of Jefferson who, Rush said, "possesses a fund of information about men and things"—to hand deliver to Burr a letter in which he declared that the man had a future. Burr's "friends everywhere look to take an active part in removing the monarchical rubbish of our government," Rush said. Friends, of course, that Burr might not have realized he had. Rush recommended Burr write to the old Boston revolutionary Samuel Adams, cousin of the vice president, to ask him to spread his name throughout the Federalist stronghold of New England.

Rush, however, could not know for sure if Burr was on his side. No one could. At a time when party affiliation was becoming nearly as fundamental as gender, Burr refused to make a public declaration. Writing to Hamilton, Gouverneur Morris likened an independent to an abstainer at a bacchanal: "You, who are temperate in drinking, have never perhaps noticed the awkward situation of a man who continues sober after the company are drunk." In New York, the line between Federalist and Republican was not so bright as elsewhere, but that blurriness ended at the border. To Burr, being an "abstainer" posed certain advantages. He could keep his head while everyone else was losing theirs to radical party positions, retaining some healthy self-interest at a time of wild political excess. Uncommitted, he was sure to receive some highly enticing entreaties from each side. Finally, neutrality would leave him perfectly positioned for a chance at national office, something that would otherwise be inconceivable for a first-term senator of so little accomplishment. At a time when the country was almost perfectly split between the parties, Burr could see that electoral success would come only to the man who appealed to more than one side of the divide.

Maintaining his distance from the party barons, Burr kept his primary political affiliation to a small band of well-positioned political operatives who soon became known as Burrites. They extended Burr's reach from his base in New York and into the Republican bastion of Virginia and even farther south, as well as north into the Federalist enclave of New England. In an era when no one actively campaigned for office, every politician relied on so-called friends to perform the humiliating political service of asking for votes from the citizenry, but few were able to enlist so many who would die for him. Soldiers of the revolution, many of these Burrites, they saw themselves as the true keepers of the flame of 1776, but then, virtually every public man did. They were distinguished in selecting Aaron Burr, hero of Quebec and Westchester County, as their Washington. Not without a trace of jealousy, Hamilton derided the band as Burr's "myrmidons," referring to the select warriors of Achilles. No one else in politics—not even

Washington—had such a crew. Besides Van Gaasbeck, they early on included such men as the vocal Anti-Federalist Melancton Smith; the one-time street brawler for the Sons of Liberty Marinus Willett; and the physician-politician Dr. Isaac Ledyard. They would soon be joined by the brass-knuckled lawyer John Swartwout, who would bring in his two brothers, and the printer Matthew Livingston Davis (later Burr's first biographer), plus the freelance politicos Theodorus Bailey and David Gelston, and finally Burr's stepson, Theodosia's Bartow Prevost, and perhaps half a dozen others. All these men had one thing in common: They would do anything for Burr, and ultimately most of them did.

→>-<-

IT WAS DR. Ledyard who provided the first political service as a Burrite, and he did so just months into Burr's term. Looking ahead to the next gubernatorial election in New York, Hamilton and Schuyler were plotting once again to topple Governor Clinton from his perch, and they were inclined to turn once again to supreme court justice Robert Yates to be their candidate. As if to demonstrate Burr's malleability, Hamilton and Schuyler tipped the Burrite Ledyard to an electrifying piece of news: Yates wouldn't run, or, as they put it, was "resigning his pretentions." Ledyard had Schuyler convey to Hamilton a better choice: Why not Burr? He'd worked against Clinton once before, as Hamilton surely recalled, as he also surely recalled that Burr subsequently served in Clinton's administration. This for-and-against quality of Burr's would surely spell victory—a claim that Burr, and Burrites, would make again. Ledyard saw the race as basically even since Clinton had won by fewer than five hundred votes the last two times around. That provided Burr's opening. Ledyard enlisted the Federalist James Watson to play up the virtues of Burr's political independence: "The cautious distance observed by this gentleman toward all parties, however exceptional in a politician, may be a real merit in a governor," Watson lectured Hamilton, unnecessarily. Anticipating Hamilton's objection that Burr wasn't enough of a Federalist for his taste, Ledyard claimed to have pressed Burr into an "artless declaration" of his political beliefs. It proved there were only two unshakable ones. Burr believed in the Union and in the "wisdom & integrity" of Hamilton.

As artless declarations go, these were pretty slick. Regarding the latter, he must have assumed that Hamilton would fall for such flattery. As for the former, what did it mean to "believe in the Union"? Which union—Hamilton's, Jefferson's, or one of Burr's own imagining? No fool, Hamilton could tell an artful declaration from an artless one, and he rejected the idea of Burr for anything. It was the first active breach between them. The two had no basis for an alliance, but the rejection confirmed their separation. Hamilton turned instead to his old friend the reliable Federalist John Jay, then serving as the chief justice of the United States, and persuaded him to take on Clinton.

And so it was on: Clinton versus Jay, the "Old Incumbent," as the long-serving Clinton was known, and the sharp, angular Jay. Burr would be on the ballot too. For when the votes were finally tallied in early May, it appeared there were some serious irregularities in the three upstate counties of New York's somewhat raucous western frontier. In one of them, Otsego County, the current sheriff had apparently not continuously overseen the sealed ballot boxes, as required by law, because there *was* no current sheriff, only a former one, Richard R. Smith, a Clinton appointee whose term had just expired. Nonetheless, he'd taken charge of the ballots—and then passed them on to his deputy, which only made a bad situation worse. The Federalists were in high dudgeon over the matter. But they had problems of their own, chiefly charges that the Federalist candidate for lieutenant governor, Stephen Van Rensselaer, the lordly upstate patroon who was Schuyler's son-in-law, had coerced his many tenants into giving him their vote. To counter that charge, Hamilton had his old friend James Kent, loyal Federalist, assert that the loyal Clintonians, the Livingstons, had driven their tenants to the polls like "sheep to slaughter."

Each side accused the other of trying to steal the election, and each side had its reasons. Under New York statutes, contested elections were left to the state's two senators to resolve, and one of them, of course, was Aaron Burr. Given all the vitriol, and his own involvement in the election, this was not a plum assignment, but for Burr, there was an extra hazard: It would force him to take sides and declare to the world whether he came down as a Republican or a Federalist. Impressively, New York's other senator, Rufus King, managed to sidestep the politics and declared that virtually all the ballots should be accepted, regardless of whether they'd been properly overseen by a sheriff or whether there was the possibility of coercion, so long as their intent was clear. This benefited the Clintonians unduly. Burr was more selective in his reasoning. He drew on an obscure English precedent to decide that consistent and proper oversight of the ballot box was essential to the democratic process. And he recommended the tossing out of hundreds of Federalist ballots where continuity was compromised, enough to hand the election to Clinton.

"I was obliged to give an opinion," he later declared, "and I have not yet learned to give any other than which my judgment directs." Thus Burr exchanged the low moral ground for the high one. What's more, he insisted that he expected no "friendship" from Clinton in return. "I have too many reasons to believe that he regards me with jealousy and malevolence." If he had, he had fewer reasons now. Republican potentates in Philadelphia could not have failed to take note that Burr had returned a loyal Republican to the governor's chair of a large and pivotal state in time for a national election. In their happiness, party elders had another thought: that Aaron Burr might not make a bad vice president after all.

THIRTY-TWO

I Have Been So Cruelly Treated

THE LAST FEW months of 1791, after Burr joined the Senate, were a frantic time for Hamilton even by his own hyperkinetic standards. He had promoted a Society for Establishing Useful Manufactures to create a demonstration project that developed an elaborate British-style manufacturing plant, harnessing the power of the surging Passaic River in New Jersey to produce state-of-the-art goods from sailcloth to beer. Hamilton was convinced that such innovation would ignite an American industrial revolution that would create economic independence just as the war had achieved a political one. It was to be backed by private interests with the blessing of the government—and it depended on some connivance, as it meant securing closely guarded industrial secrets that had been smuggled out of England by several spies who had skulked about the British factories, made precise mental models of the proprietary machinery, and returned to re-create them in America. Now, in December, he delivered his monumental *Report on Manufactures*, detailing the conceptual framework for such an initiative, and why it was so essential to American prosperity. Hamilton could see that America would never rise as a nation of farmers; it would only become a world power by industry. Of course, Republicans like Jefferson and Madison found such talk abominable. To them, it was not just contrary to the spirit of America, but positively hellish—dark, Satanic mills looming over the sylvan paradise of America. Like assumption, like his national bank before it, Hamilton's plans for American manufacturing pounded a wedge between the parties.

While that disagreement smoldered, Hamilton's other duties continued. Thursday morning, December 15, 1791, he met with George Hammond, the first British minister to the United States, to discuss the Indian wars on the western frontier; and, in response to a letter from Jeremiah Olney, the collector of taxes in Providence, Rhode Island, considered the exact duty to be leveled on imported coffee beans.

Then came another piece of business: an urgent note from Mrs. Reynolds that revealed her husband was threatening to reveal everything to Hamilton's wife.

Dear Sir

I have not tim to tell you the cause of my present troubles only that Mr. has rote to you this morning and I know not wether you have got the letter or not and he has swore that If you do not answer It or If he dose not se or hear from you to day he will write Mrs. Hamilton he has just Gone oute and I am a Lone I think you had better come here one moment that you May know the Cause then you will the better know how to act Oh my God I feel more for you than myself and wish I had never been born to give you so mutch unhappisness do not rite to him no not a Line but come here soon do not send or leave any thing in his power

Maria

The letter was a thicket of contradictions—deploring her husband's threats and endorsing them; pitying Hamilton and threatening him; wanting him and giving him all the more reason to stay away. But that was the least of it. What would come of this nightmare? By then, her husband's note had likely already arrived, giving Hamilton a first look at the hell that awaited him. If Maria's was all quivering anxiety, James's was one massive imposition, as if the man himself had burst into Hamilton's office and started shouting: "I am very sorry to find out that I have been so Cruelly treated by a person that I took to be my best friend instead of that my greatest Enimy."

And, to squeeze Hamilton a little more, he explained how he'd found out, although surely he'd known from the beginning. He'd come home to find his wife crying over a letter from Hamilton. His wife had written one back. He'd copied it surreptitiously and then secretly followed hers on its journey to Hamilton's door. Then came the confrontation and her tearfully revealing "everything."

Reynolds rounded on the treasury secretary. "And there Sir you took advantage a poor Broken harted woman. instead of being a friend, you have acted the part of the most Cruelist man in existance, you have made a whole family miserable." Lest Hamilton miss the point, he added in his next letter, "it shant by onely one family that's miserable."

As if to show Hamilton that he was dealing with a lunatic—surely a terrifying prospect for a paragon of reason—he goes on to make clear *his* family has been the one to suffer, and he is now determined to make everything worse.

"I am Robbed of all happiness in this world I am determed to leve [Maria] and take my daughter with me that She shant see her poor mother."

With some sangfroid, Hamilton invited Reynolds to come see him. When Reynolds arrived at Hamilton's Treasury office, Hamilton asked him what evidence he had of any affair. Reynolds produced none, although surely they both knew the truth of the matter, just as they both knew that the only question was the price at which it was to be resolved. Hamilton's impatience mounting, it took several more meetings, one at the George Tavern, for Reynolds to settle on the sum. For one thousand dollars, Reynolds would leave town with his daughter and go "where my Friend Shant here from me." For a secretary of the treasury who made only thirty-five hundred dollars a year, a thousand dollars was a substantial sum. Still, it was cheaper than the alternative. "To prevent an explosion," Hamilton agreed to pay it in two installments and put a "plaister on his wounded honor."

Hamilton was determined to have nothing further to do with Mrs. Reynolds. But then James wrote again a few weeks later. His wife, he wrote, "wish to see you. And for My own happiness and hers. I have not the Least

Objections to your Calling, as a friend to Boath of us." But he let Hamilton know that he would appreciate anything he had to "offer" for this pleasure.

Hamilton stayed away, and continued to, even as the entreaties mounted. Maria missed him, she was sleepless, she was agonizingly sick, sure to die, and if not from illness, by her own hand.

Finally, in March of 1792, Hamilton could stay away no longer, and he went to Mrs. Reynolds. The next morning, Mr. Reynolds wrote to express his horror at what Hamilton had done with his wife. At his request, Hamilton offered a check for ninety dollars. When good sense prevailed, and Hamilton shied away again, Mrs. Reynolds, her spelling suddenly improved, wailed that "all consolation is shut against me." That visit cost forty-five dollars, the next thirty.

Whenever his ardor ebbed, she would send him a wailing love note, her words a cacophony of high emotion and bad spelling: "I shal be miserable till I se you and if my dear freend has the Least Esteeme for the unhappy Maria whos greateest fault Is Loveing him he will come as soon as he shall get this and till that time My breast will be the seate of pain and woe adieu."

Then, a practical note. "P. S. If you cannot come this Evening to stay just come only for one moment as I shal be Lone."

And on it went: Hamilton's resistance provoked Maria's entreaties, which led to his acquiescence, James Reynolds's outrage, and Hamilton's payment. The carnival continued all through the fall of that year, and then bad became a lot worse when Jacob Clingman joined the Reynolds conspiracy. If Reynolds had been a worry, Clingman was a fright. For he was not only disreputable; he was politically connected, having been a clerk of Frederick A.C. Muhlenberg, a Pennsylvania congressman who had served as the first Speaker of the House. More audacious than the Reynoldses, but no more competent, Clingman persuaded Reynolds to join him in a hopeless scheme to pass themselves off as the executors of the estate of a Revolutionary War soldier named Ephraim Goodenough in order to divert its funds to their own account. That plot was soon discovered and the culprits remanded to jail. Clingman played his Muhlenberg connection to get out that very afternoon, but Reynolds was left to rot, much of the time spent deciding how to play the only card he had: "disclosures injurious to the head of a Department." Curiously, he did not have Hamilton in mind, but another unnamed source of privileged information in the department. When the claims came to the attention of Oliver Wolcott Jr., Hamilton's subordinate at Treasury, he arranged for Reynolds's release in exchange for his testimony.

The charges against Clingman were still pending, and, to save himself, Clingman offered up Hamilton to Muhlenberg, as someone he might "injure, very substantially." The prospect of bringing down the genius behind the Washington administration, the titular head of the Federalist Party, and the source of all the economic plans—it was irresistible, and Muhlenberg hurried the news to James Monroe. After Madison, he was the third most powerful Republican, and a tall but generally uninspiring Virginian, who drew his power from his association with the two more powerful Republicans, starting with Jefferson. Muhlenberg then shared the word with Representative Abraham Venable, a rare Virginian of the Federalist persuasion, to make any inquiry seem less of a partisan inquisition than it was. Monroe and Venable immediately had a talk with Clingman. "He affirmed he had a person in high office in his power, and has had a long time past," Monroe and Venable later reported. "That [Hamilton] had written to him in terms so abusive that no person should have submitted to it, but that he dared not to resent it." Reynolds said his information would cause the secretary to "hang."

The Virginians went to see Mrs. Reynolds, the beauty at the center of all the drama. She mentioned receiving many letters from Hamilton but did not offer them. The gentlemen assured Mrs. Reynolds that Hamilton's reputation for probity was "immaculate." She must have smiled as she replied that she "rather doubted it."

With that, the two Virginians collected Muhlenberg to see Hamilton and discuss an "improper pecuniary connection" between Hamilton and Reynolds. The thought of two powerful members of the Republican Party coming to discuss a matter that had every possibility of bringing Hamilton's career crashing down, and bringing down many of the structures he had built for the country—it must have filled Hamilton with dread. The three men laid out what they knew, and then, at Hamilton's request, agreed to meet again in the privacy of Hamilton's house that evening.

There, Hamilton confessed to what he later termed "an indelicate amour" and to paying blackmail to keep it quiet. That was the full extent of his connection to James Reynolds. With that, Hamilton hoped to put the entire matter to rest. As gentlemen, the three politicians were inclined to take his word for it. Besides, they had the documents to back it up. Still, not everyone believed they should be so trusting, as the secrets were already leaking out. "Was I with you," Hamilton's war compatriot and Burr's college friend "Light-Horse Harry" Lee wrote him, "I would talk an hour with doors bolted & windows shut, as my heart is much affected by rumor I have heard." Two of the three "gentlemen" against him, after all, were his "sworn political opponents," one of them, Monroe, a close ally of Jefferson; another conspirator was Hamilton's aggrieved mistress; and the last two utter scoundrels.

THIRTY-THREE

Louis Capet Has Lost His Caput

BY THEN, HAMILTON was being attacked headlong by House Republicans convinced that something was amiss in his handling of the large sums that the government had borrowed from Europe to pay back a loan to his new Bank of the United States. While Jeffersonians feared this money had been diverted from the nation's rightful payments to France, other critics contended that Hamilton had used it to feed the speculative frenzy. Jefferson and Madison had more insidious accusations, stemming from the whispers they'd picked up about the Reynolds affair. To nail him, the incendiary Virginia congressman William Branch Giles had insisted that Hamilton address five resolutions, each one requiring a massive detailing of international accounts, and he assigned a two-month deadline, hoping that any failure or delay would indicate guilt. Hamilton delivered the information two weeks early and festooned it with countless tables and figures. That caused Giles to pause but not to stop. He went forward with nine censure motions against Hamilton, most of them drawn from a draft of Jefferson's, but the Federalist-heavy House voted them down. Hamilton emerged victorious, but the battle had taken its toll, leaving him sleepless, skittish, irritable, barely able to distinguish between his enemies, his friends, and phantoms who might be either, and equally likely to lash out at any of the three.

※

THE MESSAGES BETWEEN the Old World and the New were not sent by just the Americans. The French sent missives, too, and in August of 1792 they were dipped in blood, as the revolution that had seemed a glorious extension of the American one took a dark turn. Mobs stormed the royal palace in the Tuileries, captured Louis XVI, and threw him in prison. The new kings, the sadistic Robespierre and Marat, soon set up a guillotine nearby to slice off the heads of more than a thousand Parisians, two hundred of them priests. Hearing the news, the Jeffersonians at first endorsed the mass executions as a necessary cleansing. Then, on January 21, 1793, the king was himself guillotined, his head stuffed in a basket between his lifeless legs, while the revolutionaries howled with delight. With that, the revolutionaries were off on a murder spree throughout the country. Among thousands of others, the Marquis de Lafayette's troops abandoned him, and he was hunted down and imprisoned. Although the revolutionaries had conferred honorary citizenship on the treasury secretary they mistakenly called "Jean Hamilton," the recipient was horrified by the turn of events—"a state of things the most cruel, sanguinary, and violent that ever stained the annals of mankind." At first, the chastened Jeffersonians simply refused to believe the newspaper accounts and persisted in regarding the revolution as "wonderful in its progress and . . . stupendous in its consequences," as Madison put it. And some made light of it. "Louis Capet," as the dethroned king was termed, "has lost his Caput," joked Freneau's *Gazette*. By 1794, the guillotine at Lyon was thought too deliberate a tool for slaughter, and hundreds were laid waste by cannon fire. At Nantes, two thousand people were loaded onto barges, tied together, taken to the middle of the Loire, and drowned. "Danton, Robespierre, Marat, and co[mpany] are furies," Adams growled. "Dragon's teeth have been sown in France and come up monsters." Jefferson was blasé. "The liberty of the whole earth was depending on the issue of the contest, and was ever such a prize won with so little innocent blood?" But the playing out of the ideological dispute internationally both expanded it and contracted it, too. Like the light from a lantern show, the American tussle between its two nascent parties was projected out into the world, and colored the view, so that all of France became Jeffersonian, and all of England Hamiltonian, almost as if those two countries had been annexed. "There are in the U.S. some characters of opposite principles," Jefferson put it, "all of them hostile to France and looking to England as the staff of their hope." And vice versa, of course. But the projection went the other way across the Atlantic, too, so that every tremor from overseas reverberated through the American political landscape, either confirming or undermining the core prejudices of either party.

The fervid revolutionary spirit paid a visit in April of 1793, when France delivered itself of a new French minister to the United States. Short but florid, he was Edmond-Charles Genet, but, in deference to the égalité of the French Revolution, he was known simply as Citizen Genet. Just thirty, he was stylish and erudite, a friend to the murdered king, and exquisitely educated. He spoke seven languages and had been fluent in ancient Greek since age six. He might have been exactly to Hamilton's sophisticated tastes, except that Genet possessed a French snobbery that rose off of him like perfume. (He left his card when paying visits to workingmen.) He may have carried with it the musk of Hamilton's bête noire, Jefferson. Beyond the stated mission of seeking a full payoff of the American war debt of 5.6 million dollars, Genet seemed bent on inflaming the differences between the emergent parties by offering an example of French democracy to counter the English aristocracy, and so drew to him a flock of Republican politicians, including Burr, who dined with him at Richmond Hill. More covertly, Genet had in his portfolio ambitions to upset Washington's careful neutrality in France's war with Britain by brazenly rounding up "privateers"—commercial fishing ships—and setting them loose to capture British merchant ships; to rouse the citizens of the adjoining foreign territories of Florida, Louisiana, and Canada to a revolution of their own; to recruit spies to infiltrate Britain; to rouse the throngs of adoring Francophiles; and to create domestic Republican versions of the rabid French political societies fueling the revolution, whose members passed around "liberty caps" and addressed each other as "Citizen." Burr found the multipronged nature of the assault intriguing, and he was not put off by the light air of menace that hung about it. Genet would prove an inspiration, reinforcing the Frenchness that had been a feature of Burr's character since he first encountered Rousseau: the multileveled approach to any endeavor, of which only the top was visible; and his lusty demagoguery, all of which explains why so many Burrites were early backers of the New York Demo-

In 1795, well into George Washington's administration, Rembrandt Peale depicted a president worn by the cares of war and government, to say nothing of his famously troublesome teeth. Little wonder Washington initially wished to limit his presidential tenure to two years.

1

Thomas Jefferson is shown here in 1791, when he was tangling with Hamilton as the other great power in Washington's cabinet. When Hamilton emerged the clear winner, Jefferson retreated into temporary retirement.

2

In this portrait done long after the fact, the boyish Hamilton idles in full military dress during the New Jersey campaign, appearing very much the "mere stripling" that one observer called him.

3

4

An idealized portrait of Hamilton, whose features were actually more rounded. As in virtually all of his portraits, his eyes do not meet the viewer but gaze out heroically into the distance, as if into the future. After this painting was completed, he would live only a few months more.

Painted by Gilbert Stuart when Burr was in his late thirties, this portrait shows Burr's seductive side, as his luminous eyes emerge from the darkness.

5

Done in stark profile, seemingly indifferent to the viewer, Burr is a year into his vice presidency at forty-six, already a pariah in the Jefferson administration, and two years from the duel. His portraitist John Vanderlyn was a recipient of Burr's patronage at Richmond Hill and would later be Burr's sole support when, in his European exile, the former vice president arrived destitute in Paris.

6

At thirty, the aristocratic Elizabeth Schuyler Hamilton—Betsey to her husband—appears in all her finery. Yet she still retains a humble affect in this portrait, done in a debtors' prison as a favor to the bankrupt Ralph Earl.

This John Vanderlyn portrait of Burr's daughter, Theodosia, in 1802 conveys all her brilliance and mystery. Left-facing to her father's right-facing portrait, it was meant as a companion piece. Burr much preferred it to the one done by Gilbert Stuart several years before. That one, he said, made her look "like a love-sick milkmaid."

Believers throughout the colonies must have been awed by the penetrating gaze of Burr's grandfather, the near divinity Rev. Jonathan Edwards.

This vision of Burr's lush Richmond Hill estate gives it a jungle aspect that is fitting for a place so thick with intrigue.

Hamilton's the Grange in present-day Harlem was well removed from the bustling city. Named for the Scottish castle he'd always claimed for his lineage, it evokes the plantation style of Nevis and Saint Croix, the islands of his childhood.

12

13

Gilbert Stuart captures the Machiavellian side of Constitution author, fourth president, and perpetual Hamilton antagonist James Madison. The forceful concentration suggests a man about to strike.

The lofty head set against a sunset glow implies a heroic view of James Monroe that Hamilton did not share. He agreed with Burr on one thing: that the future president was a total bore.

14

THE PROVIDENTIAL DETECTION

15

John Adams's attitude toward Hamilton moved from admiration to burning hatred. But in this physionotrace, all the rage among the political set, the cantankerous second president seems to be turning away from such irritations.

After losing the epic presidential election of 1800, the Federalists feared that Jefferson would abolish the Constitution. Here a Federalist eagle keeps the treacherous Republican from burning the sacred parchment as God looks on.

16

17

The highly unreliable Burr coconspirator General James Wilkinson was the highest-ranking officer in the nation, and his resplendent uniform reveals he was very proud of that fact.

Harman Blennerhassett was Burr's primary backer in his quixotic campaign to seize half of America for his private empire. To go by this miniature, the dainty, effete Blennerhassett seems destined to be taken advantage of.

18

This cartoon provides satiric commentary on the two-man brawl between a cane-wielding Roger Griswold, Federalist, and fire-tongs-swinging Matthew Lyon, Republican, on the floor of the House of Representatives. A matter of honor and politics, the fracas prefigured the duel at Weehawken.

James Van Dyck in 1834 captured the wry detachment of Burr in his final years, when his passion for adventure was finally spent and he could be amused by the world and no longer try to possess it.

19

ʘᴼ ᴛᴴᴱ ᴿᴱᴹᴼᴿᴾ ᴼᴵᴿ
· ALEXANDER HAMILTON.
The CORPORATION of TRINITY CHURCH Has erected this
ᴹ ᴼ ᴺ ᵁ ᴹ ᴱ ᴺ ᵀ
In Testimony of their Respect
FOR
The PATRIOT of incorruptible INTEGRITY.
The SOLDIER of approved VALOUR.
The STATESMAN of consummate WISDOM:
Whose TALENTS and VIRTUES will be admired
by
Grateful Posterity.
Long after this MARBLE shall have mouldered into
DUST.
He died July 12.ᵗʰ 1804. Aged 47.

20

Hamilton's grave outside Trinity Church. When his coffin was brought there by carriage through the streets of lower Manhattan, thousands of mourners from every class trailed behind, and every shop in the city was closed in tribute.

cratic Society, which took off from the French revolutionary equivalent so gloriously evoked by Citizen Genet.

The Genet invasion had its carnival aspects, but Hamilton saw it as agitprop that was invigorating Republicans who treated Genet like the Second Coming, spurring them to rapture. As one Federalist wrote, "very few body parts, if any, of the Citizen's body, escaped a salute." To the Federalists, Genet's followers were a mob, and who knew what horrors they might unleash in the name of politics. Adams rued the "terrorism" Genet inspired, recalling how "ten thousand people in the streets of Philadelphia, day after day, threatened to drag Washington out of his house and affect a revolution in the government."

Eventually hubris caught up with him. Genet proclaimed that he'd follow the will of the people and, on his own authority, commandeer American ports to rig French ships for war with Britain. Hamilton was appalled at the lèse-majesté, and even Jefferson acknowledged that he had gone too far. Washington, already outraged at the incessant Republican claims that he was a secret monarchist, was in no mood to compromise his neutrality proclamation to aid France. By now, the political discord in his cabinet on the topic had reached a nearly comical extreme, with Washington listening serenely to Hamilton's endless lectures about the Genet hazard, his little hands slicing the air, while the taciturn Jefferson fumed in his chair. In the last days of the *National Gazette*, Freneau chipped in a mock dirge for a guillotined Washington; that one left the president frothing at all the abuse he had suffered to serve his nation. "*By God* he had rather be in his grave than in his present situation," Jefferson recalled his grousing. "He had rather be on his farm than to be made *emperor of the world*." But that didn't keep Jefferson from assailing Hamilton as a "monocrat" and "Angloman," adding he was not just for a monarchy, but "for a monarchy bottomed on corruption." To the Federalists, the Republicans were all radical Jacobins, the bloodthirsty rabble behind the Reign of Terror. A vicious hater, Hamilton eviscerated Jefferson more subtly, under the pseudonyms of Catullus and the Scourge, among others. "Cautious and shy," Hamilton called Jefferson, "wrapped up in impenetrable silence and mystery, [Jefferson] reserves his abhorrence for the arcana of a certain snug sanctuary where seated on his pivot chair, and involved in all the obscurity of political mystery and deception ... he circulates his poison thro' the medium of the *National Gazette.*"

The enmity didn't end there. The two men attracted adherents like New Yorkers Rufus King and John Jay for Hamilton, and Virginians Madison and Monroe for Jefferson, and then emboldened them to spread the word to create a faction, or band of activists; they in turn accrued that broader army of believers that the Constitution preferred to overlook and Washington abhorred: parties. Two of them. Both so long evolving—a strain traced back to *Rutgers v. Waddington*—and then pushing forward through all the great political dilemmas until this one, of France versus England, which finally broke the country in two, making the next election, of 1796, the first to be settled by party, an act that split America as profoundly as the Mississippi River did the continent.

In the end, Genet simply disappeared. He gave up his ministerial post and became an American citizen. By now, he had married Cornelia Clinton, the free-spirited daughter of the governor, a Genet patron, and the couple vanished into the countryside of upstate New York.

With that, Jefferson declared that, worn out by his battles with Hamilton, he'd had enough of public life, at least for now, and wished to return to Monticello. As he wrote to Angelica Church, still a confidante: He wanted only "to be liberated from the hated occupations of politics, and to remain in the bosom of my family, my farm, and my books." He delivered a letter of resignation to Washington, who accepted it with little regret. A year or two later, when he realized the depth of Jefferson's involvement in the political intrigues bedeviling his administration, Washington restricted his correspondence to strained platitudes about the farming life until the letters stopped coming altogether three years before he died.

THIRTY-FOUR

The Best Woman and Finest Lady
I Have Ever Known

As HIS LAW practice had previously, Burr's political career now kept him from Theodosia and the children for long stretches of time. Theodosia had never been well, but her health started to deteriorate sharply once he joined the Senate. Perhaps it was merely coincidence, but it might have been the natural pain of separation, compounded by Burr's frustration with an invalid wife. "What can have exhausted or disturbed you so much?" he led off a tart letter on December 27, 1791. "You might surely have given some hint of the cause. If I had, before I left for New-York, sufficiently reflected on the subject, I would never have consented to this absurd and irrational mode of life." Living apart from her, he means. "If you will come with Mr. Monroe, I will see you to New-York again; and if you have a particular aversion to the city of Philadelphia, you shall stay a day or two at Dr. Edwards's, ten miles from town." It was that night that Burr succumbed to a migraine, and sat with his feet in warm water, his head wrapped in cloths drenched with vinegar. Two months later, he made clear he could not return to her in New York anytime soon. "It will not do for me at present to leave this place," he wrote. "I shall therefore expect you here." That "therefore" must have stung, especially when followed by this: "But the tenor of your last induces me to think that you intend a very short visit."

Theodosia had visited him in Philadelphia only once, when, in the spring of 1793, her health, always a worry, went into a steep decline, and she never left New York after that. By then, Burr, always acquisitive for real estate, had finally bought his dream house, the fine Richmond Hill estate where he'd first met Washington and briefly served as his aide-de-camp before he made an inglorious exit that would damage the relationship between the two men forever. This marked Burr's triumphant return, a trumpet fanfare with a note or two of spite in the bass register. After the war, the estate was owned by John Adams while he was the vice president. "Grand and sublime," Abigail Adams had proclaimed it. With its fine views of the "noble Hudson," she exulted, the estate afforded "a situation where the hand of nature has so lavishly displayed her beauties that she has left scarcely anything for her handmaiden, art, to perform." This earthly paradise had become available when the capital moved to Philadelphia in 1790, taking the Adamses with it. Perfect as the Adamses had found the grounds, Burr immediately set to work improving them, stopping up a creek to produce an ornamental pool by the main gate, and adding gardens seemingly everywhere.

Inside the house, the main entrance opened to two side rooms as well as the main hall; the upstairs dining room featured broad Venetian windows that looked out to that "noble Hudson" and the spreading New Jersey farmland beyond. He furnished the public rooms with two capriole sofas, a pair of inlaid card tables, an "Elegant Turkey Carpet" and a "carpet of Blue Bays," several reading tables, a dozen mahogany chairs, and a "Dutch liquor case." He filled the library with crates of his books and contracted for more from a London bookseller he trusted to select for him the finest offerings from English publishers. A place of such splendor would not have been complete without at least a few European dignitaries to stock it, and Burr had attracted the controversial diplomat Talleyrand and Jérôme Bonaparte, brother of the future emperor, as well as American nobility such as Jefferson and Madison on their New York sojourns and natives like Edward Livingston and Hamilton, who must have taken its measure for his own country estate, the Grange, which would have many of the same features. If the guests stayed over, they had the choice of the "White Room," "Blue Room," or "Little Bedroom West."

It all left Burr questing for more, but, without him, wife Theodosia must have longed for less. The sole parent of her own five, and the mother of her Burr namesake, Theodosia still had to oversee the mansion and farm, with more than a dozen slaves and paid employees, not to mention the various teachers providing young Theodosia's extensive education. For all that, as Theodosia's agonies worsened, it is doubtful she was able to rouse herself very often from the wide bed in the room Burr rarely shared with her, overlooking the front porch, to the pool. Distracted by her worsening health, his wife was no longer the intellectual helpmeet she had once been, although she still tried to pitch in with political advice, written, as requested, to him in code, and she must have noticed that, after he purchased this dream house, he didn't move in, but largely remained with the government in Philadelphia. And however many letters she sent to him in Philadelphia, fewer came back.

In early 1793, his letters took on a valedictory quality, as he fondly recalled, "It was a knowledge of your mind which first inspired me with a respect for that of your sex." Her service to him, he told her, was to elevate that status of women in his mind, thus inspiring him to undertake the campaign to educate the other Theodosia, who would soon supplant the original. "I confess, that the ideas you have often heard me express in favour of female intellectual powers are founded on what I have imagined, more than what I have seen, except in you." With that he mused yet again about Mary Wollstonecraft, the philosophical wellspring for these ideas, threw in some words of enthusiasm for their daughter, and concluded that for the foreseeable future, his letters to his wife would have to be "mere notes." Aside from some medical advice passed on from Dr. Rush at the very end of the year, that is the last letter to Theodosia saved by Davis for his collection that doesn't pertain to her condition. There are dozens to *young* Theo, though, all of them cheerful, chatty, and long.

Shortly after Burr had entered the Senate, he let his daughter know he'd placed her name, which he abbreviated to "T.B. Burr," as if she were a dignitary, on a list of those whose letters were to be answered first, up with "some of the most eminent persons in the United States." Shortly before Christmas in 1793, when her mother's health was in danger, Burr wrote to his ten-year-old daughter like a seducer: "Every hour of your day is interesting to me. What would I not give to know even your most trifling actions and amusements?"

Burr had sent the details of his wife's condition to Dr. Benjamin Rush, the Republican physician who would soon run afoul of Hamilton after the outbreak of yellow fever. It amounted to a hellish barrage of symptoms. Yet Burr relates them with such dry medical specificity, he seems almost indifferent, and it is easy to forget the patient is his wife. Or is this Burr's way, after all those deaths at age two, of distancing himself from the inevitable?

"In five or six months past," he wrote, "she has been afflicted with an almost constant choke [choking]; which is supposed to be Nephritic, & which indeed assumes all the appearances of a nephritic complaint—at Intervals of three or four weeks she has returns of Nausea and Vomiting, which have sometimes lasted six & eight Days & with such Violence as to threaten life—when these abate, the Cholic, from which she is never wholly free, returns with greater severity."* The various medical prescriptions she'd received had only brought on waves of nausea, and the dietary changes had been no help at all. "She eats with impunity whatever appetite or whim suggests—fruits, Vegetable, fresh or Salted Meats," he revealed. "Her pulse holds at about 100, although she suffers frequent chills and flushes of heat." What would the doctor, with his "inventive Mind," recommend?

A month or two later Rush arrived one evening at Burr's rooms to offer an unexpected suggestion: a small amount of hemlock. "A dose of one tenth of a grain," he recommended. "Increase as you may find you can bear it," Burr told his wife, "that it has the narcotic powers of opium, superadded to other qualities." Indeed, hemlock—a foul-smelling juice emitted from the lacy leaves of poison hemlock, a flowering plant native to the Mediterranean—can be a sedative and antispasmodic, rather like nicotine, and it was thought possibly to be helpful in tiny doses for a patient in constant pain like Theodosia. Those benefits were known to the Greeks. But the Greeks also knew, just as the Burrs must have known, that hemlock in a larger dose could be a lethal poison, one that had most famously been used to execute Socrates. Plato detailed how, after taking the poison, Socra-

---

* If, by "nephritic," he means renal, referring to some kidney failure, he is probably mistaken, as the best modern guess is that Theodosia suffered from stomach cancer, which can deliver severe abdominal pain, weight loss, and a bloody stool. It was out of the reach of eighteenth-century medicine.

tes calmly felt a paralyzing "chill" rise from his feet to his legs and ever so slowly into his torso, where it stopped his lungs. The question was, how much hemlock was too much?

At the end of 1793, Burr considered resigning to go home to his wife, but Theodosia wouldn't hear of it. As their young daughter, Theodosia, reported in January: "Ma begs you will omit the thoughts of leaving Congress." A heavy message, but Burr replied by correcting his daughter's diction. "'Omit' is improperly used here," he lectured her. "You mean 'abandon, relinquish, renounce, or abjure the thoughts/ etc.' Your mamma, Mr. Leslie, or your dictionary (Johnson's folio) will teach you the force of this observation. The last of these words would have been too strong for the occasion."

Burr inched closer to a mortal dose that winter, for the hemlock did not yield any improvement through December and into January; Rush recommended more, and Burr went along. No letters from this period survive, so it is difficult to determine the exact medical consequences, but hemlock was no remedy. In desperation, Burr tried molasses and milk, milk punch, straight milk, port wine, sweet oil, chocolate, and "bark," or quinine. Also, another highly dubious substance: mercury, which can kill by shutting down the central nervous system, or wreak a constellation of impairments—clouded thinking, impaired memory, poor balance, and queer tingling sensations throughout the body. It is no cure for anything. It was not widely known that mercury was poisonous, but there were suspicions, and Burr had picked up on them. He counseled "the most vigilant caution," but he did not veto it.

Nor did he go home to oversee the treatment. Rather, determined to salvage his political career after his embarrassment in 1792, he focused his efforts on becoming Washington's new minister to France after the departure of Gouverneur Morris, although that was certainly not a position designed for a man with an ailing wife. A committee headed by Jefferson and Madison promoted him to the president, but Washington demurred, declaring with a directness that smacked of Hamilton that he could never appoint "any person . . . in whose integrity he had not confidence." Instead, Washington picked James Monroe, even though he was a leader of the opposition.

The rejection of Burr left his ambitious friend Theodore Sedgwick mystified. "Wherefore was it that they preferred Monroe to him?" he wondered to their mutual friend Jonathan Dayton, referring to Washington and his advisers, Hamilton foremost among them. "Had they more confidence in Monroe's talent? They are not so stupid. In his integrity? no." Then Sedgwick landed on it. "They doubtless respect Burr's talents, but they dread his independence of *them*. They know, in short, he is not one of them, and of course they will never support but always effect to support him." Then again, Burr might do the same toward *them*.

Burr remained in Philadelphia as his wife's life ebbed. He drew the young Theodosia into the adult world, complex and freighted as it was, to take his wife's place. He tutored her in the mysterious potions he'd assigned her mother. "Dr. Rush thinks that bark would not be amiss," he wrote her, "but may be beneficial if the stomach does not rebuke it, which must be constantly the first object of attention. . . . Be able, upon my arrival, to tell the difference between an infusion and decoction; and the history, the virtues, and the botanical or medical name of the bark." He'd already quizzed her on the properties of mercury and praised her "disquisition" on that delicate subject as "ingenious and prettily told." She seems to have been unaware that lethality was one of its properties.

On Monday, May 19, 1794, Burr was relieved to get a letter from his daughter letting him know that her mother was "easier" and more comfortable than she had been in weeks. Then, an hour later, he received an overnight "express" from an exhausted post rider who had borne it from New York: His wife had died the day before. Burr's immediate reaction is not recorded. Toward the end of his life, he said, "her death dealt me more pain than all sorrows combined." As always with Burr, it is hard to know. He sent a letter to his uncle Pierpont Edwards a few days later, assuring him there was no need to grieve. "So sudden & unexpected was her death that no immediate Danger was apprehended until the Morning that she was relieved from all earthly cares." An oddly unaffecting way to put it. "She . . . sank calmly and without pain into her last sleep." He may have ascribed his true feelings to the young Theodosia. "My little daughter though much afflicted and distressed," he wrote a friend, "bears the stroke with more reason and firmness than could have been expected for her years." With her father in Philadelphia, it fell to Theodosia to oversee the preparation of her mother's body for burial. Theodosia Burr was laid to rest in one of Trinity Church's burial grounds, but it is not known just where— or whether her husband attended the ceremony. Shortly before he died many years later, he called her "the best woman and finest lady I have ever known."

But by then she'd had many competitors. If he hadn't taken other women by the time of his wife's death, he had certainly toyed with them, flirtations that became more serious and more numerous once she passed from the scene. To his detractors, the flirtations summed him up as a fickle man who could never commit. But Burr himself believed he was just expressing a natural hunger. It was with delight that he used to tell the story of being caught out by an unnamed lady who'd snuck up on him in his library at Richmond Hill after Theodosia's death. He was buried in a book as usual, probably with his feet up before the fire. The interloper gave him a playful slap on his cheek and asked: "Come, tell me, what little French girl, pray, have you had here?" The woman had smelled a distinctive French scent. Burr didn't furnish the name, but, in Parton's telling, he "admitted the fact," whereupon the lady "burst into loud laughter"—and Burr took no less pleasure in being discovered.

THIRTY-FIVE

Root Out the Distempered and Noisome *Weed*

E XHAUSTED BY POLITICS and intrigue, much of it of his own making, Hamilton told President Washington in December of 1794 that he planned to leave the government by the end of January. For someone so reserved, Washington's response overflowed with fatherly appreciation and pride. "In every relationship which you have borne to me, I have found that my confidence in your talents, exertions and integrity has been well placed." And more than anyone, he spoke from experience. "I the more freely render this testimony of my approbation, because I speak from opportunities of information wch cannot deceive me, and which furnish satisfactory proof of your title to public regard." He concluded with the wish that "your happiness will attend you in your retirement," and, unusually for him, closed by offering his "sincere esteem, regard and friendship."

It had been a remarkable run. Just forty, Hamilton had taken an insolvent confederacy and turned it into a dynamic union that would dominate the world. But it was time for him to go. When he'd accompanied Washington to put down the Whiskey Rebellion—a mob of five hundred, infuriated by taxes Hamilton had imposed on hard liquor—Hamilton himself had become the target of the rebels' wrath as much as his tax. It didn't help that the protests had been stoked by the Genet-inspired political societies that were a cauldron of Hamilton-hating Republicanism. Betsey had miscarried during the fighting, reminding him of the stresses of his activities on her and of the call of home. In January, he would lay out a final refinement on his epic *Report on the Public Credit* that would forever extinguish the national debt in thirty years. Although the Giles investigation was behind him, he knew the Republicans would continue to impugn his service. And he doubted the explosive Reynolds secrets would hold.

His final report offering a refinement to the bill of assumption was like everything else of his. It was designed not just to seize the objective, but to overwhelm it. It won congressional approval swiftly, delayed only by an objection from an unexpected quarter, as Aaron Burr roused himself to offer an amendment challenging one small aspect of the finance package. His motion didn't pass, but it irritated Hamilton to have Burr, of all people, crowd into view. *Hamilton* was the one true hero, not Burr. As he wrote to his ally Rufus King:

> To see the character of the Government and the country so sported
> with, exposed to so indelible a blot puts my heart to the Torture.
> Am I then more of an American than those who drew their first breath
> on American Ground? Or What is it that thus torments me at a
> circumstance so calmly viewed by almost every body else? Am I a fool—
> a Romantic quixot—Or is there a constitutional defect in the
> American Mind? Were it not for yourself and a few others, I . . . would
> say . . . there is something in our climate which belittles every Animal
> human or brute.
>
> I conjure you, my friend, Make a vigorous stand for the honor of
> your Country. Rouse all the energies of your mind, and measure swords
> in the Senate with the great Slayer of public faith—the hacknied
> Veteran *in the violation of public engagements. Prevent him if possible
> from triumphing a second time over the prostrate credit and injured
> interests of his country. Unmask his false and horrid hypotheses.
> Witness the 40 for 1 scheme a most unskilful measure, to say the best of
> it. Display the immense difference between an able statesman and the
> Man of subtilties. Root out the distempered and noisome* weed *which
> is attempted to be planted in our political garden—to choak and
> wither in its infancy the fair plant of public credit.
>
> I disclose to you without reserve the state of my mind. It is
> discontented and gloomy in the extreme.

Yes, indeed his mind is, and one could think of more adjectives, too. The letter reveals a man in such pain he will lash out at anyone. In his discontent, Hamilton seems to have made a rare but revealing mistake, conflating Burr with Connecticut senator Oliver Ellsworth, another politician-aristocrat; Ellsworth, not Burr, had been behind the "40 for 1 scheme"—the exchange rate for the conversion of inflated Continental currency. The letter's anger is striking, even for Hamilton, given that Burr is offering only a minor amendment to his bill, not threatening to reject it. But Hamilton's identification with his assumption bill was so extreme, and his frustrations with politics so vast, that a dart at his bill was an arrow at him. Nonetheless, Hamilton had plenty of fight left, and to the death he would defend America from its (and his) most dire enemy.

The view from Weehawken by the British landscape artist William Henry Bartlett in 1840. By then, it had become just another pastoral scene, albeit one with a ghoulish cast. A fourteen-foot marble monument to Hamilton had been erected here in 1806 but was soon entirely chipped away by souvenir hunters, to be replaced by a pair of rough stones engraved with the names of the two duelists and placed where each stood and fired—and one fell.

Part Three

TO THE DEATH

THIRTY-SIX

To Fight the *Whole Detestable Faction*

When Hamilton returned to New York that January, he was the hero of the city. The chamber of commerce put on a vast dinner for two hundred to honor him, and the evening culminated in nine rousing cheers for Hamilton—compared to just three for Washington and Adams. Later, Mayor Richard Varick awarded him the "freedom of the city," the highest honor he could bestow.

Hamilton settled his family in temporary lodgings before venturing north to the splendid Schuyler manse overlooking the Hudson through June. Then, after his years on a tight thirty-five-hundred-dollar salary as treasury secretary, Hamilton had to get to work. "I am not worth exceeding five hundred dollars in the world," he declared. Indeed, he had been relying on friends like Troup for small loans to stay afloat. As the former treasury secretary, he had no shortage of offers for his legal services, but he knew to be cautious. He declined Troup's offer to get in on some vast tracts of land in the newly opened Northwest Territory, since the deal originated with the vivacious, English-born Charles Williamson at a time when foreigners were still forbidden to purchase real estate under New York's Alien Act. He was more receptive to the London merchant banking house Bird, Savage, and Bird, which wrote to "beg leave to offer you our best services in whatever future walk of life you may fix on." He did help his brother-in-law Church with some of his land speculations in Pennsylvania and with more complicated transactions later. Walter Livingston, the son of the chancel-

lor Robert, wanted him to wage lawsuits against the prominent speculator
Alexander Macomb; against his own second cousin, Jonathan Livingston;
and against the bankrupt William Duer, now languishing in the New
Gaol debtors' prison. Hamilton agreed to handle only the matters involving Macomb and the cousin, steering clear of his old Treasury colleague
Duer. He didn't ignore politics. His skeletal friend, John Jay, now the
Supreme Court chief justice, had been laboring over a treaty to avoid war
with Britain, which had been "impressing" American sailors—snatching
them off their ships to toil in the royal fleet—and in the spring of 1795, he
sent back from London the final agreement, then waited for calmer seas for
his own return passage. When the treaty arrived, it was derided as a shame-
ful capitulation, as it did nothing to end the impressment, but granted the
British most-favored-nation status in American markets, among other gifts.
The Republicans saw it as yet more evil from the Anglomen. When Jay
finally sailed into New York Harbor in June, he said he could find his way
home by the light of all the burning effigies of himself.

It fell to Hamilton to defend the treaty. At Washington's request,
Hamilton delivered a lengthy endorsement, trumpeting the treaty's core
virtue that it did indeed avoid a war the United States couldn't possibly
win now, but might later. Unimpressed by that argument, masses of treaty
opponents marched on City Hall, formerly Federal Hall. Anticipating
them, the slender Hamilton climbed onto a stoop across the street and,
when Peter R. Livingston spoke up against the treaty from the balcony
where Washington had taken the oath of office, Hamilton shouted up at
him, interrupting his speech, much to the irritation of the crowd. The protesters then voted down the treaty and marched in noisy triumph down
Wall Street toward Trinity Church, torched a copy of the treaty at the Battery, and surged through the city.

A few hundred opponents stayed behind, and still perched on his
stoop, Hamilton let loose with a fusillade of oratory in favor of the treaty;
his listeners responded only with taunts. Furious, Hamilton demanded
they show him proper respect, but they replied by flinging stones at him,
one of which struck him square in the forehead. The blow stunned him,
but he stayed on his feet, finally crying out: "If you use such knock-down

arguments, I have to retire." Then, his forehead streaming blood, he staggered down the street.

The rest of the night, Hamilton wandered through scenes out of Hieronymus Bosch, as tempers flared like hellfire, everyone lost in a delirium of hate. His head bandaged, he charged back down Wall Street, spoiling for battle, until he spotted the perfidious Commodore James Nicholson, the father-in-law of Albert Gallatin, the Swiss-born Pennsylvania senator who'd been ousted as an alien, despite Burr's efforts. Nicholson had charged that Hamilton, as treasury secretary, had hidden one hundred thousand pounds sterling in a London bank. (He said he had proof, but Hamilton would have to ask him for it in person.) Now Nicholson was jawing with a Federalist backer of the treaty. Hamilton tried to calm the two men, but, seeing it was Hamilton, Nicholson wheeled around to attack him as an "abettor of Tories." When Hamilton let that pass, Nicholson accused him of base cowardice. That stood Hamilton up, and he curtly declared he would settle that charge with pistols. Too busy to make the arrangements now, Hamilton moved on to the house of Edward Livingston, brother of the chancellor, where he found his friend Judge Ogden Hoffman going at it with the treaty-hating Peter Livingston. This time, it was Rufus King who was trying to keep the peace, but Hamilton's nerves were shot, and he shouted that if the Republican argument was to be this personal, he'd "fight the *whole detestable faction* one by one." Livingston's brother Maturin coolly announced that, if so, Hamilton could start with him in a half hour, at a place of his choosing. Hamilton retorted that Maturin Livingston would have to wait. He had another duel to settle first.

The next day, when he considered his dueling obligations, Hamilton dutifully wrote out his will, with Troup to be his executor. But then he came to his senses and crafted an apology for Nicholson to sign that would spare them both. The language was strong enough to give Hamilton satisfaction without inflicting undue humiliation on the commodore. Nicholson furnished his signature, and that was it. As for Maturin Livingston, Hamilton persuaded him to withdraw any aspersions he might have cast on Hamilton's courage, and that one was finished, too.

No longer constrained by the codes of public life, Hamilton was finding freedom hazardous. His forehead healed, but his other wounds never quite did, never dissipated into that haze of the gladly forgotten. Instead, every fresh dispute awakened all the others. The frenzy of the Jay Treaty evoked Burr's theft of Jay's governorship, the abominations of France, the outrages of the Livingstons, the insolent questions about his service in Treasury, the viciousness of political clubs, the general Republican stupidity about matters of finance, the lies about his supposed monarchism, and so much more. Sensitive to challenges to his standing, he saw such challenges everywhere, and he stood ready to avenge any slight with a bullet.

As he had with the Constitution, Hamilton defended the Jay Treaty with a series of tightly reasoned essays, a dozen this time under a variety of pseudonyms that made for a sandstorm of print. His efforts allowed Washington to sign the treaty in mid-August, but he continued to crank out more afterward. Jefferson couldn't help but admire him. "Hamilton is really a colossus to the anti-republican party," he admitted to Madison in some wonderment. "Without numbers, he is an host [meaning a multitude] within himself. . . . We have had only middling performances to oppose him. In truth, when he comes forward, there is nobody but yourself who can meet him." But, of course, Madison could not "meet" Hamilton either, as Jefferson well knew.

With the treaty, Washington's work as president was complete. While there were almost universal pleas for him to stay on for yet a third term, he refused to listen. At sixty-five the great man was spent, his only thoughts of the warming fires and grand vistas of Mount Vernon. No monarch, he couldn't wait to relinquish power. Relying on material that Madison had prepared four years before, Washington made an attempt at a farewell address, and then, unsatisfied, turned the job over to Hamilton, who whittled his draft down to a core statement of Washington's belief in the importance of American neutrality in international affairs. Not only was this a clear endorsement of the Jay Treaty; it was also a not-so-subtle slap at France, which Hamilton continued to regard as a threat to American democracy. He retained much of Washington's style and never acknowledged his contribution until well after Washington's death. In keeping with Washington's disdain for public appearances, the address was never delivered but was printed in *Claypoole's American Daily Advertiser* and then reprinted in papers across the land. One Republican called it "the loathings of a sick mind," but its lessons would stand for generations.

+>-<+

WITH WASHINGTON'S RETIREMENT, the country would have its first genuinely contested election, at a time when the electorate had erupted into a near civil war between the rival parties. While Hamilton was universally acknowledged as the Federalist head, he was far too controversial and ornery a figure to contend for the presidency. If he had ever harbored any ambitions, there was the fear that the Reynolds affair would be raised against him. Without Hamilton, Vice President Adams was the obvious choice to succeed Washington, but Hamilton was not alone in his reservations about his tendency toward theatrical overreactions.

Since Jefferson was plainly the Republican candidate, Hamilton immediately set about trying to annihilate him in twenty-five essays that took on every aspect of his moral history, from his flight as Virginia governor in the face of British troops to his abandonment of his cabinet position, and then went hard at Jefferson for his ideas about race, especially such clinical assertions from *Notes on the State of Virginia* as the contemptuous idea that blacks "secrete less by the kidneys and more by the glands of the skin, which gives them a very strong and disagreeable odor." (Meaning, presumably, that blacks urinate less and sweat more than whites.) This led Jefferson to regard Africans as lower primates—"below man and above the orangutan"—that might "stain the blood" of any offspring a white might have with them. In invoking this line of argument, Hamilton was making an oblique allusion to Jefferson's relationship with Sally Hemings, which Angelica may have gossiped to him about. Jefferson was not the only one to collect embarrassing tidbits on his adversaries.

But who for vice president? In the fall of 1795, Burr made the pilgrimage to Monticello, where Jefferson had been tending his estate for nearly two years. No record survives of the conversation, and neither man was inclined to keep one. Burr might have been a minor player, but he argued that, as a New Yorker uncommitted to either party, he could pry away one or two of the states that were now out of the Virginian's reach. Whatever Jefferson replied, Burr took it to be approval, and in the summer of 1796 he was, it was said, "industrious in his canvas," pressing his case from New Hampshire to South Carolina. He concentrated heavily on his home state but held out hopes for some southern electors all the same. He unleashed his Burrites to jawbone the electors and then to buzz among themselves to tabulate their progress.

On the Federalist side, Hamilton preferred the stable, easygoing Thomas Pinckney, a revolutionary war hero who was governor of South Carolina. Hamilton imagined that, as a southerner, Pinckney might collect enough of the southern vote to edge out Adams. He tried to support Pinckney quietly, leaving no traces. But Burr had an extensive network of spies, and he sniffed out Hamilton's plans.

When Burr let Adams know of Hamilton's duplicity, Abigail was not surprised—Hamilton had always been a "Cassius" to her, ready to slide the knife into her Caesar. But her husband was shocked by the perfidy. To Burr it was perfect: The revelation was sure to pluck Hamilton from Adams's confidence and eject him from any Adams administration.

In the final balloting that December of 1796, Pinckney's bid fell short, but so did Burr's. The South had betrayed him. North Carolina gave him only six to Jefferson's eleven, and Virginia just one to Jefferson's twenty. Hamilton's maneuverings succeeded only in suppressing Adams's total, and enraging him, without depriving him of victory. Adams edged out Jefferson by just three votes but missed gaining the political power that comes from a decisive win. In the bargain, he gained a vice president who would oppose his every move. As for Hamilton, Adams vowed to keep his distance from this "puppyhood," but his anger got the better of him, and to anyone who would listen, he smeared his party chief—"as great a hypocrite as any in the U.S."—and a "Creole bastard." Except for Hamilton, Adams retained all of Washington's cabinet, so no one felt much loyalty to him. Adams's presidency was doomed before it began.

+>-<+

HAMILTON'S FRONTAL ASSAULT on Jefferson in the run-up to the '96 election had not gone unnoticed in Monticello. Jefferson was a famous repository of political tittle-tattle, much of it stored in a series of notebooks he called his Anas, an arcane term for a collection of material that characterizes an individual, and he was always collecting. It is likely that Monroe had more than a few things to tell him about his nemesis, Hamilton. For Jefferson soon turned to the slimy Republican newshound James Thomson Callender, a Scottish refugee, to consign Hamilton to oblivion. Callender's ties to Jefferson picked up where Freneau's left off; he was the sort of useful but unsavory character that Jefferson kept in the middle distance of his considerable entourage, close enough to be of service, but far enough away to be untraceable. Jefferson thought this was the right time to bid Hamilton good-bye.

The first Hamilton heard of the move against him was in a notice for a forthcoming pamphlet with the unpromising title of *Nos V & VI of the History of the United States for the Year 1796*, claiming that the Reynolds letters proved that Hamilton had indulged in illicit financial speculation at Treasury. The more electrifying charge came toward the end, almost as an afterthought: "this great master of morality... had an illicit correspondence with another man's wife." As these things go, it wasn't much. Far more salacious tidbits are routinely offered than just some "illicit correspondence." When Hamilton insisted on reviewing the letters in question, he discovered they were indeed the ones under Monroe's control.

Whatever fire there was in *Nos V & VI of the History*, it might have died down on its own if Hamilton had not tried to smother it with gunpowder. In his fury, he responded with a manic ninety-five-page broadside, elaborately titled "Observations" on "Certain Documents" in Callender's *History*, in which "the Charge of Speculation" is "Fully Refuted." "Written"—if anyone doubted—"by Himself." Hamilton went at the claims as if his life depended on it, and it may have. He asserted the charges were driven by "the spirit of Jacobinism," which posed a greater threat to humanity than "WAR, PESTILENCE and FAMINE" combined, as he declared in all caps, and stood ready to drag down "our most virtuous citizens." He reprised his heroic efforts to pass the bill of assumption, only to be attacked by base Republicans like Mr. Giles of Virginia, and do much more for the nation. And now came the chiseler James Reynolds, and his claims of "improper pecuniary speculation." Hamilton could barely bring himself to think of it. His revulsion at the vulgarity of such an "obscure, unimportant, and profligate man" came through on every page, as he averred that no one would ever use "so vile an instrument as *Reynolds for such insignificant ends*" as securing a few hundred dollars. Hamilton insisted the "reptile" cooked up the whole scheme to spring himself from prison, where he was languishing at the time.

If Hamilton had just stopped there, his life would have gone very differently. But he was faced with a terrible choice, as Jefferson must have known. Now that he was accused of financial improprieties—the few hundred dollars he'd given Reynolds—that threatened his professional reputation, the only way to clear his name was to provide the real explanation, that the money was actually payment for sex with Reynolds's wife. But he did so with such abandon that it constituted a nearly Calvinist desire to confess. He related everything that could decently be said about the affair with Mrs. Reynolds, as he always termed her, and then a good deal more.

He began the tale as if it were a romantic novel: "Some time in the summer of the year 1791, a woman called at my house in the city of Philadelphia, and asked to speak to me in private." He detailed her "seeming air of affliction," and we are off. He published every letter he exchanged with both Reynoldses—presumably copying them out in his own hand—in the course of the long, wormy business of Hamilton's buying sexual access to the wife from her husband, his letters crisply elegant, theirs a clutter of misspelled vulgarities; all of them, to and fro, defined his "amorous connection" with Mrs. Reynolds. He detailed that first tense meeting at his house on Fourth Street and his first visit to her grim abode, where he tendered her nonpecuniary "consolation" and carried it through to its discovery by the trio of Muhlenberg, Venable, and Monroe. In other words, he could either watch his professional reputation shatter or refute the financial charges by humiliating himself in the most embarrassing possible fashion. He chose the second option, but it didn't work out as he had hoped. In confessing to the sexual embarrassment, he only added a second crime. Once a figure of probity, Hamilton became an adulterer *and* a cheat.

When the pamphlet was published, a wildfire broke out, and it swept up and down the country. His Federalist allies were flabbergasted. His "Observations" had done what his enemies never could—and done infinitely worse to his long-suffering wife. "Humiliating in the extreme," declared War Secretary Henry Knox. "His ill-judged pamphlet has done him inconceivable injury," added Robert Troup. "It is afflicting to see so great a man dragged before the public in such a delicate situation and compelled to avow a domestic infidelity to an unfeeling world," said William Loughton Smith. After the Reynolds affair, it seemed Hamilton was the butt of every joke and the target of every attack.

If the Federalists were mortified, the Republicans were jubilant. Callender, the provocateur, giggled to Jefferson that Hamilton's argument had come down to: "'I am a rake and for that reason I cannot be a swindler.'" The *Aurora* put his line of reasoning: "I have been grossly . . . charged with . . . being a *speculator*, whereas I am only an *adulterer*." Jefferson took chilly satisfaction at this much-hoped-for turn of events, claiming that Hamilton's "willingness to plead guilty to adultery seems rather to have strengthened than weakened the suspicions that he was in truth guilty of the speculations."

At the White House, Abigail Adams went for a carriage ride with her friend Mrs. Pickering. She had picked up on Hamilton's predilections in Philadelphia at the start of the decade, and now the whole drive was given over to chatter about Hamilton's shameless "licentiousness" toward the ladies. A few months later, she turned philosophical, but no less damning. "Alas," she cried out to her husband, "how weak is human nature." Adams harrumphed that it wasn't *human* nature. It was Hamilton's. He'd made "audacious and unblushing attempts upon ladies of highest rank and purest virtue."

Hamilton was almost alone, but Washington did not abandon his old aide-de-camp. He sent Hamilton a wine cooler for four bottles "as a token of my sincere regard and friendship for you and as a remembrance of me." Exquisitely, he made no mention of the scandal. The Hamiltons treasured the cooler.

Unfortunately for Hamilton, the Reynolds affair did not end there, but moved on to an act two in which the three self-appointed investigators returned to the case in 1797, five years after he thought it was settled. Previously, the three congressional investigators had decided there were no fiscal improprieties. Now, to go by Callender's *History*, they'd "left [Hamilton] under an impression our suspicions were removed." *Impression?* When Hamilton asked Muhlenberg about it, he replied that he had been satisfied by Hamilton's answers and still was. Venable said the same. Monroe, ominously, did not reply.

Hamilton had already grown suspicious of Monroe. A Virginian, he naturally fell in with Jefferson. The two were nearly of the same height, but Monroe still had some of the broad-shouldered military bearing from his war days, where he'd somehow survived a musket ball to the chest. Monroe had wide-set blue eyes on an uneventful face. Like many of his contemporaries in government, Hamilton considered him maddeningly slow-witted.

When Monroe failed to respond to Hamilton's request for clarification, Hamilton inquired and discovered he was in New York visiting his in-laws just down Wall Street. Annoyed, Hamilton fired off a note demanding an interview "at any hour tomorrow forenoon that may be convenient." Knowing the conversation might grow testy, he brought Church as a witness; Monroe brought a lawyer named David Gelston, who provided a detailed report of the meeting afterward. To Gelston, Hamilton appeared "very much agitated" from the moment he came in the door, and launched into a detailed history of the Reynolds correspondence. When Monroe asked him to come to the point, Hamilton angrily delivered it: Had Monroe accepted Hamilton's explanation of the Reynolds affair back in 1792, or had he not? Hamilton took over from there, until Monroe told him to "be temperate or quiet for a moment," and he fished out of his pocket a response to Hamilton's inquiry signed by all three men, accepting Hamilton's account.

Gratifying—but what about the original Reynolds papers the three men had been given for safekeeping? Had they leaked them to Callender? Monroe said they remained "sealed with a friend in Virginia," and he, Monroe, had no intention of publishing them. To Hamilton, that was absurd—*someone* had given them to Callender. "That is totally false," he shouted.

At that, Hamilton and Monroe both leapt out of their chairs.

"If you say I am representing falsely," snarled Monroe, "you are a scoundrel."

Hamilton: "I will meet you like a gentleman."

Monroe: "I am ready to get my pistols!"

The issue would probably have required a bullet if Gelston and Church hadn't pushed between them. Hamilton remained hot, but Monroe cooled. Gelston proposed the men put aside their differences until Monroe could meet with his two confederates in Philadelphia on Friday to discuss what had happened. This was a Tuesday. Promising to forget about their "warmth" for now, Hamilton and Church left the house.

By the time Monroe reached Philadelphia, Venable had left for Virginia, leaving Monroe and Muhlenberg to reiterate in writing the joint declaration that they all three believed Hamilton's account five years before. Unsatisfied, Hamilton insisted that Monroe denounce Clingman's central claim of misconduct at Treasury—and admit that he, Monroe, had given the Reynolds papers to Callender from "motives towards me [that are] malignant and dishonorable." A large request, and no one went along. Monroe admitted only that he'd recorded Clingman's statement. Furious, Hamilton resolved to publish a full account of the matter.

On August 6, Monroe passed to Aaron Burr a copy of his Hamilton correspondence, thinking that Burr might find a way to avert a duel. Why Monroe thought that is anybody's guess. He must have known of Hamilton's hatred for Burr. Possibly, as one of the few politicians who avoided party affiliation, Burr could be thought impartial. And he did ease tensions between the two men. "I have no desire to persecute [Hamilton]," Monroe confided to Burr, "though he justly merits it." When Burr told Hamilton that Monroe had no interest in a duel, Hamilton relented. With that, Burr asked Monroe to burn his Hamilton correspondence out of "magniminity."

When Hamilton's pamphlet came out, Monroe saw in its details a fresh assault on his honor. Still, it took him months to organize a duel, with Burr as his second. Around the same time, Hamilton wrote a letter saying that he was prepared to fight, but he never sent it and Monroe let the whole matter drop. Burr's opinion of Monroe fell with it. "Naturally dull and stupid; extremely illiterate; indecisive to a degree that would be incredible to one who did not know him." If Burr had been dishonored as Monroe had, Hamilton would be dead.

When Hamilton's Reynolds Pamphlet appeared, Betsey was pregnant with the couple's sixth child after a previous miscarriage. Ever solicitous of his wife, even as he made her life hell, Hamilton often wrote her long, tender letters that ended, "Adieu, Angel." Angelica was in New York with

Church, and at the height of the scandal she joined with Hamilton to escort her sister to a sloop to sail her up the Hudson to her family retreat in Albany, safe from the madness. In his anguish, Hamilton turned to Betsey for an almost maternal comfort. "I always feel how necessary you are to me," he wrote her after she left. "But when you are absent, I become still more sensible of it and look around in vain for that satisfaction which you alone can bestow." Angelica wrote Betsey:

> *When [Hamilton] returned from the sloop, he was very much out of spirits and you were the subject of his conversation the rest of the evening. Catherine played at the harpsichord for him and at 10 o'clock he went home. Tranquilize your kind and dear heart, my dear Eliza, for I have the most positive assurance from Mr. Church that the dirty fellow [Monroe, most likely] who has caused us all some uneasiness and wounded your feelings, my dear love, is effectually silenced. Merit, virtue, and talents must have enemies and [are] always exposed to envy so that, my Eliza, you see the penalties attending the position of so amiable a man. All this you would not have suffered if you had married into a family less near the sun. But then [you would have missed?] the pride, the pleasure, the nameless satisfactions.*

While Betsey was clearly the innocent, the Republican *Aurora* treated her as if she were somehow complicit. "Art thou a wife?" the editors hissed. "See him, whom thou has chosen for the partner of his life, lolling in the lap of a harlot." As for Hamilton, the paper turned preacherly: "He acknowledges . . . that he violated the sacred sanctuary of his own house, by taking an unprincipled woman during the absence of his wife and family to his bed." As ever, Betsey clung to the image of her pious husband.

In the midst of the pamphlet crisis, the Hamiltons' oldest child, Philip, apple of his father's eye, suffered at fifteen a "bilious fever" that might be the lethal typhus, according to Dr. David Hosack, the eminence from Columbia College who was summoned to attend to him. After the onset, Hamilton had to ride thirty miles north to Rye for a court case, but his anxiety for the boy was fierce, and he "pray[ed] heaven to restore him." Nonetheless, for days, Philip sank ever deeper into a sweaty torpor and finally grew so feeble that Hosack decided to move Betsey into another room so she wouldn't have to watch Philip's death spasms. A rider was dispatched to rush Hamilton back to see his son once more before the end.

Arriving late that night, Hamilton jumped off his horse and raced into the house, where he braced himself to find a corpse, but Philip had miraculously shaken off the illness and returned to life. Hamilton was so overwhelmed at the sight, he found Hosack where he was sleeping and clasped the doctor's hand. Hosack awoke to see Hamilton's "eyes suffused with tears of joy." After that, Hamilton alone nursed Philip around the clock, "administering with his own hand every dose of medicine or cup of nourishment that was required." That was his custom for his children, and for his wife, if they fell sick. Hamilton could not have been a more devoted family man.

THIRTY-SEVEN

The Bubble of Speculation Is Burst

B Y THE TIME he returned to New York, Burr's penchant for secrecy had reached another level. It was no longer a matter of concealing the details of his legitimate activities that happened to be personal; now he was shrouding from view illicit ones, which were growing in number. He was like a mole that slunk about the forest floor, only to disappear into a labyrinth of tunnels below.

Much of his secrecy stemmed from the inherent awkwardness of his growing "pecuniary vexations," as he termed them. A financial squeeze was uncomfortable anyway, but there was the added stress of being hounded by creditors (and the greater the debt, the more the creditors), the humiliation of constantly feeling pinched, and the prospect of rotting away in some hellish debtors' prison. Burr had long taken loans from his legal clients, which was entanglement enough, but now, to escape his debts, he incurred more, borrowing more widely from friends, business relations, and relatives, much of it to fund increasingly desperate real estate speculations that were designed to free him from debt but were more likely to plunge him in all the deeper. And 1796 was no time to have bought, only to buy. "The Bubble of speculation is burst," Burr's confidant Theodore Sedgwick wrote to Rufus King, adding that Burr was "irretrievably ruined."

Burr could not have had a worse investment touch. In his desperation, he'd tried a complicated speculative scheme in the French real estate market, only to run afoul of France's moves against American ships, which had frozen financial transfers between the two countries. Then he turned to a once-wealthy financier, now little more than a confidence man, the Boston-born James Greenleaf, who'd acquired some respectability as US consul in Holland before returning to the United States in 1793 to become, briefly, the most lavish land speculator in the United States. He had purchased vast swaths of land in Washington City and in upstate New York. In partnership with Greenleaf, Burr somehow scraped up the funds to buy half the vast "Angerstein tract" north of the Mohawk River, so named for its original owner, John Julius Angerstein, the underwriter for Lloyd's who was also a renowned art collector.* Burr took advantage of New York's Alien Law prohibiting foreigners from owning any land in the state to extract his parcel from Angerstein for a very good price. Burr assumed that his partner, the illustrious Greenleaf, was good for the other half. But Robert Morris had made a similar assumption, and, for his folly, he would soon sit in the Prune Street debtors' prison in Philadelphia writing beseeching letters to his creditors. It turned out that Greenleaf had deceived Burr no less than Morris; he didn't have the money. So Burr was obliged to cough up Greenleaf's half of the twenty-four-thousand-pound sale price, or pay a huge twenty-four-thousand-pound nonpayment penalty as well. Burr frantically tried to raise the cash by selling his scant other equity stakes in land and stock, and he collected personal notes from a half dozen friends. But it wasn't enough. When word got out about Greenleaf's failure, creditors swarmed, bringing about his total ruin. Impossibly indebted, Greenleaf would join Morris in debtors' prison in Philadelphia, too.

When Burr failed to pay, Angerstein hired Alexander Hamilton to press the case against him. The matter dragged through the courts, and judgment was not rendered until 1803: Burr was obliged to pay Angerstein eighty thousand dollars, a colossal sum when the vice presidency of the United States paid a salary of just five thousand dollars annually. Hamilton marveled at the extent of Burr's debts. "He [Aaron Burr] is without doubt insolvent for a large *deficit*. All his visible property is deeply mortgaged, and he is known to owe other large debts, for which there is no specific security."

---

* His collection would form the basis of the National Gallery in London.

Meanwhile, Burr's friend John Lamb was on the hook for fifty thousand dollars. A former Son of Liberty and hero of Yorktown, Lamb was the collector of customs for the port of New York when 150,000 dollars in federal funds under his care had somehow disappeared. No one accused Lamb of malfeasance, but he was held responsible all the same, and he would be forced to forfeit his two sureties, or bonds, totaling fifty thousand dollars. None were held by Burr, but by two close Burr associates, Melancton Smith and Marinus Willett. In the interlocking network of unhappy obligations, Lamb had once loaned Burr twenty thousand dollars and then served as his surety on Angerstein, costing Lamb twice. It pained Burr to see his friend in trouble. "That your peace of mind should be distressed or personal safety endangered by an act of friendship and generosity to me," Burr confessed to Lamb, "is the most humiliating event of my life." He provided legal services, but to no avail. Lamb died bitterly impoverished in 1800.

Into this shadowy milieu strolled Colonel Joseph Brant-Thayendanegea, the Indian King, as he was known, but more exactly the Mohawk chieftain of the Six Nations of the Iroquois, and a man who came to represent the myriad of conflicts that converged in the tangle that was Burr. The image on the frontispiece of his two-volume biography from 1845 shows him adorned with a plume of feathers, thick leather belts crisscrossed over a flowing tunic, a heavy piece of ornamental silver dangling over his chest, and blowsy pantaloons below, the whole thing finished off with a tomahawk in his right hand.* But that was just for show; on government business he wore city dress, little different from Burr's own. Far from a fierce warrior, he bore the air of a burdened romantic, with soft eyes and wistful expression.

Raised in Little Falls, New York, he'd joined the British to seize Canada from the French, and proved a savvy and savage warrior. "I like the

---

* The portrait was done on a trip to London to negotiate the status of Indian lands with the Crown at the start of hostilities in 1775. Any number of English dignitaries came to gawk, but they were gawked at, too. The biographer James Boswell recalled that Brant "was struck with the appearance of the English in General, but he said he chiefly admired the ladies and the horses." Taken by the Mohawk, Boswell had a cameo done of him, as a memento.

harpsichord well, and the organ still better," he once declared. "But I like the drum and trumpet best of all, for they make my heart beat quick." Educated by Anglican missionaries, he'd become a devout Christian who later translated the Gospel of Saint Mark into his native language. After the Mohawks selected him as their chief, he led bloody raids against the Americans during the war, but he was betrayed by the British in the peace when they gave away all the Indians' western lands and expelled them to Upper Canada, a peninsula by Lake Ontario. The British had promised them clear title but never delivered it, making it impossible to resell the land to American speculators. Seeing Brant's distress, Washington tried to win his allegiance, but Brant preferred to deal with the French. He'd met with the French philosophe Compte de Volney in Albany to hear his outlandish plans to draw French soldiers up from New Orleans to steal north across the border and attack the scanty English defense. But such an ambition required money from a man desperate enough to spring for it. So when Burr, a financially strapped senator, French in orientation, long interested in Indian affairs, invited him to dinner in Philadelphia with Volney and Talleyrand, soon to assume a position in the French Directory, Brant was only too happy to attend. That dinner in Philadelphia was the beginning.

The actual scheme remains shrouded in the Burrian mystery of cryptic letters and destroyed evidence, but its outline is easy enough to discern: Talleyrand would extract money from his connections at the French Directory, presumably eager to embarrass the English, and assisted by Burr's stepson John Bartow Prevost, installed as Monroe's secretary; Volney would provide the French troops; Brant would command; and Burr would mastermind. Around this time, he put in twenty-three thousand dollars toward Canadian land purchases, and solicited poor John Lamb for much more.

To further cultivate Brant, Burr invited him to visit Richmond Hill in early 1797. Unable to be there himself, Burr left it to his daughter Theodosia, just thirteen, to handle the evening. He provided Brant a note of introduction for her. "This will be handed to you by Colonel Brant, the celebrated Indian Chief. I am sure that you and Natalie will be happy in the opportunity of seeing a man so much renowned. He is a man of education—speaks and writes English perfectly—and has seen much of

Europe and America. Receive him with respect and hospitality. He is not one of those Indians who drink rum, but is quite a gentleman; not one who will make you fine bows, but one who understands and practices what belongs to propriety and good breeding." With the chief as the guest of honor, Theodosia had invited fourteen dignitaries from New York, including New York's Episcopal bishop Benjamin Moore, one of her mother's last physicians, and Dr. David Hosack, who'd treated Philip Hamilton, and they gathered around the long table, with Theodosia at the foot and Brant at the head, the faces all lit up with candle flame.

Burr's plans, however, had not gone unnoticed by the Crown's many spies. In 1797, Robert Liston, the British envoy to the United States, told William Wyndham, Lord Grenville, that an American expeditionary force was plotting to expel Britain from Upper Canada. Burr was one of the two conspirators he named. When Hamilton got wind of the scheme, he declared that Burr's perilous financial state forced him into "unworthy expedients," including a possible "*bargain* and *sale* with some foreign power" and "probably to enlarge the sphere—a *war*." The secret out, the plan fizzled.

Crushed by his debts, sometime after that Brant dinner in early 1797, Burr had no choice. He mortgaged his house and sold all his furnishings. Out went all the ornate mirrors, the inlaid tables—everything that was not needed for his daily existence. How the vast rooms must have echoed with their emptiness. The crusty Theodore Sedgwick, now a senator, happened to be visiting when the movers came to load up all the valuables, and it must have been quite a sight, for afterward Burr wrote to apologize to him for the "chaos" of his household.

THIRTY-EIGHT

An Absolute and Abominable Lie

W HEN BURR'S TERM as senator ended that year, 1797, he did the unthinkable. He took a seat in the state Assembly, about the humblest of all elected positions in the state of New York—and relocated to up-country Albany. He'd done the political math: with New England voting as a bloc for the Federalists, and the South solid for the Republicans, that left only a few mid-Atlantic states up for grabs to decide the election. None of them was as ripe for the plucking as New York. While it was solidly Republican upstate, New York City was still Tory at heart, balancing the state for the Federalists. To Burr, it was apparent that if someone could tip the Assembly for the Republicans, the party would reap rich rewards in the Electoral College for the next presidential season—and that someone would become a Republican darling. But with Burr, there was the overt, and there was the covert. A place in the Assembly would allow him to work the machinery of state governance for his own financial advantage.

Brooding in Philadelphia, Jefferson wrote Burr one of those effusive Jeffersonian letters that rings the chimes on ambiguity, but it seemed to invite Burr into his confidence. Seeing that a few other Republicans had joined the New York Assembly with him, Jefferson hailed a "dawn of change" in the state, and then, like an evangelist, asked if Republicans might still "hope for salvation" that would "come, as of old, from the east." Could Burr "give me a comfortable solution of them?" Instead of Hamilton's rational appeals, Jefferson made emotional ones, but this was deceptive nonetheless. For Jefferson later revealed what he *really* thought of Burr during this period. "His conduct soon inspired me with distrust," he declared. "I habitually cautioned Mr. Madison from trusting him too much. I saw afterwards that under General Washington's and Mr. Adams' administrations, whenever a great military appointment or a diplomatic one was to be made, he came post to Philadelphia to show himself, and in fact that he was always at market." True enough, but Jefferson could not imagine what Burr was selling this time.

Burr replied that he agreed completely, but it would not be "discreet" to say more by letter. So he rode off again to see Jefferson as he had four years before, this time in Philadelphia. Burr was at market again. For the meeting, Jefferson brought in Monroe, just back from France, Madison, and Albert Gallatin, the Swiss-born Pennsylvanian who'd been ousted from the Senate by the Federalists for being a foreigner. This was likely the time that Monroe passed on to Jefferson a few words about the Reynolds affair, for Callender published his *History* shortly after. The rest of the meeting is a matter of conjecture, but it almost certainly involved Burr's elaborating on his plans to take back New York, and Jefferson trying to disguise his enthusiasm.

Back in the Assembly, Burr jumped right into national politics by putting forth a bill that would take away the right to select the state's presidential electors from the assemblymen and give it to the voters. Since the Federalists still controlled the Assembly, the bill was a nonstarter, but Burr knew he could win by losing, as his bill revealed that the Federalists were neither of the people nor for them. And he rounded up more Burrites, starting with John Swartwout, a blond, Bunyanesque figure from Dutchess County, who became the Burrites' Burrite, known for taking on the rough or exhausting tasks that nobody else would do. He came with three brothers—Robert, Samuel, and Henry—who became the muscle of the organization.

While Burr played politics in the Assembly, he was there for more urgent reasons. The miserable Angerstein affair had been instructive on many levels, but not the least of them was the desire of foreigners to purchase New York lands. Not only would a change expand the market and raise prices, but the foreigners would pay Burr handsomely for the privilege of getting in on the land rush. So when the land agent of the Holland Land Company approached Burr with a proposition, the assemblyman listened attentively. Holland Land was an agglomeration of Dutch banks that had, through the agent, Théophile Cazenove, purchased almost 5 million acres of virgin land in Pennsylvania and New York. The problem was, this was illegal. To get around this, Cazenove had first hired Alexander Hamilton to persuade the Assembly to throw out the Alien Law, but the best he could do was to allow ownership for a period of seven years. Not good enough. Hamilton pushed it to sixteen years—if the real estate agent in question made a 250,000-dollar loan to the Western Inland Lock Navigation Company, of which Hamilton's father-in-law, Philip Schuyler, happened to be president.

That was not much improvement, and likely to be a scandal of its own. So Cazenove turned to Burr. Somehow, even as a bankrupt, Burr had already managed to purchase one hundred thousand acres from the Holland Company, the money to be paid in installments, with a potential twenty-thousand-dollar penalty if he failed to deliver. He had yet to put down a penny, but for security, he mortgaged one of the few pieces of land that was still unencumbered and transferred a twenty-thousand-dollar bond he'd received from the lawyer for the Albany patroon, Hamilton's brother-in-law Stephen Van Rensselaer. While Hamilton had tried to be artful, Burr told Cazenove to go right ahead and bribe the key members of the legislature into doing his bidding, and he provided the names.

On April 2, 1798, the Alien Law was no more, and the state attorney general was three thousand dollars richer. Senator Thomas Morris received one thousand dollars in "legal fees," as did another legislator recorded only as "L," and doubtless there were many other recipients, too. Burr himself received a handsome loan from the Holland Company he never paid back, he was freed from the nonpayment penalty for the hundred thousand acres, and the twenty-thousand-dollar bond was returned to him.

When questioned about these transactions, Burr replied in a lengthy, detailed, and highly unpersuasive letter that concluded on a note of testiness:

By those who know me, it will never be credited that any man on earth would have the hardiness even to propose to me dishonourable compensations. This, sir, is the first time in my life that I have condescended (pardon the expression) to refute a calumny. I leave to my actions to speak for themselves, and to my character to confound the fictions of slander. And on this very subject I have not up to this hour given one word of explanation to any human being. All the explanation that can be given amounts to no more than this—That the thing is an absolute and abominable lie.

While the terms of Burr's service to the Holland Company were widely known, the only man willing to use the word "bribery" to describe them was Hamilton's hefty brother-in-law, John Barker Church. He probably heard the details from Hamilton. Apparently, Church was discussing the matter a little too loudly at a "private table in town," according to a newspaper account. As soon as Burr heard it, he demanded a duel, and Church, ever a "man of business" in Hamilton's appraisal, was not one to refuse him. Burr may have seen it as a way to burnish his Republican credentials in the run-up to 1800, for he chose the South Carolina rapscallion and noted Hamilton hater Aedanus Burke to be his second, while Church picked the former treasurer of Hamilton's Society for Useful Manufactures. The dueling ground was in Hoboken, New Jersey, and the two of them, plus their seconds, rowed across the Hudson at sunset one evening in the same boat. It was Burr's first duel, but not Church's. They both owned dueling pistols, Church's from a fine London gunsmith, but Burr's were used. They came with bullets that were slightly too small for the chambers, requiring a wrap of chamois to produce a snug fit in the barrels. Burr's man, Burke, had trouble ramming Burr's bullet into place, but Burr assured his second that it was no matter. If he missed his mark on the first shot, he would hit him with the second. The ten yards were duly measured, and the two men faced off, aimed, and fired. Burr's bullet missed entirely, but Church's clanged off a metal button on Burr's jacket, leaving its target startled but unharmed. As the seconds prepared the pistols for a second shot, Church had had enough. He stepped forward to apologize to Burr for his "indiscreet" remarks. Burr accepted the apology, the two men shook hands, and that was it. The dispute was "satisfactorily adjusted," in the words of Davis, and the party returned to New York most convivially.

That was the end of Burr's dealings with the Holland Company, but it was the beginning of another, more lasting piece of business, the creation of the Manhattan Company, which likewise combined high purpose with low skullduggery, a Burr trademark. By now, Burr watchers learned not to be distracted by the surface ripples, but to attend to the more powerful currents working below.

Ostensibly the Manhattan Company was a water company intended to deliver freshwater to a city that thirsted for it. For years, the vast majority of the citizens had had to rely on shallow well water so foul that horses shied away from it; the city's only reservoir, the so-called Fresh Water Pond, teemed with putrid filth; and its Tea Water Pump had become dangerously contaminated in 1785. Long dire, the water situation became frightening in 1798, when the yellow fever that had decimated Philadelphia in 1793 struck Manhattan, leaving many of its citizens to believe the foul water was to blame.

Burr smelled opportunity. He would provide what everyone clamored for—fresh drinking water, drawn from the still pristine Bronx River—and that surely would do much to cleanse a name that may have gotten muddied by the Holland Company business. Moreover, the proposition was likely to be highly lucrative, both for obvious reasons and for reasons that were not obvious at all. Burr left it to his brother-in-law, the physician Joseph Browne, to formally propose the notion to the Common Council, the city's governing body; the council was grateful for the suggestion but was reluctant to turn a public necessity over to a private concern. It preferred the water to be delivered by a municipal water-supply system, not by the private company Browne (and Burr) had in mind.

When he heard of the Common Council's verdict, Burr immediately secured ten days' leave from the Assembly in Albany and galloped to New York. There he collected five of the city's most celebrated men to persuade the members of the Common Council of their error and, if they failed to see their error, to overrule them. To show this appeal was above politics, Burr made sure that the six (including him) were evenly divided between three Republicans and three Federalists. For this purpose, he was one

Republican; the two others were a president of a large insurance company and the head of the Mechanics Society; the Federalists were the presidents of the chamber of commerce and the Bank of New York—and Alexander Hamilton.

Why did Hamilton join in? Having barely survived the outbreak of yellow fever in Philadelphia, he knew the risks of the disease. And he must have seen that a great city needed a reliable water supply no less than fresh capital. But there was another factor, one that blurs the differences between Hamilton and Burr. Church may have enticed Hamilton into such a potentially lucrative venture, with good money for Hamilton as his lawyer and agent in the deal. When the council refused to reconsider, the august committee met with New York's mayor Richard Varick, who asked the six members to put their thoughts in writing. Only Hamilton did, and apparently his argument was enough to persuade Varick to recommend to the Assembly that the city's water rights be assigned exclusively to the Manhattan Company.

In Albany, the session was scheduled to conclude on March 28, 1799. Burr had named himself head of the committee that would present the measure. He waited until the end of that last day to introduce his bill—and at the last moment of that last day, he introduced a slight but extremely significant change to his water bill. He added the bank clause.

> And be it further enacted, *That it shall and may be lawful for the said company to employ all such surplus capital as may belong or accrue to the said company in the purchase of public or other stock, or in any other moneyed transactions or operations, not inconsistent with the constitution and laws of this State or of the United States, for the sole benefit of the said company.*

The water company could also be a bank—a Republican bank, in point of fact, to counter the only other bank in New York City, Hamilton's Bank of New York, which was staunchly Federalist. If anyone in the legislature noticed this addition, there is no record of it. Many of them had left for home. The bill passed on a voice vote.

For passage, however, the bill needed to clear the Council of Revision, an impressive group that included Governor John Jay; Robert Livingston, the state chancellor; and all five justices of the supreme court. Of the group, only Chief Justice John Lansing said a word against the bill, protesting the bank clause. Chancellor Livingston was somewhat compromised, since Burr had already given him an option for two thousand shares of Manhattan Company stock. On April 2, 1799, Governor Jay did the math and signed the bill into law.

As a water service, the Manhattan Company was never much more than a creaky assemblage of leaky wooden pipes and overstrained pumps delivering water from a smattering of wells, the most famous of them in Lispenard's Meadow well north of the city. As a bank, it was something else again, as it finally provided for the Republicans what the Federalists had long possessed. No less than newspapers, fashions of dress, medical approaches, and European loyalties, banks were divided by party, and the Republicans had long suffered for the lack of one. The bank's political value, Edward Livingston told Jefferson, was supreme. "A very important change has been effected," he wrote, "by the instrumentality as Mr. Hamilton would call it of the New Bank." After praising the "zealous" and "active" Burr, he added, "Every thing promises a favorable issue to our labors." The Republican propagandist James Cheetham was gleeful, as he later put it: "Federalism retained its dominion until the establishment of the Manhattan Company; after that event its empire became dissolved."

Burr never intended anything less, for he stocked the board with Republicans—who were inclined to advance the prospects of fellow Republicans frozen out of credit by the Bank of New York. One of the few exceptions was his duelist John B. Church, which may be another reason why Hamilton was uncharacteristically reserved in his appraisal of Burr's deceit. The bank was a "perfect monster in its principles," he declared, but also "a very convenient instrument of profit and influence." It was for Burr, anyway. By 1802, he'd taken out almost sixty-five thousand dollars in loans from the bank.

The political benefits did not materialize, as the Federalists campaigned against the underhanded manner in which it was created. None suffered more than Burr himself, who was voted out of office in the next election by a wide margin. The presidential contest was a year away, and Burr had just been ejected from about the lowest office in the land.

THIRTY-NINE

Strut Is Good for Nothing

I**N THE WINTER** of 1798, on the floor of the House of Representatives, the stern Federalist from Connecticut Roger Griswold strode up to the hot-blooded Republican from Vermont Matthew Lyon and started caning Lyon furiously with his hickory walking stick. "He was laying on blows with all his might," wrote a fellow Federalist. Lyon tried to fend off the blows raining down on his head and shoulders and then dashed to the fireplace, grabbed the tongs, and charged at Griswold, wrote the Federalist, and "gave him one or two blows in the face" before other congressmen jumped into the fray and hauled the two men apart.

The fracas had started when Lyon accused the entire Connecticut delegation of lining their pockets with public funds; noting Lyon's dishonorable discharge from the army, Griswold taunted Lyon about his "wooden sword"; Lyon spat a cheekful of tobacco juice into Griswold's face.

The parties had been at each other's throats for some time, each side casting the other as the redcoats in a refought War of Independence. Now that the radical Jacobins had fallen to the right-wing Directory that ruled France (and to which Burr had sought to appeal), the new government had unleashed a furious assault on the upstart Americans, seizing American vessels in French ports, refusing to honor bills from American merchants, letting colonial authorities make off with American property, and, as the British had, dispatching hundreds of picaroons, or privateers, to the West

Indies to seize American vessels and impress their seamen. Then the Directory expelled the new American minister, Charles Cotesworth Pinckney, who had succeeded Monroe, broke off diplomatic relations with the United States, and started to extend its naval reach up the Atlantic to Long Island Sound, making it risky for any American ship to sail the northern Atlantic without a convoy. Trade with Britain was endangered, and the Bank of England had suspended cash payments to American merchants. Most menacing of all, perhaps, the sage young general Napoléon Bonaparte was said to be gathering an army to attack the English coast.

All this had a political cast, as usual. Since Genet, France had been the frightening symbol of mobocracy, with French-inspired democratic clubs and societies that had brought, to Federalists, a rough element to politics, which had always been left to their betters in the educated classes. Thus, Griswold was the son of the Connecticut governor, bearing degrees from Harvard and Yale, and Lyon was a loud, scrappy Irish immigrant who operated a mill in Vermont.

The squabble with France was not yet a hot war, but a Quasi-War—a matter of posturing that only portended cannon fire—and Hamilton was in the thick of it. His reputation shattered by the Reynolds affair, he hoped a war might rescue him. Hamilton advocated girding the nation for war by creating a full-scale navy and a twenty-five-thousand-man army, the rival of any on the continent. Negotiate, he told his Treasury successor, Oliver Wolcott Jr., but "prepare vigorously for the worst. "*Real firmness* is good for everything. *Strut* is good for nothing."

Alarmed by the military threat, Adams was sensitive to the politics. Even as cities along the Eastern Seaboard frantically erected fortifications to hold off a French invasion, he couldn't afford to antagonize pro-French Republicans or the anti-French Federalists, but had to somehow find the crack between them. Adams pointedly did not seek Hamilton's counsel, but enough other secretaries did that Hamilton shaped the administration's response. As of old, Jefferson worked to undermine the president's initiatives through back-channel communications. By now, Napoléon had wheeled south to crush the Austrians in Italy, and Talleyrand demanded that Adams retract his harsh criticisms of France and, outrageously, deliver massive loans instead—with a handsome bribe of £50,000 for Talleyrand himself for making all this possible.

When commissioner John Marshall's account of these negotiations finally reached Adams in March of 1798, the president was outraged. Hamilton urged *"calm defiance,"* and for once Adams agreed, requesting a congressional appropriation for the military Hamilton had been recommending. Unaware of Talleyrand's maneuvering, the Republicans charged Adams with going off half-cocked. But when Adams revealed the Marshall report—dubbed the "XYZ papers" for the coded names of three of the more irritating French diplomats in on the extortion scheme—the country flew into an uproar. The Republican leadership scrambled to justify its French allegiance; Jefferson claimed the XYZ papers had to have been faked by the Federalists. True to form, Hamilton rushed into print with a seven-part series, the Stand, slashing at the treasonous Republicans and demanding a military response.

A standing army was not a welcome idea in a country that associated such a thing with the reviled British, but, in response to the threat, Hamilton now proposed one of fifty thousand men all the same. Adams scoffed that "Mr. Hamilton knew no more of the sentiments and feelings of the people of America than he did of the inhabitants of one of the planets." He added: "Hamilton's hobby was the army." The Congress compromised on a "Provisional Army" of ten thousand men.

Eager for military rank, Hamilton longed to become the leader of his new army—except that another well-regarded general was ahead of him in line. Creaky at age sixty-six, George Washington had signaled he was willing to be lured out of retirement to protect the young nation. He'd resolved to enlist Hamilton as his number two under the title of inspector general. Adams needed only make the appointment. But Adams could be remarkably maladroit, and he could scarcely have been more clumsy in handling America's greatest hero. He appointed Washington commander without actually speaking to him first, which struck the ex-president as preemptory. Washington made clear he would be appeased only if Adams appointed Hamilton too. Adams would rather have eaten shoe leather, but he had no choice. To save his dignity, he tried to drop Hamilton below Adams's two other appointees—Henry Knox and Charles Cotesworth Pinckney—in the official announcement. "If I should consent to the appointment of Hamilton as a second in rank, I should consider it as the most [ir]responsible action of my whole life and the most difficult to justify," he wrote. He derided Hamilton as "not a native of the United States," observed that his wartime rank had been "comparatively very low," and wound up, "Hamilton has not popular character in any part of America."

In a rare case of restraint, Adams decided not to send this diatribe, but the sentiments were plenty evident, and Washington was not pleased to hear of Adams's disdain for his former aide. After Adams had worried about Hamilton's ambition, Washington called it "of that laudable kind which prompts a man to excel in whatever he takes in hand." Having irritated all the principals in this drama, Adams finally restored Hamilton to second place. However it came about, Hamilton was delighted with his lofty rank, and he immediately commissioned a bright uniform, studded with epaulets, and drew up audacious, if not grandiose, plans not just to defend America from the French, but to roust the French out of Spanish Florida and Louisiana, and, while he was at it, to remove the Spanish from land east of the Mississippi, and possibly to go marauding down the South American coast, expelling European colonists, as well. To round out his roster of brigadier generals, Adams selected a Republican: Burr. Washington was shocked about the selection of such an "intriguer." Burr? Adams was thunderstruck—he'd show Washington an intriguer. "How shall I describe to you my sensations and reflections at that moment? He had compelled me to promote over the heads of Lincoln, Gates, Clinton, Knox, and others, and even over Pinckney, one of . . . the most restless, impatient, artful, indefatigable, and unprincipled intriguers in the United States, if not in the world." It was too much, but the die was cast. "I was not to nominate Burr," Adams admitted. Secure in his own position, Hamilton was surprisingly accepting of the choice of his archrival. He could use an ally in New York City, as that would be a natural strike point for a French assault. Troup couldn't personally believe that Hamilton was coming around to Burr but acknowledged that "some conjecture that he is changing his ground." Later, he told a friend that he had seen the impossible: Hamilton and Burr actually being polite to each other. As for Burr, he lashed out only at Washington, telling Adams that he "despised Washington as a Man of No Talents, and one who could not spell a sentence of common English." That got back to Washington, and, if Burr had any chance for a commission, that spelled the end of it.

The French never did invade, confining themselves to the Atlantic and the Caribbean. That was the height of Adams's tenure. Like all victories, this one bore the seeds of future defeat, for Adams decided to make use of his new political strength to go after a runaway Republican press that had pilloried him in the French crisis. He backed a congressional bill to imprison any newspaper editors convicted of publishing a "seditious libel," meaning any "false, scandalous and malicious" statement against the Congress or the president. The Alien and Sedition Acts, the initiatives were called. They were a clear violation of the First Amendment, that great triumph of American liberty, and a nasty piece of politics besides, as they effectively criminalized dissent, and the Republicans, understandably, were apoplectic.

Burr took political advantage when he loudly supported a judge in Cooperstown, New York, who'd circulated an appeal to repeal the acts—only to be "taken from his bed at midnight, manacled and dragged from his home." But Hamilton was delighted by a law that would imprison the Scottish-born Callender, who'd revealed the Reynolds scandal. Speaking of other such editors, Hamilton asked, "Why are they not sent away?" Not that he hadn't dashed off a few libels himself.

Under the new law, the testy Republican congressman Matthew Lyon was sentenced to four months for criticizing Adams's "unbounded thirst for ridiculous pomp, foolish adulation, and selfish avarice." Another was jailed for two months for calling Hamilton's planned army a "standing army," which probably was not far off the mark. But the most memorable case involved *The Argus*, a cantankerous Republican paper in New York that had been owned by Thomas Greenleaf—no relation to the financier James—until his wife, Ann, took it over on his death. *The Argus* had run afoul of the New York district attorney for calling the government "corrupt and inimical to the preservation of liberty." But things got worse when *The Argus* reprinted a charge that Hamilton had tried to join a group to buy Brache's Republican paper the *Aurora* in order to kill it, claiming that

Hamilton had obtained his six-thousand-dollar share from the British secret service. Hamilton demanded a criminal prosecution for this "audacious falsehood." Ann Greenleaf claimed that she had merely reprinted the piece from another paper, but no matter: the editor responsible, David Frothingham, would be charged with the crime. Testifying, Hamilton made clear that his reputation was "dearer" to him "than property or life." The court was sympathetic, sentencing Frothingham to four months in Bridewell Prison. The acts, however, did nothing to discourage Republicans. While two prominent Republican papers went under, many more sprang up. General Hamilton did not cleanse American soil of foreigners as he'd threatened, but he did keep his army on alert against any possible armed insurrection by Republicans who'd sided with the French against the government. Here he had Jefferson's Virginia primarily in mind, since its legislature had moved to cancel the Alien and Sedition laws. "Put Virginia to the test of resistance," he told Theodore Sedgwick, who had loyally backed the laws. Jefferson started calling Hamilton "our Bonapart." When there was a mild stir over property taxes in western Pennsylvania, Hamilton crushed it by a massive show of force. The ringleader, John Fries, was arrested and convicted of treason. Adams thought Hamilton inclined to see a "hideous monster or phantom" in any crisis and likely to respond with "imprudent measures." Adams pardoned Fries, seeing the uprising less a rebellion than a riot. Hamilton was determined not to allow his military to be reduced in strength as the French threat receded.

→›‹←

ON THURSDAY, DECEMBER 12, George Washington came down with a sore throat after a five-hour tour of his farms in a swirl of hail that left his hair wet and his clothes damp when he sat down for lunch with visitors he did not want to keep waiting. His chest grew heavy and his voice hoarse later the next evening, and, as he settled into bed his throat was inflamed. That night, Martha was troubled to hear his labored breath, and sent for doctors in the morning. An overseer, Rawlings, bled him heavily before the doctors arrived, Washington insisting on "More, more," although the procedure was terrifically painful. The doctors drew five pints altogether, or half the body's supply, from the nation's founder, and then applied still more medieval remedies, including an enema and an extract of dried beetles. Washington could tell it was no use. Enervated, scarcely able to breathe or speak above a whisper, he told the doctors, "I feel myself going. Let me go off quietly. I cannot last long." He reached over to take his own pulse, and then, reported Washington's longtime secretary, Tobias Lear, "the General's hand fell from his wrist."

FORTY

The Lady in the Well

WHILE THE CHURCH bells in New York were still chiming Washington's death, a woman's muff was found floating in an abandoned well owned by the Manhattan Company. It was in Lispenard's Meadow, not far from Richmond Hill, where the wilderness began. After the muff was retrieved, it appeared that its owner, a Miss Gulielma Sands, lay below, in the icy depths of the well, one shoulder bare, her eyes up toward the light. Grappling hooks and then a net brought up the dripping corpse, the clothing tattered, head limp, hair in a snarl. Criminal investigations were unsophisticated, and the body was simply placed on a plank beside the well to wait for someone to identify it. That fell to Levi Weeks, a shy young carpenter and friend of Sands's from the boardinghouse where they both lived, who knew her as Elma. From there, the body was hauled to an almshouse, where it was stripped and laid out on an examination table for the coroner to examine in the presence of a grand jury that directed his work. It was out of bounds to determine if Sands was a virgin, but not to see if she was pregnant. (She was not.) Examination complete, Sands was heaved into a coffin and taken by cart to her cousin's boardinghouse, where the prosecutor's doctors discovered enough bruises around her throat to determine that Elma had been killed by "a violent pressure upon the neck" and the body dropped into the well to hide the crime. And the prosecutors identified the culprit, Levi Weeks, the young man who'd identified her. People said he'd planned to marry her, but she must have jilted him, and he'd strangled her out of jealousy. For a murder investigation, as for so much else, rumor was fact. Weeks was clapped into the abysmal Bridewell jail to await trial for Elma's murder while frenzied newspapermen spun out endless column inches with the tale of a free-spirited maiden strangled by her jealous fiancé. HORRID MURDER! BY HANDS OF A LOVER! declared *The Independent Gazetteer* of Worcester, Massachusetts. THE YOUNG LADY DRESSED AS A BRIDE, lamented *Claypoole's American Daily Advertiser* of Philadelphia. The state attorney general's office drew up an indictment: Weeks had been "seduced by the instigation of the Devil." Simple as that.

Like everyone else in New York, Aaron Burr was caught up in the case, but for different reasons. He had a financial stake in the matter. As the creator and major backer of the Manhattan Company, he couldn't let its name be contaminated by such a lurid murder involving one of its wells. Already, Levi Weeks's brother Ezra had provided much of the contracting and design work for the Manhattan Company's water project, and that was implication enough. Ezra had even constructed the very well where Sands had been found submerged. As it happened, he was now busy constructing Hamilton's new house, the Grange, on the Heights.

To defend his interests, Burr took on the Weeks case for free and enlisted Alexander Hamilton as his junior partner. As a director of the Manhattan Company, Hamilton had a stake in the outcome too. The trial was held in the former Federal Hall and presided over by John Lansing, the chief justice of the New York State Supreme Court and the one member of the review committee to object to the Manhattan Company. It was a sensation. Hundreds if not thousands of New Yorkers thronged Broad Street for a look at the prisoner, some of them climbing trees for a better angle, and many of them shrieked "Crucify him" when the hapless Weeks was escorted inside by a phalanx of constables. The luckier ones mashed their way into the visitors' gallery.

The trial went just two days, but very long ones that nearly reached morning. For the prosecution, Cadwallader D. Colden, the London-educated assistant attorney general, detailed a lurid crime of passion, presenting witnesses who claimed that Weeks had pursued Sands in a "warm courtship" that had led to their being together in a *very intimate* situation," emitting sounds of a "rustling of beds, such as might be occasioned by a man and wife." Near the well on the fatal night, someone heard the shriek of a woman "in distress" before the sound was "muffled." There were tracks in the snow from Weeks's sleigh, and the prosecutor's doctors identified "several spots pretty much in a row around her neck," proof of strangulation. An appraisal was affirmed by the celebrated Dr. Hosack, the Hamilton family physician, who had also examined the body and concluded that those indentations were the result of "violent pressure." It all led to a gruesome scenario by which Weeks had rushed out by his sleigh one night to strangle her by the well, then hurried back before anyone noticed he was gone. When Weeks was told that Elma's body had been discovered, he virtually admitted his guilt, blurting out, "Is it the Manhattan Well she was found in?"—well before he had reason to know the body's location.

True, all the evidence was circumstantial, Colden informed the jurors, but he begged them to remember the distinguished British legal commentator John Morgan's *Essays Upon the Law of Evidence*: "Circumstantial evidence is all that can be expected, and indeed all that is necessary to substantiate such a charge."

At that, all of New York seemed to breathe a collective sigh of relief that such a horrendous crime was resolved, and the murderer identified, to be expunged from the community. Burr had not yet spoken, leaving it to Hamilton to undermine the witnesses as best he could. Some of his line of questioning was harsh. He badgered one Quaker witness to explain what he meant by placing an event in the "ninth month"—even though Hamilton knew full well the answer, that Quakers regard a word like "September" as pagan. Hamilton also zeroed in on odd details like the nature of the material of the rooming house's exterior wall by the blacksmith house, and whether it was thick enough to block the sounds of children.

Having rushed down for the trial from the Assembly in Albany, and with the prospect of a frantic presidential campaign ahead of him, Burr could not have given the case his full attention, despite the financial implications. Even for him, the whole tawdry business of the corpse had to seem alien for a man who hardly specialized in criminal cases. But he may have identified with a client who was being attacked on all sides. And it was uncanny how quickly Burr was able to take hold of the matter.

When Burr finally rose, he spoke slowly, meaningfully, drawing out the contrast with the peppery, accusatory manner of the assistant attorney general. "Extraordinary means have been adopted to enflame the public against the prisoner," Burr began. "Why has the body been exposed for days in the streets in a manner most indecent and shocking? Such dreadful scenes speak powerfully to the passions: They petrify our mind with horror—congeal the blood within our veins."

With that, he started to swing the sympathies of the case toward poor Weeks and away from the lynch mob bent on hanging him. The only problem, Burr noted, with the prosecutor's tale of a love match gone dreadfully awry was that it lacked any evidence. What signs were there that there had ever been a courtship? Who had ever seen the couple together? What evidence was there of a proposal of marriage? "The story, you will see, is broken, disconnected, and *utterly impossible*." He ticked off the gaps: A strangling? The coroner had given the body a thorough going-over and found no such gruesome injuries—those were discovered only after the corpse had been well manhandled. Weeks's midnight sleigh ride? No one saw it. The sleigh tracks in the snow? They could be anyone's. Sexual relations? Who was to say *Weeks* was the man, and—he paused significantly—not someone else?

One of Burr's old law partners observed that Burr "delighted in surprising his opponents, and in laying, as it were, ambuscades for them." It was Burr's subversive streak. While the prosecution had tried to turn the circumstantial nature of the evidence in its favor, claiming that such facts never lied, Burr pointed out that every part of it had to hold up or "the whole must tumble down." And, after testing all the underpinnings, Burr pulled out the beam that held everything up. He called the blacksmith, Joseph Watkins, to the stand. Colden's premise was that Weeks had an exclusive call on Sands's affection. But Watkins revealed that another man felt the same—the boardinghouse keeper, Elias Ring, who, while his wife was off in the country, had loud, rambunctious sex with Elma. Watkins could hear them through the wall, and he recognized Ring's unmistakable voice, and told his wife. Watkins had confided what he'd heard to another boarder, a devilish man named Croucher, who had worried that his friend Ring's adultery would be found out and went about spreading "improper

insinuations and prejudices against the prisoner" to divert attention, gener-
ating the hysteria that led to Weeks's prosecution.

Now, where was this Croucher? Who was he? This was the moment
that Hamilton finally had a chance for drama, as he was the one to snatch
up a candle, push through the crowd of spectators, and hold it up in front
of Croucher's face, weirdly illuminating him. Is this the man? he demanded.
Yes, the witness answered. It was he.

After that, the prosecutors tried valiantly to resuscitate their case, but
it was hopeless. It was nearly four in the morning, and Hamilton was the
one to declare that the defense would not even bother with a summation.
The exhausted jury took only five minutes to offer its verdict: not guilty.
With just a few lines of argument, Burr had caused minds to pivot, drawing a sudden halt to a citywide crusade to hang Levi Weeks.

→►◄←

WHEN THE CASE was over, the two lawyers returned to their accustomed
roles. Hamilton opposed Burr on two insurance cases that followed, and
they both sank deeper into debt. Burr had to take a fifteen-hundred-dollar
loan, and Hamilton faced the indignity of being reminded by the Bank of
New York, *his* Bank of New York, that he was overdrawn by fifty-three
hundred dollars. He returned to savaging Burr with all the venom in his
quill.

> *These things are to be admitted, and indeed cannot be denied, that he
> is a man of* extreme *and* irregular *ambition; that he is* selfish *to a
> degree which excludes all social affectations; and he is decidedly
> profligate. He is far more cunning than wise—far more dexterous than
> able. The truth is, with great apparent coldness he is the most sanguine
> man in the world. He thinks every thing possible to adventure and
> perseverance; although I believe he will fail, I think it almost certain he
> will attempt usurpation, and the attempt will involve great mischief.*

FORTY-ONE

The Fangs of Jefferson

IT IS RARE for the turn of a century to bring in a new era. But 1800 yielded that for the young country, as it brought the first contested presidential election, one that pitted not just two rival candidates, but two rival parties against each other, both of which had evolved into warring entities that, by now, divided not just political life, but virtually all life, even the air itself, down the middle. Inevitably, the partisan newspapers only widened the divisions with their own wild bombast, the Federalists slamming Jefferson's supposed atheism, adoration of blood-soaked Jacobins, determination to shred the Constitution, and highly suspicious interest in natural history; and the Republicans firing back with attacks on Adams's supposed monarchism, slavish love of England, madness, and determination to jettison the rights secured by the glorious revolution.

With the possible exception of Adams and Jefferson, the two presidential candidates themselves, no two people were more caught up in the political warfare than Burr and Hamilton, each determined to advance his party and so to improve his political standing, which was in danger of waning. The very intensity of the dispute, and the seriousness of the stakes, seemed to inflame their characters, making Burr even more guileful and Hamilton even more dictatorial.

As Burr had divined some years before, the country's electoral map in 1800 was divided so that not just New York State, but New York City, was indeed most likely to decide the matter, in the vote-rich wards on the populous tip of Manhattan. "If the city election of New York is in favor of the Republican ticket, the issue will be Republican," Jefferson told Madison. "If the Federal ticket for the city of New York prevails, the probability will be in favor of a Federal issue." Then he turned philosophical. "The election of New York being in April, it becomes an early and interesting object."

Despite Burr's efforts in New York, the state's electors would be chosen not directly by the people, but by a majority in the state Assembly, and they would vote as a bloc. Although the Federalists had held the Assembly for much of the decade, in 1800 their majority was thinning, and it was threatened by the wild unpopularity of the Alien and Sedition Acts, which had encouraged the Republican Party they had intended to stifle. The bitter Federalist infighting led by Hamilton had not helped matters, and the country seemed to be growing tired of Federalist rule.

Everywhere, the Republicans could scarcely contain their excitement at the prospect of winning the presidency at last. Groaned the High Federalist Fisher Ames, "Every threshing floor, every husking, every part work on a house-frame or raising a building, the very funerals are infected with bawlers or whisperers against government."

In January, Burr had gone to see Jefferson in Philadelphia, where he was scheming how to depose Adams from the top spot, to let him know his plans for taking New York. Rather than rely on the usual incendiary speeches and inflamed newspaper articles to reach the voters, Burr told Jefferson he would try an entirely new approach. Even in 1800, candidates campaigned the way Washington had, relying on "friends" to put their name forward to the electorate in letters and statements to the newspapers, while they themselves professed disinterest. Now Burr proposed something far more personal. He wouldn't rely entirely on others to advance his Republican cause; he would take to the streets himself, knocking on doors to appeal directly to voters in their houses. He and his associates would fan out through every ward in the city, canvassing every last voter, cataloging his interest in the Republican Party, his ability to offer his time or his purse to the cause, his previous votes, and his intention in this election, if any, to vote Republican this time around—and assemble a detailed political dossier on every one of the ten thousand eligible voters in Manhattan.

A master of rhetoric and verbal craftiness, Jefferson was personally rather shy, with talents of persuasion that were better given to the page than to voicing in person, and certainly not with an ordinary citizen. He considered such an approach rather brazen. But he saw that Burr was clearly capable of making dramatic inroads in the critical New York vote, and this approach of his might open up Jefferson's path to the power he craved.

With Jefferson's blessing, Burr rushed back to New York and jumped right into the effort, creating the grandly titled General Republican Committee, with himself at its head. Headquartered at Burr's city house, with a fully laden table for the hungry and a mattress or two for the exhausted, the committee would serve as a command center for the military-style campaign, dispatching loyal Burrites such as Davis, the Swartwout brothers, and perhaps a dozen more, and their many minions, to every ward in the city. They would be the ones to create that dossier on every voter, making a note as to which ones should be revisited on Election Day, with a wagon to carry them to the polls if necessary. The city still had a property requirement for voters, a holdover from Federalist control, but Burr got around that with the "tontine," a banding together of tenants and others without property as collective owners of a tiny piece of legitimate real estate, even if each share was just a few square inches.

He also looked to organizations that might deliver voters in large batches, and turned first to the Society of Saint Tammany, later Tammany Hall, which was then essentially a social club for Irish immigrants who gathered regularly with their leader, the "Grand Sachem," at the "Wigwam"—also known, affectionately, as "the pig sty"—at the City Tavern. Tammany was at the other end of the social scale from Hamilton's Society of the Cincinnati, which was made up of the city's elite. And Burr would make Tammany highly functional, turning the members who gathered at the City Tavern for a glass or two of porter into workhorses of the Republican Party.

Concerned that his Federalists not look too imperious, Hamilton had stocked his list of candidates with workingmen whose democratic appeal would cut into the Republican base. But he went so far as to select political nonentities—a potter, a grocer, a shoemaker, a mason, among them—that were only a Federalist's idea of the kind of men a Republican might want to vote for. When Burr examined Hamilton's list, he "read it over with great gravity," one observer noted, "folded it up in his pocket, and . . . said, 'Now I have him all hollow.'" A morose President Adams could only agree. "Men of little weight," he called the thirteen, "obscure in name, poor in purse, mean in talents and meritorious only in [that] they were confidential friends of the great and good Hamilton." Two days later, on April 17, Burr revealed *his* list, and the contrast could scarcely have been sharper, for he had recruited some of the most illustrious Republicans in the state. His list started with the Old Incumbent himself, George Clinton, and General Horatio Gates, the hero of Saratoga, and it continued through the president of the New York Insurance Company, the esteemed Brockholst Livingston, the former postmaster general of the United States, and several more, altogether a breathtaking display of political firepower. Impressive in itself, it was all the more impressive that Burr had been able to persuade such grandees to labor for a year in virtual anonymity, for measly pay, in Albany. All is "Joy & Enthusiasm," reported one ecstatic Republican. "Never have I observed such a union of sentiment; so much zeal and so general a determination to be active," added another. More to the point, Edward Livingston told Jefferson, "there is a most auspicious gloom on the countenance of every tory and placeman." He referred to the avaricious political appointees Jefferson loved to decry.

On the day of the voting, April 29, Burr's headquarters was a madhouse of activity: Tracking reports came in from every ward in the city, dispatching campaign workers to pull out missing voters, and Burr there to oversee it all, if he wasn't dashing out into the hurly-burly himself. The Federalist *Daily Advertiser* professed to be shocked that a presidential candidate would "stoop so low as to visit every corner in search of voters." But Hamilton had not sat back. The Republican *General Advertiser* spied him all over the city—"Hurrying this way, and darting that; here he buttons a heavy hearted fed, and preaches up courage, there he meets a group, and he simpers in unanimity, again to the heavy headed and hearted, he talks of perseverance, and (God bless the mark) of virtue." The loyal Troup tried to keep up with his friend but found it nearly impossible. "Never have I witnessed such exertions before. I have not eaten dinner for three days and have been constantly on my legs from 7 in the morning till 7 in the afternoon."

A storm had been brewing for days, and it disgorged a flood of rain the day before the balloting began, leaving an unusual sheen that Federalists took to be an aura of "brimstone" that was all too portentous. Indeed, once the first of the three Election Days broke, the city had never seen such a frenzy. The streets were jammed with "carriages, chairs and waggons" bearing the party faithful to the polls, many of them escorted by partisans who kept up a stream of encouragement in one of the many languages— German, Italian, Polish, Russian—of the polyglot city. Hamilton and Burr were nearly ubiquitous presences, Hamilton aboard a handsome white horse, giving rasping speeches, sometimes almost back-to-back with his antagonist, who was doing the same on foot. Each of them tried to out-shout the other as each urged on his campaign workers and derided the opposition. In growing desperation, if not exhaustion, Hamilton turned to assailing the Republicans as "scoundrels" and "villains," but Burr, more confident, did not resort to such language. He kept at it from daybreak to nightfall, and then, when the voting was finally complete, he posted guards at all the polling places in the city to make sure that the ballot boxes were secured, the "leading Federalist gentlemen" were kept away, and the count was accurate.

After that final sunset on May 1, it was soon clear that Burr's slate had swept the entire city. Every single one of his thirteen candidates had won, by an average margin of two hundred fifty votes each—in a city the Feder-alists had taken by nearly a thousand in the last election. Hamilton had been utterly routed. One ecstatic Republican attributed the victory to "the Intervention of a Supreme Power, and our friend Burr the agent." The Fed-eralist Robert Troup saw the opposite, as he discerned "shadows, fiends and darkness" everywhere. In a fury, a disbelieving Hamilton begged Governor Jay, his longtime friend, to have the current Assembly pass a law to transfer the right to choose electors to the people after all, in hopes they might vote differently this time. Never mind that he had been appalled when Burr had recommended exactly this move scarcely more than a year before. Otherwise, he told Jay, the Mephistophelian Jefferson would likely be elected the next president. "Scruples of delicacy and propriety," he said, "ought not to hinder the taking of a *legal* and constitutional step to prevent an *atheist* in Religion and a *fanatic* in politics from getting possession of the helm of state."

But Burr's fingers were everywhere, and a Republican paper soon printed Hamilton's undemocratic appeal, creating a firestorm of outrage and blackening Hamilton's name further. Worse for him, Jay did not go along. Across the top of Hamilton's request, he wrote: "Proposing a measure for party purposes, which I think it would not become me to adopt."

→>-<-

IT WAS CLEAR that Jefferson and Adams would each top his party's ticket, but the question was—who would be their respective vice presidents? Pressed by the tireless Hamilton, the Federalists turned to General Charles Cotesworth Pinckney, the South Carolinian who was one of the three commissioners sent to negotiate with France, precipitating the Quasi-War in 1797. He still rode high on his indignant reply to Talleyrand's request for a bribe: "Millions for defense, but not one cent for tribute." He was the elder brother of Thomas Pinckney, the losing vice presidential candidate Hamilton had picked to run with Adams last time. Fed up with the erratic Adams, Hamilton would have preferred C.C. Pinckney to run at the top of the ticket, but, even if not, he hoped that Pinckney had a chance of bringing South Carolina into the Federalist column.

On the Republican side, the selection wasn't so obvious. Everyone recognized that a New Yorker would probably be needed to take the state's freshly available twelve electoral votes. But which one? The names of the ageless George Clinton and lesser-known Chancellor Robert Livingston inevitably came up in any discussion, but so did the name of the wunderkind who had made New York's votes available, Aaron Burr. Each represented one of the three major factions that held the state in their grip—Clinton and Livingston being two, both time-honored, and now Burr, with his Burrites, supplanted Hamilton's Schuyler as the third. To weigh their relative strength, Albert Gallatin was dispatched to the state to do some reconnaissance. There, Gallatin put the question first to Davis, the Burr loyalist, who was hardly disinterested. He replied that Clinton was too old for the job and Livingston too timid, and he reminded Gallatin that, if Burr were passed over, "many of us will experience much chagrin and disappointment." Gallatin would be forgiven for taking this as a threat.

Gallatin learned from his father-in-law, Commodore Nicholson, that only Clinton and Burr should be seriously considered and that Clinton himself had deferred to Burr as "the most suitable person and perhaps the only Man." But when Gallatin asked Burr, he sharply declared that he was "averse" to being a candidate since he had been humiliated by Jefferson's Virginia when their promised support in the last election had not materialized. Gallatin must have known Burr well enough to know that, of all his emotions, humiliation was the most unbearable, and drove him to say what he did not mean. Burr must have also realized that, now that he had just given Jefferson a chance to win the long-sought presidency, Jefferson was not likely to throw him over. If so, it was probably prudent not to seem overeager.

Three years later, another story line emerged, with the odd detail that Clinton told Gallatin he *would* accept the vice presidency—but only if he was allowed to resign the office shortly after the election. How this could make a winning argument for Gallatin, let alone for Jefferson, is difficult to imagine, but Clinton committed the claim to paper in 1803. Supposedly Nicholson agreed and detailed the Clinton plan to Burr. When Burr read it, he grew "much agitated," a Burrite remembered. "He declared he would have nothing more to do with the business." He would seek the New York governorship instead. Later, when Nicholson brought by two versions of a letter to Gallatin, one supporting Clinton, the other Burr, Burr charged out of the room in a fury, leaving Nicholson alone with a couple of Burr-ites, one of whom "declared with a determined voice that Colo. Burr should accept and that he was obliged to do so on principle." And, even though Burr had not been consulted, that stood as his answer. He would be a candidate in the 1800 election, not because he sought to be, but because he felt "obliged."

Nicholson told Gallatin that Aaron Burr was the best choice for the office. It could well be that the ambivalence did not extend upward from Burr's General Republican Committee but downward from the so-called Sage of Monticello, who was deeply leery of Aaron Burr. Under the Constitution, of course, Burr and Jefferson would each vie for presidency, even if they were meant to be running mates; they might well receive the same number of votes, throwing the matter to the House of Representatives. At that point, Hamilton professed to welcome the arrangement, telling his friend Theodore Sedgwick, now risen from senator to Speaker of the House, it was "the only thing that can save us from the fangs of Jefferson."

Having sabotaged every aspect of the election for the Federalists, Hamilton sallied forth to wreck the rest by cutting the legs out from under the Federalist president, Adams. Alarmed by the results from New York, Adams had decided that he needed finally to create a cabinet that answered to him, not to Hamilton, and purged the last two of the most blatantly pro-Hamilton secretaries. One was War Secretary James McHenry, and Adams did not do it gently. The president "became indecorous, and at times outrageous," McHenry reported to Hamilton. But that was Adams. McHenry observed that whether the president was "sportful, playful, witty, kind, cold, drunk, sober, angry, easy, stiff, jealous, cautious, confident, close, open," it was "almost always in the *wrong place* or to the *wrong persons*." Like Hamilton, he thought Adams was "insane." In firing McHenry, Adams directed most of his ire at Hamilton, whom he called a "bastard" and "the greatest intriguant in the world." When this flew back to Hamilton, he threw up his hands. "Oh mad! Mad! Mad!"

In Quincy for the entire summer and fall, Adams continued to peck away at Hamilton as a "little cock sparrow general," and Abigail would occasionally chime in, assailing Hamilton and his followers as "boys of yesterday." Then Adams raised the stakes, asserting that Hamilton headed an "English faction" bent on seizing the government. Outraged by the charge, even though it had been a staple of anti-Hamilton commentary since 1787, Hamilton called it "base, wicked, cruel calumny, destitute even of a plausible pretext to excuse the folly or mask the depravity that must have dictated it." If Adams had not been president, Hamilton might have challenged him to a duel. Instead, Hamilton was determined to expel Adams from his office, journeying to the capital to gain more evidence and anecdotes in support of his claims. In October, just as the voting was set to begin in several states, Hamilton published his character assassination of the president under a pseudonym as an open letter entitled *The Public Conduct and Character of John Adams, Esq., President of the United States*. Initially limited in its circulation to C.C. Pinckney's native South Carolina, the diatribe was supposedly intended just to elevate Pinckney to parity with Adams, so that he would have a shot at the presidency, but of course the effect was to provide all the more reasons for the country to dump Adams. As always, Hamilton chased his argument to the very end and produced a stunningly vicious portrait of a sitting president by a leading member of his party, one littered with cruel throwaways like his reference to "the disgusting egotism, the distempered jealousy, and the ungovernable indiscretion of Mr. Adams's temper."

If this sally was meant to be surgical, cutting away support for the president and building it up for Pinckney in his home state, it didn't work out that way. The letter got out, and not by accident. Burr got his fingers on an early copy, divined its author, and grasped the possibilities. He showed it to John Beckley, the man who'd released the Reynolds Pamphlet, and arranged for publication of choice excerpts to the Republican *Aurora*.

Stung, Hamilton responded by releasing the whole pamphlet, a move that went no better for him than it had in the Reynolds case. The revelations hurt Adams less than they damaged Hamilton, busy savaging his president for emotional instability, of which he himself was possibly more guilty. Even his friend Troup said it was Hamilton, not Adams, who was the one "radically deficient in discretion." But the revelations injured the Federalist Party as a whole more than they damaged either man, as they raised questions about its principles, decorum, reliability, and leadership. Hamilton was a battered ship in a wild storm of his own making. Adams's temper was legendary, but Hamilton's was no less, as he now flew into ever-higher rages at apparitions only he could see. It must have been unnerving to be so inept when he used to be so able. Long after others might retire from the fray, Hamilton continued to thrash about, each time hoping for a better result, and then receiving a worse one, undermining confidence while raising the stakes, which only made the issue more desperate next time. The campaign of 1800 was the most recent next time, but there would be more. He was falling, and he would continue to fall.

FORTY-TWO

The Gigg Is Therefore Up

B Y THE TIME of the election in early December 1800, the federal government had finally moved from stately Philadelphia to the onetime swamp of Washington City on the banks of the meandering Potomac, whose banks were still thick with wild turkeys. For all the efforts of Benjamin Latrobe, the architect of the original federal building in New York, to create a new Paris, Washington was a dispiriting hodgepodge of undistinguished federal buildings and mostly flimsy homes to ten thousand whites and three thousand black slaves who had been conscripted into constructing this citadel of freedom. The most impressive show buildings, the President's Mansion and the Capitol building, were still woefully incomplete, and they stood amid a shantytown of boardinghouses for Rabelaisian elected officials, their abodes rigorously separated by party.

As such, the city seemed an apt metaphor for the nation's politics. When the results of the voting were made known toward the end of December, the election had gone as the Republicans had both hoped and feared. Jefferson and Burr were tied at seventy-three votes each, and Adams and Pinckney trailed with sixty-five and sixty-four respectively. While everyone knew a tie was possible, few expected that every last Republican elector would follow party instructions and split his two votes evenly between the candidates to produce it. It was as if a coin had been flipped in the air and landed on its edge. Jefferson's ticket had swept nearly the entire South, and Adams's had taken all the North, and New York's twelve votes had indeed been the difference. It put Jefferson in a ticklish position regarding his running mate, as Jefferson could not bring himself to assert publicly that he was the preferred candidate, probably because he imagined that went without saying. For a political colossus, a man bent on shifting the course of the nation, Jefferson could be oddly lacking in confidence, and, after the vote came in, he wrote Burr a letter of congratulations that was a masterpiece of timid backhandedness. He expressed his dismay that, *as vice president*, Burr now would sadly be unavailable to serve in his administration, leaving a "chasm . . . which cannot be adequately filled up." It was praise as derision. What made Jefferson so sure that *Burr* wouldn't be president? Burr played along with this charade, offering to "cheerfully abandon the office of V.P." if he could be more useful to Jefferson elsewhere. Each man was brazenly lying to the other.

The resolution was not up to them, in any case, but to the House of Representatives, which would choose the president after all, following another ungainly process. Each vote would be cast not by an individual representative, but by the delegation of each state, as determined by the majority. Although the Federalists outnumbered the Republicans in the House, they controlled only six states to the Republicans' eight, with two other states lacking the majority needed to be officially for one candidate or the other. Some Federalists talked of maintaining the deadlock long enough to appoint an interim executive, presumably Adams, undoing the result of the election altogether. That prospect was so infuriating to Republicans that some vowed literally to execute anyone appointed to the office by such unconstitutional means, and James Monroe threatened to bring out state militias to suppress any such coup. Then the Federalists declared *their* militias would take on the Republican ones, creating the prospect of civil war. Jefferson said as much to Adams, threatening "incalculable consequences" if the Federalists tried to install a president of their own. Once they saw that the interim idea would likely lead to a general calamity, the Federalists decided to back the candidate more conducive to their interests.

At first blush, that was certainly not Jefferson. Loathed by Federalists before the election, he was loathed no less after. Many feared he was poised to destroy the financial machinery that Hamilton had assembled to generate the national prosperity, starting with the Bank of the United States.

Others were afraid that, as an atheist, he would dispatch federal agents to seize their Bibles. Rumors abounded that with devilish intent he might even introduce the Hessian fly that so fascinated him into the country.

By contrast, people did not know what to fear from Burr except his ambition, which didn't seem nearly so disturbing. For all his fears of the "fangs of Jefferson," Hamilton was appalled that anyone could possibly be so blasé about Burr, whom he declared was "selfish to a degree that excludes all social affections." He wrote this to House Speaker Theodore Sedgwick, even though he much preferred Burr's brand of selfishness to Jefferson's "pernicious theories." But Hamilton went further to claim that Burr sought "supreme Power," as one who "loves nothing but himself," and was a "voluptuary" besides. He again assailed Burr as an "American Catiline," who was not just a savage Roman conspirator, but one guilty of incest and the murder of his wife, sister, and son. He "talked perfect Godwinism," referring to the husband of Mary Wollstonecraft, who had been Burr's inspiration as a feminist to his wife and daughter, but to Hamilton all too supportive of the French Revolution and of an upheaval in the social order. Burr would go to war with Great Britain on a whim. He was no soldier, Hamilton went on, since he had abandoned the war effort at a critical period, and, as a statesman, he was "far more cunning than wise." And anyone who thought that any loyalty to the Federalist Party could possibly restrain him would be tragically mistaken. That would leave Burr "laughing in his sleeve."

By now there were two Hamiltons, a solid one and an inflated one, and the gap between them was widening. In the best of times, no one pushed Hamilton to a sputtering extreme like Burr, but the prospect of a Burr presidency positively undid him. There were no lengths that he would not travel rhetorically to remove a threat he considered mortal. If the Hamilton of old was known for his temperate, well-reasoned, and persuasive arguments, now he was given to shameless hyperbole and foolish bombast. Did he imagine that anyone had forgotten what he'd said about Jefferson, and how *he* was the real danger to the country?

Gouverneur Morris knew Burr well enough to know that he was not the end of the world. He asked Hamilton straight out: How could Hamilton now support a man he'd always considered to be utterly "void of principle"?

In reply, Hamilton conceded that he ought to "hate" Jefferson and like Burr, with whom "I have always been personally well." But he continued to denigrate Burr at every opportunity—to little effect except to further marginalize himself in the party. He was leading a parade, but there was no parade behind him.

Throughout the period of maneuvering before the formal vote in February, most of the congressmen lived in that clutch of boardinghouses near the Capitol, where, over meals or drinks, they did their best to persuade their colleagues to switch positions and break the tie. But since the boardinghouses, like so much else, were divided by party, there were limits to what anyone could do to alter the outcome.

Jefferson remained in Monticello, although he was closely attuned to the political proceedings. Burr was in Albany, and he was so out of touch he might have been removed from the country altogether. One reason was that his daughter, Theodosia, had found a mate and was due to be wed on February 2, nine days before the House was to vote, and Burr could not bring himself to change the wedding day, even if his chances for the presidency hung in the balance. If Hamilton's personality inflated during this period, Burr's deflated, all passion spent. Rather than returning to that level of maniacal hyperactivity he'd reached for the New York elections, he settled into a mystifying state of quiescence in which he was scarcely heard from at all.

But his children had always been his country, and at eighteen, Theodosia might have been his own first lady. She had already been wooed by the painter John Vanderlyn, who'd lived with them at Richmond Hill through her teens, and whom Burr had packed off to Paris when his ardor got the better of him. Meriwether Lewis, the dashing twenty-six-year-old explorer whom Jefferson would soon dispatch to explore the American Northwest, had pursued her as well. But she finally settled on a gentlemanly twenty-one-year-old, Joseph Alston, who, by virtue of a bequest from his paternal grandfather, was one of the richest men in South Carolina, with vast rice holdings in the Georgia District and more than two hundred slaves to tend them. Dubbed the "Palmetto Plutocrat," Alston had a softness to his cheeks and cheerfully curly hair that proved to be misleading, as it did not reflect the bearer's stiff and overbearing personality, which only slowly revealed itself. Alston had met Theodosia on a languid northern tour the previous summer when Burr was traveling about New England in search of votes. Burr hoped that such a wealthy young man might be right for her, but he had his Boston friend Dr. William Eustis "anatomize him soul & heart & body." Eustis gave Alston a good report, but Alston was probably better suited to the needs of Theodosia's father, who soon enlisted him as his political emissary to the southern states, entrusting him with a letter to carry to Jefferson at Monticello. As satisfying as Alston was to Burr, he left Theodosia pining for something more, even if he was rich and well educated. He seemed brusque and standoffish. Well into their courtship, when she was impatient for a marriage proposal, Theodosia wrote him to say she'd "be happy to see you whenever you choose; that I suppose is equivalent to very soon." She added, teasingly, "My father laughs at my impatience to hear from you, and says that I am in love; but I do not believe that to be a fair deduction." After describing her plans through February, she declared, "My movements will after that depend on my father and you." She concluded, "Adieu. I wish you many returns of the century."

She was right about her father's claim of love—it wasn't a "fair deduction," but the marriage proceeded just the same. A notice in the *New-York Commercial Advertiser* listed the details: the couple were married by the minister of the Dutch Reform Church in Albany as planned on February 2. Theodosia was listed as "the only daughter of Aaron Burr, Esq.," with no mention of her late mother or his political accomplishments.

Alston soon proved to be insufferable. "The most intolerable mortal I ever beheld," in the estimation of George Washington's step-granddaughter Nelly Custis, who knew him socially. Added Maria Nicholson, the savvy daughter of Burr's ally the commodore, the one pumping him for the presidency: "He is a great dasher, dissipated, ill-tempered, vain, and silly." And: "He is ugly and of unprepossessing manners." Troup suspected that Burr's massive debts played a role in the marriage: "The money in question was the predominating motive." But there was politics, too, and Burr hungered for South Carolina's eight electoral votes, the ones that Hamilton hoped Pinckney would bring to the Federalists. He imagined the politically connected Alston could help secure them (as, in fact, he did). All of which made Maria Nicholson fly into despair: "Can it be that the father has sacrificed a daughter to affluence and influential connections?"

Burr had given Theodosia a husband—and won himself a Burrite.

→>-<←

WHILE JEFFERSON MONITORED developments in Monticello, Burr remained in Albany and did nothing to stop the speculation that he was after the presidency—or to encourage it. He did not need to declare himself either way, since voters could not distinguish between the candidate they wanted for president and the one they wanted only for vice president. It was solely a presidential election, with the runner-up to be the winner's vice president. This ambiguity served Burr's purposes perfectly, as it allowed him to maintain his usual detachment from the events he had unleashed. It was as if he imagined himself merely an observer of this epic drama, when he was the one on whom all eyes were trained. There were other characters— Jefferson foremost among them—but unlike Burr, his position was fixed, leaving him almost no room to maneuver to win Federalist votes. He was obliged to be Jeffersonian. Not so Burr. To call Burr a Burrite was hardly to ascribe to him any political philosophy. He was what he always was—a code that could be read one way by one key, and another by another. Because any political position was available to him, he was free to redefine himself however he liked, even as a Federalist, and no one would have accused him of inconsistency. Burr was what he was not. As Theodore Sedgwick described Burr to his son: "He is not an enthusiastic theorist. He is not under the direction of Virginian Jacobins. He is not a declared infidel." More to the point: "He would not be able to administer the government without the aid of the Federalists and this aid he cannot obtain unless his administration is Federal[ist]." In short, Burr was an opportunist, and others could find opportunity in that.

If Burr took no active role in securing the presidency, he did nothing to discourage the speculation that he might, and he expressed irritation that anyone might try to constrain him. Irked at the Republican insistence that he resign rather than be a pawn to Federalist ambitions, he let Samuel Smith, Jefferson's lieutenant in the House, know that he considered such a request "unnecessary, unreasonable and impertinent." Strong words that were sure to get back to Jefferson, which was doubtless his intent. The idea that the Federalists could play him was so preposterous that there was no need to deny it. Which, of course, *was* a denial, and an unconvincing one. Beyond that, he left it to surrogates to express his disavowal. Absent any Burr thunder from Albany, other theories rushed in to fill the vacuum, many of them feeding on Burr's reputation as a man made for darkness.

The truth was that Burr had refused to disavow all interest in the presidency for the simple reason that he didn't want to. Burr had always been an arrow pointed up, and he was not about to point down now. Besides, he had the vice presidency in his pocket, so what was there to lose? He said as much to General Smith when the two men met in Philadelphia one evening in early January, and Smith was plainly eager to gallop back to Washington City with the good news that Burr was backing Jefferson. The Federalists controlled the outcome, either by denying Jefferson the presidency and handing it to Burr, or by denying them both by holding out for a Federalist president, come what may. In response, Burr declared, "We cannot be without a president, our friends must join the federal vote." Meaning that if Republicans wished to foil the Federalist plot to delay long enough to install a Federalist president, some of them would have to abandon Jefferson and join with the Federalists to elect Burr. Then Smith's associate Gabriel Christie of Maryland had to ask: "Who is to be our vice president then?"

"Mr. Jefferson," Burr replied.

That did not sit well in Monticello.

Still, it is one thing to desire an outcome, and another to make it happen, and there is no evidence that Burr made the attempt—overtly. But covertly? Hamilton suspected that Burr had enlisted the New Yorker Edward Livingston as a double agent, appearing to talk up Jefferson's candidacy on Burr's behalf, even as he actually was pushing Burr as president to the impressionable New York delegation. A New Jersey congressman was said to be working for Burr from the same angle. Hamilton wasn't above doing a little double-dealing himself. He had the plan to try to entice Burr into backing a small piece of Federalist policy to win some Federalist votes, then leak the news of his perfidy to Jefferson and "lay the foundation of dissension between the two chiefs." Then there were the many Burrites, such as Matthew Davis and the hearty Swartwout brothers, who scuttled about trying to find the soft places of the influential. More ominous for Hamilton, his own law partner, the loyal Federalist David A. Ogden, had been seen moving among the New York delegation, possibly with the aim of getting it to swing to Burr. But it was a shadowy time, this presidential season. No one knew who was up and who was down, and a hundred speculations bloomed in the darkness. Amid the feints and counterfeints, it was impossible *not* to suspect Burr of midnight skullduggery.

The fact is, for all his frustrations with party regulars trying to push him into doing their bidding, Burr never did the one thing that would have closed down the political carnival and brought about what Burr, along with virtually every prominent Republican, professed to want, namely, a Jefferson presidency. That was for Burr to announce publicly and emphatically that he wanted that too, and that enough of his votes should be transferred to Jefferson to make him president on the first ballot, while reserving enough of his own to secure the vice presidency. Then, having demonstrated his loyalty to the leader of his party, he could wait eight years until he could succeed Jefferson for his heroic sacrifice. But this he did not do, and so the Federalists continued to believe that Burr was up for sale, and the Republicans continued to fear that too, and Jefferson built up such a revulsion at the very name of his vice president that Burr effectively removed himself from the administration before it even began, to say nothing of his presidential aspirations eight years later.

Altogether, it was a baffling performance—not just a terrible miscalculation, but a kind of political suicide, one that among political contemporaries was equaled only by Hamilton in his outlandish response to the revelation of the Reynolds affair. For it wasn't a quiet going, a Roman bloodletting in the bathtub, but a screaming leap from a great height. It was the kind of death-seeking performance that called into question the many death-defying ones that preceded it.

Burr became something he had never before been, a negative, an empty space left to others to fill. And, mystified by his intentions, no one budged. In a desperate last attempt at getting Burr to commit, his old friend Gallatin wrote him in Albany to say that three key representatives in Maryland,

New Jersey, and New York were prepared to defect to him and hand him the presidency, but to secure these gentlemen's votes he needed to come down to Washington "without an instant's delay." In Albany, his "friends" urged him to do just that, posthaste. According to Burr's ally and fellow assemblyman Peter Townsend, Burr "agreed to do so." Then, in the shorthand of a New York merchant to whom Townsend hurriedly told the tale: "His friends left him—went to the legislature—Burr did not come—they supposed he was preparing—after the House adjourned, they called at his lodgings—they found his luggage packed and he ready—*but at the critical moment his heart failed him*—he remained in Albany."

→>‑<‑

No haven anyway, Washington had been enduring a long, brutal winter that February. In the Executive Mansion, the Adamses had kept all thirteen fireplaces blazing around the clock but still could not dispel the icy damp. When, in the officials' efforts to warm themselves, small fires broke out in the War offices and Treasury, Republicans charged that the Federalists were burning evidence of their corruption.

For the first count on February 11, a blizzard enveloped the city in a whirl of white, impeding the passage for so many congressmen that some observers figured the tie would be broken by Mother Nature. But everyone arrived, even Maryland representative Joseph H. Nicholson, who, stricken with a raging fever from his pneumonia, was carried on a litter for two miles through the snow, his wife trudging alongside.

At one o'clock that Thursday, Speaker Sedgwick called the House to order for the balloting. Despite all the stratagems, speculation, and politicking, the vote remained where it had stood after the election, with Jefferson winning the eight Republican delegations and Burr the six Federalist ones; the remaining two yielded majorities for neither man. It seemed impossible that such a tenuous tie would remain one, and countless rumors flew of backroom deals sending Jefferson votes to the Burr camp, or the reverse, to settle the matter. But no. Six more votes were taken in rapid succession, with the same result. At that, Sedgwick released the congressmen for one hour "to eat a mouthful," as one representative put it. The balloting then went on through the night, one vote every hour, each one more tedious and predictable than the last, until eight the next morning. Nothing changed. After one more try to break the deadlock at noon, Sedgwick banged his gavel and recessed the House until Friday at eleven. "What the Feds...mean, I cannot tell," Republican representative John Dawson wrote Madison. "We are resolved never to yield, and sooner hazard everything than to prevent the voice and wishes of the people being carried into effect." He concluded, "I have not closed my eyes for 36 hours." When the Federalists left, they endured taunts from Republican hecklers gathered by the doors. One Federalist newspaper urged their representatives to chastise any defectors from Burr to Jefferson as "consecrated to infamy."

While it was obvious that the shift of a single delegation would change the outcome, it was also apparent that the movement of one man would have made that unnecessary. That was Burr, of course. But he remained silent in Albany, although he doubtless was following the proceedings by post rider from the capital. "Had Burr done anything for himself, he would long ere have been President," wrote Federalist representative William Cooper. The air was so thick with intrigue that Madison installed a relay system of militia riders to convey up-to-the-minute reports to him in Richmond. For all the speculation, no vote changed on Friday or Saturday. The House had gone through thirty-three ballots, and no one had given ground.

And then someone did: James A. Bayard, Federalist representative from tiny Delaware, who had, with his party, voted diligently for Burr. He finally concluded that the Republicans would never yield from electing Jefferson and that Burr would never dare offer the concessions that would win enough Federalists over. "Burr has acted a miserable paltry part," Bayard groused. "The election was in his power, but he was determined to come in as a Democrat, and in that event would have been the most dangerous man in the community." Bayard came to this conclusion over the weekend, but he needed some reassurances from Jefferson before he was ready to crown him on Monday. Would he continue Hamilton's system of finance, maintain the navy, and leave Federalists in their government jobs? If the answers were yes, he would be president. He revealed his thinking at a party caucus on Monday morning. "The clamor was prodigious. The reproaches vehement," he wrote a cousin. "We broke up in confusion."

The Federalists needed time to discover Burr's intentions—and Jefferson's. In the meantime, everyone continued to vote the party line through the thirty-fifth ballot. Jefferson's answer had been cloudy, giving the Federalists hope that Bayard would not go for him after all. But Burr, at long last, became crystal clear: Words he should have spoken immediately after the popular election, he now said after a calamitous and protracted House procedure had almost split the nation in two. He "explicitly resigns his pretensions" to the presidency, Sedgwick reported bitterly to his son. "The gigg is therefore up."

And so it was. The Federalists never did cast a single vote for Jefferson, but on the thirty-sixth ballot, at one o'clock on Tuesday afternoon, February 17, enough of them, starting with Bayard, abstained to make Thomas Jefferson the third president of the United States, with Aaron Burr his vice president. In an irony, it was the vote of Matthew Lyon, the Vermont representative who had been bludgeoned on the House floor, that put Jefferson into office. When the electrifying news went out, Republicans burst forth with parades, cannon fire, banquets, bonfires, and fireworks, a celebration rivaled only by the announcement of the peace agreement after the American Revolution, which, to Republicans, it closely resembled.

It wasn't until two days after the vote, on February 19, that Burr, still in Albany, got word of the result, and he set out to Washington immediately, but not hastily, stopping over in New York City, Philadelphia, and Baltimore, where he collected Theodosia and her husband, to bring them back to Washington for the inauguration on March 4. It was held in the Senate chamber, where Burr would preside for the next four years as his sole governmental duty. Tellingly, at the ceremony, Burr spoke only to take the oath of office. In his address, Jefferson delivered the memorable line, "We are all Republicans, we are all Federalists." A statement that the election had shown to be manifestly untrue, as would his presidency. Rather than attend the ceremony in a show of national unity, Adams and Speaker Sedgwick had fled the capital by stagecoach at four o'clock that morning, headed into retirement.

FORTY-THREE

A Damn'd Rascal

WHILE JEFFERSON SETTLED in to the still-chilly President's House that March, Burr himself took up residence in Georgetown, a separate township of five thousand people, three miles upriver. Roads connected the two, but they were often too rutted and muddy to offer easy passage to the capital. If Washington was a boomtown of ramshackle boardinghouses, Georgetown provided more stately residences and so was the preferred home for foreign dignitaries, of whom Burr might have been considered one. To him, Washington City might as well have been a foreign capital, a city clotted with dignitaries who harbored dark suspicions about the sitting vice president.

By starting the year as an assemblyman, Burr had made a political ascent worthy of the Montgolfier brothers,* but, as with any balloonist, he had only air under him when he was at his height. He had not been lifted by anything like the national groundswell that had elevated Jefferson. Peo-

---

* Joseph-Michel and Jacques-Étienne Montgolfier invented the *globe aérostatique*, or hot-air balloon, in 1783, when they stitched together an orb of tightly buttoned sackcloth seventy-five feet high and fifty feet across, and colorfully decorated with signs of the zodiac and the royal monogram of Louis XVI. Standing in a basket below, Jacques-Étienne was the first to be lifted off the face of the earth, leaving the outskirts of Paris's Bois de Boulogne, rising three thousand feet, floating five miles outside of Paris, and landing safely beside a windmill half an hour later.

ple knew Jefferson. People knew nothing about Burr except that his machinations had nearly won him the presidency. Burr had been lifted not by the people, but by his Burrites. So there was almost no one to catch him when he fell.

The peak moment of his term as vice president occurred as the inauguration ceremony began, when Burr had graciously offered the incoming president his chair and Jefferson had taken it. A simple gesture, it was nonetheless duly noted and praised as a lovely, if belated, acknowledgment by Burr of Jefferson's superior position. It would be the last such moment between the two men ever. For Burr was still falling, a calamitous drop that would take him not just down to the ground, but, as in a tale from Greek mythology, into the underworld below, where he would stagger about the dead. Burr himself professed to be oblivious of his dire circumstances. Some of this was his aristocratic disdain of unpleasant truths; some his disbelief that anyone would ever take such political shenanigans seriously; and some his conviction that he should pay no penalty because he had done nothing wrong.

Writing to party chieftain Albert Gallatin from Philadelphia shortly before the inauguration, Burr had scoffed at the idea that anyone would be troubled by all the preposterous rumors about a supposed Burr intrigue for the presidency: "They are now of little consequence, & those who had believed them will doubtless blush at their own weakness." Unfortunately for Burr, President Jefferson was one of the ones who believed them, and with good reason. As early as April 24, Samuel Osgood—the Massachusetts merchant who'd supplied Washington with his executive mansion in New York, now the Speaker of the New York Assembly—wrote Madison to warn him that he had proof that Burr had indeed intended to seize the presidency. "Strong evidence," Osgood called it, although he did not reveal any in the letter. "[The Burrites] are entirely devoted to the Vice President; and had it been in their Power we have reason to believe Mr. Jefferson would not have been President."

Jefferson was set to take his revenge with his usual stealth, leaving no evidence of his complicity. He did not even make a show of consulting his vice president when selecting his cabinet; nor did he take the slightest interest in Burr's views on a single matter of policy or politics. It was as if Burr had somehow ceased to exist. Most wounding of all, when Burr sought to capitalize on all the federal offices opening with the change of administrations— rewarding his key Burrites, who had worked so hard in the campaign, with plum appointments, and providing himself with a power base for his own future run for the presidency in the bargain—Jefferson did not even give him the favor of a reply. Burr specified posts for five of his closest associates, including John Swartwout and Matthew Davis, whom he was pushing to be naval officer of New York. In truth, Jefferson did quietly make two of the appointments, installing the two Burrites with demonstrable talent. But the question of the remaining three, Davis especially, dragged on through the summer. In increasing frustration, Burr made inquiries of everyone but the president, confiding to Gallatin, now secretary of the treasury, his fear that the appointments had been sidetracked by "Jesuit machinations." For someone normally so cautious about what he wrote, it was an indelicate construction to apply to an avowedly atheistic president, especially since he was likely to see Burr's letter. But the issue was far less about Davis than about Burr. As Gallatin put the matter to Jefferson: Did he want to oblige his vice president at all, and, more to the point, would he support a Burr presidential bid when his own term was up? Jefferson was not one to commit the answers to such questions to paper, but they would have certainly been no in both cases. The truth was, he'd had quite enough of Burr and would have liked nothing more than to excise him from his administration at the earliest opportunity.*

Jefferson's antipathy was only amplified by events in New York, where the state's politics were now running sharply against Burr. In the fall of 1801, the indefatigable Governor Clinton had defeated Hamilton's brother-in-law, the patroon Stephen Van Rensselaer, to win the governor's chair for yet another term, and had placed his cunning nephew, DeWitt Clinton, just thirty-two, at the head of the state's Council of Appoint-

---

* Gallatin also imagined that Jefferson might be seeking a way to weaken Burr to the point that he could drop him for his second term, clearing the way for the loyal Virginian James Madison to take over.

ments. There he emptied all the Federalists out of state offices and installed loyal Clintonians and not a single Burrite. Following the developments from Washington, Jefferson could see this meant that Burr was persona non grata in his home state, offering even less reason to reward any of his people with federal jobs.

To press his cause for employment, Davis rode to Monticello to plead his case with Jefferson. It did him no good. "Nothing is decided," Jefferson wrote Gallatin afterward. And nothing would ever be decided, which is to say, the decision was no. Burr was rarely frightened, but this was one of those times. Knowing that a decision about Davis was a decision about him, Burr wrote Jefferson twice more that fall, but the president did not deign to respond until mid-November. His tone could scarcely have been colder. He curtly informed his vice president that, as a general rule, he did not answer letters "relating to office." If Burr sought a response, "The answer is to be found on what is done or not done with them." In other words, Jefferson would not even lift a pen to oblige his vice president on a matter of supreme importance to him. The post of naval officer of New York remained occupied by a Federalist.

→-◄-

BURR WAS NOT alone in seeing his influence wane both federally under the new president and in New York State under a new governor. Hamilton had the same miserable experience. Having created national policy under Washington and influenced it under Adams, he was now reduced to watching Jefferson from the balcony seats, hoping that he would not kill off the financial programs he'd slaved to create. Happily, many of Jefferson's positions proved rhetorical. He did not in fact try to shrink the bloated federal bureaucracy—of 130 employees, no less—to "a few plain duties to be performed by a few servants," as he had pledged, although he did scuttle the navy, to the country's regret later. Of particular interest to Hamilton, he left in place the Bank of the United States he professed to loathe, and when Jefferson dispatched Gallatin to uncover any frauds hidden in the archives of Hamilton's Treasury Department, Gallatin duly investigated and then confessed he could not find any. "I have found the most perfect system ever formed," Gallatin reported. "Any change that should be made in it would injure it. Hamilton made no blunders, committed no frauds. He did nothing wrong." For Jefferson, that was not good news. As he later groused, "we can never completely get rid of [Hamilton's] financial system."

In the governor's race, Hamilton had shouted himself hoarse with campaign speeches that pushed his brother-in-law and the Federalist cause, but they may have only contaminated both with the Hamilton toxin, and Van Rensselaer had been routed by a wide margin, making a clean sweep of Federalist losses since the Washington administration.

With the Federalists in retreat nationally and on the defensive in the state, Hamilton moved to create a vibrant Federalist paper to fend off the propaganda spewed by the various Republican sheets in town. The *New-York Evening Post*, it was to be called. Hamilton himself put up a thousand dollars of the ten thousand needed to start it, and he picked the editor too: William Coleman, a ruddy-cheeked Irishman from Boston who'd met Hamilton when he had barnstormed New England in the 1796 campaign. Coleman was convinced he had seen God. "The greatest statesman beyond comparison of any age," he declared. Then he won Hamilton's heart by accusing Jefferson of pulling down the Federalist cathedral of order and putting up "a foul and filthy temple consecrated to atheism and lewdness."

The *Evening Post*'s first issue, on November 16, 1801, struck an elevated tone, offering readers "correct information" with an eye toward promoting "just principles." It proved to be a handsome publication, which quickly established the standard for newspapers across the country. None other than James T. Callender, who had done more than anyone to ruin Hamilton's reputation, called it "the most elegant piece of workmanship that we have seen in either Europe or America." Principled as the publication might be, Hamilton would rely on it as his preferred place to run his vitriolic indictments of the Jefferson administration.

He had scarcely settled into his new role as a publisher when, on November 23 of that year, the *Evening Post* was obliged to cover an unspeakable tragedy involving his family. Hamilton's nineteen-year-old son, Philip, had been killed in a duel with a young Republican lawyer named George I. Eacker. Tousle haired and quick-witted, if somewhat impetuous, a recent graduate from Columbia with high honors, Philip was said by his father to be the family's "eldest and brightest hope." He was the adored one. Hamilton had overseen Philip's studies almost as assiduously as Burr had Theodosia's, and when Philip had fallen sick that time as a teenager, his father had never left his side, administering his medicine around the clock.

As part of the July Fourth festivities, promoted by Jefferson to make his party the source of the American religion, New York had been thrilled by cannon fire and bell ringing—and also by speeches on Broadway, many of them quite partisan. Strolling about, Philip Hamilton happened to hear Captain Eacker loudly blaming the notorious XYZ Affair on England, not France, and declaring that General Hamilton's army had been raised not to defend America, but to intimidate Republicans.

That was irritating, but Philip forgot about it until he spotted Eacker at the Park Theater in Manhattan a few months later. Outraged to see him there chatting with some friends before the show, Philip and a friend named Price barged into George Eacker's box and started ragging him about his July Fourth oration. Eacker insisted they take this up in the lobby. As Eacker made his way there, he muttered: "It is too abominable to be publicly humiliated by a set of rascals."

"Who do you call damn'd rascals?" Philip snapped. To a gentleman, "rascal" was a terrible insult.

Eacker grabbed Philip by the collar and yanked him close, nearly bringing them to blows right there in the theater. They continued on to the lobby, where more harsh words were exchanged, and still more in a nearby tavern. Finally Eacker had had enough. "I expect to hear from you," he told Philip as he left.

"You shall," Philip replied.

Eacker stormed back to his box in the theater. Before long, Price scrawled out a challenge and delivered it to Eacker in his seat. Eacker accepted immediately.

Philip was more cautious; he knew the political implications of a Hamilton dueling with a Jeffersonian. He consulted his uncle John Barker Church, who, after his duel with Burr, and quite likely some others, knew a

bit about dueling, and he recommended trying to come to some accommodation. While Philip pondered what to do, Price and Eacker rowed across
the Hudson to fight their duel in New Jersey. At the field, they each fired
off two shots. None hit. Eacker considered the matter closed. Price was not
his target.

It was Alexander Hamilton, who was riding a knife's edge—keen to
protect his son's reputation, and his own, but also desperate to see Philip
survive. Paralyzed, he left the matter to Church, but the negotiations he
advised stalled. Eacker refused to retract the inflammatory word "rascal"—
even if Philip apologized for charging into his box, as he offered to do.
Left with no choice, Philip agreed to meet Eacker at three o'clock the next
afternoon at the field of honor at Paulus Hook, down the coast in New
Jersey. When the duel was on, Hamilton counseled his son to rise above the
foolishness of dueling and "throw away" his ball, shooting in the air. That
way, he would demonstrate his gentlemanly virtues to Eacker, encouraging
him to do the same. They would settle the disagreement peacefully, their
honor intact, as Eacker had with Price.

It sounded reasonable and high-minded, but unilateral disarmament is
a dangerous approach to an armed man bent on vengeance. Besides, if the
point is to protest the barbaric custom of dueling, why not just refuse to
participate?

At Paulus Hook, the seconds paced off the distance and the two men
faced off. When a second shouted out to fire, Philip did not raise his pistol,
and neither did Eacker. The two of them stared at each other, pistols down,
for a small eternity. Then Eacker slowly raised his pistol and aimed it at
Philip, and Philip mirrored him, aiming his pistol at Eacker. Then Eacker
fired, and the bullet cracked into Philip's right side. With Philip standing
sideways to minimize exposure, the bullet slammed sideways through his
entire abdomen, wreaking havoc on his internal organs, and finally broke
through the other side to lodge in his left arm. In shock and overwhelmed
with pain, Philip slumped to the ground, firing his ball uselessly as he fell.
He lay on the ground unmoving as his second rushed to him. Philip was
carried to shore and rowed hurriedly across the choppy Hudson to Manhattan, where bearers carried him to Hamilton's in-laws, the Churches,
whose house was close by, and settled him on a bed. The eminent Dr. David

Hosack, who had saved his life once before, rushed to his aid, but the case was hopeless.

When Hamilton rushed into the room, he took his son's pulse, then, stricken, he turned to Hosack. "Doctor, I despair," he told him, Hamilton's face a river of tears.

"Never did I see a man so overwhelmed by grief as Hamilton," his friend Troup recalled. Betsey came in, heavy with her tenth pregnancy, and stared down, disbelieving, at her son, who was white, scarcely able to breathe. Both parents lay down beside him and held their son all night long. A friend recorded the scene:

> *On a bed without curtains lay poor Phil, pale and languid, his rolling distorted eyeballs darting forth the flashes of delirium. On one side of him on the same bed lay his agonized father, on the other his distracted mother, around [him] his numerous relatives and friends weeping and fixed in sorrow.*

Philip survived only until daybreak.

It was pouring the day of the burial, but a great throng turned out to pay their respects. His father was so weighed down by grief, he was speechless and unable to walk. He had to be supported by friends as he approached his son's grave.

Hamilton had been afraid that Betsey would miscarry from the strain, but she carried the child to term and bore him safely in June. They christened him Philip, and the family sometimes called him "Little Phil."

Philip's sister Angelica, the third born, named for Betsey's flamboyant sister, had always been devoted to her big brother, and she never recovered from his death. Sensitive and artistic, she may have been too delicate, and when her brother died, she lost touch with reality altogether. Hoping to bring her comfort, Hamilton had C.C. Pinckney, the onetime presidential candidate, send her some watermelons and parakeets, since she'd always been fond of birds, from South Carolina. But instead of being pulled out of her misery by such kindnesses, she retreated ever deeper into it. She remained a child even as she aged; she sang the songs she used to play on the pianoforte with her father when she was young; she referred to Philip in the present tense; she sometimes failed to recognize her parents; and she remained under a physician's care for the rest of her life.

→►◄◄

BURR READ THE account of Philip Hamilton's death in the new *Evening Post*, interested that the violence had stemmed from a political conflict. Burr faced the same in Washington, and increasingly in New York, where the ancient factions that he had always played in his favor were now allied against him. In both places, he was being squeezed out. New York's politics was a familiar triangle, but now with the Clintonians and the Livingstons in an uneasy alliance on one side, and the Burrites, having deposed Hamilton's Schuyler faction, at an increasingly lonely apex on the other. As in Washington, power was measured in the ability to produce jobs for important constituents, and on that score, Burr was proving to be embarrassingly feeble. While DeWitt Clinton freely distributed appointments by the thousand, Burr made only the most modest request of DeWitt's uncle, the governor, for eight positions, of which five were granted. Five slots for the vice president of the United States. Worse, he was outmaneuvered by the Clintons, who rammed through a change in the state constitution that drained away his little remaining chance to offer jobs through the Council of Appointments. And then his nemesis DeWitt Clinton was given a Senate seat to fill a sudden vacancy. The younger Clinton could scarcely have been more disdainful of his predecessor. "Little or no consequence is attached to him in the general estimation," he declared.

Burr himself would not have disagreed with this assessment. "I dine with the president about once a fortnight, and now and then meet the ministers in the street," Burr wrote Joseph Alston dryly. "They are all very busy: quite men of business. The Senate and the vice president are content with each other, and move on with courtesy." Avoiding him.

He did continue to occupy the chair of the Senate president, and his vote was needed to break a deadlock regarding the Republican-inspired repeal of the Federalists' Judiciary Act from the Adams administration, which would have added a number of Federalist "midnight judges" to the court. Jefferson had swept into office determined to reverse the measure, and most vice presidents would have obliged him automatically. But Burr hinted that he respected the Federalist point of view and believed the Constitution forbade repeal, infuriating Jefferson but thrilling the Federalists, who thought he might be one of theirs after all. In a preliminary vote, however, Burr broke a tie by siding with Jefferson after all. Then, on a vote whether to send the measure back to a Senate committee for yet more agonizing consideration, he broke with Jefferson to vote yes. Burr insisted he did this on the merits, claiming he wished only "to ameliorate the provisions of the bill, that it might be rendered more acceptable to the Senate," but Jefferson was not assuaged. He knew an enemy when he saw one. Ultimately, the Republicans rescued it from committee and forwarded it to a vote, which this time they carried, and did on the House side, too, by a substantial majority that did not require Burr's vote. A man who could never miss now could never hit.

With suspicions raised everywhere against him, his every move was subject to the darkest speculation. When it came time to celebrate the birthday of the revered Washington at the end of February 1802, a swarm of Federalists gathered at Stelle's Hotel, for what a Republican newspaper derided as "Bacchanalian orgies" in memory of the country's late founder. With all the guests loyal Federalists, they all enjoyed a boisterous dinner with ample quantities of wine when, by one account, some "gentle taps" were heard at the door. The crowd quieted and then turned completely silent as the door swung open to reveal the vice president of the United States. No one knew if he was representing Jefferson or signaling a switch in party. But they were galvanized by his presence either way.

Newly humble, Burr apologized for intruding on the merriment, but he reached for some wine and said he would like to propose a toast. Permission granted, he raised his glass and offered this: "An *union* of all *honest* men."

If his remark was received with some bafflement in the hall, Jefferson knew exactly what it meant. His vice president was declaring war on him. If so, war he would have.

As if newspapers were not savage enough in the Federalist administrations, they became bloodthirsty under Jefferson, in large part because the two parties had drawn to rough parity among the electorate, so few issues or elections were so one-sided that they could not be tipped by a broadside attack. It was in this spirit that John Wood, a Scottish journalist of low repute, created a five-hundred-page pamphlet attacking the Adams administration, and then larded it with ancillary material, including a peripheral assault on Burr. "Thirty pages of high eulogium"—Burr put it in the teasing fashion he had come to affect in these brutal years. To avoid the stain, he offered to buy up the whole run of 1,250, and, suddenly worried the British edition would haunt him, dispatched the brig *Recovery* to fly to London to bag that one too. For good measure, Burr prepared to write a new edition of the pamphlet that was cleansed of the animadversions against him. For a fee, Wood delivered the offending edition to the home of Burr's henchman, the lawyer and political operative William P. Van Ness, where it was promptly burned, so no new one was called for.

But then the infamous James Cheetham intervened. Burr himself had brought him over from the British Isles, seeing him as the sort of unscrupulous and conniving editor who could be of some use, and Burr chipped in half the purchase price of the Republican paper called *The Argus* for him. In 1801, Cheetham swapped that for a half share in the *American Citizen*, along with DeWitt Clinton's wealthy cousin David Denniston. In switching papers, Cheetham shifted his political loyalty from Burr to the man emerging as his most dangerous enemy, the nefarious young Clinton. Worse for Burr, Cheetham decided it would help to stay on Jefferson's good side by giving him a few morsels of malicious gossip about Burr to snack on. By now Cheetham had managed to secure an unburned copy of the Wood pamphlet, complete with its revelations about Burr, along with the juicier bit about Burr's elaborate attempts to suppress it—attempts that now seemed rather comical. Jefferson was delighted to have it. He thanked Cheetham for sending news of his vice president that was so "pregnant with considerations." Ever cautious about leaving behind evidence of his dirty dealing, Jefferson asked that Cheetham destroy the letter, which Cheetham was not the sort of man to do.

Cheetham then went at Burr hard, labeling his next pamphlet *The Narrative of the Suppression of Colonel Burr of the History of the Administration of John Adams*. This retailed the revelation of the original Wood pamphlet and Burr's hilarious attempts to conceal it. It was succeeded by four more pamphlets attacking his former benefactor, all on the theme that

Burr was an American Napoléon, an untrustworthy scoundrel who'd schemed to steal the presidential crown from its rightful owner and place it on his own head.

This action inspired an equal and opposite reaction, as John Wood, of all people, rose to Burr's defense, as did a number of Federalist papers, including Hamilton's *Evening Post*. But Burr's reputation could not be unsullied. Whatever influence he might have had in Washington had evaporated. Even the loyal Burrite William P. Van Ness's congressman brother, John, had to note that Burr's "influence & weight with the administration is in my opinion not as much as I could wish." Leaving Burr even further adrift, the *Evening Post* claimed that the New York Republicans were furious with Burr for—shades of the glorious 1800 campaign—advancing a slate of Burrites on the Republican side of the ledger in the coming election. This provoked Cheetham to disavow any such move by Burr. He was wanted by neither Republicans nor Federalists. Robert Troup hoped that the whole imbroglio would embarrass Jefferson, since everyone would assume he was behind it. Maybe so, but it left Burr in that middle place where few politicians want to be—scorned by both parties.

The anger didn't just smolder, but flared into fire. As the editors of the leading two papers on the two sides of the partisan divide, Coleman and Cheetham started to go at it with new fury. Outraged by something Cheetham had written, Coleman challenged him to a duel. Not wishing to be killed over a few stray words, Cheetham avoided any lethal confrontation by promising not to repeat such charges. When the New York harbormaster claimed that it was Coleman who had backed off, Coleman called him out to the dueling ground—and shot him dead. Then the towering Burrite John Swartwout weighed in to declare that DeWitt Clinton was the one behind Cheetham's denunciations of Burr. That accusation sent Clinton into a frenzy, calling Swartwout "a liar, a scoundrel, and a villain." That earned them a trip to Weehawken, across the Hudson. There on the narrow rocky ledge that had become the prime dueling ground for antagonists from the city, Clinton waited for his second's cry of "Present!" then leveled his pistol at Swartwout and blasted him in the leg, dropping him to the ground in obvious agony. When Swartwout finally hauled himself up, he insisted the matter was not settled, and he called for another round. The pistols were duly reloaded, the order to "Present!" repeated, and Clinton cracked Swartwout in the same leg again, and dropped him, howling, once more. When he managed to hoist himself onto his feet once more to stand unsteadily on a ruined leg, Swartwout bravely insisted the duel proceed. And it did, for five rounds altogether. None of the bullets found their mark, purposely, one imagines, on Clinton's side. Finally, Clinton refused to continue, and, declaring that he "wished he had the principal here," namely Burr, he quit the field.

But Burr did not enter that fray or any other. For someone who'd always been so scrappy, he had turned oddly defeatist, as if he was so overwhelmed with so many woes that he could only retreat into his shell. He did start another newspaper, installing the vivacious Peter Irving to edit it, with an eye to promoting Burr. He let the many verbal assaults go unanswered, and he instigated no duels against the many men who questioned his reputation. He did rouse himself to sue Cheetham for libel regarding his actions in the presidential election. For the case, he solicited depositions from James Bayard and Samuel Smith to acknowledge that Burr had done nothing wrong. But he placed these documents in a drawer, where they languished until 1830; he never pursued the case. The top of the world had become the bottom of the world, and there would be no inverting it.

→>-<←

INSTEAD, HE RETREATED from the world altogether, into a place where he found only comfort, the arms of women. After his initial stay in Georgetown, Burr moved into a handsome suite of rooms near the Capitol, where he dined frequently with his good friend Dr. William Eustis, who had come down from Boston as a representative. Still, for someone used to accomplishment, the lack of it must have been exasperating. "My life has no variety, and of course no incident," he told his daughter, Theodosia, twenty days away in South Carolina. To fill the gap, he embarked on a series of affairs with women he wooed under various playful *noms d'amour*: "Celeste," "La Planche," "Madame G." (also dubbed "La G."), and "Inamorata." Because Burr's literary executor, Davis, destroyed most of his love letters, it is hard to say who these objects of his desire were, what he did with them and when, how much the affairs may have overlapped, and how they concluded. While he tended to be secretive about his amorous activities, he did confide in Eustis, his uncle Pierpont Edwards (only six years his senior, and a man very much after his own heart), and his daughter, Theodosia, whom he had raised in a manner that went beyond Mary Wollstonecraft, to think as coolly as a man.

Two of the women believed to be in his life as vice president were American exotics, Susan Binney and Madame Leonora Sansay. Binney may have been Celeste. She was just twenty-three when Burr was vice president, the daughter to an established Boston physician, and sister to a Philadelphia lawyer. Sansay seems to have been older. American-born, she spoke fluent French and styled herself as a European, freely carrying on affairs during her marriage. Whatever relationship Burr may have had with Binney, it was brief. He mentions her in a letter to William Eustis in June 1800, urging his friend to look in on a Miss Binney of Boston "if you have not forsworn all Virtuous women." Burr had closed off relations by the time of the inauguration, telling Binney the "plain truth and quit honorably." In his judgment, anyway. One letter to Binney survives, as it pertains to a book he'd sent her on the differences between the sexes, a favorite Burr subject. Burr himself had been unimpressed, finding the author had succeeded only in the "jumbling and confounding of sexes," and was "as remote from the truth as the arrogant pretension of male superiority." He thought he would write it better.

As for Sansay, Eustis may have been in on this one, too. Burr seems to have met her as early as 1797, well before Binney, getting serious sometime before her marriage in 1800 to a much older French merchant, Louis Sansay, from New York. Marriage seems not to have inhibited Leonora Sansay very much. In 1802, as she and her new husband prepared to move to Santo Domingo, she traveled to Washington to meet with Burr, ostensibly to request letters of introduction for her trip. Burr was thrilled by the encounter. As he told his uncle Pierpont Edwards: "you may speak very highly of her talents, her acquirements and her accomplishments—She speaks & writes French & has more sense & information than all the women to be found in St. Dom." He had his protégé John Vanderlyn paint Madame Sansay in oil when she was next in New York. Once the Sansays were ensconced on their island home, Louis Sansay confided to Burr that he was afraid his beguiling young wife would run off with another man—although he never suggested that the man might be Burr himself. M. Sansay wanted Burr to offer her twelve thousand dollars upon his death if she stayed with him. So Burr played marriage counselor and lawyer—and rival. On that basis, the Sansays remained together. On Santo Domingo, she fashioned herself a connoisseur of love, writing for Burr the romantic adventures of a certain "Clara" on the island, much as Burr might have written of his for her. Eventually Leonora did leave her husband and return to America, where she settled in Philadelphia and ran an artificial flower shop and published racy novels. She may have been Burr's mistress there. It is hard to know.

One last woman in Burr's orbit in his vice presidential years was Susan Reynolds, just a teenager, daughter of the infamous Maria Reynolds. Since Burr had handled Maria's divorce from the abusive James, Maria was returning for another favor—to help her find a place for Susan to live. In December of 1800, Burr passed her request on to his friend Eustis to help. "I repeat & do assure you," wrote Burr, "she is to my belief, pure and innocent as an angel." By this he meant that she was a legitimate child, and not, as Eustis, knowing Burr, might suspect, Burr's own daughter. It is remotely possible that Susan might have been Hamilton's, since she was conceived after Reynolds came to know him. If so, it was surely a remarkable coincidence for such hot-blooded political adversaries. Burr addressed Eustis's obvious first question head-on: "she has not the most remote affinity to me." Instead of a familial connection, he had "a sacred obligation to protect her." Burr placed Susan in a boarding school in Boston, but she had other ideas. In 1803, she eloped with Francis Wright, a rake, said Eustis, "educated to dissipation without acquiring any one decent trait." He dumped Susan three weeks later, and she ended up in a house "frequented by young men"—a brothel. "I see nothing to be expected of our unfortunate charge," Eustis wrote, "but a gradual declension from reputable life down to what lengths or depths God knows." Thus ended the Reynolds affair.

While Burr betrayed European attitudes toward his gallantry, taking pleasure where he could and avoiding attachments where possible, his political enemies were not quite so sanguine. In May 1801, a handbill appeared all over New York City entitled AARON BURR! It called Burr a

"Catiline," a familiar charge that referred to the lustful conspirator of the Roman Republic, who had "confessed in all his villainy." But this one added a NEW TRAIT—Burr's "abandoned profligacy," as demonstrated by all the "wretches" the vice president had supposedly seduced and betrayed, many now reduced to prostitution, others fallen to poverty, disease, and death. Like most of the images summoned up in the partisan wars, this handbill was satire, but it was not without foundation. For Burr had indeed left more than a few wretches in his wake. His friend Eustis was in on it; he wrote once from Boston to update the vice president of the doings of a Mrs. Werring and a "reported daughter of B——," both of them Burr connections, presumably, one as a hired partner, the other as issue. A Mrs. Hayt in New Haven, however, could scarcely have been clearer. She wrote the vice president plaintively to remind him she was "in a state of pregnancy and In want . . . only think what a small sum you gave me, a gentleman of your connections. I don't wish to crowd you tou hard Because I know your short of money by your small complyments to me. Neither do I wish to expose you. But I would thank you if you wuld Be so kind as to send me a little money."

Burr had come to this.

FORTY-FOUR

Tant Mieux

DESPITE THE FEDERALIST fears that Jefferson would spell the end of the Republic, he had governed far more from the center than from the edge, presiding over a nearly noiseless administration that retained much of the Hamilton financial system even as he reduced the federal debt on which it was based. To top it off, although he had vowed to observe every particle of the Constitution and to reduce spending, on his own authority he'd spent 15 million dollars from the US Treasury on the Louisiana Purchase, a stack of prairie in the middle of the continent that would double the size of the country. Like most successful presidents, he succeeded more by what he was not than by what he was. He was not the overheated Adams, and he let the despised Alien and Sedition Acts expire, unmourned.

Since 1802, there had been alarming rumors about a continuing sexual liaison between Jefferson and one of his slaves, Sally Hemings, but the spreading of those charges seemed more a mark of the Federalist desperation than of any lapse in Jefferson's character. By the close of 1803, Jefferson was confident enough about the 1804 election that he could contemplate a move that might, under other circumstances, seem drastic: shedding the perfidious Aaron Burr as vice president. He decided to replace him with the old warhorse George Clinton, once Clinton assured Jefferson he wouldn't seek the presidency himself, since Jefferson wished to reserve that for his current secretary of state and fellow Virginian, James Madison.

Clinton obliged, terming the vice presidency a "respectable retirement." When the plan was put to the Republicans' nominating caucus, it was passed without a single dissenting vote. No one spoke up for Burr.

It was as a dying man that Burr sought an interview with Jefferson on January 26, one that Jefferson recorded in his Anas in unusual detail, to plead with him to be kept on, and, failing that, for him to offer the slightest endorsement of the man who had secured him the presidency. Burr could scarcely have been more unctuous in his professions of loyalty to the president, as he recalled that he had accepted being named as vice president only "from a desire to be with me," Jefferson wrote, "whose company & conversation had always been fascinating to him." His pen must have dripped acid in inscribing that sentence. If, before, Jefferson had offered Burr a cabinet position to withdraw from the vice presidency, Burr asked now only for "some mark of favor" from the president, whose eminence was nearing Washington's. On such matters, Jefferson had to remind him that it was his policy to remain "merely passive"—always the most comfortable position for him anyway. Hoping to come away with something, Burr complained about the pamphlet wars in New York, which were shredding his reputation in his home state and the base of any political power he retained. Surely, Jefferson could restrain the Republican newspapers, at least. But no. Jefferson admitted that, while he had noticed the attacks on Burr, they were "as the passing wind." And, regrettably, he had "never thot it proper to interfere for myself, & consequently not in the case of the Vicepresident."

It was all over. A few days later, snow had blanketed the Northeast, and, exchanging his coach's wheels for runners, Burr sleighed up the coast to New York to throw himself into the election for the governorship that Clinton was abandoning. This time, he would run neither as Federalist nor as Republican, but as an independent, a rare category in that bifurcated age. The Republican machine was in the hands of the hateful DeWitt Clinton, who'd given up his Senate seat to take over the mayor's office and run the Clinton faction from there, where it could be amplified by the heavy patronage in the city. That Clinton put forward the perennial Morgan Lewis, a Livingston by marriage, united two sides of the political triangle.

As ever, Hamilton ran the embattled Federalist Party, but it wasn't until February 16 that he was able to organize a grand Federalist banquet at

Lewis's City Tavern in Albany to choose a candidate. Since the Federalists had been so battered the last time around, no one of substance wished to get involved. After the fiasco of the 1800 election, and the Reynolds scandal before it, Hamilton's political standing was almost as low as Burr's. Like his rival, he saw the election as his best chance to recoup. But he would never consider Burr a Federalist, not after 1800, and would never support him for anything. Instead, he threw his weight behind the current New York chancellor, former chief justice John Lansing, unaware that Lansing had chosen not to run. As Burr summarized it in a dispatch to his daughter, Hamilton was "for any candidate who can have a chance of success against A.B." This time, however, Hamilton's usual attacks on Burr went for naught. The Federalists declared Burr their candidate anyway. And so did the Republicans who gathered at Tontine's in Albany. As did a political group that gathered at Mechanics Hall in New York City. And so it went almost county by county. Hamilton looked like yesterday's man. It seemed as though the state would elect Burr by acclamation.

While New York seemed to be coalescing around Burr's candidacy, there was another movement afoot, a clandestine one, as befit Burr's style, pulling Burr, and the state, in a drastically different direction. It appeared that Burr was appealing simultaneously to sharply different constituencies for radically different ends: Even as he was campaigning for governor, he was also listening to the entreaties of a group of northeastern Federalists who were in such despair over Jefferson that they were starting a movement to secede from the Union. The bedrock Federalist states of New England would join with New York to create an independent nation, provisionally called the Northern Alliance. Because of its size and economic strength, New York was key to the venture. And the backers imagined that Burr was key to New York. Massachusetts's Senator Pickering, thought to be the ringleader of the scheme, dined with Burr half a dozen times, accompanied by one or another of the other New Englanders in on the plot. Burr never committed himself to such a treasonable project, but he did listen and let the conspirators imagine he was with them. But as they later went back over his statements, they couldn't find a syllable that indicated he actually was. As a mystified Senator William Plumer put it: "No man's language was ever more apparently explicit, & at the same time so covert and indefinite."

In the conversations, Burr freely bashed the "Virginia faction" that had treated him so abominably, making no distinction for the president, but that didn't necessarily mean that he was willing to break the Union apart to be free of it. "He has the spirit of ambition and revenge to gratify," said the conspirator Senator Roger Griswold, the one previously famous for his cane, "and can do little with his 'little band' alone." The more Griswold pressed, however, the more Burr retreated. It was the election of 1800 all over again. If Burr was to be king, he had to seize the crown, but this he would not do. And who could blame him? The scheme called for him to win the governorship first and then inform the voters they'd actually elected him president of a whole new country—and face the consequences from Jefferson.

Burr professed to his daughter that he could scarcely be less interested in the outcome of an election that would, in fact, determine his political future. "They are very busy here about an election between Morgan Lewis and A. Burr," he wrote in a teasing fashion that revealed an effort to put some distance between himself and events. "The former supported by the Livingstons and Clintons, the latter per se." By himself alone. The remark was meant to be humorous, but there was considerable truth, and pathos, to it. The campaign was vicious, unhampered by any serious discussion of the issues. Indeed, the casual observer might think the election wasn't between Burr and Lewis, but between Burr and Hamilton, with the scurrilous editor James Cheetham bent on playing up every point of dispute between them. Burr went so far as to file a lawsuit for libel against Cheetham, but the editor replied that any criticism had come from Hamilton, drawing the two men even more tightly into conflict. A Burr newspaper revived the hoary charge that Hamilton sought to install the son of George III as an American king, claiming that Governor Clinton, of all people, retained a letter of Hamilton's to that effect. Surprisingly enough, Clinton could produce no letter, only a recollection of it. Hamilton struck back by accusing Burr of plotting to destroy the Union with his scheme of a northern confederacy, which Hamilton had gotten wind of. Undaunted by any threat of a libel suit, Cheetham's *American Citizen* went after Burr for a sexual licentiousness that was monstrous, by its account. The newspaper assembled a list of "upwards of twenty women of ill fame" who had supposedly dallied with Burr, and another of respectable married women whom Burr had betrayed. Thousands of handbills posted all around the city took up the theme. Many of them penned by Cheetham, they told bitter stories of the deflowered who were now descending on New York to seek their revenge, or of business associates who had been cheated out of their money. But by far the most scandalous claim was Cheetham's that Burr had seduced a bosomy black woman at a "nigger ball" hosted by a black servant at his Richmond Hill. It was all shockingly personal, a public shaming that relied, not on truth, but on the credibility of any appalling story about the vice president.

Burr responded by dispatching his Burrites throughout the state to push the cause and seek endorsements of the influential. One new convert was Martin Van Buren, just twenty-two, who proved so adept that the other side sought to disparage him as Burr's illegitimate son, an imputation that lingered. Burr professed to be unaffected by the "new and amusing libels" that were daily published against him, and did not respond in kind. In his own literature, he styled himself a "plain and unostentatious citizen" and made sure his own attacks on Lewis stayed well within the bounds of political decorum. He hoped that voters would reward him for his high-minded restraint.

The tumult finally came to a close when the voting began. Despite the acclaim he'd received at the start of the campaign, Burr was not sanguine about its end, telling his daughter that he'd never gone into an election with "so little judgment about the outcome." Hamilton was likewise darkly pessimistic, declaring himself "disgusted" by politics.

This time, there proved no reason for him to be. The election was a disaster for Burr. He lost to Morgan Lewis by almost nine thousand votes, sixty percent to forty percent, making it the worst defeat in the history of New York gubernatorial elections. "The storm in New York is thoroughly allayed," observed John Randolph of Virginia, referring to the Burr forces, "never to rise again from the same quarters, or rather from the same men."

If this was his political demise, Burr did not acknowledge it. A long, chatty letter to Theodosia written shortly after the election was filled mostly with tales from his romantic life, describing how he had not been received by the mistress he called Celeste, but had been by the "good-natured" but lamentably "flat-chested" "La G." (Given the tenor of the campaign, it is surprising that any woman would entertain his advances.) It wasn't until the end of the letter that he added as a postscript, "Election is lost by a great majority: *tant mieux*." So much the better.

But that was merely Burr's surface aristocratic disdain. Down deeper, he was not nearly so accepting. He had lost everything worth having in the public life to which he had committed himself for the last fifteen years, and one that might have brought him to the presidency. The defeat had been so sweeping, it could not be blamed on any one factor. Burr's behavior in 1800, the ferocious newspaper attacks, and the rumors about the northern conspiracy—all these were immensely destructive. But the Burrites instinctively attributed the loss to one man: Hamilton. "If General Hamilton had not opposed Colonel Burr," groused Burr's ally Charles Biddle, "I have very little doubt but he would have been elected governor of New York." Burr himself believed that, even if Hamilton had not cost him the election, he was behind the vicious newspaper attacks that ruined his reputation. This was an immensely public defeat, and every aspect of Burr's life, public and private, had come under assault. The result would burn. First the presidency, then the vice presidency, and now this. He who once had everything within his reach if not in his grasp now held nothing at all.

Rage was never a Burr characteristic. He was far too controlled and far too fond of his pose of heroic detachment. Coolly methodical, he was far more likely to seek revenge. For him, it was a form of communication: His enemy would get to know his pain by feeling it as his.

→>-<←

HAMILTON KNEW RAGE very well. He flew into it often, although he usually expressed it in such artful language that it lost much of its communicative force. By 1804, however, his rages were starting to subside, the passion spent in too many tirades against too many malefactors, real and imagined. Burr had scarcely known defeat before 1804, but it had been a commonplace for Hamilton ever since he left the Treasury in 1795. None of his

Federalist candidates had won. This fact didn't stop him, but it surely diminished the fury he might have felt if the fates were against him less regularly. By 1804, Hamilton was largely finished as a party manager. And his joy was gone, too, after the death of his favored son, murdered for defending his father's name. If his daughter Angelica never recovered from the shock, the same could be said of her father. A darkness descended over him. He was not angry.

FORTY-FIVE

A Still More Despicable Opinion

HIGHLY PUBLICIZED DUELS enjoyed something of a revival in New York City at the turn of the nineteenth century, owing largely to the combustible mix of politics and the press—and a cadre of gentlemen willing to kill or die for their reputations. The whole notion of a duel—from *duellum*, a contraction of *duo bellum*, or war of two—descended from the medieval contests of rivalrous knights that developed in Europe in the early sixth century. Frustrated by the inability of courts to dispense justice, combatants started whacking at each other with heavy truncheons to resolve criminal disputes between them, the loser to be hung. Over the centuries, the disagreements branched out into romantic rivalries, and, in an oddly festive tournament setting, a pair of especially eager suitors would fight to the death with swords or daggers, if they didn't joust on horseback, to win a lady's hand—not that the lady always rejoiced at the outcome. But by the time the duel had migrated to America in 1800, the traditional weapons of chivalry had been exchanged for dueling pistols, often quite handsome ones—engraved, hand finished, and long barreled for greater accuracy—that were frequently kept as a pair in a velvet-lined mahogany case. And the animating sentiment had fluffed out into a grander sort of masculine pride that wasn't intended to impress the courts, women, or the Crown, but to awe a small circle of gentlemen who shared their particular notion of personal honor, one that ran so deep that they, almost alone, would be willing to face down a loaded pistol—coolly, without the slightest trace of fear—at ten paces to defend it.

An "affair of honor," as this tiny war was termed, was as tightly regulated as the president's ball and advanced according to precise steps. The precipitating event could be almost anything: The code of honor was no statute book, and any offense was subjective. It may be as seemingly minor as calling someone a "rascal," as Eacker did to Philip Hamilton; or as fierce as accusing someone of engaging in bribery, as John Barker Church did Burr. Whatever, the offender is rarely surprised to receive notice. Every gentleman had a feel for the limits of acceptable behavior. The transgressor was officially made aware of his transgression when the aggrieved party called him out by issuing a "challenge." While there was some wiggle room, the recipient was generally obliged to accept. Both parties appointed seconds to handle the details of place and time and to serve as the principals' surrogates as needed. For the final "interview," the two antagonists met in some out-of-the-way spot, usually in New Jersey, where duels were no less illegal than in New York, but the laws were less likely to be enforced. There, the seconds marked out ten paces, loaded the pistols, and set them out for the participants. The two men then took up their positions, standing sideways to the line of fire to diminish their profile. They awaited the cry "Present!"—their cue to fire when ready; it was possibly the last word one of them ever heard.

For a gentleman of a certain sort, his honor was everything he most prized about himself—his prestige, valor, cultivation, masculinity, self-regard. The very notion might seem ridiculous in an uproarious period when the vilest insults filled the streets, newspapers, coffee shops, taverns, and halls of Congress. But this very chaos may have fostered it, as honor alone separated a gentleman from all this rampant vulgarity. As abstract as honor might seem to those who scoffed at it, to a gentleman his honor was like his manhood. It could never be surrendered without a fight. Because of their comfort with arms, military officers were probably the first to call an assailant out to the dueling ground over a slight, but politicians were soon close behind. The political rivalries of the day were so fierce as to provoke genuine outrage, and more than in other fields, a politician's career rested largely on his reputation.

Opposed in so many things, Hamilton and Burr were united in the recognition that by 1804 their honor was about all they had left. As public figures, they had reason to be preoccupied with it; their careers largely rested on their reputation, and for each of them, that reputation lay in tatters—making it, paradoxically, all the more important that it be salvaged. For both of them, tales of sexual transgressions were the fundamental indignities; the fact that the charges were mostly true only added to the sting. Their financial affairs were in ruin. And they had both been largely discarded by the party they had either created or transformed. Once serene or haughty in the face of attack, both men had grown twitchy, hypersensitive to slights that they might once have brushed off. To an extent, each had the other to thank for that. As the world tightened around them, it left them less room to maneuver and exposed them to the irritations of a closed-in life in which each had only the other for company, or so it may have felt. They were a pair of wolves in a tight cage; eventually they became all fangs. As the aggravations mounted—political, social, moral, personal—they bred still greater hostility and dealt injuries that scarred over but never healed.

Yet if they agreed on the value of honor, the two disagreed about the necessity of killing to defend it. Having sacrificed a son to the practice, Hamilton was bound to consider the ritual "abhorrent," even though he had participated in it countless times. "We do not live in the days of chivalry," he reminded his friend, a certain Dr. Gordon. "The good sense of the present times has happily found out, that to prove your own innocence, or the malice of an accuser, the worst method you can take is to run him through the body or shoot him through the head." But Hamilton also recognized that, after the Reynolds affair, the Adams pamphlet, and other follies, what was left of his reputation needed to be protected at all costs. Hamilton would be involved in eleven duels, most of them toward the end of his life, but only the last involved potentially lethal gunfire. Burr was involved in only two, both against members of the Hamilton family, and both required pistols to resolve.

But, of course, in a freighted matter like a duel, no decision is ever purely rational, a careful weighing of pros and cons. For all of Hamilton's cool reasoning, his most fateful decisions were made impulsively, seemingly without any consideration at all, whether it be to give up on Princeton, to abandon Washington, to fight at Yorktown, to pursue Maria Reynolds, or to defy Burr in 1800. But there was another side to him beside the quicksilver one, and that one was prone to a leaden despondency that was evident after sharp reverses, such as in Jefferson's famous description of him as being morose and disheveled as he lurked by Washington's door when he was afraid his bill of assumption would never pass. Facing the prospect of a duel, he seemed caught between the two sides of his nature, one impetuous, the other sluggish.

Burr had his periods of lethargy, especially when he recovered from bursts of action during the war, but for the most part his rarely deviated from a full-on posture. A duel was no time for cowardice. If anything, a duel appealed to his war-faring side, first expressed in Quebec and repeatedly throughout the revolution, which seemed as genuine for him as it was artificial for Hamilton. Ever since his days on the Elizabeth River, straight through to the Manhattan election campaign of 1800, Burr relished adventure. For Hamilton, soldiering was military uniforms and histrionic displays of valor. His greatest contributions to the war came seated at his writing desk in Washington's headquarters. Burr found glory in the field.

It is remarkable that the two men came to this shared conviction about affairs of honor from such different places as the island of Nevis in the West Indies and Elizabethtown, New Jersey. That one was a solitary immigrant of unknown ancestry, the other a scion of a nearly divine American lineage. That one burned with the fire of the dispossessed, the other displayed the coolness of an aristocrat. That one was determined to attain the highest rank in his adopted country, and the other, confident of his place in society, cared merely to follow his whim. That one created the first American political party, and the other nearly served as president in the second American political party. And on it went, the bright contrasts between these two, extending from their schooldays in the Elizabethtown of 1775 to a fatal disagreement in New York City in 1804. They were two men of nearly the same age, physique, talent, and magnetism. It seemed, ultimately, as if the country had room for only one of them.

→>-<←

THE FATAL DUEL found its most immediate origins in that dinner hosted by the grim Judge Tayler in Albany in February 1804, when his son-in-law, the interloper, Dr. Charles Cooper, jotted down his recollections of Ham-

ilton's table talk. For a man like Hamilton, that was a hazard, for comments he would make only to friends would be repeated to those who were
not his friends. And on the subject of Burr, Hamilton had not been able to
say a civil word since at least 1792. When the word "dangerous" emerged, it
meant even more than Cooper imagined, for it drew on everything that
had come before—the schemes to gain entrance to the presidential contests
of 1792 and 1796, not to mention the brazen efforts to win the Manhattan
vote, and with it the presidential vote, in 1800, and, most dastardly of all,
his flirtation with the High Federalists to create a northern confederacy
that would crack the fabled Union in two. All of these acts, audacious on
their own because of what Hamilton viewed as Burr's singular lack of
accomplishments, were made, to Hamilton, even more reprehensible by the
fact that Burr's great cause was only Burr. He had done nothing for the
country, in Hamilton's view, other than get himself elected. He stood for
no principles of governance beyond his own self-aggrandizement, as Hamilton had said any number of times and would freely say again, and thus made
a mockery of those who, like Hamilton, had convictions and stuck by them.
Because of its menacing implications, "dangerous" went well beyond the
standard critique of Burr being aloof and ambitious. In Hamilton's usage, it
evoked someone far more wicked, someone capable of crimes more threatening for being unspecified. It was code for everything evil about Burr.*

If the word as commonly understood didn't actually fit Burr—who was
no more "dangerous" than, say, Governor Clinton and probably a good deal
less—it fit Hamilton's understanding of him, which was the whole point. At
least since 1792, when Hamilton first started to single out Burr as a threat to
the new nation, Hamilton had become hyperreactive where Burr was con-

---

* For some time, there has been the competing theory that Burr was outraged not by anything Hamilton said about his political behavior, but because he had accused Burr of having an incestuous relationship with his daughter, Theodosia. A tempting idea, since it
would certainly explain the duel, but there is no evidence that Burr had done anything so
abominable, or that Hamilton had said he had. Such a remark would have been so inflammatory, and so consequential, that someone would have passed it along to history, but no
one has. As it is, only Gore Vidal has asserted it in print, and he did so in his *Burr*, a satiric
novel. Fiction, of course, is not fact.

cerned, amplifying any hazard to an inordinate degree. Hamilton's very impreciseness—one that Burr would be desperate to pin down—created its power and helps to account for why Burr, who could ignore so much, could not ignore this. It didn't help that Cooper, in defending himself from Schuyler's charge that he had fabricated Hamilton's comments, had chipped in with a yet more inflammatory—and tantalizing—notion that he could relate a "still more despicable opinion" that Hamilton held of Burr.

Hamilton had called Burr a "dangerous" man in February, during the election campaign that was filled with such insults. Shortly afterward, in one of the strange twists that were forever conjoining the two men, Burr had ridden through the snowdrifts for several hours by moonlight from Richmond Hill up to the Grange, Hamilton's country seat high above the Hudson. The sun had still not risen when he arrived at his rival's lovely two-story house, a soft yellow that would have been a ghostly pale before sunrise.

Hamilton's son John recalled being awakened by a "violent" ringing of the bell. A servant roused his master from his bed. In the front hall, Hamilton was not entirely surprised to see a somewhat haggard Burr before him, a man "agitated," recorded John, in his need for "immediate pecuniary assistance." Ten thousand dollars, it appeared, if Burr was to save his house. It was a sum twice Burr's salary as vice president, and the inevitable result of his ruinous spending, but Hamilton did not snicker, as he might have. Indeed, he seems not to have taken any pleasure in his rival's predicament. Instead, he made some notes and told Burr he would see what he could do. Burr returned the way he had come. Ultimately, Hamilton would turn to his brother-in-law, who—despite his own nearly lethal run-in with Burr—agreed to float Burr a loan that tided him over, but only temporarily.

On returning to his bed, Hamilton wryly asked his wife, "So who do you think that was?"

She couldn't guess.

But that was then. The Cooper account didn't get into Burr's hands until four months later, well after Burr was struck by his sweeping defeat, which must have made Hamilton's adjective read all the harsher. By then, Hamilton's kindness was long forgotten. It was to reverse that fresh defeat, or at least obtain some shred of satisfaction, that Burr was determined to assault Hamilton now. He'd been the victim of Hamilton's slurs long enough.

Through his own legal minion, the twenty-eight-year-old William Peter Van Ness, Burr demanded to know from Hamilton what that "more despicable" opinion might be. Caught out, Hamilton was in the same bind he'd experienced in the Reynolds affair. He had the choice of admitting it or engaging in a lot of legalistic hairsplitting that was not likely to convince anyone of anything except Hamilton's cleverness. In Letter II he opted for the latter, with predictable results:

> *The language of Dr. Cooper plainly implies, that* he *considered this opinion of you, which he attributes to me as a* despicable *one; but he affirms that I have expressed some other,* more despicable, *without, however, mentioning to whom, when, or where. 'Tis evident that the phrase, "still more despicable," admits of infinite shades, from very light to very dark. How am I to judge of the degree intended? Or how shall I annex any precise idea to language so indefinite?*

The casuistry is stunning here—the parsing, the redefinitions, the logical shifts—and all of it completely beside the point, and worse. It is remarkable that Hamilton should attempt these pirouettes before a firing squad anyway, but it shows a startling tone deafness that he could possibly imagine that Burr wouldn't regard this legal lecture of his as a monstrous insult. In that respect, it might as well have been a suicide note. But Hamilton was in a bind from which there was no escape. He could not deny these slurs against Burr, for too many people had heard him say them, and he had therefore based his reputation on them. But if he admitted them, then Burr had due cause for a duel.

Burr's reply was alarmingly brief: He found in it "nothing of that sincerity and delicacy which you profess to value." Then he gets right down to it. "The question," Burr writes icily, "is not whether [Dr. Cooper] has understood the meaning of the word, or has used it according to syntax, and with grammatical accuracy; but whether you have authorized this application, either directly or by uttering expressions derogatory to my honor." Honor. Both men knew what that meant.

Hamilton had to feel the gravity of the situation. Not only was Burr raising the prospect of a duel, but he was acting like a man who intended to kill.

Burr closed by demanding "a definite reply."

Here in Letter III, the roles are set: Burr is predator, Hamilton his prey.

Burr had Van Ness deliver that one to Hamilton's office, too, and he waited while Hamilton read it. Stunned by its ferocity, Hamilton immediately told Van Ness that he found it "rude and offensive," but he knew better than to commit that thought to writing. He said instead that he needed time to consider his reply. Van Ness told him he'd return in the evening, and he set a time.

Hamilton alerted his own "friend," a lawyer named Nathaniel Pendleton, to the developments; he urged Hamilton to hold firm. Outraged, Hamilton fired off an angry letter for Pendleton to take to Van Ness, rather than receive him again, and for Van Ness to convey to Burr. In this one, Hamilton took the tone of a man who was sick of being bullied, and so became a bully himself. "Your first letter, in a style too peremptory, made a demand, in my opinion, unprecedented and unwarrantable," he began, and he charged on from there to conclude that he had nothing further to say. "I have no other answer to give, than that which has already been given."

Alarmed at the direction, and the speed, that things were going, Pendleton did not deliver that letter as Hamilton asked, but held on to it for several days while he got in touch with Van Ness, hoping the principals would cool down while their seconds figured out a way to avoid catastrophe. In the company of each other, Pendleton and Van Ness were reasonable men; they knew the stakes. Pendleton thought it might help if Burr could let Hamilton know what bothered him so much about the Albany conversation. Perhaps Hamilton could recall the conversation for him, to let him know that, despite Dr. Cooper's account, nobody said anything disrespectful of Burr? To that end, Pendleton prepared a "memorandum" of Hamilton's recollections for Van Ness to give Burr. Unfortunately, this account of the dinner was so anodyne as to amount to an affront of its own, as Hamilton claimed that the guests confined themselves only to Burr's "political principles" and said nothing about his "conduct" or "character." Not too likely. Seeing that, Van Ness urged Pendleton to press Hamilton further to be more specific, and more credible, by assuring Burr that no one accused him of any "dishonorable conduct," and thinking this a way out, Hamilton did just that.

On June 26, eight days after the first letter from him, word came back from Burr. Not good enough. If Hamilton could so clearly say he'd said nothing disrespectful at the Albany dinner, then why not clear the air and make similar assurances about other times? About *all* other times, in fact. If he couldn't do that, or wouldn't, Burr could only conclude that Hamilton had indeed been spreading "injurious opinions" of him. And Burr wanted details. Exactly what horrible things had Hamilton said about Burr, when, and to whom?

Where to begin, Hamilton had to think. Just to consider the question was to answer it, for it raised the specter of countless exchanges, some starting with Hamilton, some with others, but for all of them Hamilton was a hearty contributor. And each one was boundless in its animosity, as each word had a tone, association, history, and implication that, to exacting literary minds like theirs, created a cannonball of meanness, bristling with sharp points.

Burr was enraged, and now nothing would appease him. He had never before loomed quite this large, not even in the presidential campaign of 1800. He was immense, and Hamilton was tiny. The original inquiry related to the Albany dinner had now expanded to cover *all* of Hamilton's conversations about Burr *ever*. It was an impossible request, calculated to antagonize, as Burr surely knew. Could Hamilton swear he'd never, ever said a harsh word? Of course not. Hamilton was *always* deriding Burr; everyone knew that.

Pendleton told Van Ness that no one would ever oblige such a request, and especially not Hamilton. He prayed that the two men could reach an "honorable accommodation," but he doubted they could. Burr's letter, Pendleton could not help noting, smacked of "predetermined hostility."

Van Ness delivered a reply the next evening. *Burr* was the injured party, not Hamilton. "He feels," Van Ness wrote, "as a gentleman should feel when his honor is impeached or assailed, and without sensations of hostility or wishes of revenge he is determined to vindicate that honor at such hazard as the nature of the case demands."

Honor, again.

Hamilton must have been stunned. Did Burr really want to kill him? To risk *being* killed? The answer came back swiftly. Yes.

→-◄-

IN THE TWO-WEEK period from the close of the negotiations on June 27 to the duel on July 11, Hamilton and Burr carried on with their lives as though everything was normal. Hamilton continued to live in his law office downtown, venturing to the Grange for only a few days at a time. He never told his wife of the duel, sure that she would forbid it. Just a week before, Hamilton hosted a ball for seventy-five, including the artist John Trumbull, who had done his full-size portrait, and, in the warm weather, Hamilton had encouraged the guests to spill out to the garden and the wood beyond, where musicians hid among the trees. A widower, Burr spent most evenings at Richmond Hill, some of the evenings shivering in front of a fire, even in July. But Hamilton and Burr both passed the evening of July Fourth at the Society of the Cincinnati, a club for old soldiers of the Revolutionary War, of which Hamilton was president and Burr a member. Everyone noticed that the two men were not their normal selves, but no one knew the cause. Trumbull was there, and he noticed that "contrary to his wont," Burr "was silent, gloomy, sour." Hamilton, by contrast, "entered with glee into the gaiety of a convivial dinner party." The evening called for drinking songs, and both men obliged, Hamilton actually climbing a table to deliver his in a pleasant tenor, while Burr gazed up at him, rapt.

> *Why, soldiers, why*
> *Should we be melancholy, boys?*
> *Why, soldiers, why?*
> *Whose business 'tis to die?*
> *What! Sighing? Fie!*
> *Damn fear, drink on, be jolly boys!*
> *'Tis he, you, or I.*

It was up to Hamilton to select the pistols, since he was the challenged party, and he chose the very pair his son had used. Made by Wogdon, the London gunsmith, they were owned by Church. Flintlock pistols, they were heavy, each one weighing several pounds, and featured dark-walnut stocks and handsome brass barrels of menacing length. They were not weapons for the unpracticed.

That last night before the duel, Hamilton had been up late at his town house on Cedar Street, completing his will, creating a rather grim financial accounting of his estate, tidying up other affairs, and writing a last round of letters to friends. And he stole some time to write an explanation of his conduct in the run-up to the duel, one that, as he may have known, would shape the campaign to secure his reputation in the case of his death. He insisted he would "throw away" his "first fire" and possibly his second—the same tactic he had recommended to his son—the better to encourage Burr to "pause and reflect." Before firing, presumably. Since this had led to the death of his son, it is surprising that Hamilton would think of it this time. More, it hints at a fatalism that verges on the suicidal, as Hamilton planned to stand defenseless before Burr, leaving it to his worst enemy to shoot him dead.

He finished with a note to his wife, which was to be delivered to her only in the case of his death. Up at the Grange, she had no idea of her husband's plans. An orphaned boy was staying with him, and late that night, Hamilton found him reading a book in Hamilton's study. Hamilton laid his hands on top of the boy's and recited the Lord's Prayer; then he settled back in a chair, and the child soon fell asleep in Hamilton's arms. Roaming the house, he woke his son John, who was with him, to tell him he would be going later to the Grange so the boy wouldn't worry to find him gone in the morning. Finally he returned to his own bed.

Hamilton rose before dawn and arrived first at the Manhattan docks. From there four oarsmen rowed him across the Hudson, with the loyal Pendleton, who would serve as his second, and Dr. Hosack, who had attended to his dying son, Philip. Hamilton had wanted him along; Burr professed not to see the point of having a doctor present.

Burr had passed the night at Richmond Hill, much of it writing a long, chatty letter to Theodosia, always his favorite correspondent, that said nothing of the duel. Instead, he informed her husband, asking him to keep up her academic studies if he didn't survive. He waited out the days until the duel with increasing impatience. "From 7 to 12 is the least pleasant [time]," he told Van Ness, who was making the arrangements. "Anything so we *but* get on." But when, on the fateful morning, Van Ness came to walk with Burr down the hill to the dock, he found Burr sound asleep on the couch in front of the fire.

The sun was just dawning when the men reached the bluff at Weehawken, and the seconds set about to clear away some brush that had gathered on the dueling ground. They were the ones to pace off the distance and to throw the lot to determine whose second would shout, "Present!," the signal to fire. That fell to Hamilton's man. With no other preliminaries, the two men took their positions across from each other. In the rosy light, at that distance, each could get a good look at the other, to check for a tightening of the eyes or a flickering of the cheek that might betray the obvious tension of the moment. By the code, calmness in the face of annihilation was essential, even as they stood across from each other, in a classic fencer's pose, right foot forward, body sideways, right shoulder up high over the chin. The better, that way, to narrow the profile and protect the vitals from a one-ounce ball of lead that would strike like a tiny cannonball at this distance. Both men wore heavy topcoats to obscure the contours of their bodies. Standing so close, with an index finger curled around the trigger of his pistol, each could scrutinize the other's face—one by now nearly as familiar as his own—for gratifying hints of distress.

It had to have been a singularly terrifying moment, but neither man is said to have betrayed any emotion as he stared the other one down. Finally, Hamilton's second cried out, "Present!"

Each leveled his pistol at the other, and two blasts sounded, with puffs of smoke, in close succession.* Burr's ball caught Hamilton on his right

---

* The shots were not almost simultaneous, as one might expect, but according to the two eyewitnesses were about four or five seconds apart. It is an unusual gap. It takes considerable sangfroid to hold back one's fire and hope the other man's ball flies past harmlessly. Aside from separating the calm from the impatient, the delay suggests a divergence in strategy that says something about the otherwise mysterious mind-sets of the two men at this climactic moment in their lives. Who shot first? That has never been clear, and competing narratives have sprung up to support either position. Was it Burr, the more soldierly one, firing immediately to deliver a mortal wound that was, in fact, just an inch from a near miss? Or was it Hamilton, immediately "throwing away" his fire, as he had

side. He gave out a cry of pain as the impact of the bullet twisted him onto the balls of his feet and then sent him sprawling back onto the ground. He lay there stunned, ashen faced, gasping. Burr took a step toward his fallen enemy, a flash of "regret" on his face, said his second, before he hurriedly left the field without a backward glance.

"I am a dead man," Hamilton told his own second, Pendleton, and added to Dr. Hosack, who rushed to his aid, "This is a mortal wound."

And so it was. The bullet had cracked through his ribs, shredded his lungs, and pierced his liver before lodging tight against his lower spine, leaving him paralyzed all down his legs as blood pooled in his gut. Pendleton and Hosack eased him down the steep slope and into the rowboat, which conveyed him back to Manhattan, every stroke of the oars excruciating.

The news from Weehawken went up as a bulletin at the Tontine coffee-house, a gathering spot for the city's business class. GENERAL HAMILTON

---

claimed he would—and then leaving it to Burr to shoot him at his leisure if he chose? Both sides labored mightily to persuade the world that the other man fired first. The Hamilton forces insisted that Burr did and that Hamilton's gun had gone off only by a spastic reflex after he was shot and his bullet went up into the trees. Pendleton returned to the dueling ground the next day and claimed to find a cherry tree branch "at about twelve and a half feet" up from where Hamilton stood that had supposedly been drilled through by his bullet. "General Hamilton did not fire first, and he did not fire at all at Col. Burr," Pendleton argued. The Burr camp insisted that Hamilton did and that Burr had no way of knowing that Hamilton hadn't shot to kill. "The falsehood 'that H. fired only when falling & without aim' has given to very improper suggestions—the fact does appear to me to be important—'You never before doubted'—is it possible you can now doubt?" Burr later wrote Van Ness in an unusually clipped style that revealed his anxiety about the matter. When Hamilton's ball missed, it left Burr time to wait for the smoke to clear, take precise aim, and fire. What's more, to show that Hamilton fully intended to shoot at Burr, the Burr camp contributed the detail that Hamilton stopped the proceedings after the distance had been paced off, and the two men faced each other down, to say that the sunlight was glinting off his glasses, obscuring his vision. He needed to adjust them. John McLane Hamilton, however, insisted his grandfather didn't wear glasses.

Burr was determined to show that he had followed the prescriptions of the code *duello* and upheld his honor; the Hamilton people insisted that Burr had killed a defenseless man in cold blood. If the evidence favors the former, it has been the latter position that has won the day. In this, the dead Hamilton outdid the living Burr.

WAS SHOT BY COLONEL BURR THIS MORNING IN A DUEL, THE GEN-ERAL IS SAID TO BE MORTALLY WOUNDED. The electrifying news spread quickly in every direction, and an eerie quiet settled over much of the island. Much of the city's business stopped, and on the street, people were desperate to find out what others had heard.

Despite his agony, as he lay on his deathbed at a friend's house in Manhattan, Hamilton tried to comfort his delicate wife, who'd rushed to his side from the Grange, thunderstruck at the news. She'd dissolved into a fit of explosive weeping the moment she saw him. "Remember, my Eliza, you are a Christian," Hamilton urged her. To soothe herself, she fanned him throughout the rest of the hot day. Her beguiling sister Angelica came and crumpled into tears, too.

Hamilton sought Communion, but neither minister he summoned would oblige a man dying from a duel. "I have no ill will against Colonel Burr," he assured the second one, the Episcopal bishop Benjamin Moore. "I met him with a fixed resolution to do him no harm. I forgive all that happened." With that, Bishop Moore gave Hamilton the sacrament after all. He labored through the night, and in the morning Betsey brought in his seven children and stood them at the foot of his bed, a sight that left Hamilton unable to speak. More friends came, twenty in all, a scene of desperate grief. Only Hamilton, it appeared, was able to keep his composure. His last words were political: "If they break this union, they will break my heart." He died so easily, his wife weeping beside him, that people did not immediately realize he was gone.

Afterward, Betsey opened the letter that he'd written her in the event of his death. He concluded stirringly:

> *Fly to the bosom of your God and be comforted. With my last idea, I shall cherish the sweet hope of meeting you in a better world.*
> *Adieu best of wives and best of women. Embrace all my darling children for me.*

→>-<←

NEWSPAPERS OF EVERY political slant were filled with the story of the death, the ones favoring Hamilton's Federalist Party framing their accounts with borders of funereal black. The city was consumed with grief. "The feelings of the whole community are agonized beyond description," wrote one New Yorker, who added that there was a greater outpouring for Hamilton than there had been even for Washington upon his death five years before.

A state funeral was staged two days later. While massive guns boomed along the Battery, and church bells rang sorrowfully all about the city, the New York militia marched through the city in formation, their muzzles pointed downward in memory and respect, leading Hamilton's mahogany casket east along Beekman, down Pearl, past Whitehall, and to Broadway, carving a line around what would be the financial center of the world that Hamilton had largely created. The casket was borne by eight pallbearers, with Hamilton's wife and children trailing behind, and then Hamilton's riderless horse, the boots reversed in the stirrups. At Trinity Church, the mourners packed the pews to hear a stirring eulogy by the stylish Gouverneur Morris, the longtime friend of Hamilton who'd also given the eulogy for Washington, and from there the mourning spread throughout the country, declaimed in pulpits and retailed in newspapers, until it seemed that everyone knew that Alexander Hamilton had been murdered by Aaron Burr.

This cipher letter—sent by Burr to his coconspirator General James Wilkinson on July 29, 1806—contained Burr's secret plan to establish himself as the emperor of the American West. It proved Burr's undoing when Wilkinson passed the letter to President Jefferson, who had Burr arrested for the capital crime of treason.

Part Four

———•———

AND THEN
THERE WAS
ONE

Have No Anxiety About the Issue of This Business

AFTER BURR CROSSED the water from Weehawken following the fateful interview, he climbed up to his retreat, Richmond Hill, in full confidence that everyone would recognize he had done nothing wrong. Hamilton had sullied Burr's honor, and Burr had dispatched him according to the code.

As it happened, a cousin had come for a visit that very morning from Connecticut, arriving shortly after Burr. He was directed to the library, where he found Burr engaged in what an early biographer called "his usual avocations." Reading, presumably. Burr greeted him warmly, and the two chatted for a few minutes, until it was time for breakfast, which they enjoyed together, the young relative not thinking for a moment that there was anything amiss for his cousin. "Neither in his manner nor in his conversation was there any evidence of excitement or concern," he noted. It wasn't until the cousin bade Burr good day and took a stroll down Wall Street that he noticed an unusual stirring, and a friend rushed up from the crowd to ask if he'd heard the terrible news about Hamilton. "Colonel Burr has killed him in a duel just this morning!" he cried.

Nonsense, the cousin replied. He'd just come from seeing Burr, and he hadn't said a thing about it.

But then, as he walked farther, the cousin heard more and more people saying the same thing. Colonel Burr had killed General Hamilton. And the cousin came to realize that Burr's blithe insouciance was the queer proof that the gossip must be true.

Burr had planned to stay on in Manhattan, and why shouldn't he? He'd gone into the duel confident that the people were with him, whatever happened. Unlike Hamilton, he'd tested his popularity. *He'd* stood for election, after all, and he'd held offices, increasingly higher ones—assemblyman, state attorney general, senator, and now vice president of the United States. Others might belittle the post, and he might himself, but it was still an impressive title. And what was Hamilton? With the ascendancy of Jefferson, he was yesterday's man, and his many efforts of late to revive his reputation—including that ridiculous pamphlet about Maria Reynolds—only confirmed that impression.

Burr did summon Dr. Hosack—the doctor who had attended Hamilton—to Richmond Hill to give him an account of Hamilton's condition. But that didn't stem the wild stories of raucous celebrations at Richmond Hill, the claims that Burr wished he'd shot Hamilton in the heart, and the suggestions that he'd been practicing his marksmanship for weeks. Federalist stories, perhaps, but they spread. If Burr had hoped people would take his side, he was so grievously disappointed he thought it safer to stay inside.

Meanwhile, the Manhattan coroner was driven by the public outcry to investigate the case. More than forensics, such an investigation usually turned on atmospherics. If it looked like a crime, it was. And the coroner was not likely to let a possible murderer go free.

"I propose leaving town for a few days," Burr airily wrote a friend a few days into the ordeal, "and meditate also a journey of some weeks, but whither is not resolved." To his son-in-law, Alston, he was more candid, writing that the duel "has driven me into a sort of exile, and may terminate in an actual and permanent ostracism." With rising anxiety, he hung on at Richmond Hill for a few more days, and then slunk away in the darkness, a house Negro carrying his bags, his loyal friend Sam Swartwout for company. There was a pier on the water at the foot of the gentle slope of the hill, and there a rowboat with a pair of oarsmen was waiting for him.

They rowed through the night and in the morning pulled in to Perth Amboy on the Jersey shore, where Burr figured he would be safe for a while,

New Jersey being less likely to prosecute duelists. Besides, the state's governor, Joseph Bloomfield, was a friend, or had been. In Perth Amboy, he'd come to see another friend, Commodore Thomas Truxtun, in hopes of securing horses to carry him on to Philadelphia. Truxtun greeted the vice president warily. He'd been friends with Hamilton, and it was hard for him to know what tone to take with his murderer. When Burr asked for "a dish of good coffee," Truxtun brought everyone up to the house for a full breakfast. Burr asked about horses, but Truxtun said he was sorry, but he couldn't possibly arrange a carriage and four until Monday, two days off.

It didn't help that Truxtun let slip that he'd loved Hamilton "as a brother." He quickly added that he had "an unfeigned and sincere regard" for Burr, too, but the damage was done. Burr was clearly troubled by what happened, Truxtun thought, not that he said anything. For his part, Burr had to wonder—was his old friend deliberately trying to hold him up?

Finally Monday came, Burr and his party boarded Truxtun's carriage, and they hurried on to Bristol, and from there across the Delaware by ferry to Philadelphia. Truxtun, aware of the sensitivities, rushed to furnish his account of the visit to the newspapers, lest someone else do it for him, and he let the world know that, while he had done Burr a favor, he'd always been a Hamilton man.

Burr arrived in darkness in Philadelphia and made his way to a local tavern, instinctively pulling a cloak around him and drawing his brimmed hat low. But the tavern keeper recognized him and called out his name, sending a bolt of fear through Burr and his compatriots. That encounter proved harmless, but Burr never knew. Word of his crime—that was now the term—had spread from New York, and, courtesy of lurid newspaper accounts, shocked letters, and salacious gossip, it was moving through the surrounding states like an infectious agent. A vice president was normally fairly anonymous in those days, but not Burr. When he ventured out into Philadelphia one night, cloaked as usual, a correspondent for a Federalist paper spotted him and then marveled in print that a murderer had the "hardihood to show himself in the streets." This was doubly troublesome, for he had received word of a plot by anonymous agents to assassinate him. In a letter to Theodosia, he assured her the claims were "mere fables," bravely adding, "those who wish me dead prefer to keep at a very respectful distance." He would carry on just as before, he assured her. "No such attempt has been made or will be." But he later weakened, begging her not to be "dissatisfied with me . . . I can't just now endure it."

His associates were in worse trouble. At the end of July, warrants had been issued for them to testify or be clapped in jail, a fate that befell his close friends Matthew L. Davis and Colonel Marinus Willett. The crippled John Swartwout, who'd left Burr for New York, and the ever-loyal Van Ness had both gone into hiding. But after a few days Swartwout smuggled out a letter to Burr with the news that a grand jury had delivered a verdict of "willful murder by the hand of A.B.," with Van Ness and Hamilton's Pendleton as "accessories before the fact." Stunning news—a vice president accused of a capital crime. Swartwout was trying to keep the bulletin out of the papers, but it was not to be stopped. Shortly after came word that New York's governor Lewis, who had trounced Burr in the last election, was set to enlist the governor of Pennsylvania to enforce the warrant for Burr's arrest.

Burr remained defiant. "I shall remain here some days," he told his son-in-law, Joseph Alston, "that I may better know the enemy." He closed on a note of iron to fortify Alston—and possibly himself. *"Have no anxiety about the issue of this business."*

Still, it must have been troubling to see a copy of the grand jury's verdict, which declared that the vice president, "not having the fear of God before his eyes, but being moved and seduced by the Instigation of the devil . . . feloniously and willfully did kill and Murder [Alexander Hamilton] against the peace of the People of the State of New York and their dignity."

Aaron Burr was now officially a wanted man.

FORTY-SEVEN

A Good Many Incidents to Amuse One

B URR HAD ALWAYS had a plan.

Late on the night of May 23, 1804, just days before Burr fired off his opening salvo in what would prove to be his fatal correspondence with Hamilton, the vice president received a visitor at his mansion on Richmond Hill, a man who had insisted on arriving in total darkness—"without observation," as he put it in a letter to Burr setting up the interview—and on leaving that way too. It was Brigadier General James Wilkinson, a man of middling height, but bulky and heavy walking, with a confident manner and a rough voice that he kept low when Burr ushered his guest into the library and closed the door behind him. Wilkinson was the commander and highest-ranking officer of the American army, just a few thousand strong, but still the most powerful force in North America. His title had previously been held by Washington in 1798, when Adams had raised an army to face down the rising French threat in the Quasi-War, and then by Hamilton. He in turn bestowed it on Wilkinson in 1800.

No one mistook Wilkinson for a canny general or a decent fellow. He was little more than a ruddy-faced braggart, but there was something solid within his bluster, even if it raised doubts about his fundamental character. Wilkinson was not a man to cross, and Hamilton had realized that, as dangerous as it might be to promote a man like Wilkinson, it was more dangerous not to. "He will apt to become disgusted if neglected," Hamilton explained. "And through disgust may be rendered really what he is now only suspected to be." He was being rendered really now, for Wilkinson had suffered a wrenching comedown, too, when Jefferson had unceremoniously trimmed Wilkinson's army by a full third, making it, to Wilkinson, little more than a militia. And Jefferson also let it be known that he wasn't so sure that Wilkinson needed a grand title like brigadier general. The moves "awakened me from a dream," Wilkinson seethed. Burr, of course, had his own reasons to hate Jefferson.

Burr knew Wilkinson from their days in the Continental Army, when they had both served in Benedict Arnold's ill-fated campaign to liberate Quebec from the British. And it may be that the specter of America's preeminent traitor hung over them now as they huddled in Burr's library, for the two were dreaming of sedition, which could be charted in the half dozen rolled-up maps that Wilkinson had brought with him. For they were all of the American West, which Jefferson had recently acquired from Napoléon, a faraway place at least two months' ride from New York, assuming a safe passage across the Alleghenies. Burr unrolled the broad sheets over the library table and set about candles to light them. As he searched from one to the next, he could see these lands weren't like any place he knew. There wasn't anything there! It was like staring at the Pacific—endless, but empty. Burr wasn't much of a traveler, but he was open to the possibilities of the West. Jefferson loved to spin tales of tribes of gigantic Indians, river bluffs carved into sculpture as fine as Michelangelo's, endless prairies seeded with bumper crops, and whole mountains made of salt. (The Federalist editor Coleman scoffed that the president had left out the "lakes of molasses" and the "vales of hasty pudding.") And the fancies had taken hold. It would be some time before they would be replaced by the harsh truth of a barren landscape, hostile Indians, and extreme weather.

As Burr and Wilkinson peered at their maps, they could see that the lands ran from the Mississippi, fed by countless twisting tributaries including the Ohio and the Missouri, down to New Orleans on the Gulf of Mexico; west to the "Montagnes de la Roche," as the French called the Rockies, rendered only as a blunt and unimposing ridge snaking along the edge of the Pacific Ocean; and then up to what was termed the British South Wales

Possessions to the north. Most of this was terra incognita, even to its inhabitants. Jefferson had just that month sent out the roughhewn explorers Meriwether Lewis and William Clark to hunt up a passage to the Pacific and to find out what they could of the lands along the way.

While the geological features were all crudely depicted, none of the maps showed any human habitation. Not a town, village, fort, settlement. But Burr knew that would change. He knew the inexorable surge of easterners eager for land and opportunity. He'd engaged in enough land speculation to have the feel of it. If the West was empty now, it would not be empty long. And if it was empty now, that meant it was his for the taking.

If Burr was the man for that, his guest was the man to help him. The plan that Burr had in mind required soldiers, and a commander to lead them. And it would require unusual talent for deception, since it had to unfold in secrecy if it was to unfold at all. Such deception created a unique intimacy, as each man could ruin the other. This created an odd fondness at least on Wilkinson's part: "I think of you always my handsome and dear devil."

The plan would evolve, but the rudiments were set: to seize the nearly 1 million square miles of the Louisiana Purchase—all the new western lands from the Mississippi across to the Rockies—and to turn them into Aaron Burr's personal empire. The ambition was inspired by Napoléon, then overrunning Europe. Burr would call himself emperor as well, with Theodosia his empress, and her son, Aaron Burr Alston, the heir to the throne. Burr of course was no Napoléon. He'd never commanded men in battle, and he had nothing like Napoléon's vast army of a half million men. But then, the land that he sought to conquer was undefended, and westerners might welcome Burr's arrival as a liberator from the strictures emanating from Washington. On the western side of the Alleghenies, settlers sent their goods down the Mississippi, not east through the Alleghenies, so few felt much commercial connection to the Atlantic states. To many in the West, the American government was an occupying force, its governors appointed by a distant Congress like the Crown of old.

By the middle of June, Wilkinson left for his headquarters at Fort Massac, and from then on, the two communicated only by cipher—a fitting medium for such a shadowy duo.* The first step was to raise some money. As always, Burr was mired in debt, and his beloved Richmond Hill was soon to be seized by his creditors—ultimately to be claimed by John Jacob Astor. It was the last of his assets. Burr insisted to Theodosia that this was all to the good. "A huge weight it has taken from the head and shoulders, and every other part, animal and intellectual, of A.B." But it added a huge weight, too.

Burr imagined that King George III might pay for the chance to take revenge on his runaway colonies, and thought his hearty, knockabout friend Charles Williamson might be just the man to plead their case. English by birth, he'd become an American citizen after the war and served with Burr in the Assembly, where they'd joined in some lavish land speculations in New York. More recently, Burr had helped him secure a divorce from his American wife. Burr had a passion for Williamson, he told Theodosia, one "such as had I with no other man living, and such as it is utterly improbable I should ever have with any one again."

When he learned of Burr's plan, Williamson passed him on to the British ambassador, Anthony Merry, in Philadelphia. But he had some other conspirators to round up first. One of them was that Commodore Truxtun. While Burr had ostensibly visited Truxtun to find a place of refuge, he was actually soliciting him to join their secessionist cause. When Truxtun put it out in the newspapers that he had received Burr with misgivings, since his greater loyalty was to Hamilton, that was cover, for Truxtun's greater loyalty always was to Burr, which is why Burr had gone to him. He hoped Truxtun would provide at sea what Wilkinson had agreed to deliver on land, commanding Burr's navy to project power out from the

---

* Burr's encryption had evolved into an elaborate process involving an ever-changing key drawn from an unrelated text, like a passage from the Bible, to encode messages letter by letter, translating, for example, an *e* into a *g,* and a *j* into an *l,* and then decoding them back. Encoded, the message looks like a crossword puzzle created by a lunatic, with no proper words, and a highly perplexing proposition for anyone who found it. By modern standards, however, such encryption is so light a teenager with a cell phone could penetrate it.

Gulf of Mexico, not across the Atlantic. But when asked, Truxtun rather sensibly equivocated, preferring to see how events unfolded.

With that, Burr hurried on to Philadelphia, where he addressed secret number three—Celeste, who had signaled that she might be open to his advances after all. Despite his suits for La G and La Plante, among other anonymous beauties, he returned in secret to Celeste, whom he'd swooned over ever since he first laid eyes on her at a dinner of her father's. Of late, she'd been tormenting him with declarations that she could never, ever marry him, never marry *anyone*, only to beg him to come back, *please*, so he could continue his delightful advances. Recently, though, she had turned enticingly "pliant" after an exchange of letters, and now he made his way to her Philadelphia town house, attempting to renew his courtship once more.

But Celeste declared that she had decided, irrevocably, that she would never marry after all. With that, her door was shut to him. "Nothing can be done with Celeste," he told Theodosia wearily. "There is a strange indecision and timidity which I cannot fathom." *Basta!* "The thing, however, is abandoned." In fact, he was giving up "all such things"—meaning women—for the duration; under the circumstances, such romantic follies were all too much even for him: "If any male friend of yours should be dying of ennui," he told his daughter, "recommend to him to engage in a duel and a courtship at the same time."

Now he paid his call on Williamson's friend Anthony Merry, the British minister who was the king's personal representative in the United States. Despite his name, Merry was a dour, grim-faced creature who was aquiver with fussy English proprieties. He'd been appalled that, when he paid a call on the president at the Executive Mansion, Jefferson had greeted him in bedroom slippers. It was a political statement, of course, but Merry took it as a dire insult. So when Burr approached him with his proposal to take his revenge, he listened attentively. Rearranging the cartography of North America—who wouldn't smile at that? To have a chance to teach that insufferable Jefferson a lesson? And for Anthony Merry, far too long overlooked, to emerge as the power broker?

Merry passed along to his royal minders Burr's offer: Burr would resign the vice presidency and serve the British in any capacity it wished—if the

British government would do what it could to detach the American West from its current owners, specifically: "To effect a Separation of the Western Part of the United States from that which lies between the Atlantick and the Mountains, in its whole Extent." The sensitive question of what would become of the American West when it was liberated, whether it was to be British or Burr's, that was left for Williamson, who would be sailing for London shortly, to discuss with members of the British cabinet in person. Merry prudently cautioned his superiors about the "profligacy of [Burr's] character," since that was as well-known on that side of the Atlantic as it was on this. But he did trumpet Burr's "talents and activity" and "connections" and urged His Highness not to overlook Burr's "spirit of revenge against the present administration."

With that, Burr moved on farther south. Ostensibly this was to evade a murder warrant, but that imperative eased with each mile. Gradually, he was treated less like a fugitive and more like a conquering hero who had stood up to dishonor. But he wasn't seeking relief. He'd gone south to Spanish Florida to seize it.

→‹‹

SPAIN HAD BEEN a subject of speculation for ambitious Americans for two decades. With the Treaty of Paris that ended the Revolutionary War, England had retreated from all North American territory south of Canada, surrendering to the United States its lands in the Ohio Valley and giving to the Spanish all its lands along the Gulf Coast. Spain thus had a chokehold on the agricultural goods that descended the Mississippi, and it was thought to be hoping to reach to the north and west from there. That was irritant enough, but the deeper antagonism with Spain stemmed from the years after the revolution, when ambitious Americans—Hamilton among them—sought to liberate South America from the Spanish as they had done against the English. Adams could see that Americans had enough to handle in North America and had put a stop to such an adventure, but Jefferson was determined to drive Spain out of the continent.

Neither Spain nor the United States, however, was willing to risk open war. The Americans did not have a sufficient military, and the Spanish did not want to fight a war across the Atlantic. So, instead, both sides undertook a war of maneuvering—of intrigues, essentially—that would gain them geopolitical advantage without gaining actual territory.

At this point, the Spanish had attracted to their cause any number of key figures who were putatively on the other side. Unknown to Burr, one of the most outrageous traitors was Wilkinson, who served as Spanish Secret Agent "No. 13" reporting directly to the king of Spain. His task was to enlighten the king on American political developments and troop movements, and also to shift the western allegiance toward the Spanish by playing up any antagonism with Washington and playing down any problems with Spain. At the same time, of course, Wilkinson was also working covertly with Burr to advance an entirely different agenda.

For now, Burr was attending only to Spanish Florida; he would go after the rest of the Spanish lands later. He told everyone, even Theodosia, that he was in Georgia just to pay a visit to his friend Pierce Butler, whom Burr knew from their days together in the Senate, on the windswept barrier sea island of Saint Simons off the Georgia coast. With his vast acreages of rice and cotton, Butler was one of the wealthiest men in America, possessing a thousand slaves to tend his plantations.*

Saint Simons was a delight, and Burr regaled Theodosia with the retinue in his lavish guesthouse: a personal housekeeper, cook, chambermaid, seamstress, and two footmen, not to mention the pair of fishermen and four bargemen he also had at his disposal if he wished to return to the water. The plantation islands themselves were garden paradises that extended from horizon to horizon, growing everything from turkeys to pomegranates, not just cotton and rice.

He would use Butler's plantation as a secure base of operations from which to launch some preliminary investigations of this foreign territory— its population centers, serviceable roads, political organization. He'd origi-

---

* When Butler had been a representative at the Constitutional Convention, he was the one to advance the insidious constitutional rule that, for purposes of apportioning House seats, a black slave, even though nonvoting, counted as three-fifths of a white citizen, substantially inflating the political power of the South. Without that provision, the historian Garry Wills has argued, Jefferson and Burr would most likely not have been elected in 1800.

nally set aside five or six weeks for the purpose. But he'd been delayed coming south and was obliged to head north again sooner than he had intended. So now, to his frustration, he would be in Florida for only two weeks at most. Since he had no horse, he feared he wouldn't be able to penetrate deeply into the peninsula, but have to cling to the coast, with Saint Augustine, one of the larger settlements, his likely target.

He was just preparing for his first foray over the border when, around noon one day, the winds suddenly rose and then started ripping at the trees and slamming his guesthouse. By the afternoon, the furious hurricane was at its height, smashing against the length of the island's shoreline and sending up huge seas, seven feet above the normal high tide, to crash on the beach. The winds shattered outbuildings and ripped live oaks out of the ground to smash them down on frail rooftops. Burr watched the devastation through storm-splattered windows from inside his guesthouse, where he could feel the structure "shake and rock"; he was afraid the whole building might go over and be scattered to the winds. As it was, a chimney toppled over onto the roof, and the tide surged up the beach and burst through the front door to flood the ground floor.

The ironic Burr professed detachment to Theodosia. "You may imagine, in this scene of confusion and dismay, a good many incidents to amuse one if one had dared to be amused in a moment of much anxiety." A neighbor insisted that Burr take refuge in a nearby storehouse that was more secure—well back from the water, solidly built, and lower to the ground. With others from the plantation, Burr huddled around lanterns as the storm swirled around them. The winds eased off briefly in the midafternoon but then regained their fury and pounded the island for the rest of the night.

By morning, the storm had passed. The skies were clear and the seas quiet. As Burr stepped about to survey the damage, he could see that dozens of houses had been flooded and discovered that hundreds of acres of Butler's rice fields had been ruined, costing him a fortune in lost rice. Nineteen slaves had drowned. Most of the local roads were washed out, and virtually all the boats along the shore had been reduced to kindling.

Because of the devastation, it would be some days before Burr could return once more to his mission. He hesitated to write anything more about it to Theodosia, for fear that the letter might be intercepted. As it was, it would be taken in hand by a black slave, who'd have to swim "a half a dozen creeks," and it was easy to imagine the letter might get loose. Burr hated to think it might end up in the newspapers, not because it might reveal his plot for Spanish Florida, but because it would reveal the latest details of his romance with "pauvre Celeste," who had still not let go her hold on him.

With that, he secured one of the still-intact boats for a trip down the Florida coast. He'd hoped to reach Saint Augustine, but he got no farther than Saint Johns, about fifteen miles shy. Whatever intelligence he gleaned from this trip, all that survives is this one observation: "It is a fact that the Spanish ladies smoke segars," he declared, explaining that the lady "takes a few puffs" then hands the cigar to her lover "as a mark of great kindness."

→>-<+-

RETURNING TO SAVANNAH, Burr was delighted to be serenaded by a band outside his hotel window, as part of an effort by local citizens to get the vice president to come out and say a few words. This Burr did, only to be tendered yet more invitations for more appearances. Was it possible, he wondered, he had misjudged the popular response to Hamilton's death? Might he not emerge as the hero of that tale after all? And might he not be able to convert such heroism into yet more magnificent grandeur?

From there, he continued by boat up the coast to Washington City to perform his last official act as vice president: to preside over the Senate's impeachment trial of Supreme Court Justice Samuel Chase. If the Federalists had attempted to go after the Republicans through the Alien and Sedition Acts, Jefferson would now retaliate by calling for the impeachment of Federalist judges who did not adhere to his interpretation of the Constitution. Of them, by far the most prominent was Chase. By the time Burr arrived in Washington, he learned that he had been indicted for murder in New Jersey, too. So a man wanted for murder in two states would stand in judgment over a Supreme Court justice.

To see that he had his way, Jefferson had his vice president several times to dinner and, at Burr's urging, added a couple of sweeteners: He named Burr's brother-in-law Dr. Joseph Browne to the office of secretary of all of

Louisiana, and, obviously unaware of the plot against him, made General Wilkinson governor of the entire Louisiana Territory. Jefferson had already made Burr's stepson John Bartow Prevost the federal judge in New Orleans. Through these men, Burr would gain political influence over much of the region, and even more in New Orleans, which he envisioned to be the capital of his empire.

Despite Jefferson's inducements, Burr proved an even-handed judge, never once veering off the course of legal probity, although he occasionally revealed traces of bitterness. "He conducted with the dignity and impartiality of an angel," wrote the *Washington Federalist*, "but with the rigor of a devil." At one point, he called out a senator for nibbling cake during the proceedings and derided another for breaking decorum in the Senate chamber by wearing a heavy coat against the blasts of arctic air seeping in around the window edges.

When the trial was done, Burr tendered a verdict of not guilty, much to Jefferson's fury, leaving himself one last task as vice president, to give an envoi to the Senate where he had served his term. It was the first time in the short history of the nation that the vice president had not been returned to high office, and the Constitution held no provision for a speech. He selected a moment in the Senate's executive session, and, waiting until the senators fell silent around him, he stood ramrod straight and, speaking extemporaneously, adopted the solemn tone of a Roman valedictory. Gesturing to the hall about him, he called the Senate chamber:

> *a sanctuary and a citadel of law, of order, of liberty—and it is here—*
> *in this exalted refuge—here if anywhere will resistance be made to the*
> *storms of popular frenzy and the silent arts of corruption; and if the*
> *Constitution be destined ever to perish by the sacrilegious hands of the*
> *demagogue or the usurper, which God avert, its expiring agonies will be*
> *witnessed on this floor.*

It was an extraordinary performance, one that left many of the senators weeping, they were so moved by his words. But it is a wonder they weren't speechless with indignation, instead. For flights of rhetoric, this had to have been one of the more preposterous heard in that young chamber. While it was intended to exalt the Senate, it could as easily be heard as Burr's self-pitying tribute to himself as a political refugee. In hailing the Senate as an "exalted refuge" and a "citadel of law," he meant *for him*. If anyone was desecrating the Senate, it was himself, a fugitive from the law at that very moment! For "corruption" he had no equal. And if anyone was threatening the Constitution—Hamilton's Constitution, one might add—it was Burr himself, by virtue of the conspiracy he had already begun and would return to shortly. If Burr were speaking ironically, his words would have the advantage of humor, but instead these high-flown sentiments seem to have emerged from that part of his moral imagination that turned black into white, and back again, as needed, so that Aaron Burr need never be in the wrong, whatever he did. It was a handy skill, and he would use it often.

→>-<-

WITH BURR'S TERM now complete, he was free to pursue his dream of sedition in earnest. He added another confederate to his little band—Jonathan Dayton, whom he'd known from Elizabethtown, New Jersey, and the school they'd attended there before Princeton, a locus that bound up the Burrs and the Daytons, and another family, the Ogdens, in the elite. Matthias Ogden married Dayton's sister Hannah after the war, and Burr had guided Dayton's speculation in frontier land, chiefly in southwestern Ohio, where he became tight with General Wilkinson. Dayton had gone into politics, although as a Federalist, and helped push Burr's abortive presidential bid in 1796. Given all this, it was probably inevitable that Burr should bring Dayton into his scheme. Having journeyed to New Orleans in 1803 in advance of the Louisiana Purchase, Dayton had seen for himself that the United States did not have a firm hold on these territories and that the underlying uncertainty would work to the advantage of the French, who could play the eastern states off against the western ones. Dayton, in short, was a believer, and he made Ogden one too.

But it wasn't always easy to know who would be attracted to Burr's scheme, who would be helpful, and who would be a risk. Matthew Lyon, the irascible former congressman from Vermont, was a possibility. He'd made a name for himself in Washington for his use of those fireplace tongs.

Now relocated to Kentucky, Lyon wanted to persuade Burr to move south too. In 1796, there had been few more staunch backers of Tennessee's bid for statehood than Burr, and Lyon imagined Burr could easily call in that marker now. He need only set up a nominal law practice in Tennessee, give a few speeches, and Lyon was sure that Burr could be elected congressman before a year was out, and senator shortly after that. He would be back in the game.

Lyon had said as much to his sleazy confederate, General James Wilkinson, in Washington, and Wilkinson claimed to have been overjoyed at the idea, either because he genuinely was pleased to think of a way to get Burr back into a sphere of political influence, or because he was just concealing the true intentions of the man he referred to as "the little counselor." Lyon recalled, "He clapped his hands on my shoulders, exclaiming with an oath, 'This will do!—it is a heavenly thought—worthy of him who thought it!' He rang the bell, ordered his boots, and said he would go instantly and inform the little counselor, and would call on me in the House in the course of two or three hours."

Lyon went to see Burr at Mr. Wharton's, an elegant boardinghouse patronized by government men, where it took several pulls on the bell before a servant came, only for Lyon to discover that Burr was deep in company. Lyon was about to leave his card, with plans to return another time, when Burr emerged from the room and said it would be just half an hour more, and please wait. This time, when the door opened, he recognized the voices of Wilkinson and Dayton, which was a surprise since Dayton was not thought to be in town. Burr explained that the meeting was about "some land concern in the Western country," as Lyon put it. When Lyon revealed to Burr his proposition, he could see immediately that Burr was nowhere near as "enamored" as Wilkinson had been of the project.

Burr did allow that he was planning a western trip that would take him to Pittsburgh and west from there. One imagines a significant pause here, as Burr waited for Lyon to ask the obvious question, "Why?" And that, in turn, would let Burr give the barest hint of his true intention, so as to gauge Lyon's reaction and determine if it was safe to proceed any further with a conversation that could get him hanged if it went awry.

Either because he couldn't imagine there was anything more to Burr's travel plan, or because he could, Lyon said only that he was headed the same way and offered him passage on his boat. If Burr wanted to get into Tennessee politics, he shouldn't waste any time on western travels.

By now, Burr must have determined that Lyon would be of no particular use to him, for he made clear he had his own boat waiting for him in Pittsburgh. But, leaving the door ajar, he allowed that perhaps they could travel a ways together down the Ohio.

FORTY-EIGHT

Motives of Profound Political Importance

B URR WAS MAKING some progress with his seditious plans, but his was not a pretty situation. "In New York I am to be disenfranchised, and in New Jersey hanged," he acknowledged to his son-in-law from his Washington boardinghouse. "Having substantial objections to both, I shall not, for the present, hazard either, but shall seek another country." True enough— but the sentiment was so ironic and roundabout that it amounted to another form of encryption. The short of it was, of course, he was indeed seeking another country—to seize. And what he said next had its own truth too.

"There is no reason to think that I shall this season visit either New-York or New-Jersey," he teased Theodosia. Then he laid out a detailed itinerary: first to Philadelphia, then west to "Fort Pitt," better known as Pittsburgh, and down the Ohio clear to Saint Louis, then across to Tennessee, and finally float down the Mississippi to New Orleans. "This tour has other objects than mere curiosity," he admitted. "An operation of business which promises to render the tour both useful and agreeable." He did not, however, say what it was. "As the objects of the journey, not mere curiosity . . . may lead me to [New] Orleans, and *perhaps further*, I contemplate the tour with gayety and cheerfulness."

If Theodosia had anything to write him, he told her, she should send it to him in Philadelphia, since he would not have any fixed addresses after that. Philadelphia because the alluring Celeste was there. Yes, that Celeste.

Burr could not free himself of her. Just the year before she had sent him packing, but since then she had sent some timid feelers that had raised his hopes that she had reconsidered, and he'd made time to renew his suit now.

To Theodosia, he chortled at the thought that everyone in Washington would assume he was going to Philadelphia for politics, when in fact it was for Celeste. "How little is this truth suspected by the hundreds who are at this moment ascribing *to the movement motives of profound political importance*." This, of course, is the benefit of secrecy: People misapprehend.

The visit, however, went no better than the previous ones. Once again, Celeste refused to see him. While he must have been perplexed, if not infuriated, Burr professed to take the defeat in stride. "The affair of Celeste is forever closed," he told Theodosia, "so there is one trouble off hand."

Thus unburdened, he continued on to Pittsburgh, joined for this portion of the trip by Mr. Gabriel Shaw, a New York merchant eager to do business in the West, and Shaw's wife, all three on horseback. Burr's purpose was an unusual one, to take possession of an elaborate houseboat he'd purchased to float down the Ohio. A "floating house," he called it; sometimes his "ark." He'd bought it for the relative pittance of 133 dollars, and it was probably paid for by Theodosia's wealthy husband, Joseph Alston, who was starting to pick up some of Burr's expenses. Sixty feet by fourteen, it was on the scale of a Philadelphia row house, and it contained a dining room, kitchen with fireplace, two bedrooms, and, as Burr put it, was "roofed from stem to stern," with a slender staircase up to a widow's walk that ran the whole length. Flat bottomed and squared off, it was propelled only by the flow of the river and required bargemen to fend off rocks and shore as the house descended. The vessel was ready for him when he arrived, and he boarded it the next day.

He'd hoped to bring General Wilkinson along. There would have been no more private place to discuss their strategy than bobbing along the Ohio. But Wilkinson was on his way to Saint Louis, bound for New Orleans, where he would assume his new appointment from Jefferson as governor of Louisiana. Burr had planned to meet Matthew Lyon, the congressman who was wooing him to Tennessee, and after a day's float, the ark caught up with Lyon's barge, and the two men lashed their very different crafts together, and, conjoined, they continued to float down the swift

Ohio, sweeping along at eight miles an hour, the rushing river water slowed by the wide oxbow bends that required some careful pole work by the bargemen to keep the ark from running aground. On either side, the Ohio's banks showed no sign of human life; it was as if they had returned to an earlier time. The banks heaped up to hills behind, and some to small mountains, some steep, some rounded, that were a lush green of leaves and grass and vines that grew everywhere. For hundreds of miles, Burr and his three companions could not see a soul.

Finally—Wheeling, a pretty little village where Burr noticed, as he drifted by, that some of the women had a decided "air of fashion" reminiscent of the cities of the Atlantic coast. Farther down, there was a more substantial settlement, Marietta, named for Marie Antoinette. It had been the first in the territories, and it boasted a boat works that built gunboats, highly maneuverable and well-armed ones. Burr couldn't help noting that it might be fitting to employ a western firm to free the West. While he was here, he took a contemplative stroll about its prehistoric burial ground of aboriginal Indians, but nonetheless he made time for several gentlemen who were eager to strike up conversation with such an eminence.

With that, Lyon untied his barge from the ark, and, taking the Shaws with him, he went on ahead, leaving Burr to continue downriver alone. Lyon was left scratching his head about Burr's true intentions. "There seemed to be too much mystery in his conduct," he wrote later. "I suspected him to have other objects in view, to which I could not penetrate."

When the bargemen cast off, the ark was soon enclosed in wilderness again, that endless green that was broken only by the blue of the sky and the churning blue-green water. Finally, about twenty miles along, the ark curved around a wide bend, and there, straight before him, was a long but slender strip of island, overspread by tall trees, and bright with gay colors that must have seemed to Burr almost inconceivable in such a wilderness. A fine house stood on it, done of stone, and Georgian in balance and symmetry, one that would not have been out of place in London, its two wings rounded into a perfect semicircle like a pair of arms in greeting. A spreading lawn ran before it, bounded by shrubbery and flowers and interrupted only by the carriage road that served the entrance. Barely visible behind were acres of pretty flower gardens in the English style, as well as long rectangular patches of well-tended vegetables, and beside the house were lovely espaliers of peach, apricot, quince, and pear trees, with walkways snaking all about. An early writer, William Harris Safford, likened it to the sight of "the Moorish palaces of Andalusia," which conveys the spirit of improbability of finding such a mansion on the Ohio River.

Or of finding Harman Blennerhassett. Tall, with a knobby face, and stooped from a nearsightedness so extreme that a servant had to aim his gun when he shot game, Blennerhassett was Irish by birth, foolish by nature, and immensely rich by virtue of a legacy bestowed on him by his father, an extremely wealthy manufacturer. In midlife, Blennerhassett had set out across the Atlantic to make a name for himself in the New World. For the sum of sixty thousand dollars, he had created this paradise on the sliver of land that became known as Blennerhassett Island, settling here eight years before with his wife, who also happened to be his niece. Here he devoted himself to scientific investigations—chemistry, astronomy, botany; the list was almost limitless—that he hoped would yield him some marketable secrets of life.

But hadn't. And the bitter truth was, for all the boldness of Blennerhassett's ambitions, he was not bold at heart. His electrical studies, for example, were compromised by the fact that he was so terrified of lightning that, at the first darkening of the skies, he shut all the doors and windows, rushed into his bedroom, locked the doors behind him, and huddled in the middle of his bed, where he believed any flickers of lightning were least likely to get him. He soothed his nerves with music, playing both the violin and violoncello.

If Blennerhassett had hoped that his scientific discoveries would revive his declining fortunes, the truth was that they had only depleted them further, making him an increasingly desperate man in an increasingly desperate situation. Which is why Burr had come.

After the bargemen secured the ark, Burr stepped out and, rather than making for the house, he took a languorous turn about the gardens to examine the wide variety of flowers, as well as the abundance of ripe fruit hanging off the trees in the orchard. He might have continued his tour for some time, but a servant approached him and told him that Mrs. Blennerhassett would be delighted if he would favor her with a visit to her house.

Nonplussed, Burr took out his personal card and wrote a note to say that he regretted he must decline. He'd stopped only for a brief tour of the gardens, and he would soon be on his way. He signed it "A. Burr." Seeing that, Mrs. Blennerhassett was stricken, sending back a note of her own that she could not bear to be inhospitable to a former vice president, and although her husband was away, she *insisted* on welcoming him in their house. To that, Burr could do nothing but assent.

The interior proved to be no less magical than the exterior, not least because it brought a cool, high-ceilinged elegance to the hot lushness of West Virginia in late summer. Mahogany tables, gilt mirrors, velvet-cushioned furniture, classical paintings, Chinese vases—it was almost more than Burr could take in.

While Blennerhassett obviously had his limits, it seems his wife did not. Safford, that early writer, does not just term her the most extraordinary woman west of the Alleghenies; he acclaims her one of the finest women in all of history—extolling her fluency in French and Italian, brilliance at Shakespeare, exquisite Grecian features, graceful yet dignified manner, and flowing dark hair swept behind an exotic, richly colored silk headdress worn à la Turque.

Burr was not one to be immune to such charms, and the realization that Mrs. Blennerhassett was married with three children would not likely have held him back either. But the fact that she was married to a man with a sizable fortune—Burr did not know yet just how sizable—that he was attempting to make a little less sizable would certainly have cooled his ardor. And that was the nub of it. Knowing that other people were interested in Blennerhassett for his money made it imperative that Burr make it seem he wasn't. Hence the charade about his being uninterested in her invitation. He certainly was interested, but his resistance would only encourage his hostess to greater eagerness, which would work to his advantage. Then again, stratagems aside, it was possible that the very fetching Mrs. Blennerhassett could simply not resist someone so bewitching as a former vice president who was wanted for murder.

Whichever, Mrs. Blennerhassett did not demur when, over wine, Burr started to inquire—no, press her—about her husband's business affairs, and, more pertinent, his financial standing. So attractive to so many, Mrs.

Blennerhassett was probably not used to being the one to reveal more than she intended. So she was unable to do anything except to answer the questions he asked, all of them put to her so delicately, with those wide, curious eyes of his, and when their conversation was concluded, she begged him to stay for dinner, which he agreed to only with great reluctance, and it wasn't until almost midnight that, sated, he quit the house with professions of the greatest gratitude to his hostess. When the door shut behind him, he crossed the lawn and made his way down to the dock, where he boarded his floating house, settled into his bedroom, and slept, the waters of the Ohio sliding gently past.

→><←

WHEN BURR CAST off from Blennerhassett Island the next morning, he continued down the Ohio in his ark, gathering backers as he went. It seemed there was no shortage of the prominent who were willing to sign on with a serenely self-confident adventurer who offered the allure of riches beyond measure without actually specifying their form, quantity, or source. In Cincinnati, he collected a twenty-five-thousand-dollar loan from the Indiana Canal Company, which operated as a bank in imitation of Burr's Manhattan Water Company, and then met two senators, one being Ohio's mirthless John Smith, a former Baptist minister turned speculator whose land agents had been the fabled Kemper brothers, who'd tried, and failed, to conquer Spanish West Florida; and the other New Jersey's Jonathan Dayton, Burr's kinsman from Elizabethtown, who had vast landholdings along the Miami River in the Northwest. He revisited the persistent Lyon, who once again tried to persuade Burr to run for office in Tennessee and, failing, fell disenchanted with this man of "too much mystery." He tried to hit up the canal company's major backer, Senator John Brown, for funds, and spent nights with Kentucky's wealthiest insurer in a hunt for further financing. Burr gave every indication his venture was military. He visited shipyards to discuss boats to carry soldiers down the Mississippi. While he never came right out and said that he was planning an assault on Mexico that would seize Spanish gold mines and all its territory, freeing America to expand throughout the continent, few people doubted that was his intention—or at least one of them. And if this was a violation of the 1798

Neutrality Act, and unlawful under the Constitution besides, the audacity was, if anything, all part of the appeal west of the Alleghenies, a corner of the backwoods that was more likely to look for inspiration down the Mississippi than east across the Alleghenies.

As Burr's ark progressed, the excitement over this would-be Napoléon only increased, and when he arrived at Nashville, Tennessee, the city exploded with booming cannons and a festival of flags. "I have been received with much kindness and hospitality," he wrote Theodosia. "I could stay a month with pleasure." He spent time with Andrew Jackson and his beloved Rachel at their country mansion, the Hermitage. Not yet the brave heart of his military days, Jackson was known more for his earnestness. "One of the frank, ardent souls I love to meet," Burr termed him, although his appeal doubtless included the two-thousand-man state militia he controlled.

At star-shaped Fort Massac, a lonely outpost guarding the junction of the Ohio and Mississippi Rivers, he paid a call on his burly coconspirator, General Wilkinson, and disappeared with him for more than a day and a half, likely to discuss plans to invade Spain, either to the west, past the Louisiana Purchase, or to the east, in Spanish Florida, if not both. Wilkinson raved to his Spanish minder in New Orleans that Burr was "brave, learned, eloquent, gallant, honorable . . . and rich in the affections of the human heart." Meaning, Spain had nothing to fear from such a paragon. Meaning, it absolutely did. Then Burr traded in his ark for a military barge crewed by ten oarsmen, receiving a "cordial reception," he told his daughter, wherever he anchored.

Finally, Burr reached New Orleans, the city that would figure in his dreams. Hot, fragrant, mysterious, it was a southern New York, a city into which all rivers emptied, and which all seas touched. Its spicy cosmopolitanism matched Burr's ambitions perfectly, as he envisioned it the takeoff point for any assault on Mexico and the capital of any western empire he assembled. Through his shifty New York friend Edward Livingston, who'd fled to New Orleans to escape his debts, Burr tried to forge an alliance with the Mexico Association, a three-hundred-member organization that dreamed of liberating Mexico with a mass of troops drawn from Kentucky and Louisiana. They told him of the fifty-five guns abandoned by the

French, a prospect that made him almost giddy. He was introduced to the merchant Daniel Clark, who was as eager to see him then as he was to disavow him later. Burr also made an overture to the Catholic Church, whose backing would be necessary, and was a particular hit with the Ursuline nuns he conversed with through a grate.

The trek back was a strain—through several hundred miles of "vile country," he told Theodosia, "destitute of springs and of running water—think of drinking the nasty puddle-water, covered with green scum and full of animalculai." Nonetheless, he included a map so she could follow along the route known as the Natchez Trace.

While he was still buried in the forest, word of Burr's true intentions leaked out in the pages of the *Gazette of the United States*, the one that had been devoted to Hamilton, and was now, to his memory. It declared that Burr was not Republican, or a Federalist, but the head of a "revolution party on the western waters" that was bent on drawing the western lands under a separate government, those lands to pay off the revolutionaries, to lure further inhabitants, and to raise funds for liberating Mexico, aided by British ships. It was the first of the many published rumors about Burr, and it spread to other papers across the country, many of them Jeffersonian. It was a sufficiently accurate assessment of Burr's ambitions that it likely came from a person in a position to know, probably the Spanish minister Marqués de Casa Yrujo, who gleaned them from Wilkinson. The rumors did not take hold with the Jefferson administration, or with the public, where the very mystery that hung about Burr seemed to counter any particular suspicions. Burr himself, of course, could never be sure what purchase the newspapers stories might have had. The British were distressed to think that Burr was enacting his plans without them, and the Spanish were outraged to think that Burr might try to seize their land. A follow-up report put Wilkinson on the spot, as it linked him publicly with this Burr conspiracy to seize the western lands, and his Major James Bruff resolved "to watch the motions of General Wilkinson and Burr." And Bruff was somewhat suspicious, when the two men came calling, to hear Burr tease Wilkinson about his "military notions" with a "consciousness of superiority." Burr was just a private citizen—but he had put himself above the commander of the army? Wilkinson was obviously not pleased to be teased about his rank, and Bruff right to wonder about the awkward tightness of the relationship between the two men. Later, Burr, through an intermediary, tried to solicit Bruff into heading up a private expedition to Santa Fe, a strategic outpost for any western gambit. Bruff sensibly declined. He'd keep his distance.

Another batch of rumors hit closer to home, as the newspapers were declaring with ever-greater precision the Burr plans to foment secession, focusing on Kentucky, Tennessee, Ohio, part of Georgia, and Carolina. Burr professed to be unperturbed, focused on what he viewed as the main chance: a war with Spain over its lands in Florida, and, to the west, its boundary with the United States near the Sabine River, which had not been exactly specified in the agreement with Napoléon. Jefferson coveted the territory and had dispatched James Monroe to Madrid to win it, to no avail. To Burr, this raised the wonderful specter of war, which would rouse the nation against Spain, allowing him to steal into New Orleans amid the din and then launch his attack on Mexico from there in the name of liberation. The United States would be broken like crockery. "Once Louisiana and the western country become independent," he told the fussy British minister, Merry, "the Eastern States will separate themselves immediately from the Southern." To make this happen, he dispatched Charles Williamson, his man in London, to make a small request of King George III: funds to raise a fifty-thousand-man army that Burr himself would command to march on Mexico, plus British ships to patrol the mouth of the Mississippi. He gave the king a three-month deadline, leaving Burr time to coordinate his battle plan to the east and west once the warships were offshore. If England didn't help, Burr threatened to turn to France, bringing the specter of Napoléon to sweep over the continent.

To appraise Jefferson's military intentions, Burr had a remarkable two-hour meeting with him at the President's House, surely one of the more strained, in which Burr regaled Jefferson with details of western fauna and extracted the bitter news that Jefferson had no plans for war with Spain, even if it might announce to the world that he was a man of "Quaker principles." Worse still, King George III let the deadline pass, leaving Burr to try to enlist Spain's help in detaching the western lands from the United

States with the promise of securing them for its king. He sent his man Senator Dayton to make the request of Spain's incredulous American representative Yrujo, while glossing over the small fact, by now widely reported, that Burr intended to steal away the rest of Spain's North American holdings. Though he professed interest, Yrujo's offer of support said otherwise. Just three thousand dollars—a small price for intelligence of Burr's obvious desperation, just enough to keep more Burr information coming. Things were turning farcical.

More humiliating still, a shady South American revolutionary named Miranda was lurking about the United States in an effort to mount an identical mission to liberate Spain's American possessions and had made far greater headway. He'd actually collected a small force of 180 men to sail off from Philadelphia in the *Leander*, backed by Burr's own kinsman Samuel Ogden and William Smith, son-in-law of John Adams. While Jefferson had initially supported the venture, he turned with public opinion and had Smith and Ogden indicted for violating the Neutrality Act, which forbade such adventuring against foreign governments. Nonetheless, the move was grating for Burr, as it showed how little he had to show for his two years of maneuvering. More galling still, the Royal Navy escorted the *Leander* through the waters of the Caribbean, while the British government wouldn't even answer Burr's letters.

The whole thing was maddening, and Burr responded with a rare tantrum that revealed the fire that always burned below the cool demeanor. He let Yrujo know, through Dayton, that if Jefferson would not oblige Burr with war, he would bring war to Jefferson, a very particular war, assassinating him, kidnapping his vice president and the president pro tem, turning Congress "neck and heels out of doors," seizing the Treasury and the navy, and declaring himself in charge of the government. It is hard to know how seriously Yrujo took this news, which amounted to nothing, and stands best as a mark of Burr's towering frustration with the mystery man who had by now eclipsed Hamilton as the bête noire of Burr's existence. Unfortunately for Burr, he had caught Jefferson on the upward slope of his power trajectory, while Hamilton had been on the downward. By the time he shot Hamilton, he had little to fear from him. Now, of course, was another matter, as Hamilton's ghost loomed over Burr's every move as he sought to rebuild his reputation by dismantling Hamilton's legacy of a thriving, intact country. Jefferson would not be undone so easily.

While Jefferson never got wind of any assassination plan, he was apprised of the hazard that Burr posed to the configuration of the country. He read the newspapers, assiduously, but he valued more a report from the US attorney in Kentucky, Joseph Hamilton Daviess, who wrote on January 10, 1806, that "We have traitors among us," and went on to describe Burr's now-familiar plan to detach west from east. Jefferson asked for names.

Throughout the winter, Burr scrambled to mount his insurrection, but it was a castle built on air, like so many of his plans, and nothing that he erected stood up. As always, money woes plagued him. He depended heavily on his son-in-law, Alston, but his fortunes were at a low ebb after a flood had swamped his rice fields. Burr was so desperate that he went crawling back to Jefferson, of all people, to ask him if he could deliver the high-level post he had promised him after the 1800 election. Otherwise, as Jefferson recorded in his Anas, "he could do me much harm." This was not a winning approach, and Jefferson overlooked the possibility that Burr could dismember his nation, instead declaring that Burr's days in public office were over, as the people had lost confidence in him. "Not a single voice" urged him to keep Burr on as vice president in 1804, he added cruelly.

Uncaring that his conspiracy had long since gone public, Burr redoubled his efforts to round up coconspirators, with little success. Commodore Truxtun wisely declined to take over any Burr navy, as yet unbuilt, and the swashbuckling soldier William Eaton was put off by Burr's plans for a coup, plans he forwarded to Jefferson, who was not particularly impressed.

So Burr turned instead to yet another stratagem, likely with money borrowed from the long-suffering Alston, purchasing land in what was called the Bastrop Tract along the disputed Spanish border, in hopes both of stoking a war and of disguising his interest in doing so. Consisting of a million acres along the Ouachita River, which drains, ultimately, into the Mississippi, well north of New Orleans, the tract was named for the dastardly Dutch-born Baron de Bastrop, who claimed to own it. In fact, Bastrop possessed only a concession from the Spanish king to sell farm plots to five hundred families; if he could do that, which it proved he couldn't, he would be granted the remainder. If he could secure legitimate title, Burr imagined this was a sound real estate investment, or sound enough to look like it was, and convey that Burr was, despite all appearances, a peaceable man who wanted only to settle down. Beyond the possibility of using it to provoke Spain into an overreaction that would mean war, it provided Burr with yet another potential line of attack to confuse his adversaries about his true intentions, and to keep his options open even more widely. There were now five: taking Mexico, seizing New Orleans, detaching the West, grabbing Spanish Florida, and settling in Bastrop. Or some combination. There were so many, and Burr's known resources so anemic, that the very scale of his ambition, even without a presidential coup, was its best disguise.

FORTY-NINE

A Terrible Whirlpool, Threatening Everything

THROUGH THE SUMMER of 1806, Burr continued to make the rounds of his coconspirators, hoping to expand the roster and shore up any of the wavering. He drew the architect Benjamin Latrobe back into his camp, as he gave him the plum assignment of digging a canal at the Falls of the Ohio; he recruited the German-born Erich Bollman, who'd rescued Madame de Staël from a Parisian mob and tried to free Lafayette from prison. He lavished attention on the flighty Yrujo, loyal Dayton, and standoffish Merry; and he brought his former traveling companion, the young Sam Swartwout, back into the fold. But he gave General Wilkinson his heaviest consideration, since he was the man on whom the great enterprise rested most fundamentally. And with that, toward the end of August, Burr issued the order to put his plans to capture the American West into effect.

He might have announced his intentions directly to the editors of the *Western World* of Frankfort, Kentucky, so quickly were they to appear in its pages over thirteen installments, which described not only Burr's venture but named other conspirators, including Livingston and Dayton, and detailed the tangled allegiances of General Wilkinson. Shown the series by an anxious Latrobe, Burr laughed it off as the work of John Marshall, the Federalist whose family owned the paper. Republicans in the state were so outraged that one of them shot one of the paper's editors, Joseph M. Street, grazing his side. (Undaunted, Street chased after his assailant with a dagger.)

On the strength of the articles, Kentucky's US attorney Daviess besieged the president again with Burr accusations. He had already followed up with more details on the conspiracy and had even interviewed Wilkinson, who professed he'd never seen anyone so admired as Burr. If he'd been president, "Burr would have had all the country before now." That sentiment was not likely to please Jefferson. Now Daviess insisted that Burr was planning to invade Mexico and steal the West. Jefferson preferred to ignore these charges too.

Although the publicity was not to Burr's advantage, developments with Spain were. It appeared that the United States might go to war with Spain after all. Picking up news of Spanish troops rampaging across the Sabine River into America's Louisiana Territory, the secretary of war told Wilkinson to repel the Spanish king's advances there and in Spanish Florida as well. It was just what Burr had been waiting for, but, unaccountably, Wilkinson did not move. He remained in Saint Louis, claiming he needed to tend his ailing wife. It wasn't until the end of August that Wilkinson finally descended the Mississippi bound for New Orleans, and Burr was determined to meet him there with fifteen hundred men, dozens of his handpicked lieutenants, a veritable armada of boats, and himself in the place of glory at the head. To that end he'd been scouring boatyards, recruiting soldiers, acquiring supplies, assigning tasks.

So far, absolutely nothing had come of it, except that it had brought him back to the place where he had started, on Blennerhassett Island, with the befuddled Harman Blennerhassett and his bewitching wife, Margaret. His dreams were at this point nothing more than fantasies, and the Blennerhassetts' fantasies had never been anything less. To appeal to them, Burr promised Blennerhassett that when he took the West, becoming Aaron I, Imperator, or some other suitably Roman title, he would in his first act name Blennerhassett his ambassador to England, thereby puffing up his patron's prestige in two countries. While Alston had supposedly offered to underwrite the expedition, Burr would turn to Blennerhassett for more immediate expenses, like the boats that were still to be constructed for the men who were yet to be recruited to take down the river, and the so-far-unbuilt kilns to dry the unsourced corn to feed them. Burr went beyond this, scouring the nearby territory for volunteers, and did his best to counter the alarms in the newspapers about a Burr conspiracy by offering soothing advisories about the upside of any secession. The locals were not persuaded, and there was talk of mustering the local militia to descend on the island to put a stop to it. To discourage hostility, Burr wrote an open letter to the people of Cincinnati declaring himself unaware of any "design to separate the western from the eastern states" and saying he couldn't imagine how such a scheme could be advanced if it were not in the interests of the people.

After Burr had taken the island as the base for his operations, he invited Theodosia down with her husband, Alston, and their four-year-old son, Aaron Burr Alston, whom "Gampy" had selected to be his successor. This was the clearest sign that he was preparing his last move. Burr scarcely overlapped with his daughter before he was off down the river again, in hopes of securing the lasting allegiance of Andrew Jackson now that they had a new bond. Jackson had recently killed a man in a duel but had taken a bullet to the chest that would remain there for life. But Jackson would not be won. He had heard the rumors and also learned more about the involvement of the duplicitous Wilkinson, whom he had come to detest. "It rushed into my mind like lightning," Jackson said, that Burr might be a traitor.

Then the first hammer blows struck. If before the accusations were confined to the press, now they reached the courts. The irrepressible Daviess had seen to that. On November 4, he asked Judge Henry Innes of the US District Court in Frankfort, Kentucky, to issue a warrant for the arrest of the former vice president, accusing him of a "high misdemeanor" by plotting to attack Mexico. Under the Constitution, only a domestic insurrection is considered treason, a felony punishable by hanging; foreign "filibusters" like these are misdemeanors if they do not occur in the context of a declared war. Innes rejected the request, since Daviess had provided only hearsay evidence and his own personal conviction that it was so. Daviess, a devout Federalist, was hoping more for political advantage than any legal victory, and he was inclined to let it go at that. But when Burr got wind of it, he insisted on having his day in court. With future senator Henry Clay his lawyer, Burr made mincemeat of the charges and walked out of the room to the cheers of the faithful. One newspaper marveled at Burr's "calmness, moderation and firmness."

Two weeks later, Daviess was at it again, this time with three witnesses to support his charges, although unfortunately only one showed up for the grand jury. Eager for details, the grand jury subpoenaed the two editors of the *Western World* for their personal knowledge of the case, but they admitted they had none beyond what had been told them by their correspondents. With that, the Daviess case against Burr collapsed again, Burr emerged from the courthouse to a roar of approval, and a great ball was held in his honor. His good name temporarily restored, Burr returned to the business of conspiracy. Whatever he had been able to assemble in boats and men and material, now was the time to deploy it and move on New Orleans at last. Wilkinson would be waiting, and their armies would be joined.

For a public man, Burr was always strangely solitary, a conundrum to everyone but his daughter. It meant that people never fully knew him, leaving them to be surprised by his mercurial shifts in mood and ambition. But it also meant that he rarely knew others. No one did he know less than the puffy, grandiose General Wilkinson, the man upon whom he depended most in this grand misadventure. Given that nearly everyone else (Jefferson excepted) considered Wilkinson a walking hazard, it is a wonder that Burr didn't. Every aspect of his person and character may have shouted that he was untrustworthy, but Burr gave him his trust time and again.

For Wilkinson, it was less a question of whether he would betray Burr than when. For a man who traded on information, he had some material on Burr that was far too valuable not to cash in. The moment of crisis for him came on October 8, 1806, when Wilkinson was with his army a hundred miles west at Natchitoches, in the Red River valley near Louisiana's western border, where he was leading his army against the Spanish insurgents that were proving to be a constant irritant along the Sabine. But not pushing his men too hard, of course, lest he offend his Spanish keepers. That evening, a boat docked on the river shore, and Burr's enthusiastic young emissary Swartwout hurried to Wilkinson's quarters, delighted finally to have located the general. He fumbled in his pack to pull out a sealed letter for him that Burr had written at the end of July. Wilkinson waited until nightfall to open it, alone. The letter was written in three different codes, one of them relying on a key drawn on the 1800 edition of

Entick's New Spelling Dictionary, by which a pair of numbers referred to the page and position of each word. That was supplemented by a set of pre-assigned numbers to refer to individuals (Burr was 14, 15, and 16), and an array of symbols represented key elements such as England, France, and Spain.

The decipherment was such a labor that Wilkinson couldn't piece out the whole thing right then, but he got enough of it to know that Burr said he had the funds and the participants to move ahead. On to New Orleans and Mexico, sweeping up the western lands along the way. Or so it seemed to say; between the code and Burr's natural reticence, it was hard to tell. But Burr clearly expected to meet Wilkinson in Natchez, 250 miles up the Mississippi, by December 15, for an assault on New Orleans. Brimming with confidence, the missive ended with a rousing huzzah Burr passed on from Dayton: "Are you ready?" he nearly shouted. "Are your numerous associates ready? Wealth and glory, Louisiana and Mexico."

It must have made Wilkinson's heart sink. Which side was he on? Was he a wholehearted coconspirator of Burr's? Or a dutiful agent for Spain? Or an American patriot? Or was he simply a Wilkinsonian, for lack of a better term, who would do whatever best advanced his personal interests? The answer was: whichever was better for Wilkinson, full stop. But here was the dilemma: If Wilkinson went at the Spanish, he could create the smoke screen war Burr craved and leave New Orleans wide open for Burr, or he could go to New Orleans himself and arrest Burr as a traitor. With the first, he would antagonize his patron and be known forever as Burr's coconspirator, which would be an issue only if Burr failed. With the second, he stood a chance of emerging as a national hero, increasing his standing for further deceptions. In the balance hung his own fortune, and also Burr's, not that that mattered, particularly.

He was torn and might have remained so but for one line in Burr's message—"Wilkinson shall be second to Burr only." It reminded him of the slur with Bruff. Wilkinson would be second to no man. That tipped the balance decisively from Burr to himself, and he immediately set about to act on it. He made peace with Spain, and he did his best to drain the obliging Swartwout of everything he knew of Burr's plans. The respiratory illness of Wilkinson's wife that had delayed him over the summer had turned fatal, but as she lay wheezing beside him, he stabbed Burr in the back. He wrote two letters to President Jefferson laying out all the particulars of the plot and included a copy of Burr's cipher letter, albeit one that he slightly altered to disguise his own involvement. To conceal them, he had his courier, a lieutenant named Thomas Smith, sew them into the soles of his boots for the grueling fifteen-hundred-mile overland journey to Washington City.

By then, Burr's movements were starting to create havoc. Some essays that the hapless Blennerhassett had written to defend a western initiative were raising alarms, which were not allayed by Blennerhassett's efforts to sell some land in the Bastrop Tract. Some of his neighbors threatened to torch his house, sending his wife into a frenzy of anxiety. Benjamin Latrobe reported that Burr was having military bateaux built to rush down the Ohio to the Mississippi. But for every potential recruit, it seemed that countless more were appalled by the prospect of Burr's military adventure, whatever it proved to be.

Burr had meanwhile enlisted Blennerhassett to go ahead with plans to make his island a staging area for his military assault, in whatever direction it might go. He loyally went about erecting kilns to dry corn for the journey, but did little more. He stockpiled no weapons or agricultural tools that would presumably be needed for any new settlement, and he failed to oversee the boatbuilding. By December 9, eleven boats were finally at hand, each one a good fifty feet long, and most of them covered against the elements. They were built for fifty men, so there were nowhere near enough soldiers to fill them all. By then, the Ohio militia, alarmed by the developments on the island, was mustering to stop them. Their authority ended at the eastern shore. On the Virginia side, it was worse: Vigilantes were swarming there to administer even rougher justice. Even Blennerhassett could see it was now or never, so he had slaves load on his five trunks, and, after midnight on December 10, ordered all the men, who numbered little more than thirty, to board the boats and shove off, the rapturous Mrs. Blennerhassett distraught behind him.

Vigilantes descended on the island at dawn and tore through the house, but they came too late to catch Burr's men. By then, they were well down the Ohio and would continue for more than two weeks, watched only by an occasional curiosity seeker, docking along the way to take on supplies and some men, until the numbers swelled nearly to eighty, far short for an invasion of just about anything, as they felt their way toward Burr, whose location was still unknown, but nearly ubiquitous in the public imagination, which was on fire over this man who'd been accused of treason and remained wanted for murder in two states. By then, Burr had joined up with his men where the Cumberland flows into the Ohio. There were only a hundred, a far cry from the seven thousand he'd pledged Wilkinson, and which the newspapers had announced. When the men were billeted onshore, Burr went about to each of them to shake hands and say a few words. But this would-be Washington said no more, no grand inspiring speech or statement of purpose.

When, on November 25, Lieutenant Smith arrived in Washington City, much bedraggled, Jefferson ushered him into his private study and watched in some fascination as Smith plucked off his boots, now well worn, ripped open the soles, and handed him the secret documents on which Jefferson's legacy would turn. While Wilkinson could be pompous, he could also sound the right note when necessary, and he began with a clarion call: "A numerous and powerful association, extending from New York through the Western states to the territories bordering on the Mississippi, has been formed with the design to levy and rendezvous eight or ten thousand men in New Orleans."

This did it. Two days later, Jefferson delivered a proclamation to the nation, warning of an unnamed conspiracy against Spain. He soon followed it with an address to Congress in which he declared that the conspiracy was led by Aaron Burr. He directed that Burr be indicted and arrested for the hanging offense of high treason. Having killed the leader of one party, Burr now risked being killed by the leader of the other.

Back on the very day that Jefferson received Smith, Wilkinson marched into New Orleans, a city on edge with the uncertainty about Burr's plans. To reassure them, and to establish his bona fides, Wilkinson immediately strengthened the city's defenses, and he soon crowed to Jefferson that despite "stupendous" difficulties, and his "time short," he was working "wonders." He offered a federal Indian agent five thousand dollars to capture Burr and strung along Burr's henchmen, feigning sympathy to the cause, before he pounced, ordering the arrest of two of Burr's men, Sam Swartwout and Peter Ogden, even though this required releasing a copy of the heavily ciphered Burr letter as evidence—with those critical emendations to conceal his own complicity. Upon arrest, Swartwout wanted a sword to dispatch himself, a request that was denied. And then Wilkinson arrested two more Burrites who were already in the city. When the grounds were questioned, Wilkinson argued the point in court in full military dress, "his scabbords rattling along the floor," which made for an argument all of its own. After he won that one, Wilkinson arrested two Burr lawyers, the editor of the *Orleans Gazette*, and Burr confidant General John Adair, the former senator who was now head of the Kentucky militia. Wilkinson had him held in a swamp for three days and then dispatched to Baltimore to stand trial. Altogether, Wilkinson had twenty men arrested for the crime of being friendly to Burr.

On January 10, Burr was in the settlement of his friend Judge Peter Bryan Bruin in the Mississippi Territory, inland from the river. It was so fiercely cold that blood oozed from the fingertips of his rowers. It was there that he finally caught up with the newspapers and realized that the great game was up. No war with Spain, Jefferson in a fury, New Orleans under military occupation. All he could think of was Wilkinson. "The greatest traitor on the face of the earth," he rasped. His fellow adventurers were drifting away daily, and now he put it to them: Who would like to go on with him? The men saw little choice but to see the project through, but before they could cast off again, the Mississippi militia showed up, three hundred strong. Burr had his men row to the New Orleans side and tried to sweet-talk the Mississippi Territory's acting governor, Cowles Mead, out of posting any charges, but Mead insisted on riding to the town of Washington, near Natchez, to discuss the matter with federal judge Thomas Rodney.

That required a few days' wait, and Burr was placed under house arrest at Windy Hill Manor, where he spent most of his time courting his comely neighbor Madeline Price, a widow's daughter. According to one account, Burr practiced "his witchery night after night, and [she] loved him with all the fervor of a Southern nature."

Unfortunately for Burr, he was not able to snow Rodney quite so effectively. As in Kentucky, the grand jury had declined to charge Burr with any crime, but Rodney, a Jefferson appointee, insisted on holding Burr's bond all the same, guaranteeing his return to face any further indictments. Burr thought it best to leave. He returned to his men, explained the situation, and advised them all to divide up what property they could and to disperse. Sixty of them were soon arrested by territorial authorities, although all of them were freed. All but the unlucky Blennerhassett, who was sent to Richmond to stand trial.

Burr disappeared on horseback into the pine barrens of central Mississippi. Exactly where he went is not known. Possibly he returned to Price: according to lore, the two exchanged marriage vows, leaving her pining for him for years after. But he was wise not to stay, for Wilkinson had dispatched five rough men, four of them soldiers and all of them armed to the teeth, to capture him. He remained in hiding for two weeks, before emerging on February 18 outside the little town of Wakefield two hundred miles west of Natchez. According to Wilkinson, Burr was "disguised in an old blanket coat begirt with a leathern strap, to which a tin cup was suspended on the left and a scalping knife on the right." Also a beaver hat with a broad brim pulled down low over his forehead. Burr had a companion with him, a Major Robert Ashley, and they paused for a moment to ask directions of a local man to the Hinson place, a homestead some two miles distant. The local proved to be Nicholas Perkins, the land commissioner, and he had seen the governor's offer of a two-thousand-dollar reward for the fugitive vice president, which had mentioned that Burr's eyes "sparkled like diamonds." The brim of Burr's beaver hat was not pulled low enough that Perkins couldn't see the preternatural shine of Burr's eyes. Perkins told the two men that the bridges were out and they'd do better sleeping at the local tavern. The two ignored the advice and pressed on. That confirmed it: No honest man would pass up a bed close by for one more distant. Perkins hurried to the sheriff, rousting him out of bed to pursue the two strangers. The two tracked the men to the Hinson place, and then Perkins split off to borrow a canoe to paddle to Fort Stoddert for reinforcements. There, Lieutenant Edmund Gaines immediately provided a file of soldiers to gallop back with Perkins to the farmhouse. By then, the two strangers had already set out, but the soldiers caught up to them on a hill a few miles distant. It was there that Lieutenant Gaines placed Burr under arrest. Seeing all the soldiers, the former vice president accepted his fate quietly, ending any hope of a western empire.

After a brief stay at the fort, Perkins was selected to lead an eight-man team to escort Burr to the courthouse in Richmond, fifteen hundred miles north, much of it along a narrow track through dark wilderness said to be thick with Indians. At night, Burr was awarded the only tent. It was a grueling journey of more than a month, covering more than forty miles a day regardless of the brutal winter weather. Burr was flanked by escorts on every side. He wore the ridiculous frontier getup the whole way, humiliating as it must have been. In the town of Chester in South Carolina, Burr finally jumped down off his horse, cried out to the local citizens who he was, claimed he'd been abducted illegally, and begged for their protection. But no one moved to save him, and Perkins lifted the little man up and dropped him back down on his saddle once more. At that, Burr burst into tears. President John Adams called Burr's ill-fated expedition "a kind of waterspout, a terrible whirlpool, threatening everything." But it was over.

FIFTY

A Slight Expression of Contempt

W‌HEN BURR ARRIVED in Richmond, he was billeted at Mr. Epps's hotel on Main Street while he awaited trial. He put aside his tattered, homespun clothing and moved to black silk, with his queue fashionably tied, as if he were to appear in a ballroom rather than court. It was an appearance of sangfroid that would henceforth never leave him, no matter how dire the circumstances. Right now, those circumstances could hardly be worse, as he was on trial for his life, mired in debt, hounded by creditors, a subject of ridicule throughout the country. Still, he counseled Theodosia, always his proxy, not to give in to self-pity. "I beg and expect it of you that you will conduct yourself as becomes my daughter, and that you manifest no signs of weakness or alarm."

It would be a criminal trial, a case of treason, pitting a coolly vengeful Jefferson against his nefarious vice president, a man who had personally threatened to do him harm and nearly did. The two men, once linked in office, were each distant yet intimate. As Jefferson's powers had grown, so had his prickliness, and he took personally Burr's plans to dismember his empire. If Jefferson had once viewed Burr's activities with an airy unconcern, now he was a man obsessed. "I never indeed thought him an honest, frank-dealing man," he wrote of Burr, "but considered him as a crooked gun, or other perverted machine, whose aim or stroke you could never be sure of." He dispatched agents to interrogate witnesses, from New York

State down to Nashville, with forty-six questions, sought loyalty tests of soldiers possibly drawn to Burr's gambit, directed the prosecution in packet after packet of detailed instructions, and had Burr's confederate Erich Bollman taken from prison directly to the President's House for a personal interview.

But it was a political trial too. The divisions that split the country over banks and wardrobe did not stop at the courts, and Jefferson was convinced that no Federalist judge would ever see anything his way. As if to confirm his worst fears, the Burr trial would be presided over by the brilliant, folksy John Marshall, Supreme Court chief justice who had been appointed by Adams solely for the purpose of tormenting his successor, or so Jefferson believed.

Treason is the only crime defined by the Constitution, and the framers were careful to do so because they didn't want the president to follow European monarchs and invoke loose notions of treason to slaughter their political opponents in the name of the state. The Constitution delineates treason narrowly: It requires an overt *act* of war against the nation, not just the creation of a conspiracy or the formulation of a plan, and any act must be witnessed by at least two people. So the law wasn't helpful to Jefferson's desire to see Burr swing.

And John Marshall wasn't either, as he quickly revealed in his ruling on the case of the two Burr functionaries, Bollman and Swartwout, who'd been caught up in the Burr hysteria. To him, treason had to be "visible," and when he saw that the only evidence against the two men were vague affidavits from Wilkinson and his ally Eaton and a copy of the cipher letter from Burr, Marshall had the men released, since none of that indicated any witnessed overt act against the United States. This boded ill for the president, who redoubled his efforts to scour the countryside for two people who could testify to seeing an overt act of treason by Aaron Burr.

Marshall did leave an opening for the president, however, as he indicated that an "assembly" of men to levy war might be sufficient, and there could be little doubt that a fair number of men had assembled on Blennerhassett Island, although it would be hard to say for exactly what purpose. But this was the meat of the matter when the case was finally convened at the biggest hall in town, the neoclassical Hall of Delegates behind the Virginia state capitol, which happened to have been designed by Jefferson. What happened at Blennerhassett Island that might constitute treason?

By now, the legal teams were in place, and they were formidable on both sides. Burr's was led by Edmund Randolph, Washington's attorney general, assisted by Richmond's own John Wickham, and the prolix Luther Martin, who was better known as "Lawyer Brandy-Bottle" for his primary indulgence, but who had also won the sobriquet "impudent federal bulldog" for his work defending Supreme Court Justice Samuel Chase from impeachment. But Burr himself would direct the effort and come to be recognized as the ablest lawyer in the room. For the prosecution, Jefferson's attorney general Caesar Rodney, nephew of the Rodney who had weighed in on the case in Mississippi, helped by the US Attorney George Hay. Theirs would be the harder job.

The first order of business was to request indictments of a grand jury, which was a matter of the prosecution presenting enough evidence to show it had a case. When Marshall took the bench and gaveled the court into session, Burr looked far more the lawyer than the client. "There he stood," one commentator marveled, "as composed, as immovable, as one of Canova's living marbles." He had the simpler case to make: He planned no hostilities against the United States, only against Spain, and that would wait for an American action, making it a legal "filibuster," not a violation of the Neutrality Act. Without a war, he would simply move to his land in the Bastrop Tract. And Burr was blessed in this: Any witnesses who might say different were tight allies such as Bollman and Swartwout, who would never dream of such disloyalty. Moreover, Burr had a lovely knack for legal histrionics. When George Hay begged the court put Burr on "the same footing with every other man charged with a crime," Burr sprang to his feet. "Would to God that I did stand on the same ground with every other man! This is the first time I have been able to enjoy the rights of a citizen."

No sooner had the court begun than it halted again, waiting for the appearance of the only man capable of solving the mystery of Burr's intentions and his acts to advance them. That was General Wilkinson, and the court had already waited on him a month but would have to wait three weeks more, the legal talent getting itchier by the day. But Burr went on the offensive, demanding the original letter that Wilkinson sent Jefferson, not his copy, and the military orders that Jefferson issued in response. When Jefferson refused to hunt them up, citing the demands of his position, Marshall allowed Burr to issue a subpoena, thus turning the tables on the chief executive. Jefferson insisted that some of the requested papers were simply too sensitive to reveal—and he would be the sole judge of that. Or so he wished. "Executive privilege," as it came to be called, was not as sweeping as he might like, and Marshall required him to deliver the essential documents or face contempt like anyone else. That did not sit well with the president, but he acquiesced.

While that was still being argued, Wilkinson appeared magisterially, as if from the ether, in a gold-trimmed uniform, a sword dangling from his belt. "Like a turkey cock," wrote future novelist Washington Irving, who was attending the trial, "and bracing himself up for the encounter of Burr's eye."

By now, the city of Richmond had doubled in size, people jamming hostelries for miles around, all the ladies swooning over the image of the moody sorcerer at the lawyers' bench. It was the moment everyone was waiting for, when the accused faced his accuser. Irving watched closely: "At the mention of his name, Burr turned his head, looked him full in the face with one of his piercing regards, swept his eye over his whole person from head to foot, as if to scan its dimensions, and then coolly resumed his formal position, and went on conversing with his counsel as tranquilly as ever." He had to marvel at Burr's performance. "There was no appearance of study or constraint in it; no affectation of disdain or defiance; a slight expression of contempt played over his countenance, such as you would show on regarding any person to whom you were indifferent, but whom you considered mean and contemptible."

Wilkinson of course saw it differently, as he told Jefferson. "My eyes darted a flash of indignation at the little traitor," and saw a Burr laboring under "the weight of conscious guilt, with haggard eyes in an effort to meet the indignant salutation of outraged honor."

When it came to his testimony, Wilkinson had the worst of it, as much of it was so suspicious that the grand jury nearly indicted him as well. But it did indict Burr and Harman Blennerhassett, and five of Burr's intimates, including his kinsman Senator Dayton of New Jersey. The trial would commence on August 3. Until then, Burr would be transferred to a special suite in the Richmond penitentiary, which was hardly pleasant, but did come with a servant, and the ladies vied to see who could furnish him with the most sweetmeats and ice.

When the trial finally resumed, it fell to the slow business of collecting jurors and drawing witnesses. When arguments began, it became clear that the government would follow the indictments and place the scene of Burr's supposed levy of war at Blennerhassett Island on December 10 of the previous year, even though Burr was in Kentucky at the time. To put that one over, the prosecution had to create a doctrine of "constructive treason," meaning that Burr was in the middle of it, even if he was miles away. It would also hope to show that everything that came after was somehow embedded in the island activities as well. But witness after witness went by without anyone being able to say that he had actually seen what the Constitution demanded—an overt act of war against the United States—and some of them, like Commodore Truxtun, declared the opposite, that *he* was more ready to take on Spain than Burr was. And so it went—much reported conversation, scene setting, rationalizations. And more bloviation on the part of the large-lunged lawyers present. But nothing the prosecution could say would produce the evidence of war making, and it went even worse for them when Marshall delivered his opinion that, under the indictment, any act of war had to occur on the island on the tenth; anything elsewhere or after was irrelevant. In short, it had to be visible, and it had to be there, just as he said all along. "The overt act must be proved . . . by two witnesses. *It is not proved by a single witness.*" And when the case was finally given to them, the jury had no choice but to agree, promptly finding Burr not guilty "by any evidence submitted to us." At that, Burr leapt to his feet and insisted that the reference to any evidence was mere editorializing, and Marshall agreed that the bit about evidence should be struck. He was not guilty, and that was all he was.

"Marshall has stepped between Burr and death," wrote embittered prosecutor William Wirt.

With Burr found innocent, the district attorney saw no reason to press the case against Blennerhassett and the rest. Free, Blennerhassett felt nothing but revulsion at Burr as he paraded about town with Theodosia, who had come to comfort her father during his ordeal, and he schemed to retrieve the heavy loans he'd extended Burr for his adventure, hopeless as that would prove to be. As it was, the poor man lost everything—his mansion, his enchanted island, his fortune. Despite the thunderous rejection of his claims of treason, Jefferson insisted on proceeding with the lesser charge of making war on a foreign country, a misdemeanor. "The criminal," as Jefferson called Burr, "is preserved to become the rallying point of all the disaffected and worthless of the United States." But it went no better for him. Wilkinson testified for five days, leaving even the prosecutors flummoxed as to what to make of his story. It came as a blessing that Marshall issued a ruling on a motion that brought a halt to the fiasco, instructing the government to "desist from further prosecution," as Burr gleefully wrote his daughter. And that was it. Whatever he'd actually done, Burr's legal calamities were over.

FIFTY-ONE

G.H. Edwards

I F BURR HAD hoped that his legal victory would somehow make him a national hero, he was mistaken. After Weehawken, he'd had to slink south from New York, a fugitive from justice, and now he'd had to creep north from Richmond, an obvious scoundrel. When he arrived in Baltimore, he was greeted by angry crowds who were ready to hang him in effigy and who dragged a proxy of him "habited for execution" about the city "in full huzzah in fife and drum playing the 'Rogue's March.'" The streets were papered with hundreds of handbills making dire threats against "his Quid majesty," and fifteen hundred citizens surged down Chestnut Street breaking windows in their hostility toward the diabolical ex–vice president. Burr had to sneak out to Philadelphia by mail stage to avoid being seized by a mob.

Burr's financial woes were so desperate that some friends had to cobble together emergency loans to keep him out of debtors' prison. At fifty-three, he was weary and impoverished, spurned by virtually all, without political prospects or the grand plans that had always saved him before. In Philadelphia, he holed himself up in a dreary French boardinghouse, so depressed with the "fiend ennui" that his Philadelphia friend Charles Biddle feared Burr would "end his sufferings with a pistol." He received some satisfaction in learning that New Jersey had decided to quash the murder indictment against him, but a congressional investigation led by John Quincy Adams determined that Burr would have caused "a war of the most horrible description . . . both foreign and domestic," and decided that only legal technicalities saved him. Burr concluded that if America could offer him nothing except hostility, he would sail to England to raise funds from the Crown to remount his campaign against Spanish Mexico after all. If he had not considered treason before, he would consider it now.

He boarded the packet *Clarissa Ann*, bound for England under the alias G.H. Edwards—after his reverend grandfather—on June 9, 1808; ever devoted, Theodosia was there to see him off with "tears and reproaches" for his embarking on such a hazardous voyage. He told her to take a pseudonym as well, selecting "Mary Ann Melville" (although the novelist would not be born for more than a decade). Intended as a martial quest, his "grand Hegira" would be more a spiritual journey, "a sort of non-existence," more inward than outward, and, for a man of action, it would pose psychic challenges that dwarfed the practical ones. Intended as a brief sojourn, it ended up lasting four years, each one more hellish than the last, until it seemed that he might never return. If the rest of his life is shrouded in secrecy, his years of exile are quite literally an open book.

Hamilton's letters generally took the form of a legal brief, charging straight ahead, but Burr's always tended to be more looping, only occasionally touching down at the matter at hand. For this journey, he kept an immense journal for Theodosia, the person he loved most, and perhaps only, and he often addressed it directly to her. He brought her picture with him, too, always to keep on view in his rooms. The journal amounted to a thousand-page letter to her. More than the likeness, the journal had the effect of bringing him *her*, but it also allowed a man of secrecy an obligation of disclosure. It presents an exhaustive view of his daily rounds, with special emphasis on his parties with the European elite, whose quality, to be sure, eroded slightly as the months went by and Burr's gloss dimmed. Still, the book is a blizzard of names:

Arrived at Dr. Lettsome's at 6. They had but that moment sat down to dinner. Colonel Elliott; Smith, avoc. [advocate] solicitor to Board of Ordnance; Norris, surgeon; Cooke, physician; Temple, physician. Very gay and social. Dinner and wines excellent. Norris engages me to dine on Monday. To William Godwin's at ½ p. 9.

Godwin was the widower of Burr's sainted Mary Wollstonecraft, and, like her, a staunch believer in the rights of women. But Burr's greatest catch was the utilitarian philosopher Jeremy Bentham; as a man who brought clarity to the mysteries of right and wrong, he was hailed as the "Newton of the moral world." Burr giddily passed several days with him in spirited conversation about "tattooing, how to be made useful; of infanticide; of crimes against Nature, etc. etc." It was to Bentham that Burr let slip his first recorded words about the duel. Burr revealed he was "sure" he'd kill Hamilton—a notion that left Bentham appalled. "I thought it little better than murder," he admitted. Nonetheless, Bentham was intrigued by Burr enough to consider moving to the American Southwest to take part in a renewed effort of conquest—until wiser friends persuaded him otherwise.

Interspersed in the social gossip, however, are the more intimate details Burr had always withheld from view. Some are charmingly domestic, as he revealed that he left his room a mess, with his clothes piled on every chair but one, and everything else scattered across the floor; that he was always losing his watch, gloves, house key, and umbrella; and that he was terrible with money, besotted with luxuries that frequently left him destitute.

It is charming that Burr would choose to divulge such homely details to his daughter; the revelation to her of his many sexual affairs, less so. The constant flaunting of his sexuality verges on epistolary incest, forcing Theodosia to see what her father did in the dark. The women are countless. As a single man on the prowl, Burr distinguished between the eligible, the ineligible, and those for hire—but then had at all three. He looked longingly on a woman of sixty-three, dubbing her the best-looking woman of that age he'd ever seen, and he lusted for one "she animal." But it was the rare woman under thirty whom he did not call "comely," "lovely," or "beautiful." He was insatiable. Even when he was nearly starving, he still found the money for sex. One German lady described his lunging impetuosity as a cross between *gauche* and *halbwilde*, or "half-wild." Burr used the French term *muse*, referring to an animal's rutting period, as in this Copenhagen tryst: "The chambermaid, fat, not bad; *muse* again." Or this one in France: "From across the hall, the maid came. *Muse.* I couldn't send her back."

He was capable of some seduction himself. In a Paris theater, he gaily chatted up the lady in the adjoining box. Declaring her "full of genius," he asked, "Upon which of your talents do you rely most?" She replied with raised eyebrows. "I have cultivated only the art of pleasing." Unfortunately for Burr, things devolved from there. She offered him supper at her home the next evening, but he preferred to call on her in the afternoon. But when he arrived, he found that she came encumbered with two children. Burr fled this "dangerous siren."

Unfortunately, his other conquests did not go nearly as well. His quest for an audience with a minister of the king to obtain funding for his Mexican adventure, referred to in his journal as "X," already hampered by Burr's failure in America, was now done in by the Spanish would-be conquistador Miranda. He had just tried the Mexican gambit with the king's money and come up empty. This was communicated to Burr by silence, which had an increasingly portentous edge.

Then early on the morning of April 4, 1809, at his modest lodgings at 35 Saint James Street in London, he awoke early with "a confused presentiment that something was wrong." Two months before, he'd been sued by an irate London bookseller for a four-year-old debt, which Burr lacked the money to pay. He'd disappeared to Saint James Street, where he lived under yet another assumed name, Mr. Kirby (he had accumulated a half dozen pseudonyms by now), this time with a Madame Prevost, a morsel of twenty-eight (unrelated to his late wife) "sent by the Devil to [seduce] Gamp." Burr did not resist.

On the fateful morning of the fourth, he tried to evacuate, but too late: "At 1 o'clock came in, without knocking, four coarse-looking gentlemen," bearing a warrant to seize him and his possessions. Lord Liverpool, secretary of state for home affairs at the British ministry, wanted Burr out of the country, probably at the behest of the Spanish envoy, who did not take kindly his ambitions against his country. The intruders hustled Burr to the Alien Office, and he was placed under a loose house arrest with a Mr. Hughes. Burr was unfazed:

> To Wedgewood's; paid 25 shillings for sundries. To Flaxman's. The Italian wife! To Achaud's to inform them of the postponement of my journey. (Mem.: At 3 got mutton chop and potatoes at D. M. R.'s.) Mem.: On leaving 35 James street bid dom. to get something for my

dinner at 6, and to buy coal, &c. At 6 at Madame Onslow's. T: Tea
and two games chess, &c. Par. a 101. At 11 chez D. M. R.; alone.
Couche on his sofa.

Meanwhile, the British government was trying to decide how to get rid of Burr. He himself wished to return to America and hoped that his passage to England under the name of Edwards would be no impediment, any more than his posing as a Mr. Kirby now. Since he was born before the revolution, he cheekily claimed that he was a British subject and should be free to come and go—a position that cut no ice with the ministry. It floated the notion of banishing him to a remote island in the North Sea, but in the end he was allowed to sail to Sweden—on the condition that he never come back.

In his journal, Burr does not react to this news. His is largely an accounting of his activities, making one wonder if, after being buffeted about for so long, he was even capable of a reaction anymore. He sailed from Harwich on April 24, 1809, aboard a British packet, the *Diana*. He had anticipated a relatively brief stay of a few weeks while he engineered his return to America, but when he received no letters from his confederates, he assumed that Britain was intercepting his mail. In any case, Jefferson had remained vigilant against the return of a man he continued to regard as an arch traitor. Burr ended up in Sweden for five months, long enough to pick up some of the language, tour the country, and sample many of its ladies. As his journal attests, he gained free access to the Swedish elite, which is startling for a man in such bad odor. When he finally left, he sailed to Germany, with the idea of working his way across the continent to France, where he hoped to gain an audience with Napoléon and lay before him what he now termed his plan X.

Theodosia did not take the developments nearly so well. She was "stupefied" to learn her father had been expelled from England and aghast at the prospect of his vagabond life in Europe. "You appear to me so superior, so elevated above all other men; I contemplate you with such a strange mixture of humility, admiration, reverence, love and pride, that every little superstition would be necessary to make me worship you as a superior being." She concluded: "I had rather not live than not be the daughter of such a man." Even as Burr religiously detailed his every expense, he rarely expressed much concern for his financial state, which was growing more perilous by the day. Theodosia could scarcely sleep for worry about him. Once when he sent her a letter in cipher, he failed to provide her with the key, sending his daughter into a paroxysm of distress. "I have worked and wept, and torn the paper and thrown myself down in despair, and rose full of some new thought, and tried again to fail again, till my heart is worn out." She had tried to scrounge up a loan for him from one of the few mon-eyed friends who was not tapped out. The fact that she evidently hadn't turned to Alston for the money shows how tired her husband must have grown of his father-in-law's follies. That, in turn, may account for a daugh-ter's panegyrics for a father who hardly seems worthy of them. What she means is, *I still love you, even if no one else does.* And every line of his jour-nal says back, *I love you more than anyone.* In Theodosia's desperation, she'd gone so far as to ask Burr's old flame Dolley Madison, once she became first lady, if there was anything her husband could do to help. She received no response.

In Germany, he settled for a time outside Hamburg, then under French control, in a community thick with Americans who did not take to the former vice president. "What a lot of rascals," he complained, "to make war on whom they do not know; on one who never did harm or wished harm to a human being." That, of course, was an exaggeration. He pushed on through other German principalities and then took it as a summons to Paris when Napoléon called for the liberation of Spain's American colo-nies. His application to the police for a passport to Paris was wry, declaring that he was acting "from motives of curiosity and amusement only." Per-mission denied, Burr was left in limbo for months, in which he suffered dental agonies that led to the extraction of one tooth, which only passed the pain to the "neighbors of the departed." He spent the next few days with his head wrapped in bandages, boiled figs pressed against his inflamed gums. Burr would eventually be left with hardly any teeth in his head. For three more months, he was not allowed to enter the French capital, proba-bly done in by the American minister, General John Armstrong of the

DeWitt Clinton faction. A month later, that judgment was mysteriously overturned, and Burr found himself en route to Paris, "my head so full of X matters."

In Paris, he stayed at the Hotel de Lyon at 7, Rue Grenelle in the Saint-Honoré district, and he got to work collecting maps of Mexico and lining up friends in Paris such as the Compte de Volney and the painter Vanderlyn. The diplomat Talleyrand refused to see him. Having considered Hamilton the greatest man of the age, he could not possibly welcome his murderer. Burr prepared for the emperor a lengthy, four-part memorandum of his plans and had it translated into courtly French. It finally detailed what he had always intended—an attack on Spanish Pensacola, on the Gulf, a brisk sweep across to New Orleans, gathering recruits as he went, and then the sailing down the coast for the long-awaited assault on Mexico, which would pull away the American West. As if that were not enough, Burr also planned to liberate Canada from the British, snatch its island of Jamaica, and return Louisiana to French control. These were all acts of liberation, not conquest, he emphasized, although that difference was not made clear. To call this bold was an understatement, but it wasn't necessarily lunacy to pitch such a sweeping campaign to an emperor who had conquered much of Europe. Still, there were obvious objections: The British navy would likely close down any naval transport into the Gulf or out to Veracruz; the United States was not likely to be any more receptive to Burr's plot this time, especially if it was under the aegis of Napoléon; Burr had never displayed any talent for military leadership, only for audacity, and he had no soldiers, supporters, or funds. Finally, he lacked what he always lacked—a wider rationale for his efforts beyond the prospect of his own aggrandizement. While this might be done in the name of liberation, it was not in the cause of liberty, freedom, self-determination, or any of the other ideals that cause people to risk their lives. It was to give Burr a reason to live.

Napoléon must have considered Burr's plan preposterous, if it came to his attention at all, for he never responded to it. Burr did see him once, or thought he did. He was attending a concert in the Tuileries, and the emperor was said to be above him in the balcony, "but that not being lighted, we could not distinguish him." Burr waited for months in increasing desperation for an answer and finally decided there was nothing for it but to give up on plan X and return to the United States. Once again, however, no passport was forthcoming. Now his funds had just about run out. "I am a prisoner of the state, and nearly penniless," he wrote in French in July of 1810. He walked fourteen miles a day to make his supplications to various bureaucrats "and all for nothing." He thought he'd found some luck when the chief of police, the Duc d'Orante, seemed sympathetic enough to his military plan to request details, but Napoléon discovered that Orante had opened back-channel communication with the British. Orante fled for his life, but not before an aide had revealed his private correspondence with Burr. "This, Madame, is rather grave," Burr wrote Theodosia, revealing the first signs of anxiety. "Winter approaches, no prospect of leave to quit the empire, and still less of any means of living in it. So must economize most rigidly." He realized he faced "starving in Paris." He moved out of the hotel to a room of a family named Pelough, lived on a cup of tea, some bread, and a single egg for dinner. Even so he purchased seven francs' worth of a certain mademoiselle named Flora, whom he deemed "pretty good, voluptuous." Winter was on. Only by turning his oversize fireplace into a jury-rigged Franklin stove was he able to heat his room to 41 degrees—but even so, he had to lie flat on the floor when icy winds blew down the chimney. He placed a candle on either side of him and read a book, the only diversion he allowed himself. He slept hardly at all, suffered from chronic diarrhea, walked with a limp on a painfully swollen foot, and gradually became unmoored. After dragging himself into the city one bitter afternoon, he lost track of everything. "I then stood some minutes to discover where I was. In what country I was. What business I had there. For what I came abroad. And where I intended to go." Terrified for him, Theodosia could send him nothing. Any money he borrowed, he spent on lavish presents for her—and then, to live, had to sell the presents for a fraction of the sum he paid for them. He made a stab at learning Spanish. He tried to pick up with the Holland Company, whose bidding he had done as an assemblyman, to some effect. He made a little money translating English books into French. One of them was a political diatribe containing "a quantity of abuse and libels on A. Burr." Nonetheless, he translated them faithfully.

He was cursed. In April 1811, Burr discovered that the French had relented and issued a passport, but it was lost in the bureaucratic maze and would take months to replace. On his own, he located a sailing ship, the *Vigilant*, captained by a New Englander, to take him across the Atlantic, except it was out of commission for legal reasons. When those restrictions eased a month later, he still had no passport. Finally, toward the end of July, the Duc de Bassanno—a friend he'd met over oysters at the home of the French museum director—became minister of foreign affairs, and he knew a lady who possessed unusual influence over the American minister, Mr. Russell, who'd placed a hold on Burr's passport. Moments after she paid a call on Russell, Burr's passport materialized. By then the *Vigilant* had been released from purgatory, and Burr paid all but his last few Louis to book passage. He wrote Theodosia: "I feel as if I were already on the way to you, and my heart beats with joy."

But no. The British seized the ship as a potential prize of war and docked it in England. Burr was waylaid there with the three hundred books he'd purchased in Europe and thirteen steamer trunks of his belongings for seven months. Finally, in February 1812, the *Vigilant* was released—but this time bound for New Orleans, not Boston. And New Orleans was not likely to be receptive to Burr. "A bad, bad day," he wrote. Finally, in March, he found another ship, the *Aurora*, to carry him across, but, unable to retrieve the original fare, he was twenty pounds short for passage. By the time he was able to scrape it up, the *Aurora* had set sail. Burr scrambled into a wherry to row after it, but, without a coat, he found the icy winds so fierce, he had to stop to pitch some straw on the bottom of the boat for insulation.

Finally, he reached the *Aurora*, and it made an uneventful passage. On May 5, Burr arrived safely in Boston under the "incog" of Mr. Adolphus Arnot. Fearing the "implacable wrath" of Bostonians, he concealed himself in a wig and heavy whiskers when he limped about the city's streets, but no one noticed him. Three weeks later he returned to New York. By then he'd written to tell Theodosia of his safe return. A month later, he received a letter back: "A few miserable days past my dear father & your late letters would have gladdened my soul, & even now I rejoice at their contents as much as it is possible for me to rejoice at anything—but there is no more joy for me, the world is a blank, I have lost my boy, my child is gone forever—he expired on 30th June."

His grandson, Aaron Burr Alston, who once was to inherit his Gampy's throne as emperor, had died of fever at age ten. To her husband's dismay, Theodosia decided to sail north to see her father, in hopes that their reunion would lighten both their hearts. To be safe, Burr sent a friend to accompany her. The two left from South Carolina aboard the *Patriot* on New Year's Eve 1812. The ship never it made it to Boston, and although there have been rumors of the ship having been seized by pirates, it was most likely lost at sea. None of the passengers or crew were heard from again.

For Burr, it was the cruelest blow. He wrote Alston that he felt "severed from the human race."

→>-<←

BURR WAS FIFTY-SEVEN. He lived more than twenty more years, most of them uneventful, none of them successful. The light had gone out of him, and he shrank in size. William Seward, the future secretary of state, worked a case against him in Albany and discovered Burr in one of the "fourth-rate houses" there. Seward was shocked to find Burr "shriveled into the dimensions almost of a dwarf." Like many, he debated whether to shake the hand that "laid low Alexander Hamilton."

While Burr rarely spoke of the duel, it was clear it was never very far from his mind. Some years before he died, a friend persuaded him to revisit Weehawken, where he had never been since that July morning in 1804. It was a bright summer day, but Burr seemed unusually quiet, lost in thought, as they rowed over to the Jersey shore. After they clambered up the cliff, he had his friend stand where Hamilton had squinted into the sun. As the memories tumbled forth, Burr's voice rose, according to his first biographer, James Parton. He recounted how much he'd had to put up with from that popinjay, until he could bear it no longer. Either he would have to "slink out of sight, a wretch degraded and despised," or make a stand against this slanderer, who would keep at it until he was cornered. "When he stood up to fire, he caught my eye, and quailed under it; he looked like a convicted felon." Burr had heard the claims that he had fired first, but they weren't true. Hamilton had. He heard the bullet whistle past, and as for

Hamilton's own assertions to his wife about the duel from the night before? "It reads like the confessions of a penitent monk." The friend couldn't help noting that, as he spoke, Burr didn't seem little anymore. "His very form seemed to rise and expand."

While the Burrites who confined themselves to politics were unharmed by the association, several of his coconspirators suffered unduly. The Blennerhassetts were driven to dirt farming to survive, and Senator John Smith was nearly expelled from the Senate before he withdrew of his own volition. Wilkinson survived three investigations and died in Mexico in 1825.

Burr himself sailed on. He set up house with a couple of his late wife's Bartow relatives, plus two of his own children, Aaron Columbus Burr and Charles Burdett, by other women. On July 1, 1833, when he was seventy-seven, he married again, to Eliza Jumel, a former prostitute, it was said, who had been the wife of a wealthy wine merchant, Stephen Jumel. But Burr continued to see a young beauty named Jane McManus, among others, and, incensed, Eliza divorced him for adultery and plundering her assets. He accused her of adultery back. Her charges proved more credible in court, as a witness had spotted Burr and McManus sitting together on a settee "as close as they could set." Peering through a window blind, he could see "Colonel Burr had his hand under her clothes . . . his trousers all down."

Back in 1830, Burr had suffered a stroke that disabled his right side, and four years later, shortly after the divorce, he had another stroke that proved completely debilitating. Friends moved him to the Jay Mansion, named for his Federalist nemesis, now a dilapidated boardinghouse on the Battery. When that was condemned, Burr was moved to the Hotel Saint James near Port Richmond on Staten Island. He was placed by the window on the second floor, where he could watch the boats at harbor. It was here that he died alone at age eighty on September 14, 1836.

If Hamilton's death had triggered a nationwide outpouring of grief and a massive funeral parade that wound through New York, Burr's death occasioned only a tepid oration by the president of Princeton. He was buried at the college beside the monuments to his father and grandfather, in an unmarked grave.

FIFTY-TWO

In the End

EMPIRES RISE AND fall, and so do the men who build them. Hamilton came from so little to make so much, winning a war, creating a constitution, establishing a financial system, before he fell to scandal and despair. Burr's ascent is not so marked, in part because he began at such a height: He gave good service in the revolution, proved an able lawyer, initiated a democratic style of campaigning, and nearly won the presidency. Their lives, Burr's and Hamilton's, stand now on the distant horizon like a pair of mountains of different heights but similar shapes. The one behind is higher and mightier, but it is obscured by the lower mountain in front. And their ridgelines cross, the one in front appearing to rise where the other descends.

Front and back, up and down, relative standing was everything to these two men—fatal for Hamilton, and hardly less ruinous for Burr. Hamilton was well into his decline while Burr was climbing to the presidency. Just when Hamilton was diminished by his failures, Burr was enlarged by his success, exacerbating all the latent tensions between the two—until Burr missed the presidency and he started his own plunge. His bitterness shaded into wrath, and he took his revenge on a fallen man.

→>‹←

THE FORTUNES OF both men turned at Weehawken. Today, it is a town of a little over ten thousand. Just north of Hoboken, it is best known as the western terminus of the Lincoln Tunnel. Up on a bluff above a ferry landing, there is a small park off Hamilton Avenue purporting to mark the spot of the fatal duel. It is actually well below it, as the original dueling ground rested on a rocky ledge that stood above, until it collapsed sometime in the nineteenth century. The memorial park's chief feature is a sizable boulder that Hamilton supposedly rested on after he was shot, and a plaque that describes the basics of the duel. Adjoining is a park devoted to Hamilton alone, clearly the favored combatant, that offers a proud bust of him on a high pedestal.

But of course, the real monument to Hamilton does not lie on the Jersey shore, but on the shore across, where the financial towers of Wall Street that he inspired have turned an island wilderness into a built paradise that is the envy of the world, one that has extended from New York to Pittsburgh to Kansas City to Des Moines to San Francisco and to hundreds of cities more, in the steady advance of prosperity across the land. Great men do great things. As he made himself out of nothing, he created a country out of nothing.

There is no bust of Burr. If a visitor were to look out from Weehawken, scanning the horizon in search of Burr's lasting contribution to the country, let alone to the world, he might detect a certain glow of roguery that, at this distance of time, can seem charmingly American. But that's vaporous. If our visitor were to seek something more solid, he could look everywhere in this vast country, from the east to the west, and be very hard-pressed to find anything at all.

ENVOI

A ND THAT LETTER from Hamilton to Theodore Sedgwick from July
10, 1804, the night before the duel?

New York July 10. 1804

My Dear Sir

*I have received two letters from you since we last saw each other—that
of the latest date being the 24 of May. I have had in hand for some time
a long letter to you, explaining my view of the course and tendency of
our Politics, and my intentions as to my own future conduct. But my
plan embraced so large a range that owing to much avocation, some
indifferent health, and a growing distaste for Politics, the letter is still
considerably short of being finished—I write this now to satisfy you,
that want of regard for you has not been the cause of my silence—*

*I will here express but one sentiment, which is, that
Dismemberment of our Empire will be a clear sacrifice of great positive
advantages, without any counterballancing good; administering no
relief to our real Disease; which is <u>Democracy</u>, the poison of which by a
subdivision will only be the more concentrated in each part, and
consequently the more virulent.*

King is on his way for Boston where you may chance see him, and hear from himself his sentiments—

God bless you
AH

T Sedgwick Esqr

It's a strange letter to dash off in haste to an old friend, and all the more so considering the harsh destiny awaiting him in the morning. It's almost breezy, as if Hamilton has refused to acknowledge the gravity of the occasion. Under the circumstance, it is peculiar that he doesn't mention the duel, or Burr, a man Sedgwick knew well.

Instead, Hamilton offers up a kind of political sermon. It was not the first time he had expressed these sentiments, but it was the first time that he had put them so starkly, as if, on the eve of his "interview," Hamilton was finally answering Burr's snarling question to him: What do you find so despicable about me?

In this note, Hamilton doesn't get on Burr for the usual reasons, that he is ambitious, self-serving, unscrupulous. But rather he reaches for larger perils that he associates with Burr but that transcend him, making him a greater peril still. The claim against democracy is the more problematic. It is at the very least unseemly for a founder of America to inveigh against democracy. But, in context, the charge may be as much against Burr's version of democracy as it is against democracy itself. There is no question that Hamilton had a prejudice for a government of the elite—one that would include Sedgwick and, of course, Hamilton himself. But it is certainly possible that Hamilton was embittered by Burr's ability to manipulate popular sentiment for his own ends, and suspected that such manipulation would be even more pervasive, or "virulent," if the country was divided into smaller bits. Hamilton was gratified to fight off Burr's last assault on elective office, but he must have found it galling that, in his campaigns, the aristocrat had the popular touch, not the immigrant. If Burr could pass himself off as a man of the people, anyone could represent himself as anything, unconstrained by truth or principle. Hamilton detested that, and feared it.

*Alexander Hamilton's last letter, written on the night of July
10, 1804, to Theodore Sedgwick in Stockbridge,
Massachusetts. Despite the occasion, the penmanship is as
elegant as ever, and the thinking as clear.*

Hamilton's concern for the union was hardly misplaced, as Burr had flirted with that northern conspiracy and would soon direct a far more threatening western one. And that, in turn, may have inspired the southern one that nearly ended the entire American enterprise. As the country expanded to fulfill its manifest destiny, it was prone to breakings off by the disaffected; any significant split threatened to undo Hamilton's fiscal union, which underlay the political one. If Hamilton's laments about democracy referred to Burr's history, his fears about "dismemberment" alluded to Burr's future. And correctly, as it turned out.

It is impossible to say whether these ideas impelled Hamilton to take on Burr—to stop him either by killing him or being killed by him—or whether they were simply a proclamation to the world of his political values, which he might have written at any time. If the former seems a bit too melodramatic, the latter seems a little loose. But either way, they were Hamilton's last words on the subject, and Sedgwick never replied. For the sender was no longer here.

ACKNOWLEDGMENTS

I would like to claim that I retraced every footstep of my duelists, buried myself in their musty archives, and, as my manuscript inched along, solicited editorial comments from countless historians and celebrities, all close friends. But in fact I worked on this book almost entirely alone in my third-floor office in Brooklyn's Park Slope. As it happened, this was where Washington's callow soldiers—led by Hamilton and Burr among others—fled the onrushing redcoats in the first battle of the revolution. I took a lesson from that and let that distant period of the nation's founding come to me. Since generations of scholars had scrutinized the Federalist period, I quickly divined I was better off trying to make sense of the mountains of existing material than hunting for more scraps that had not yet been gathered. Besides, most of the original documents were almost instantly available to me by means of the two great boons to modern historians: Amazon Prime and the Internet. In a twinkling, I could surround myself, virtually speaking, with practically all of the known papers of Hamilton and Burr—an astonishing twenty-seven volumes of letters for Hamilton, although just four for Burr (who lost many more at sea, and to the fire courtesy of his prissy executor, Matthew L. Davis)—as well as those of Washington, Adams, Jefferson, Madison, and many others, all of them perfectly transcribed with brilliant annotations. I also pulled down from the metaphorical shelves any number of rare books from the period—Catherine Schuyler's chatty memoir, a biography of Hamilton's friend James Kent, an early history of Albany—that Google had extracted from the dusty corners of eminent libraries, scanned, and delivered to my screen, gratis.

Of the hundreds of more recent books I consulted, I need to pay tribute to the authors of two. First to the unparalleled Ron Chernow for his comprehensive biography of Hamilton, which is a wonder of research and writing, and then to Milton Lomask for his two-volume life of Burr from a generation ago that is still the gold standard account of that complicated figure—readable, compelling, and accurate.

But of all the books from the period, the one I found most illuminating was not a work of fact, but of fiction. I speak of Gore Vidal's *Burr*. Snide, skeptical, scoffing, it did more to evoke the humanity of our all-too-revered Founders than a library of factual accounts. Vidal traffics gaily in the flaws of these eminences, showing the petty, tyrannical, jealous, and duplicitous interior that lies below the glossy surface of the standard waxworks version. Paradoxically, their flaws revealed their virtues, as the struggles of their lives became more evident. No one wants an unblemished hero, in any case. Vidal inspired me to consider Hamilton and Burr as if I'd heard them gripe about money or squabble with their wives, or smelled their cologne. Since each got under the skin of the other, I imagined a parallel biography, showing their tightening trajectories, would reveal features that would otherwise be concealed, and provide a truer account than if I'd placed either man up on a pedestal alone. To the extent that I have succeeded I have Vidal to thank.

I've come to view history as the journalism of another time, and as such would like to reach back a few years to thank my editors at *GQ*, chiefly its late editor in chief Art Cooper, and my longtime editor Marty Beiser, who taught me more about fresh, vigorous writing than I ever learned anywhere else. While it may seem to be a desecration to the hallowed tradition of historiography, I often thought of this book as an immensely long *GQ* piece. But I'd also like to thank the various biographers I have come to know—I don't want to name any for fear of leaving others out—for opening the door for me to the past and showing me how to enter into it through detailed research and careful writing. Properly considered, the past is never over.

Beyond that, I'd like to pause a moment to remember my late friend Steve Richardson, who read this book in manuscript before he died and whose enthusiasm for it still stuns me. Thanks, also, to Lisa Dietrich, whose early rapturous comments on the book could not have been more welcome. The learned Steven Ellstrom, M.D., was very generous in explaining the various illnesses and injuries of my historical characters in modern terms. Jonathan Blackman, a partner at Cleary Gottlieb Steen & Hamilton LLP, penetrated for me some of the mysteries of the transition from English law to an American one after the revolution. And Peter Dunning, general manager of the terrific Golden Rock Inn on Hamilton's Nevis, where I went *solely for research*, was a wonderful host and guide. On Saint Croix, Robert White of the Alexander Hamilton Society showed me around the island, taking me to Hamilton's mother's lonesome grave site at the Grange, among many other places.

I'll always be grateful to my agent, Dan Conaway at Writers House, for believing in this project from the beginning, and to my editor at Penguin, Charlie Conrad, for quickly getting behind it, seeing its possibilities, and making them manifest in the present volume. His assistant, Pieta Pemberton, has been wonderfully able in helping to make it all happen. I have been greatly aided by my photo researcher, Carol Poticny, who has done yeoman's work to collect all the images that are here so beautifully displayed.

As ever, my daughters, Sara and Josie, have been lovely, constant supports in my writing life as in my non-writing life; as he rounds past one, my tiny grandson, Logan, is growing into the role of charmer-in-chief; and my fairly new step-children, Darya and Alex, are adorable presences, bringing cheerful voices and pattering feet to the house where I work upstairs. Overarching all is my wife, Rana Foroohar, about whom I would say what Aaron Burr said of his adored wife Theodosia—that she is "the best woman and finest lady I have ever known."

NOTES

I WELCOME SCHOLARLY ATTENTION, of course, but I have assumed that this book will be read primarily by the public. So I have not filled the notes with the chapter-and-verse references of academe, allowing intrepid scholars to track each fact and quotation back to its source, but instead sought to provide guides for readers who might want to know where to turn for further reading. In the Google era, of course, most information, especially material pertaining to the Founding Fathers, can be traced without scholarly citations anyway. Google offers free scans of entire books from the period; they are in the public domain because they were published before 1923.

What follows is what Google cannot offer: an accounting and appraisal of the sources from which I drew this book. I have cited them usually by author and title, but the full citation can be found in the bibliography. All of these sources were helpful, some invaluable, and I hope that readers will draw as much instruction and delight from them as I have.

AUTHOR'S NOTE

Hamilton's letter to Theodore Sedgwick from July 10, 1804, is posted on the website of the Massachusetts Historical Society, appearing as a yellowed photographic image, and in transcript. See: masshist.org/database/207.

INTRODUCTION: THE FATAL DINNER

The letters leading up to the duel have been widely republished, but I relied on the wide-ranging compendium of William Coleman—the editor of Hamilton's *Evening Post*—that he titled *A Collection of the Facts and Documents Relative to the Death of Major-General Alexander Hamilton*; it also includes material on the run-up, the national reaction to the tragedy, and the arrangements for the stately funeral procession in New York. The quote from Burr about the malignant Federalists comes from the *Memoirs of Aaron Burr, Complete*, edited by his longtime associate Matthew L. Davis, a book hereafter referred to as Davis. For more on John Tayler, see *The History of the City of Albany, New York, from the Discovery of the Great River in 1524, by Verrazzano, to the Present Time*, by Arthur James Weise, which well describes the Albany of 1804 as well. The quotes relating Hamilton's increasingly severe attitude toward Burr can be found, like so many Hamilton quotations, in many places on the Internet, but most reliably in *The Papers of Alexander Hamilton*, edited by Harold C. Syrett, hereafter referred to as PAH.

PART ONE: THE ROOTS OF THE HATRED

1: IN THE HANDS OF AN ANGRY GOD

The best single source on Burr's religious antecedents is the monumental biography *Jonathan Edwards: A Life*, by George M. Marsden, a book whose detailed scholarship is a marvel in the often-cloudy prerevolutionary era. Marsden well illuminates the entry of Aaron Burr Sr. into the Edwards lineage, and with him, of course, Aaron Burr Jr. Edwards's famous "Sinners in the Hands of an Angry God," preached at Enfield, Connecticut, on July 8, 1741, can be found all over the Internet. It was James Parton, the early biographer of Burr, who noticed "lofty style" being widely commented on. For background on the early years of Princeton, see *History of the College of New Jersey:*

From Its Origin in 1746 to the Commencement of 1854, by John Mclean, a later president of the college. Milton Lomask, in the first volume of his two volumes on Burr, supplies the essential overview, and, as the single best source for all things Burr, reappears frequently in these notes. The quotations from Esther Burr are from Davis, but Lomask records her letters to Sally Prince about her "Mr. Burr." Marsden relates the fear of slaughter. The letters of Esther's that are not in Schachner or Lomask can be found in *The Works of President Edwards*. For a line or two about the inoculation attributed to Cotton Mather, see *The Puritan Tradition in America, 1620–1730*, edited by Alden T. Vaughan. Elizabeth Fenn's *Pox Americana* has the gruesome details of death by smallpox; Marsden supplies the deathbed account of Rev. Edwards.

2: CONTENTMENT

For the Faucettes, the geography of Saint Croix, and the court case, see Chernow's *Alexander Hamilton* and Flexner's *Young Hamilton*. Atherton supplied the exquisite "mouth of a shark" in her fully researched but novelized account, *The Conquerors*. The sniffing Hamilton descendant is John Church Hamilton, Alexander's third born. Chernow, in his *Alexander Hamilton*, made the observation about the multiple spellings of Levine, and countless other things that are tallied farther on. On Saint Croix, the Christiansted fort still stands, and Rachel's low-ceilinged cell is open to visitors. Chernow is the best source on the Hamilton lineage, although I supplemented his account with Flexner. Robert White, of the Alexander Hamilton Society on Saint Croix, provided the observation about the limestone blocks, and several other things related to the island. The history, geology, economy, race relations, and natural history of Nevis are well evoked by Vincent K. Hubbard in his *Swords, Ships and Sugar*, right down to the metal-plated iguanas and the observations of the Reverend Robertson. The broader context of the sugar economy is laid out in the breathtaking *Sugar in the Blood: A Family's Story of Slavery and Empire*, an account of the global sugar trade by Andrea Stuart.

For Hamilton's far-seeing gaze, I am thinking primarily of Trumbull's standing portrait from 1791, but it is true of nearly all of the renderings; even the famous bust by Giuseppe Ceracchi seems to be looking past the viewer. Jefferson purchased a copy and placed it opposite one of himself in the entrance hall at Monticello so the two of them, he joked, would be opposed in death as in life. Flexner noted that the Danish court found the children "obscene," and that Lavien called them "whore children."

3: PLATONIC LOVE IS ARRANT NONSENSE

For the early years of Burr, Lomask is the unrivaled source, and he is the source here for Burr's early rebellious streak. Davis, as always, is the ur-source of the Burr quotes. For more on Elizabethtown, see *As We Were: The Story of Old Elizabethtown*, by Theodore Thayer. Parton shed the light on Burr's early education and relationship with Reeve and Burr's sister, Sally. Lomask recounted the tale, widely repeated, of Burr's determination to escape from home and later to enter the College of New Jersey, and his life there. Davis makes much of Burr's sexual history in his *Memoirs*. For more on the Cliosophic Society, see *The Halls: A Brief History of the American Whig-Cliosophic Society of Princeton University*, by Wallace J. Williamson III.

4: THE PRODICTIOUS GLARE OF ALMOST PERPETUAL LIGHTNING

Chernow charted Hamilton's Jewish connection and his patched-together education on Nevis. John C. Hamilton recorded the remark "It's a dog's life." Allan McClane Hamilton added Hamilton's lament about his father. Chernow detailed the resemblance to Ned Stevens, and its implications, and looked into Hamilton's work at Beekman and Cruger. The dailiness of the work is captured in the letters and documents from the period in PAH. His poem and life-changing essay are also there, as is Hamilton's famous wish for a war in his letter to Ned Stevens. For more on Hamilton's emergence from Saint Croix, see Richard Brookhiser's *Alexander Hamilton, American*.

5: REFINEMENT

For a close-up view of life in New York when Hamilton arrived, I have turned to that marvelously compendious volume *Gotham: A History of New York City to 1898*, by Edwin G. Burrows and Mike Wallace, which is a fund of statistical details, impressions, and insights, starting with the word "refinement" and proceeding from there. The steady march of the colonies toward war will come as no surprise to most readers; for the basics I have relied most heavily on *A Leap in the Dark*, by John Ferling, among countless other sources. For the details of Hamilton's involvement with Rev. John Rodgers, I have relied on Chernow. For the suspicion that Rodgers alerted Hamilton to Burr's existence, setting the two in competition, this is only my surmise, based on the facts that it seemed like a natural topic of conversation, and that Hamilton changed his behavior and his age shortly afterward.

6: IN THE ROSEATE BOWERS OF CUPID

For details of life in Elizabethtown, I have relied on Thayer's history of the town. The frivolities of life at Liberty Hall are well recounted in the biography *John Jay: Founding Father*, by Walter Stahr, as Jay was an active participant. Chernow delved into the personalities of William Livingston and his brother-in-law Lord Stirling. As ever, see PAH for that scrap of Hamilton's effulgent poesy. Among others, Chernow delineates how Hamilton's politics guided his switch from the College of New Jersey to King's.

7: SIX SLAYLOADS OF BUCKS AND BELLS

Lomask provides all the basics on Burr's curricular and extracurricular pursuits at Princeton. For Theodore Sedgwick in Stockbridge, see Welch, *Theodore Sedgwick, Federalist*, and my own family memoir, *In My Blood: Six Generations of Madness and Desire in an American Family*. The account of Burr's frustrations with Rev. Bellamy is amply detailed in Burr's many letters to Ogden, all of them collected in Davis; and Davis follows through with letters pertaining to the switch to his brother-in-law Tapping Reeve. Lomask has the best single account of the affair with the future Dolly Hancock, but I have also drawn on Unger's biography of Hancock. Davis has collected Burr's many dishy letters with Ogden relating his romantic exploits, along with Ogden's tepid responses.

8: HOLY GROUND

For Hamilton's years at King's College, I've turned to Flexner as well as Chernow. *Gotham* is best at setting the general scene of that part of New York.

John C. Hamilton recorded Troup's observations of Hamilton in the college chapel, noting Troup's ideas about Hamilton's political beliefs at the time. For the earlier relationship between the colony of New York and the Crown, see *The Memorial History of New-York*, vol. 2, by James Grant Wilson. The Boston Tea Party is everywhere described; I took my details from Ferling. Flexner describes Hamilton's early efforts to come to terms with the new politics, to take on Samuel Seabury, and to save Myles Cooper.

9: A FEVER FOR WAR

Burr's response to the Battles of Lexington and Concord is well recorded in Davis's collection of his letters. For the perilous assault on Quebec, the most reliable sources—beyond Burr's own few letters—are two biographies of Benedict Arnold, James Kirby Martin's and Willard Stern Randall's. As for some indications of the psychological dimensions of the journey, I have turned to *Fallen Founder*, by Nancy Isenberg, who is especially good at highlighting the legendary aspects of Burr's role in the tragedy in the poetical works of Spring and Brackenridge.

10: LIBERTY OR DEATH

Flexner tells the tale of Hamilton's practicing to be a soldier, and John C. Hamilton recited the topics of his father's paybook. Nathan Schachner described Hamilton's efforts with his young charges in his *Alexander Hamilton*. Chernow laid out Hamilton's ideological assault on British rule and then detailed Washington's defense of New York, Hamilton's rescue of Rivington, and his retrieval of the patriots' sole cannons from the reach of the mighty *Asia*.

Burr's impatience is well documented in Davis; for his fateful meeting with Washington, I have relied on Lomask's account.

11: WHEN IN THE COURSE OF HUMAN EVENTS

The Hickey conspiracy is nicely described in Chernow's *Washington* and in his *Hamilton*. In both, he relates the terrifying invasion of the vast royal armada, adding the charming bit about Hamilton missing his purse on the nation's first Fourth of July. For the ensuing battles, it was not only the generals who were hidden behind

a fog of war—historians have been, too. To penetrate it, for the first full year of war, I have found McCullough's account in the oversize *1776*—complete with maps, reproductions, and charming facsimiles of the correspondence of the principals—immensely helpful, especially in re-creating the Battle of Brooklyn. The precise movements of Burr and Hamilton can never be known for sure, only guessed at from fragments, but I have relied most heavily on the detective work of Lomask and Chernow and done my best to coordinate their somewhat divergent accounts. Their actual intersection at Bayard's Hill Redoubt is a matter of some conjecture, as neither referred to it in his letters, but in Davis's compendium, Burr mentioned the story years later, adding that he knew the area because of his many visits to Mrs. Thomas Clarke, then Mary Stillwell, an aunt of Burr's future wife, Theodosia Bartow Prevost. (In a quirk, the Clarkes' daughter Charity married Benjamin Moore, the Episcopal bishop who gave Hamilton his last rites.) Chernow guided me through Hamilton's involvement with the surprise attack at Trenton, then Princeton, emerging as Washington's aide-de-camp at Morristown. Hamilton's own letters from early March 1777, in PAH, revealed his early duties. The story of the dashing John Laurens is best told in his sole biography, *John Laurens and the American Revolution*, by Gregory D. Massey. I took Hamilton's remarkable confessional letter to Laurens from PAH, although it has now been picked up by gay rights activists and distributed widely about the Web. Theodore P. Savas and J. David Dameron's *Guide to the Battles of the American Revolution* was indispensable in penetrating the fog of that war. That said, I found that Chernow provided a clear description of Hamilton's daring skirmish with the British along the Brandywine—leaving Massey to detail Laurens's fight at Chadd's Ford—and the battle's implications for the Continental Congress in Philadelphia.

12: THE MALCOLMS

Davis records the letters regarding Burr's appointment and his efforts to educate and lead the raw recruits of the Malcolms to guard the gap in the Ramapo Mountains, and Lomask provides a helpful overview. The events pertaining to Saratoga, with Hamilton's negotiations with Gates, and the looming Conway Cabal—all this has been a staple of Hamilton lore since Henry Cabot Lodge brought it to general attention in 1884, but many political nuances and emotional subtleties have been added by Flexner and Chernow. The convergence of Burr and Hamilton at either end of Valley Forge is depicted by each man's biographers, neither side, tellingly, taking notice of the other. Chernow provided the salient details of Laurens's extraordinary duel with Charles Lee.

13: A LADY WITH A BEAUTIFUL WAIST

Again, Chernow sets the scene for Hamilton's romantic life in camp, but it's the extraordinary letter to Laurens that penetrates Hamilton's tortured heart. That can, again, be found in PAH.

14: BEAUTY IS WOMAN'S SCEPTRE

Mary Wollstonecraft is indispensable to an understanding of Burr's relations with women. For the Moncrieffe affair, I turned to Davis, who recorded the whole thing, rather uncomprehendingly. The brutal duty in Westchester County is well described by Lomask. For the detail about Burr's escapade to New Jersey, I have relied on Lomask, who adds a ditty called "Aaron Burr's Wooing" from *Harper's* magazine of 1887:

> Eight miles to the river he gallops his steed,
> Lays him bound in the barge, bids his escort
>   make speed,
> Loose their swords, sit athwart, through the
>   fleet reach yon shore;
> Not a word! not a plash of the thick-muffled oar!
> Once across, once again in the seat, and away—
> Five leagues are soon over when love has the say;
> And "Old Put" and his rider a bridle-path know
> To the Hermitage Manor of Madame Prevost.

15: THE SCHUYLERS

Flexner gives a good account of Hamilton's headlong plunge into matrimony, with Chernow adding important details about the family he was marrying into. But of course it is the letters of the bridal couple—plus the *Memoir of Lieutenant Colonel Tench Tilghman* and the biography of Catherine Schuyler by Mary Gay Humphreys—that fully evoke the scene. For the matrimonial tendencies of the Schuyler family, I found the biography of Catherine Schuyler particularly

evocative. An earlier account of Hamilton and Burr, Arnold A. Rogow's *Fatal Friendship*, was particularly good on the subject of Betsey's older sister Angelica's rash romance with John Barker Church.

16: BUT A SINGLE WORD, *BURR*

Isenberg was helpful at revealing the clandestine origins of Burr's attachment to the woman who was then Mrs. Prevost. Parton is the most blunt of the biographers in appraising her, and the most credible. Davis has included much of the correspondence of the two lovers, pining for each other in their separation, with Burr in Albany and Mrs. Prevost in Paramus. And Davis, of course, tosses his own approving comments into the mix, obviously pleased that his friend was done, at least temporarily, with his philandering ways. The sad story of Major André is well told in James Kirby Martin's biography of André's coconspirator, Benedict Arnold. Lomask recounts the betrothal of Mr. and Mrs. Burr.

17: A LITTLE SORCERESS

The exchange between Hamilton and Schuyler is recorded in PAH, as are Hamilton's letter to his new wife about being bewitched, the two to Laurens complaining about his service in the army and then denying his request for more troops, and Laurens's letter of anguish back. Chernow gives the fullest description of the famous staircase altercation between Washington and his chief aide. For Hamilton's participation in the siege of Yorktown, I turned to Savas and Dameron's battle guide. For Hamilton's comments to Betsey, see PAH.

18: IN ILL HUMOUR WITH EVERY THING BUT THEE

Davis records the letters to Theodosia, as well as the journal entries. Lomask and Chernow both place their men in Albany, although not at the same locale. Davis has the letters regarding Burr's bid to alter the opinion of the New York State Supreme Court—interspersed with letters to Theodosia about what he'd prefer to think about. Lomask has the details of the wedding. See Brookhiser's *Madison* for Hamilton's encounter with him in Philadelphia. For Hamilton's last letters to Laurens, see PAH.

PART TWO:
THE BATTLE IS JOINED

19: COMMENTARIES ON THE LAWS OF ENGLAND

The marvelous and indispensable *Gotham* set the scene of New York City after the war, and I relied on Herbert S. Parmet and Marie B. Hecht's *Aaron Burr: Portrait of an Ambitious Man* to establish the movements of Burr in the city, while Chernow did the honors for Hamilton. The ecological details of early New York come from Eric W. Sanderson's *Mannahatta: A Natural History of New York City*. For coffee shops as the center of city life, see William Ukers's 1922 *All About Coffee*. Schachner best compared the legal styles of Burr and Hamilton. Isenberg detailed Burr's legal practice. Parton had the item about Hamilton's returning one fee as too much.

I drew the complicated matter of Rutgers and Waddington from Davis, who likewise finds the source of American political parties in this seemingly obscure case. Brookhiser picked up the matter as a failure of the Articles of Confederation. The quote from Chancellor Robert Livingston can be found in Edwin Brockholst Livingston's *The Livingstons of Livingston Manor*. A good look at the impregnable George Clinton can be had in *George Clinton: Yeoman Politician of the New Republic*, by John P. Kaminski. Davis also rounds out the story, with Clinton's failed effort to take revenge on Mayor Duane.

20: CHILDREN OF A LARGER GROWTH

Lomask is the most sweeping in his account of Burr's nascent legal career, including the details about his "nice, new, beautiful little chariot," Burr's insistence that his was Ver Plank's house, and the growing debt that ensued, despite the activity of his law office. Davis provides the inner story that comes from the tender letters between Burr and Theodosia that were as clear in feeling as they were in expression. Mary Wollstonecraft's *A Vindication of the Rights of Woman* provides the basis of Burr's understanding in the matters of gender that fascinated him, and Lord Chesterfield's *Letters to His Son on the Art of Becoming a Man of the World and a Gentleman* a point of ignorance. The extraordinary moment at Fort Johnson comes from Davis.

21: COME MY CHARMER AND RELIEVE ME

Chernow wonderfully details the domestic scene of the Hamiltons, with Allan McLane Hamilton adding a sprinkling of comments from his *Intimate Life of Alexander Hamilton*. The contrasting letters to Betsey and Angelica are in PAH. The Kent anecdote is from his memoirs, compiled by his son, William.

22: YOU WILL BECOME ALL THAT I WISH

For an insightful account of the growth and development of young Theodosia Bartow Burr, I have relied on the biography by Côté, supplemented by letters in Davis.

23: TWO MEN OF POLITICS

Burr's early political career is well told in Lomask; Chernow handles Hamilton's, supplemented by the many insightful letters in PAH. Chernow and Kaminski present the early phase of the loathing between Hamilton and Clinton, from the opposing points of view. Two biographies of Madison—by Richard Brookhiser and Gary Wills—rounded out for me the oft-told tale of the Constitutional Convention. The biography of Gouverneur Morris shed light on that stylist and his contribution to the hallowed document. The Federalist Papers proved invaluable to understanding Hamilton's thought. I turned to Broadus Mitchell for some of the details. As always, the quotations from Hamilton can be found in PAH. Chernow evoked the federal ship *Hamilton*.

24: A DREADED DILEMMA

To get a sense of Washington's mind-set, I turned to Chernow's *Washington*, well deserving of its Pulitzer Prize for evoking such a taciturn man in full. The letters of solicitation are in PAH, as are Hamilton's tepid remarks about Adams. Kaminski reveals Clinton's anxiety from the other side, and Adams's fury is recorded in the Adams papers at the Massachusetts Historical Society. Kaminski is invaluable on Hamilton's fight to remove Clinton from office; the Parton tripartite division is, justly, a staple of political commentary on the period. Chernow picks up the Yates campaign—and Lomask introduces Burr into the matter, which Kaminski helps sort out. For the larger economic environment, and Hamilton's role in it, see, among the other predictable accounts, "The U.S. Panic of 1792: Financial Crisis Management and the Lender of Last Resort," by David J. Cowen, Richard Sylla, and Robert E. Wright.

25: TO A MIND LIKE HIS NOTHING COMES AMISS

McCullough, in *Adams*, well depicts the scene of Washington's inauguration at Federal Hall. Allan McLane Hamilton picks up the tale from his grandparents' perspective, and Chernow runs through the humorous business of choosing a title for the new president. Brookhiser has an eye for the social subtleties of state dining. The Charles Rappleye biography of the brilliant, doomed financier Robert Morris offers a helpful perspective on Hamilton's candidacy for Treasury. Chernow fills in the rest, about the politics of disappointing the Livingstons. In Robert F. Jones's *"The King of the Alley,"* William Duer is a monarch all of his own, although ultimately a toppled one, and, like Morris, he provides a useful gloss on the early years of economic expansion under Hamilton. Mitchell retails Hamilton's efforts to get the Treasury Department up and running, and the economy along with it. Fisher Ames's comments, widely quoted, come from the second volume of the 1837 two-volume *Life of George Washington*, by John Marshall. Angelica's letter to Hamilton regarding her husband, the exchange over the garter, and the Hamiltons' sorrowful letters to the departed Angelica are all in PAH. Hamilton's to-the-penny calculation of the debt is in his *Report on the Public Credit*, which is the source of the other quotations, as well. I used the handsome Library of America edition, although the text is also in PAH. The gossipy William Maclay recorded his observations of Hamilton's "funding system" in his surprisingly tart *Journal of William Maclay*. Hamilton's own version of the disagreement is in PAH.

26: ANOTHER LONG NOSE

If it takes one biography to understand Washington, it takes hundreds to understand Jefferson, and even then the view in is only partial. Of the many to pick from, I relied most on Fawn M. Brodie's *Thomas Jefferson: An Intimate History* and Joseph J. Ellis's *American Sphinx: The Character of Thomas Jefferson*. Both were written before the DNA confirmation of the two centuries of

rumors about his relationship with Sally Hemings, but even though Brodie wrote in 1974, she was better prepared, and better positioned, for the news. Jon Meacham's more recent biography of Jefferson ferreted out fresh details regarding the Cosway scandal, which previously seemed to have been milked dry. The account of Hamilton's appearance at Cherry Street is taken from Jefferson's Anas.

27: AND WE HAD A BANK

The most complete account of the development of Hamilton's doctrine of implied powers comes from *The Age of Federalism: The Early American Republic, 1788–1800*, by Stanley Elkins and Eric McKitrick. Betsey Hamilton's charmingly abridged version is in PAH. Her husband's observations will, of course, be found there, too. I found *Every Man a Speculator* to be a helpful guide to the period kicked off by Duer, as was the biography of William Duer himself, *"The King of the Alley."* It shed light on his role in the Panic of 1792, as does the article cited earlier, "The U.S. Panic of 1792."

28: BOTANIZING

There are many accounts of the famous sightseeing trip of Jefferson and Madison right through Troup's prophesy, but I have gotten some of the color of this one from Brookhiser's biography of Madison. The Federalist angle is quite well-known; the Burr not so much, and I have relied on Lomask to see it his way, and then to follow that narrative line through to its conclusion, with Burr a senator.

29: EMBRYO-CAESAR

It was Parton who supplied the wonderful vignette of Hamilton at dinner. For the lowdown on Burr's presidential ambitions in 1792, I have turned to Kaminsky, who revealed them from Clinton's point of view. Hamilton's assessments of his rival can all be found in PAH.

30: OTHER THAN PECUNIARY CONSOLATION

Chernow captured the social scene in Philadelphia that may have contributed to Hamilton's losing his sense of moral balance. But the best account of Hamilton's affair with Mrs. Reynolds is indubitably his own from the so-called Reynolds Pamphlet, in PAH.

31: SOBER AMONG THE DRUNKS

Burr's mysterious letters to Gaasbeck can be found in the collections of Peter Van Gaasbeck in the Senate House Museum, Kingston, New York. The consoling ones to Theodosia are in Davis, as are Theodosia's complaints. Lomask details the effects of the yellow fever epidemic on the woman who would become Dolley Madison, and Gutzman's *James Madison and the Making of America* supplied some of the humanizing details. For details of the disease itself, I relied on two books with very similar names: *The American Plague: The Untold Story of Yellow Fever, the Epidemic That Shaped Our History*, by Molly Caldwell Crosby, and *An American Plague: The True and Terrifying Story of the Yellow Fever Epidemic of 1793*, by Jim Murphy. For Dr. Rusk and the early wooing of Burr, I depended on Lomask, who provided the early tally of Burrites. Morris's letter to Hamilton about political sobriety is in PAH. Parton steered me through the futile efforts of Dr. Ledyard to win Hamilton's backing. For the intricacies of Otsego balloting regulations, I depended on Lomask.

32: I HAVE BEEN SO CRUELLY TREATED

Much of Hamilton's plans for the Society for Establishing Useful Manufactures were laid out by him in his lengthy *Report on Manufactures*, available in the Library of America edition. PAH establishes that he was busy on the fateful morning when the Reynoldses both charged back into his life. His Reynolds Pamphlet gives a full rendering of all the letters back and forth. In his Hamilton papers, Syrett's lengthy editorial note on Oliver Wolcott Jr., Hamilton's successor as secretary of the treasury, offers the best and most judicious guide to the players, their backgrounds, and their motivations in this tawdry but high-stakes melodrama, which was now only in its opening act.

33: LOUIS CAPET HAS LOST HIS CAPUT

The events of the French Revolution are well-known. In sculpting my own version—the one that was most pertinent to Hamilton, Burr, and Jefferson, among other American politicians—I have relied on Simon Schama's magisterial *Citizens: A Chronicle of the French Revolution*. To see these events from the American perspective, I turned to Elkins and McKitrick's *Age of Federalism*, which also laid

out the triumphal American tour of Citizen Genet. Chernow recorded the denouement. Hamilton's comments are in PAH.

34: THE BEST WOMAN AND FINEST LADY I HAVE EVER KNOWN

For Abigail Adams's fervid admiration of Richmond Hill, see Charles Felton Pidgin's 1907 biography, *Theodosia, the First Gentlewoman of Her Time*. Pidgin also calls the roll of the famous guests to the Burr mansion. The death of Theodosia is recorded in the letters collected in Davis, most of them from Burr as Theodosia went into ever-steeper decline. Côté's *Theodosia Burr Alston* picks up the story, once it turned to the other Theodosia, and Parton tells the tale of the unnamed woman in Burr's library.

35: ROOT OUT THE DISTEMPERED AND NOISOME *WEED*

Hamilton's resignation letter to Washington is in PAH, as is the tender one back from his fatherly commander in chief. PAH also has Hamilton's long, anguished letter to Rufus King about his bête noire, Burr.

PART THREE: TO THE DEATH

36: TO FIGHT THE *WHOLE DETESTABLE FACTION*

The various offers for Hamilton's legal services are related in PAH. Chernow recounts the raucous evening Hamilton spent defending the Jay Treaty on the streets of an inhospitable New York. As always, the quotes are in PAH. The two Madison biographies above, by Brookhiser and Wills, chronicle the struggle to write Washington's farewell address. The various Jefferson quotes about racial differences can all be found in his *Notes on the State of Virginia*.

Although it is one of Callender's more notorious efforts, *Nos V & VI of the History of the United States for the Year 1796* has fallen out of print, but the contents are widely cited, and the facts of Callender himself can be found in Michael Durey's biography, *"With the Hammer of Truth,"* which details the wrecking-ball life of this Scotsman. Hamilton's famous Reynolds Pamphlet, again, is in PAH, as is the commiseration of his friends.

Chernow rounds out the tale with the quotations from Abigail Adams, and then the go-around with Monroe, Muhlenberg, and Venable. The account of the set-to with Monroe was the one set down at the time by his associate Gelston; I relied also on Harry Ammon's Monroe biography. Angelica's sympathetic letter to Betsey is in PAH. Chernow recounts the tale of Philip's illness.

37: THE BUBBLE OF SPECULATION IS BURST
The fullest and most reliable account of Burr's various financial misadventures—but especially with Angerstein and Lamb—will be found in a lengthy editorial note in Kline's two-volume edition of the public letters. Hamilton's delight in Burr's debt is in PAH. For Joseph Brant-Thayendanegea, the Indian King, I relied on William L. Stone's two-volume 1845 biography, *Life of Joseph Brant-Thayendanegea*; also on Côté; and on a long and fascinating entry in the online *Dictionary of Canadian Biography*. It is Parmet and Hecht who penetrate most deeply into the true nature of Burr's relationship with the Indian King.

38: *AN ABSOLUTE AND ABOMINABLE LIE*
The fulsome letters from Jefferson to Burr are in the *Papers of Thomas Jefferson*. Lomask details Burr's efforts in the Assembly, both for the common good and for Burr's singular advantage. Davis records his indignant response to the many reasonable questions about his bill. Chernow reports Burr's ensuing duel with Church. Among others, Parmet and Hecht relate the creation of the Manhattan Company. Brian Phillips Murphy's "A very convenient instrument," an award-winning article about the bank in the *William and Mary Quarterly*, is particular insightful.

39: *STRUT* IS GOOD FOR NOTHING
Elkins and McKitrick relate the famous brawl between Griswold and Lyon, according it the balance of horror and hilarity that it deserves. They are also very good at showing the overlap between foreign concerns and domestic ones and relating the balance between sensible caution in regard to France and paranoia, and also the fine distinction, for Hamilton, between a healthy sense of duty and shameless self-aggrandizement. Lomask ably gives the Burr angle on all this and on the misguided

Alien and Sedition laws that ensued. I was also very glad to consult Dunn's *Jefferson's Second Revolution*, which sets the scene for his election. For Washington's death, I relied on Chernow's biography of the first president.

40: THE LADY IN THE WELL
To recount this peculiar tragedy, I turned to Paul Collins's *Duel with the Devil*, which tells the tale and makes much of the odd fact that Burr and Hamilton made up the defense team. For further details, I depended on Kleiger's *Trial of Levi Weeks*, which offers a transcript of the case, drawn from the newspapers of the time. Hamilton's derision of Burr is in PAH.

41: THE FANGS OF JEFFERSON
To recount the tumultuous election of 1800, from Burr's effort to wrest a majority from the state Assembly to the Manhattan street fight of the election itself, I depended on a range of accounts of this signal event in American history: *A Magnificent Catastrophe*, by Edward J. Larson; Susan Dunn's *Jefferson's Second Revolution: The Election Crisis of 1800 and the Triumph of Republicanism*; John Ferling's *Jefferson and Hamilton*; and Ferling's *Adams vs. Jefferson*. The Larson was especially enlightening. It was the indefatigable Lomask who dredged up the odd story about how Clinton would accept the vice presidency, but only if he was allowed to resign it shortly afterward.

42: THE GIGG IS THEREFORE UP
As with the previous chapter, I was impressed with Larson, Dunn, and Ferling, all of whom do yeomen's work to bring clarity to a very murky period of American political history. For the correspondence with Theodore Sedgwick, I turned to our kinsman Richard Welch's biography. Hamilton's bitter comments toward Burr are in PAH. Isenberg helps sort out why Burr might have attracted this particular type of vituperation in this period. Along with Pidgin, from an earlier day, Côté tells the grim story of young Theodosia's misguided marriage. For the pivotal anecdote about how Burr packed but did not come—this comes from the dogged Parmet and Hecht.

43: A DAMN'D RASCAL
Parmet and Hecht, along with Lomask, are the best on Burr's miseries as vice president. Davis

reveals Burr's letters dismissing the suspicions against him. Kline's edition of *Political Correspondence and Public Papers of Aaron Burr* is good on the sad saga of Davis's attempt to get a job with the new administration. Chernow provides a useful gloss on Jefferson's administration by providing the Hamilton angle. And he gives the most poignant account of the unbearably tragic death of Philip Hamilton at the hands of Captain George I. Eacker.

Of all Burr's biographers, Isenberg was the most diligent in tracking down Burr's many paramours, from Celeste to Sansay. Lomask dug out the two women Burr seduced into prostitution while vice president.

44: *TANT MIEUX*

In his trenchant character study of Jefferson, Ellis lays out the continuing appeal of the Jefferson presidency. Kline offers the most succinct account of the falling-out between Jefferson and Burr. Lomask is terrific on the governor's race, being fair to both sides—Hamilton's and Burr's—while sliding in the wild card of the allure of the Northern Alliance for Burr. Burr's postmortem to Theodosia is in Davis.

45: A STILL MORE DESPICABLE OPINION

For the history of dueling in New York, and more generally, by far the most spirited are *Gentlemen's Blood: A History of Dueling, from Swords at Dawn to Pistols at Dusk*, by Barbara Holland; *The History and Examination of Duels: Shewing Their Heinous Nature and the Necessity of Suppressing Them*, by John Cockburn; and a curious *Essay on the Practice of Duelling, as It Exists in Modern Society*, by James Sega, LL.D., in 1830, occasioned by the death of a friend.

Hamilton's line about popular opinion regarding duels is in PAH. For sources regarding the Albany dinner, see those in the introduction, when the dinner is first introduced. Coleman offers the best compendium of the letters between Burr and Hamilton, and of the consequences that followed. Chernow follows Hamilton's movements once the duel is set. The descendant of the original Manhattan Company, now called JP Morgan Chase & Co., possesses the original pistols in its archives at its Manhattan headquarters but is lamentably chary of showing them to

the public. The New-York Historical Society possesses nearly perfect facsimiles. For the line of inquiry behind the footnote regarding the timing of fire, I found Joseph Ellis's *Founding Brothers* to be the most compelling on a point that is often overlooked. The sad lines of farewell from Hamilton to his wife are in PAH.

PART FOUR: AND THEN THERE WAS ONE

46: HAVE NO ANXIETY ABOUT THE ISSUE OF THIS BUSINESS

Lomask tells the odd story of the visit of Burr's cousin. Kline has Burr's letter of uncharacteristic concern to his son-in-law. Lomask relates the bit about Truxtun but misses the shading that Truxtun is potentially a Burr ally, and he carries the tale through the shadows of Philadelphia. The letters of Burr's to and from his confederates are all in Davis.

47: A GOOD MANY INCIDENTS TO AMUSE ONE

For the full story of the remarkably untrustworthy James Wilkinson, I have turned to Andro Linklater's *Artist in Treason*, which details the dawn of the Burr conspiracy, which began over maps in Burr's library. It is unknown what maps Burr and Wilkinson were poring over, but one of them might have been the exquisite Faden map of the United States from 1796, which shows the known world ending at the Mississippi, with mostly blank spaces beyond. Burr's reassuring letter to Theodosia is in Davis. In volume 2 of his big Burr biography, Lomask nicely lays out the secession plan, as does David O. Stewart in *American Emperor*, a fine account of Burr's career as a traitor. Burr's bouquet to Williamson is in Davis, as are Burr's many complaints about his various amours. For the Truxtun negotiations, as well as the Merry mission, the complications with Spain, and the other preliminaries, I turned to Stewart, Lomask, and Parmet and Hecht, but Lomask offers the best understanding of Burr's sojourn farther south before he doubled back to preside over the Chase trial. Burr's brave and blustery letters to Theodosia are in Davis. Lomask is essential to following the story of Burr's recruiting efforts in Washington.

48: MOTIVES OF PROFOUND POLITICAL IMPORTANCE

In general, I preferred Lomask's version of Burr's tour down the Ohio, although Stewart's *American Emperor* provides a good guide to the territory, filling out the details on what he terms the "high-spirited" Kemper brothers, elsewhere considered notorious desperadoes. All the commentators go to town on poor Blennerhassett, but William H. Safford's 1850 *The Life of Harman Blennerhassett* gives a good sense of how Blennerhassett's near contemporaries might have viewed this eccentric. Burr's letter to Theodosia, in which he extols Jackson and his hospitality, is in Davis. Wilkinson, again, is best understood through the biography *An Artist in Treason*. His own interminable autobiography is, like the man, overstuffed, showy, and not to be relied on. The complicated interplay among Burr, Wilkinson, and the rightly suspicious Major James Bruff is difficult to piece out, but I found that Stewart has the best close-up view of the later stages of the plot, while Lomask is better at providing the overview of the goals of Burr's conspiracy, which are otherwise hard to discern, especially as they came into conflict with his hopes for extracting a political appointment from Jefferson, and his investment in the Bastrop Tract.

49: A TERRIBLE WHIRLPOOL, THREATENING EVERYTHING

Lomask's account of the endgame of the Burr conspiracy is the most thorough and convincing, as he recounts how the unwanted newspaper publicity aroused the determined Kentucky US attorney Daviess. Linklater does his best to render Wilkinson's objectives, which were no more transparent than Burr's. Safford helps out with poor Blennerhassett. Stewart describes Burr's fling with Madeline Price, drawing the quote about his "witchery" from Claiborne's *Mississippi*, and on through the various court cases, until Burr hit a judge who was not taken in by him.

50: A SLIGHT EXPRESSION OF CONTEMPT

The Burr letter to Theodosia is in Davis. For Jefferson's, see the *Papers of Thomas Jefferson*. For Marshall, there are several biographies of this remarkable jurist, of which Jean Edward Smith's 1996 *John Marshall: Definer of a Nation* offers the fullest account of Marshall's life, and not just his public life. Linklater, however, does the best at bringing to life a long, meandering trial with quotations he collected from skeptical observers such as Washington Irving. Lomask ably represents the trial's basic shape.

51: G.H. EDWARDS

When Burr fled to Europe, he was, for the first time, on his own, and, rather than sending letters, he recorded his ample thoughts and sentiments in *The Private Journal of Aaron Burr*. It was intended as one immensely long account of his travels for his daughter, Theodosia—nearly a thousand pages altogether, in two volumes. As it included the few, often heartbreaking letters from Theodosia back, this has had to suffice as virtually the sole source for most accounts of those years, as it has been for my own. After his much-delayed return to America, Burr's life thinned out considerably, and I have relied on Lomask—along with Parton, Stewart, and Schachner—to provide the grim essentials.

BIBLIOGRAPHY

Adams, Henry. *History of the United States of America During the First Administration of Thomas Jefferson*. Vol. I. New York: Charles Scribner's Sons, 1889.

———. *The Life of Albert Gallatin*. Philadelphia: J.B. Lippincott, 1879.

Adams, John, and Abigail Adams. *The Letters of John and Abigail Adams*. Edited by Frank Shuffelton. New York: Penguin, 2004.

Ambrose, Douglas, and Robert W.T. Martin. *The Many Faces of Alexander Hamilton: The Life and Legacy of America's Most Elusive Founding Father*. New York: New York University Press, 2006.

Ames, Fisher. *Works of Fisher Ames, Compiled by a Number of His Friends*. Boston: T.B. Wait, 1809.

Ammon, Harry. *James Monroe: The Quest for National Identity*. New York: McGraw-Hill, 1971.

Atherton, Gertrude Franklin Horn. *The Conqueror: Being the True and Romantic Story of Alexander Hamilton*. New York: The MacMillan Company, 1902.

Baldick, Robert. *The Duel: A History*. 1965. New York: Barnes and Noble Books, 1996.

Bernstein, R.B. *Thomas Jefferson*. New York: Oxford University Press, 2003.

Biddle, Charles. *Autobiography of Charles Biddle, Vice-President of the Supreme Executive Council of Pennsylvania*. Philadelphia: E. Claxton, 1883.

Boswell, James. *Life of Samuel Johnson, LL.D. Comprehending an Account of His Studies, and Numerous Works*. N.p., 1857.

Brady, Joseph P. *The Trial of Aaron Burr*. New York: Neale, 1913.

Brands, H.W. *The Heartbreak of Aaron Burr*. New York: Anchor Books, 2012.

Brodie, Fawn N. *Thomas Jefferson: An Intimate History*. 1974. New York: W. W. Norton, 2010.

Brookhiser, Richard. *Alexander Hamilton, American*. New York: Touchstone, 1999.

———. *Gentleman Revolutionary: Gouverneur Morris—The Rake Who Wrote the Constitution.* New York: Free Press, 2003.

———. *James Madison.* New York: Basic Books, 2011.

Brown, T. Allston. *A History of the New York Stage from the First Performance in 1732 to 1901.* Vol. 3. New York: Dodd, Mead, 1903.

Burdett, Charles. *Margaret Moncrieffe; the First Love of Aaron Burr. A Romance of the Revolution.* New York: Derby and Jackson, 1860.

Burr, Aaron. *Memoirs of Aaron Burr, Complete.* Edited by Matthew L. Davis. Miami: Hard Press, n.d.

———. *Political Correspondence and Public Papers of Aaron Burr.* Edited by Mary-Jo Kline with the assistance of Joanne Wood Ryan. 2 vols. Princeton, NJ: Princeton University Press, 1983.

———. *The Private Journal of Aaron Burr.* Vol. 1. N.p., 1903.

———. *The Private Journal of Aaron Burr During His Residence of Four Years in Europe.* Vol. 1. Edited by Matthew L. Davis. New York: Harper and Brothers, 1858.

Burrows, Edwin G., and Mike Wallace. *Gotham: A History of New York City to 1898.* New York: Oxford University Press, 1999.

Cary, Edward. *George William Curtis.* New York: Houghton Mifflin, 1899.

Cheetham, James. *Nine Letters on the Subject of Aaron Burr's Political Defection, With an Appendix.* N.p., 1803.

———. *A View of the Political Conduct of Aaron Burr, Esq. Vice-President of the United States.* N.p., 1802.

Chernow, Ron. *Alexander Hamilton.* New York: Penguin Press, 2004.

———. *Washington: A Life.* New York: Penguin Press, 2010.

Claiborne, John Francis Hamtramck. *Mississippi, as a Province, Territory and State....* Jackson, MS: Power and Barksdale, 1880.

Clark, Daniel. *Proofs of the Corruption of Gen. James Wilkinson, and of His Connexion with Aaron Burr....* N.p., 1809.

Clemens, Jeremiah. *The Rivals: A Tale of the Times of Aaron Burr, and Alexander Hamilton.* Philadelphia: J.B. Lippincott, 1860.

Cockburn, John. *The History and Examination of Duels: Shewing Their Heinous Nature and the Necessity of Suppressing Them.* London: privately printed, 1720.

Coleman, William. *A Collection of Facts and Documents Relative to the Death of Major-General Alexander Hamilton.* 1804. Austin, TX: Shoal Creek Publishers, 1972.

Collins, Paul. *Duel with the Devil: The True Story of How Alexander Hamilton and Aaron Burr Teamed Up to Take on America's First Sensational Murder Mystery.* New York: Crown Publishers, 2013.

Coombs, J.J. *The Trial of Aaron Burr for High Treason....* Washington, DC: W.H. and O.H. Morrison, 1864.

Cooper, James Fenimore. *New York.* N.p., 1864.

Cornwall, Bernard. *Redcoat.* 1987. New York: Perennial, 2003.

Côté, Richard N. *Theodosia Burr Alston: Portrait of a Prodigy.* Mount Pleasant, SC: Corinthian Books, 2003.

Cowen, David J., Richard Sylla, and Robert E. Wright. "The U.S. Panic of 1792: Financial Crisis Management and the Lender of Last Resort." Paper for the NBER-DAE Summer Institute, July 2006.

Crosby, Molly Caldwell. *The American Plague: The Untold Story of Yellow Fever, the Epidemic That Shaped Our History.* New York: Berkley, 2006.

Daniels, Jonathan. *Ordeal of Ambition: Jefferson, Hamilton, Burr.* Garden City, NY: Doubleday, 1970.

Davis, Joseph Stancliffe. *Essays in the Earlier History of American Corporations.* Cambridge, MA: Harvard University Press, 1917.

Desjardin, Thomas A. *Through a Howling Wilderness: Benedict Arnold's March to Quebec, 1775.* New York: Saint Martin's Griffin, 2006.

Disch, Lisa Jane. *The Tyranny of the Two-Party System.* New York: Columbia University Press, 2002.

Dungan, Nicholas. *Gallatin: America's Swiss Founding Father.* New York: New York University Press, 2010.

Dunn, Susan. *Dominion of Memories: Jefferson, Madison and the Decline of Virginia.* New York: Basic Books, 2007.

———. *Jefferson's Second Revolution: The Election Crisis of 1800 and the Triumph of Republicanism.* New York: Houghton Mifflin, 2004.

Durey, Michael. *"With the Hammer of Truth": James Thomson Callender and America's Early National Heroes.* Charlottesville: University Press of Virginia, 1990.

Dwight, Timothy. *The Folly, Guilt, and Mischiefs of Duelling: A Sermon, Preached in the College Chapel at New Haven.* . . . Hartford: Hudson and Goodwin, 1805.

Edwards, Jonathan. *The Works of Jonathan Edwards, A.M.* Vol. 1. London: Paternoster-Row, 1839.

———. *The Works of President Edwards, in Four Volumes.* Vol. 1. New York: Leavitt and Allen, 1852.

Elkins, Stanley, and Eric McKitrick. *The Age of Federalism: The Early American Republic, 1788–1800.* New York: Oxford University Press, 1993.

Ellis, Joseph J. *American Sphinx: The Character of Thomas Jefferson.* New York: Knopf, 1998.

———. *Founding Brothers: The Revolutionary Generation.* New York: Vintage, 2002.

———. *His Excellency: George Washington.* New York: Vintage, 2004.

———. *Passionate Sage: The Character and Legacy of John Adams.* New York: W. W. Norton, 1993.

Fenn, Elizabeth A. *Pox Americana: The Great Smallpox Epidemic of 1775–82.* New York: Hill and Wang, 2001.

Ferling, John. *Adams vs. Jefferson: The Tumultuous Election of 1800*. New York: Oxford University Press, 2004.

———. *Jefferson and Hamilton: The Rivalry That Forged a Nation*. New York: Bloomsbury Press, 2013.

———. *A Leap in the Dark: The Struggle to Create the American Republic*. New York: Oxford University Press, 2003.

Fischer, David Hackett. *Washington's Crossing*. Oxford: Oxford University Press, 2004.

Fleming, Thomas. *Duel: Alexander Hamilton, Aaron Burr and the Future of America*. New York: Basic Books, 1999.

Flexner, James Thomas. *The Young Hamilton: A Biography*. New York: Fordham University Press, 1997.

Fraser, Steve. *Every Man a Speculator: A History of Wall Street in American Life*. New York: HarperCollins, 2005.

Freeman, Joanne B. *Affairs of Honor: National Politics in the New Republic*. New Haven, CT: Yale University Press, 2001.

Gallatin, James. *A Great Peacemaker: The Diary of James Gallatin, Secretary to Albert Gallatin 1813–1827*. New York: Charles Scribner's Sons, 1914.

Gaylord, Irving C. *The Burr-Hamilton Duel, with Correspondence Preceding Same, etc.* N.p., 1889.

Gordon-Reed, Annette. *The Hemingses of Monticello: An American Family*. New York: W. W. Norton, 2008.

———. *Thomas Jefferson and Sally Hemings: An American Controversy*. Charlottesville: University of Virginia Press, 1997.

Gutzman, Kevin R. C. *James Madison and the Making of America*. New York: St. Martin's, 2012.

Hamilton, Alexander. *The Revolutionary Writings of Alexander Hamilton*. Edited by Richard B. Vernier. Indianapolis, IN: Liberty Fund, 2008.

———. *Writings*. Edited by Joanne B. Freeman. New York: Library of America, 2001.

Hamilton, Alexander, John Jay, and James Madison. *The Federalist Papers*. A Public Domain Book. Amazon Digital Services, n.d.

Hamilton, Allan McLane. *The Intimate Life of Alexander Hamilton*. London: Duckworth, 1910.

Hamilton, John C. *The Life of Alexander Hamilton*. 2 vols. New York: D. Appleton, 1841.

Hardy, Thomas. *Far from the Madding Crowd*. N.p., 1874.

Harrison, Samuel Alexander. *Memoir of Lieutenant Colonel Tench Tilghman, Secretary and Aid to Washington. . . .* Albany, NY: J. Munsell, 1876.

Hitchens, Christopher. *Thomas Jefferson: Author of America*. London: HarperCollins, 2005.

Hofstadter, Richard. *The Idea of a Party System: The Rise of Legitimate Opposition in the United States, 1780–1840*. Berkeley: University of California Press, 1969.

Holland, Barbara. *Gentlemen's Blood: A History of Dueling from Swords at Dawn to Pistols at Dusk*. New York: Bloomsbury, 2003.

Holmes, David L. *The Faiths of the Founding Fathers*. New York: Oxford University Press, 2006.

Hubbard, Vincent K. *Swords, Ships and Sugar: History of Nevis to 1900*. Placentia, CA: Premiere Editions, 1996.

Humphreys, Mary Gay. *Catherine Schuyler*. New York: Charles Scribner's Sons, 1901.

Isenberg, Nancy. *Fallen Founder: The Life of Aaron Burr*. New York: Viking Penguin, 2007.

James, William. *Pragmatism: A New Name for Some Old Ways of Thinking*. N.p., 1907.

Jefferson, Thomas. *Autobiography*. N.p., 1821.

———. *The Complete Anas of Thomas Jefferson*. Edited by Franklin B. Sawvel. Charleston, SC: BiblioBazaar, 2009.

———. *The Garden and Farm Books*. Edited by Robert C. Baron. Golden, CO: Fulcrum, 1987.

———. *Memoir, Correspondence, and Miscellanies, from the Papers of Thomas Jefferson*. Vol. 2. N.p., n.d.

———. *Notes on the State of Virginia*. New York: Digireads.com, 2009.

Jenkinson, Isaac. *Aaron Burr, His Personal and Political Relations with Thomas Jefferson and Alexander Hamilton*. N.p., 1902.

Jones, Robert F. *"The King of the Alley": William Duer, Politician, Entrepreneur, and Speculator, 1768–1799*. Philadelphia: American Philosophical Society, 1992.

Jusserand, Jean Jules. *With Americans of Past and Present Days*. New York: Charles Scribner's Sons, 1916.

Kaminski, John P. *George Clinton: Yeoman Politician of the New Republic*. Madison, WI: Madison House Publishers, 1993.

Kendall, Joshua. *The Forgotten Founding Father: Noah Webster's Obsession and the Creation of an American Culture*. New York: Berkley, 2010.

Kennedy, Roger G. *Burr, Hamilton and Jefferson: A Study in Character*. New York: Oxford University Press, 2000.

Kent, William. *Memoirs and Letters of James Kent, LL.D.* Boston: Little, Brown, 1898.

Kilmeade, Brian, and Don Yaeger. *George Washington's Secret Six: The Spy Ring That Saved the Revolution*. New York: Sentinel, 2013.

King, Charles R., ed. *The Life and Correspondence of Rufus King*. Vol. 1, *1755–1794*. New York: G.P. Putnam's Sons, 1894.

Kleiger, Estelle Fox. *The Trial of Levi Weeks or The Manhattan Well Mystery*. 1989. Chicago: Academy Chicago Publishers, 2001.

Knott, Stephen F. *Alexander Hamilton and the Persistence of Myth*. Lawrence: University Press of Kansas, 2002.

Lancaster, Bruce. *The American Revolution*. Boston: Mariner Books, 2001.

Larkin, Jack. *The Reshaping of Everyday Life, 1790–1840*. New York: Harper Perennial, 1988.

Larson, Edward J. *A Magnificent Catastrophe: The Tumultuous Election of 1800, America's First Presidential Campaign*. New York: Free Press, 2007.

Leake, Isaac Q. *Memoir of the Life and Times of General John Lamb, an Officer of the Revolution, Who Commanded the Post at West Point....* Albany, NY: Joel Munsell, 1850.

Linklater, Andro. *An Artist in Treason: The Extraordinary Double Life of General James Wilkinson*. New York: Walker, 2009.

Livingston, Edwin Brockholst. *The Livingstons of Livingston Manor*. New York: The Knickerbocker Press, 1910.

Lodge, Henry Cabot. *Alexander Hamilton*. Boston: Houghton Mifflin, 1884.

Lomask, Milton. *Aaron Burr: The Conspiracy and Years of Exile, 1805–1836*. Toronto: McGraw-Hill Ryerson, 1982.

———. *Aaron Burr: The Years from Princeton to Vice President, 1756–1805*. Toronto: McGraw-Hill Ryerson, 1979.

Maclay, William. *Journal of William Maclay*. Edited by Edgar S. Maclay. New York: D. Appleton, 1890.

Maclean, John. *History of the College of New Jersey: From Its Origin in 1746 to the Commencement of 1854*. Vol. 1. Philadelphia: J.B. Lippincott, 1877.

Maier, Pauline. *American Scripture: Making the Declaration of Independence*. New York: Random House, 1997.

Marsden, George M. *Jonathan Edwards: A Life*. New Haven, CT: Yale University Press, 2003.

Marshall, John. *Life of George Washington*. Philadelphia: C.P. Wayne, 1804.

Martin, James Kirby. *Benedict Arnold, Revolutionary Hero: An American Warrior Reconsidered*. New York: New York University Press, 1997.

Mason, John Mitchell, D.D. *An Oration, Commemorative of the Late Major-General Alexander Hamilton....* New York: Hopkins and Seymour, 1804.

Massey, Gregory D. *John Laurens and the American Revolution*. Columbia: University of South Carolina Press, 2000.

McCaleb, Walter Flavius. *The Aaron Burr Conspiracy: A History Largely from Original and Hitherto Unused Sources*. New York: Dodd, Mead, 1903.

McCraw, Thomas K. *The Founders and Finance: How Hamilton, Gallatin, and Other Immigrants Forged a New Economy*. Cambridge, MA: Harvard University Press, 2012.

McCullough, David. *John Adams*. New York: Simon and Schuster, 2001.

———. *1776: The Illustrated Edition*. New York: Simon and Schuster, 2007.

Meacham, Jon. *Thomas Jefferson: The Art of Power*. New York: Random House, 2012.

Merwin, Henry Childs. *Thomas Jefferson*. New York: Houghton Mifflin, 1901.

Miller, James R. *Early Life in Sheffield, Berkshire County, Massachusetts: A Portrait of Its Ordinary People from Settlement to 1860.* Sheffield, MA: Sheffield Historical Society, 2002.

Miller, John C. *Alexander Hamilton: Portrait in Paradox.* New York: Harper and Row, 1959.

Mills, W. Jay, ed. *Glimpses of Colonial Society and the Life at Princeton College, 1766–1773.* N.p., 1903.

Mitchell, Broadus. *Alexander Hamilton: A Concise Biography.* 1976. New York: Barnes and Noble, 2007.

Monroe, James. *Calendar of the Correspondence of James Monroe.* N.p., n.d.

Morse, John T., Jr. *Observations Suggested by John T. Morse, Jr.'s Life of Alexander Hamilton.* N.p., 1876.

Munsell, Joel. *The Annals of Albany.* Vol. 4. Albany, NY: J. Munsell, 1853.

Murphy, Brian Phillips. "'A very convenient instrument': The Manhattan Company, Aaron Burr, and the Election of 1800." *William and Mary Quarterly,* April 2008.

Murphy, Jim. *An American Plague: The True and Terrifying Story of the Yellow Fever Epidemic of 1793.* New York: Houghton Mifflin, 2003.

Nolan, Charles J., Jr. *Aaron Burr and the American Literary Imagination.* Westport, CT: Greenwood Press, 1980.

Oliver, Frederick Scott. *Alexander Hamilton: An Essay on American Union.* New York: G.P. Putnam's Sons, 1921.

Onuf, Peter S. *The Mind of Thomas Jefferson.* Charlottesville: University of Virginia Press, 2007.

Parmet, Herbert S., and Marie B. Hecht. *Aaron Burr: Portrait of an Ambitious Man.* New York: The Macmillan Company, 1967.

Particulars of the Late Duel, Fought at Hoboken, July 11, Between Aaron Burr and Alexander Hamilton, Esqrs. . . . Containing All the Papers Relating to That Event. . . . New York: A. Forman, 1804.

Parton, James. *The Life and Times of Aaron Burr, Lieutenant-Colonel in the Army of the Revolution, United States Senator, Vice-President of the United States, Etc.* Boston: James R. Osgood, 1877.

Pasley, Jeffrey L. *The First Presidential Contest: 1796 and the Founding of American Democracy.* Lawrence: University Press of Kansas, 2013.

Pearson, Jonathan. *Early Records of the City and County of Albany, and Colony of Rensselaerswyck (1656–1675).* Albany, NY: J. Munsell, 1860.

Pidgin, Charles Felton. *Theodosia, the First Gentlewoman of Her Time: The Story of Her Life, and a History of Persons and Events Connected Therewith.* Boston: C.M. Clark, 1907.

Randall, Willard Sterne. *Benedict Arnold: Patriot and Traitor.* New York: William Morrow, 1990.

———. *Thomas Jefferson: A Life.* New York: Perennial, 2014.

Rappleye, Charles. *Robert Morris: Financier of the American Revolution.* New York: Simon and Schuster, 2010.

Renwick, James. *Life of Dewitt Clinton.* New York: Harper and Brothers, 1840.

Reports of the Trials of Colonel Aaron Burr, Late Vice President of the United States, for Treason.... Philadelphia: Hopkins and Earle, 1808.

Rogow, Arnold A. *A Fatal Friendship: Alexander Hamilton and Aaron Burr.* New York: Hill and Wang, 1998.

Roman, James. *Chronicles of Old New York: Exploring Manhattan's Landmark Neighborhoods.* New York: Museyon, 2012.

Sacks, Oliver. *Migraine.* New York: Vintage, 1992.

Safford, William H. *The Life of Harman Blennerhassett. Comprising an Authentic Narrative of the Burr Expedition....* Chillicothe, OH: Ely, Allen and Looker, 1850.

Sanderson, Eric W. *Mannahatta: A Natural History of New York City.* New York: Abrams, 2009.

Savas, Theodore P., and J. David Dameron. *A Guide to the Battles of the American Revolution.* New York: Savas Beatie, 2010.

Schachner, Nathan. *Alexander Hamilton.* New York: Appleton-Century, 1946.

Schama, Simon. *Citizens: A Chronicle of the French Revolution.* New York: Knopf, 1989.

Sedgwick, John. *In My Blood: Six Generations of Madness and Desire in an American Family.* New York: HarperCollins, 2007.

Sedgwick, Theodore, Jr. *A Memoir of the Life of William Livingston, Member of Congress... and Governor of the State of New Jersey from 1776 to 1790.* New York: J and J Harper, 1833.

Sega, James. *An Essay on the Practice of Duelling, as It Exists in Modern Society.* Philadelphia: N.p., 1830.

Shorto, Russell. *The Island at the Center of the World: The Epic Story of Dutch Manhattan and the Forgotten Colony That Shaped America.* New York: Doubleday, 2004.

Simon, James F. *What Kind of Nation: Thomas Jefferson, John Marshall, and the Epic Struggle to Create a United States.* New York: Simon and Schuster, 2002.

Sleigh, William Willcocks. *Abolitionism Exposed! Proving That the Principles of Abolitionism Are Injurious....* Philadelphia: D. Schneck, 1838.

Smith, Barbara Clark. *After the Revolution: The Smithsonian History of Everyday Life in the Eighteenth Century.* New York: Pantheon Books, 1985.

Smith, Jean Edward. *John Marshall: Definer of a Nation.* New York: Henry Holt, 1996.

Stahr, Walter. *John Jay: Founding Father.* New York: Hambledon and Continuum, 2006.

Stevens, John Austin. *Albert Gallatin.* Boston: Houghton Mifflin, 1884.

Stewart, David O. *American Emperor: Aaron Burr's Challenge to Jefferson's America.* New York: Simon and Schuster, 2011.

Stone, William L. *Life of Joseph Brant-Thayendanegea: Including the Border Wars of the American Revolution....* 2 vols. New York: Cooperstown: H. and E. Phinney, 1845.

Stuart, Andrea. *Sugar in the Blood: A Family's Story of Slavery and Empire*. New York: Knopf, 2013.

Syrett, Harold C., ed. *The Papers of Alexander Hamilton*. Charlottesville: University of Virginia Press Digital Edition, 2011–2015.

Syrett, Harold C., and Jean G. Cooke, eds. *Interview in Weehawken: The Burr-Hamilton Duel as Told in the Original Documents*. Middleton, CT: Wesleyan University Press, 1960.

Thayer, Theodore. *As We Were: The Story of Old Elizabethtown*. Elizabeth, NJ: Grassmann, 1964.

Thompson, Keith. *Scoundrel! The Secret Memoirs of General James Wilkinson*. Vol. 1, *The True Spirit of '76*. Bedford, IN: NorLights Press, 2012.

Todd, Charles Burr. *Life of Colonel Aaron Burr, Vice-President of the United States. . . .* N.p., 1879.

Trial of Aaron Burr for Treason. New York: James Cockroft, 1875.

Trial of Jacob Barker, Thomas Vermilya, and Matthew L. Davis, for Alleged Conspiracy. New York: N.p., 1827.

Truman, Major Ben C. *The Field of Honor: Being a Complete and Comprehensive History of Duelling in All Countries. . . .* New York: Fords, Howard, and Hulbert, 1884.

Tuckerman, Bayard. *Life of General Philip Schuyler, 1733–1804*. New York: Dodd, Mead, 1903.

Ukers, William H., M.A. *All About Coffee*. New York: The Tea and Coffee Trade Journal, 1922.

Unger, Harlow Giles. *The French War Against America: How a Trusted Ally Betrayed Washington and the Founding Fathers*. Hoboken, NJ: John Wiley and Sons, 2005.

———. *John Hancock: Merchant King and American Patriot*. New York: John Wiley and Sons, 2000.

———. *The Last Founding Father: James Monroe and a Nation's Call to Greatness*. Philadelphia: Da Capo Press, 2009.

Vaughan, Alden T., ed. *The Puritan Tradition in America, 1620–1730*. New York: Harper and Row, 1972.

Vidal, Gore. *Burr: A Novel*. New York: Vintage, 1973.

Walton, John. *The Duel for America: Jefferson vs. Hamilton*. N.p., 2012.

Weisberger, Bernard A. *America Afire: Jefferson, Adams, and the First Contested Election*. New York: Perennial, 2000.

Weise, Arthur James. *The History of the City of Albany, New York, from the Discovery of the Great River in 1524, by Verrazzano, to the Present Time*. Albany: E.H. Bender, 1884.

Welch, Richard E. *Theodore Sedgwick, Federalist*. Middletown, CT: Wesleyan University Press, 1965.

Williamson, Wallace J., III. *The Halls: A Brief History of the American Whig-Cliosophic Society of Princeton University*. Princeton, NJ: The Society, 1947.

Wills, Garry. *James Madison*. New York: Henry Holt, 2002.

Wilson, James Grant. *The Memorial History of the City of New-York, from Its First Settlement to the Year 1892*. Vol. 2. New York: New-York History Company, 1892.

Wollstonecraft, Mary. *A Vindication of the Rights of Woman*. 1792. New York: Dover Publications, 1996.

Wood, Gordon S. *Empire of Liberty: A History of the Early Republic, 1789–1815*. New York: Oxford University Press, 2009.

PHOTO INSERT CREDITS

1. George Washington by Rembrandt Peale, 1795. National Portrait Gallery, Smithsonian Institution / Art Resource, NY.
2. Thomas Jefferson by Charles Willson Peale, from life, 1791–1792. Courtesy of Independence National Historical Park.
3. Alexander Hamilton in the Uniform of the New York Artillery by Alonzo Chappel. © Museum of the City of New York, USA/Bridgeman Images.
4. Alexander Hamilton by John Trumbull, c. 1804. © Collection of the New-York Historical Society, USA / Bridgeman Images.
5. Aaron Burr by Gilbert Stuart, ca 1792–94. From the Collection of The New Jersey Historical Society, Newark, New Jersey.
6. Aaron Burr by John Vanderlyn, 1802. © Collection of the New-York Historical Society, USA / Bridgeman Images.
7. Elizabeth Schuyler Hamilton, Wife of Alexander Hamilton by Ralph Earl. © Museum of the City of New York, USA / Bridgeman Images.
8. Theodosia Burr (Mrs. Joseph Alston) by John Vanderlyn, 1802. © Collection of the New-York Historical Society, USA / Gift of Dr. John E. Sitwell / Bridgeman Images.
9. Reverend Jonathan Edwards, c. 1750–1755, by Joseph Badger, Courtesy Yale University Art Gallery, Bequest of Eugene Phelps Edwards.
10. A view of the present seat of his excellency, the Vice President of the United States, Tiebout, Cornelius and Sidney Lawton Smith, 1901. Picture Collection, The New York Public Library, Astor, Lenox and Tilden Foundations.
11. Hamilton Grange, from 'Old New York, Volume I', Samuel Hollyer, 1802. © Collection of the New-York Historical Society, USA / Bridgeman Images.
12. Portrait of James Madison by Gilbert Stuart, 1804, The Colonial Williamsburg Foundation. Gift of Mrs. George S. Robbins.

13. James Monroe by Samuel F.B. Morse, 1819. White House Historical Association (White House Collection).

14. John Adams by Charles B.J. Févret de Saint-Mémin. 1800–1801. Conté crayon, charcoal (?), and white-chalk heightening on off-white laid paper coated with gouache 21 1/2 x 15 1/8 in. Gift of William H. Huntington, 1883 (83.2.470). The Metropolitan Museum of Art, New York, NY, U.S.A. Image copyright © The Metropolitan Museum of Art. Image source: Art Resource, NY.

15. 'The Providential Detection', cartoon depicting Thomas Jefferson trying to destroy the Constitution, American School, (18th century) / American Antiquarian Society, Worcester, Massachusetts, USA / Bridgeman Images.

16. James Wilkinson, Anonymous, 19th Century. National Portrait Gallery, Smithsonian Institution / Art Resource, NY.

17. Miniature portrait of Harman Blennerhassett, c. 1795–1796. Courtesy of Blennerhassett Island Historical State Park.

18. Congressional pugilists, Congress Hall in Philadelphia, 1798. Library of Congress Prints and Photographs Division Washington, D.C.

19. Aaron Burr by James Van Dyck, 1834. © Collection of the New-York Historical Society, USA / Bridgeman Images.

20. Monument at Alexander Hamilton's Grave, Kent G. Becker, 2012.

INDEX

Page numbers in *italics* indicate illustrations.

presidential campaigns of, xxi, 253–54, 286–88,
    290–93, 295–98, 300–305, 322–23, 357*n*, 374
press on, 203
Quasi-War and, 275
racism of, 253
Revolutionary War and, 202, 253, 286
Reynolds affair and, 230, 257, 268
sexuality and love life of, 110, 192–95, 253, 322
sightseeing trip of, 202–203
state secretaryship and, 183, 191, 196, 198, 203, 207
threats against, 373–74
West and, 352–53
Jeffersonians, Jeffersonianism, 192–93, 200, 202,
    217, 230–31, 267, 300, 311, 371
Jews, 13, 28
Judiciary Act, 314–15
Jumel, Stephen, 402

Kemper brothers, 369
Kennedy, Dennis, 91
Kent, James, xviii–xix, 136–37, 143, 151, 158, 222
King, Rufus, 203–5, 222–23
    Burr and, 205, 208–9, 262
    Hamilton and, *iv*, 184, 203, 208–9, 234, 243
    Jay Treaty and, 251
King's College, 42, 155, 260, 311
    Hamilton and, *xxiv*, 33, 45, 51–56, 70–71,
        170, 179
    physical appearance of, 51
    Revolutionary War and, 54–56, 70–71, 78
Knox, Henry:
    provisional army and, 277
    Revolutionary War and, 71, 75, 77
    as secretary of war, 183, 185, 207–8, 256
    and withdrawal of British troops, 135
Knox, Hugh:
    Hamilton and, 35–36, 39–41, 52, 80

Lafayette, Marquis de:
    French Revolution and, 231, 376
    Hamilton and, 85, 95, 110, 118–20, 130
    Revolutionary War and, 85, 87, 95, 110, 118–19,
        121–22, 130
    wound of, 87
Lake George, fort at, 9
Lamb, Caroline, 148
Lamb, John, 147, 264–65
Lansing, John, 273, 282, 324
Last of the Mohicans, The (Cooper), 8*n*
Latrobe, Benjamin, 211, 295, 376, 381
Laurens, Fanny, 83, 101
Laurens, Henry, 83, 87, 119*n*

Laurens, John:
    Burr and, 82
    death of, 130
    duel between Lee and, 95
    Hamilton and, 82–85, 95, 97, 99–101, 107–10,
        118–19, 122, 130, 158*n*
    physical appearance of, 82–83, 85
    Revolutionary War and, 82–87, 99, 110, 118–19,
        122, 130
Laurens, Martha Manning, 82–83, 100–101
Lavien, Johann Michael, 13–16, 18–19, 30, 32, 44
Lavien, Peter, 13, 30–31, 44
Leander, 373
Lear, Tobias, 280
Ledyard, Isaac, 221
Lee, Charles, 72, 93–95, 104
Lee, Henry, III "Light-Horse Harry," 26, 86,
    198, 229
Leeward Islands, 12–17, 35
Le Guen v. Gouverneur and Kemble, 140
L'Enfant, Pierre Charles, 181
Lewis, Meriwether, 298, 353
Lewis, Morgan, 136–37
    gubernatorial campaign of, 323, 325–26, 350
    Hamilton and, 142
Lexington, Battle of, 56–58, 67–68
Liberty Hall, 42–43, 45, 47, 128
Lispenard's Meadow, 273, 281
Liston, Robert, 266
Liverpool, Lord, 395
Lives (Plutarch), 28
Livingston, Catharine "Kitty," 42–43, 109
Livingston, Edward, 236, 251, 273
    Burr and, 301, 370, 386
    and election of 1800, 289, 301
Livingston, Henry Brockholst, 26, 136–37, 142, 289
Livingston, Jonathan, 250
Livingston, Maturin, 251
Livingston, Peter R., 250–51
Livingston, Robert R., 110, 142–44, 250–51
    on American political landscape, 143–44
    Constitution and, 172
    and election of 1800, 291
    Hamilton and, 184, 204
    Manhattan Company and, 273
    Washington's inauguration and, 181–82, 184, 250
Livingston, Walter, 249–50
Livingston, William, 51, 72
    Burr and, 128
    Hamilton and, 41–43, 45, 47, 128, 142
Livingstons, 43, 142, 144–45, 178, 184, 212, 222,
    252, 323, 325

Courtesy of Josephine Sedgwick

John Sedgwick is a journalist, novelist, memoirist, and biographer who has written or cowritten numerous books ranging from his psychological thriller, *The Dark House*, to his multigenerational family memoir, *In My Blood*. He has also written many articles for *GQ*, *The Atlantic*, *Newsweek*, *Vanity Fair*, and other magazines. He lives with his wife, the *Time* columnist Rana Foroohar, and her two children in Brooklyn.

CONNECT ONLINE

johnsedgwick.biz